studies in jazz

Institute of Jazz Studies
Rutgers—The State University of New Jersey
General Editors: Dan Morgenstern and Edward Berger

1. BENNY CARTER: A Life in American Music, *by Morroe Berger, Edward Berger, and James Patrick, 2 vols., 1982*
2. ART TATUM: A Guide to His Recorded Music, *by Arnold Laubich and Ray Spencer, 1982*
3. ERROLL GARNER: The Most Happy Piano, *by James M. Doran, 1985*
4. JAMES P. JOHNSON: A Case of Mistaken Identity, *by Scott E. Brown;* Discography 1917–1950, *by Robert Hilbert, 1986*
5. PEE WEE ERWIN: This Horn for Hire, *as told to Warren W. Vaché Sr., 1987*
6. BENNY GOODMAN: Listen to His Legacy, *by D. Russell Connor, 1988*
7. ELLINGTONIA: The Recorded Music of Duke Ellington and His Sidemen, *by W. E. Timner, 1988; 4th ed., 1996*
8. THE GLENN MILLER ARMY AIR FORCE BAND: Sustineo Alas / I Sustain the Wings, *by Edward F. Polic;* Foreword *by George T. Simon, 1989*
9. SWING LEGACY, *by Chip Deffaa, 1989*
10. REMINISCING IN TEMPO: The Life and Times of a Jazz Hustler, *by Teddy Reig, with Edward Berger, 1990*
11. IN THE MAINSTREAM: 18 Portraits in Jazz, *by Chip Deffaa, 1992*
12. BUDDY DeFRANCO: A Biographical Portrait and Discography, *by John Kuehn and Arne Astrup, 1993*
13. PEE WEE SPEAKS: A Discography of Pee Wee Russell, *by Robert Hilbert, with David Niven, 1992*
14. SYLVESTER AHOLA: The Gloucester Gabriel, *by Dick Hill, 1993*
15. THE POLICE CARD DISCORD, *by Maxwell T. Cohen, 1993*
16. TRADITIONALISTS AND REVIVALISTS IN JAZZ, *by Chip Deffaa, 1993*
17. BASSICALLY SPEAKING: An Oral History of George Duvivier, *by Edward Berger;* Musical Analysis *by David Chevan, 1993*
18. TRAM: The Frank Trumbauer Story, *by Philip R. Evans and Larry F. Kiner, with William Trumbauer, 1994*
19. TOMMY DORSEY: On the Side, *by Robert L. Stockdale, 1995*
20. JOHN COLTRANE: A Discography and Musical Biography, *by Yasuhiro Fujioka, with Lewis Porter and Yoh-ichi Hamada, 1995*
21. RED HEAD: A Chronological Survey of "Red" Nichols and His Five Pennies, *by Stephen M. Stroff, 1996*
22. THE RED NICHOLS STORY: After Intermission 1942–1965, *by Philip R. Evans, Stanley Hester, Stephen Hester, and Linda Evans, 1997*
23. BENNY GOODMAN: Wrappin' It Up, *by D. Russell Connor, 1996*
24. CHARLIE PARKER AND THEMATIC IMPROVISATION, *by Henry Martin, 1996*
25. BACK BEATS AND RIM SHOTS: Th⌐ ⌐ W. Vaché Sr., 1997*

26. DUKE ELLINGTON: A Listener's Guide, *by Eddie Lambert, 1998*
27. SERGE CHALOFF: A Musical Biography and Discography, *by Vladimir Simosko, 1998*
28. HOT JAZZ: From Harlem to Storyville, *by David Griffiths, 1998*
29. ARTIE SHAW: A Musical Biography and Discography, *by Vladimir Simosko, 2000*
30. JIMMY DORSEY: A Study in Contrasts, *by Robert L. Stockdale, 1998*
31. STRIDE!: Fats, Jimmy, Lion, Lamb and All the Other Ticklers, *by John L. Fell and Terkild Vinding, 1999*
32. GIANT STRIDES: The Legacy of Dick Wellstood, *by Edward N. Meyer, 1999*
33. JAZZ GENTRY: Aristocrats of the Music World, *by Warren W. Vaché Sr., 1999*
34. THE UNSUNG SONGWRITERS: America's Masters of Melody, *by Warren W. Vaché Sr., 2000*
35. THE MUSICAL WORLD OF J. J. JOHNSON, *by Joshua Berrett and Louis G. Bourgois III, 1999*
36. THE LADIES WHO SING WITH THE BAND, *by Betty Bennett, 2000*
37. AN UNSUNG CAT: The Life and Music of Warne Marsh, *by Safford Chamberlain, 2000*
38. JAZZ IN NEW ORLEANS: The Postwar Years through 1970, *by Charles Suhor, 2001*
39. THE YOUNG LOUIS ARMSTRONG ON RECORDS: A Critical Survey of the Early Recordings, 1923–1928, *by Edward Brooks, 2002*
40. BENNY CARTER: A Life in American Music, Second Edition, *by Morroe Berger, Edward Berger, and James Patrick, 2 vols., 2002*
41. CHORD CHANGES ON THE CHALKBOARD: How Public School Teachers Shaped Jazz and the Music of New Orleans, *by Al Kennedy,* Foreword *by Ellis Marsalis Jr., 2002*
42. CONTEMPORARY CAT: Terence Blanchard with Special Guests, *by Anthony Magro, 2002*
43. PAUL WHITEMAN: Pioneer in American Music, Volume I: 1890–1930, *by Don Rayno, 2003*
44. GOOD VIBES: A Life in Jazz, *by Terry Gibbs with Cary Ginell, 2003*
45. TOM TALBERT—HIS LIFE AND TIMES: Voices from a Vanished World of Jazz, *by Bruce Talbot, 2004*
46. SITTIN' IN WITH CHRIS GRIFFIN: A Reminiscence of Radio and Recording's Golden Years, *by Warren W. Vaché, 2005*
47. FIFTIES JAZZ TALK: An Oral Retrospective, *by Gordon Jack, 2004*
48. FLORENCE MILLS: Harlem Jazz Queen, *by Bill Egan, 2004*
49. SWING ERA SCRAPBOOK: The Teenage Diaries and Radio Logs of Bob Inman, 1936–1938, *by Ken Vail, 2005*
50. FATS WALLER ON THE AIR: The Radio Broadcasts and Discography, *by Stephen Taylor, 2/2006*
51. ALL OF ME: The Complete Discography of Louis Armstrong, *by Jos Willems, 4/2006*
52. MUSIC AND THE CREATIVE SPIRIT: Innovators in Jazz, Improvisation, and the Avant Garde, *by Lloyd Peterson, 8/2006*

MUSIC AND THE CREATIVE SPIRIT

Innovators in Jazz, Improvisation, and the Avant Garde

Lloyd Peterson

Studies in Jazz, No. 52

THE SCARECROW PRESS, INC.

Lanham, Maryland • Toronto • Oxford

2006

SCARECROW PRESS, INC.

Published in the United States of America
by Scarecrow Press, Inc.
A wholly owned subsidiary of
The Rowman & Littlefield Publishing Group, Inc.
4501 Forbes Boulevard, Suite 200, Lanham, Maryland 20706
www.scarecrowpress.com

PO Box 317
Oxford
OX2 9RU, UK

British Library Cataloguing in Publication Information Available

Library of Congress Cataloging-in-Publication Data
Music and the creative spirit : innovators in jazz, improvisation, and the avant garde /
[edited by] Lloyd Peterson.
    p. cm. — (Studies in jazz ; no. 52)
  Includes bibliographical references (p.   ) and index.
  ISBN-13: 978-0-8108-5284-6 (pbk. : alk. paper)
  ISBN-10: 0-8108-5284-5 (pbk. : alk. paper)
  1. Jazz musicians--Interviews. 2. Creation (Literary, artistic, etc.) I. Peterson, Lloyd,
1955- II. Series.

ML395 .M
781.65092'2—dc22   2006002651

∞ ™ The paper used in this publication meets the minimum requirements of American
National Standard for Information Sciences—Permanence of Paper for Printed Library
Materials, ANSI/NISO Z39.48-1992.

For my parents, Kim and Lloyd; my stepfather, Paul;
my brother and his wife, Steve and Kerri;
and my nephews, Brent and Kasey.

"Bebop was about change, about evolution. It wasn't about standing still and becoming safe. If anybody wants to keep creating, they have to be about change."

—Miles Davis

"I don't want to be modern, futuristic and neither do I want to be hung by the plaintiveness of something that we might have done years ago, even with success. I have no ambition to reach some intellectual plateau and look down on people and by the same token, I don't want anyone to challenge my right to sound completely mad, to scream like a wild man, to create the mode melody of a simpering idiot or to write a song that praises God."

—Duke Ellington (Special thanks to Ray Anderson)

"Improvisation is not the expression of accident but rather of the accumulated yearnings, dreams, and wisdom of our very soul."

—Yehudi Menuhin

CONTENTS

Editor's Foreword   Edward Berger   ix

Preface   Dave Douglas   xi

Acknowledgments   xiii

Introduction   xv

1 Fred Anderson   1

2 Derek Bailey   2

3 Joey Baron   9

4 Tim Berne   19

5 Peter Brotzmann   29

6 Regina Carter   34

7 Chicago Roundtable   43

8 Marilyn Crispell   56

9 Jack DeJohnette   66

10 Dave Douglas   75

11 Hamid Drake   86

12 Bill Frisell   93

13 Fred Frith   103

14 Annie Gosfield   109
15 Mats Gustafsson   112
16 Barry Guy   121
17 Dave Holland   132
18 Susie Ibarra   138
19 Eyvind Kang   140
20 Steve Lacy   146
21 George Lewis   148
22 Pat Martino   160
23 Christian McBride   169
24 Brad Mehldau   178
25 Myra Melford   184
26 Pat Metheny   191
27 Jason Moran   199
28 Ikue Mori   207
29 David Murray   211
30 Paal Nilssen-Love   215
31 Greg Osby   221
32 Evan Parker   233
33 William Parker   243
34 Joshua Redman   252
35 Maria Schneider   261
36 Wadada Leo Smith   271
37 Ken Vandermark   279
38 Cuong Vu   293
39 David S. Ware   297
40 Otomo Yoshihide   306
41 John Zorn   315
42 Pat Metheny   Closing   317

Index   325
About the Author   333

EDITOR'S FOREWORD

In this important work, Lloyd Peterson takes a refreshingly broad view of jazz. If one thing becomes clear in reading this rich collection, it is that the word "jazz" can no longer (if it ever could) describe the vast array of diverse styles that fall under the general description of creative improvised music. As Dave Douglas eloquently points out in his preface, this work eschews categories and recognizes that contemporary artists are not limited by artificial boundaries and draw inspiration from a wide range of sources.

Peterson lets the musicians speak for themselves. He is obviously a skilled interviewer and elicits frank and insightful testimony about the creative process with frequent and intriguing digressions into politics, religion, literature, and many other areas. Peterson is also a careful listener and knows when to deviate from the "script" in order to follow a promising thread or open new vistas. He has also chosen his subjects well, for these forty innovators are astute and articulate observers of contemporary culture and respond enthusiastically to the author's stimulating questions.

The list of interview subjects includes several important European innovators. One of the book's strengths is its examination of the evolution of a distinctly European identity in improvised music and its relationship with (or independence from) the traditional roots of jazz. In addition, while some of the artists are household names, others are lesser-known but equally important experimenters whose views rarely make it to print. *Studies in Jazz* is pleased to present this fascinating and provocative addition to the series.

Edward Berger
Series Editor

PREFACE

The recent publication of *Dear Professor Einstein* demonstrated the warmth and candor with which Albert Einstein responded to letters from children. He got this in a letter from a sixth-grader in 1952: "There are a few people in our room that do not understand why people are classed as animals. I would appreciate it very much if you would please answer this and explain to me why people are classed as animals."

His answer suggested an approach to the question that has been tearing jazz apart.

"We should not ask 'What is an animal' but 'what sort of thing do we call an animal?' Well, we call an animal something that has certain characteristics: it takes nourishment, it descends from parents similar to itself, it grows, it moves by itself, it dies if its time has run out."

What sort of thing do we call jazz? It helped me to analyze my own work, and to contextualize the great work that I hear from the contemporary artists all around me. And it brought me to a clearer sense where music is coming from and where it's going.

Not everyone in this book plays jazz. In fact, all kinds of musical languages have become fair game for use in conjunction with improvised music. This is not the kind of book that proposes a classification of music. Rather, it gathers together the broadest array of people involved in creative music and collects their words about process, their thinking, their world. One could say that this book is a compendium of characteristics we may consider in thinking about jazz, improvised music, and culture.

"Creative music" is another term often used to describe new music involving improvisation. To me, it refers to those engaged in the search for a personal language. Creative musicians search for an expression of their own realities on the planet and choose music as the medium. Jazz, as an American music, has given body to the idea that each musician can speak or his or her self, that freedom resides in the degree to which we allow each other to be free, that each musician must have the right, the responsibility, to pursue his or her own voice. Creative music as I understand it drinks from that same well, and perhaps is a more apt name for much of the music discussed here.

One thing is clear. The kind of thing we call jazz has undergone an enormous transformation over the last forty years, and there is no question that the existence of jazz has engendered the incredible wealth and variety of music that we are now blessed with.

Does music spring from an unknown creative force and emerge in the crucible of the moment, or does it grow from the fertile soil of tradition? Does jazz represent a cultural lineage belonging to the African American community that created it, or is it the fruit of personal expression by talented, hardworking individuals? Are new developments in jazz part of a continuum, or are they an adulterous aberration? As we grapple with these questions, we also have to recognize that these issues continue to tear at the entire world of culture and art.

Ultimately, the creative process leaps over the arguments in the act of creation. We are now blessed with this collection of thoughts from some of the most protean personalities involved in contemporary music, proposing answers to some of the perennial questions of our culture.

What sort of thing do we call creative music? Read on.

Dave Douglas 2005

ACKNOWLEDGMENTS

During a time when projects such as this are not given much opportunity, I would like to thank Bruce Phillips, former senior acquisitions editor, and Sam Grammar, former editorial assistant, along with my current editor, Renée Camus, assistant editor with Scarecrow Press. Also, Dan Morgenstern and Edward Berger, codirectors of the Institute of Jazz Studies, Rutgers University. Thank you for believing in the importance of forward-thinking work.

My sincere appreciation to Dave Douglas, Ken Vandermark, and John Zorn, who took the risk and were there with their personal support from the very beginning.

I would also like to thank Patti Kiyono, who provided her expertise when it was very much needed. Patti is the former communications and development manager with the Densho organization (www.densho.org/) which is responsible for educating and preserving the testimonies of Japanese Americans who were unjustly incarcerated during World War II. Through their tireless efforts, they continue to promote justice, equity, and democracy for all Americans regardless of ancestry. Appreciation must also go to Executive Director Tom Ikeda and Scott Oki for their vision in making Densho a reality.

Importantly, I would also like to thank the Executive Development Institute in Seattle (www.ediorg.org) and the Leadership Education for Asian Pacifics in Los Angeles (www.leap.org/) for their education, leadership, and inspiration. A special thanks to Scott Oki and John Kobara for caring about passion. And, to J. D. Hokoyama, thank you for your vision. Without these experiences, this book may have never happened.

A sincere thank you to Earshot Jazz Executive Director John Gilbreath for your passion and support. To Paul Debarros, author of *Jackson Street Blues*, jazz writer for *Downbeat* magazine and the *Seattle Times*, for your early vision of Earshot and your inspirational writings. To Rob Perry and staff at Jazz Alley; Henry Hughes and Peggy Sartoris-Belaqua for their vision in making Polestar Music Gallery a reality; Ken Pickering and the Vancouver Coastal Jazz and Blues Society (perhaps the most diverse festival anywhere in the world); Brad Winter with the Portland Creative Music Guild; Cory Franklin and staff with the Triple Door; Jason Koransky, editor of *Downbeat* magazine; Terry Currier of Music Millennium; Andy Laird of Timbuktunes; Justin Wright, Herb Sieler, and Chris Pugh with Silver Platters; and Peter Monaghan, editor of *Earshot Jazz*. Thanks for keeping the music alive!

Appreciation must also go to my friend and writing mentor, Michael Read. To my friends and supporters who I sincerely appreciate: Hirut Nicodimos, Neil Conklin, Nick Parisi, Dana Harmon, Al Parisi, Johnny Hahn, Michael Mitchell, Hannah Wong, Ralph Northrup, David Armstrong, Jane and Dave Emerson, Les Hutchinson, Jeff Akutsu, Mike Leonard, Tyler Fisher, Tim Sorrenson, Nancy Rivenbaugh, and to all those who have supported me at Boeing. To MM, thank you for Green Lake. Matt Butchko, Rafa Evolante, Michael Hale, Giorgio Aschiero, and Lisardo Maggipinto, thanks for the music. To Dawn Zervas, the "original" visionary behind Torrefazione Italia coffee; I will always appreciate your encouragement and confidence in me. To Norm Lockett, who rests in peace but will always be with me.

To Anne Lamott for "Bird by Bird." To the wonderful Pulitzer-awarded photographer, Daniel Sheehan. To Marianne Gontermann, my very special friend who stood by me with your positive thoughts, your encouragement, your forward-thinking ideas, and especially your patience, which I will always treasure. My lifelong best friend, Roger Volk, who has always been there when it mattered most. And lastly, to my mother and father, for caring. It means more than you will ever know. I love you both.

INTRODUCTION

My earliest memories of music come from growing up in Seattle in the late fifties and sixties. When I was three or four years old my mother, who is from Kumomoto, Japan, would play Japanese folk songs on her guitar, and the beauty and warmth of those memories still resonate within me today. She also played records from the Motown sounds of the Supremes and Shirelles, and I watched with wonder as my father, mother and their friends would dance to this music with joy.

When I was eight years old, my father, whose family is from Norway, began taking me to Grand Ole Opry concerts that were part of the tours coming out of Nashville. I was completely engulfed and mesmerized by the shades of sounds and lights cascading like waterfalls over the stage in rich lustrous colors of blues, reds, and greens. I vividly recall a young Loretta Lynn dancing in a flowing red dress, the southern elegant grace of Kitty Wells, and the imposing stature of Ernest Tubb. These still remain a part of my fondest childhood memories.

I was introduced to my first instrument, the violin, by my 5th grade teacher, Ms. Dorothy Watson. Through her encouragement, I began playing the ukulele and soon the cello, guitar, drums, and saxophone. I was finally able to recently meet with Ms. Watson again after 38 years. Amazingly, now 86, she's as energetic and sharp as I recall her in 1965. She spoke about how married women were not allowed to teach in public schools in the forties and how many of her friends had to lie in order to do what they loved. She also taught public school in Bainbridge Island, Washington, where the very first Japanese Americans were taken from their homes, their businesses, and even children from her classroom and placed in internment camps at times apart from their families. Ms. Watson will always remain a source of strength and inspiration.

Like most kids in the mid-sixties, I was interested in the Beatles, but something quite strange, unique, and powerful came along during the summer of 1967. I was twelve and visiting an older friend who would sometimes invite me over to his parents' house to listen to music. Jean turned me on to Janis Joplin, Otis Redding, the Doors, and Blue Cheer, but on one particular warm summer afternoon, I became enraptured by sounds that pulled at my guts and reached into my soul. Jimi Hendrix created something I had never heard before, but seemed somehow familiar. Not only could I feel his passion, but also his pain.

Growing up in a neighborhood as one of the only children of color was an experience that has contributed much to who I am today. As difficult and painful as it could be, I have no regrets. It has provided me greater sensitivity and tolerance along with a desire to understand people and cultures globally. This project gives me the opportunity to give back the support that music provided during a very challenging time of my life.

After being honorably discharged from the U.S. Army in 1976, I renewed a friendship with a former schoolmate, Margaret Trautmann. Margaret's mother had an extensive jazz collection and Margaret would bring her mother's jazz records over to my apartment and we would listen to this incredible music for hours. I didn't understand Trane's music right away but his powerful voice, spoken in a highly emotional, complex language was a revelation I wanted to know, to understand.

I would spend most of the eighties working with disadvantaged children, and though my job and community work were important, I never lost my passion for music. I was introduced to new music with other passionate music listeners from around the world, but also became more frustrated that more was not being documented about these brilliant artists—some of the most creative in the history of music.

We are in a creative period unlike that of any other era. Our culture is influenced by society and, ironically, is a victim of the overwhelming complexities and pace of that same society. But like the most innovative art forms of previous generations, contemporary creative music is rarely understood or accepted in its own time. Crowds rioted upon the early performances of Stravinsky's "Firebird"; Louis Armstrong would call the new bebop sounds of Charlie Parker and Dizzy Gillespie, "Chinese music." And we must not forget that both Ellington and Parker preferred that their music not be called jazz. Duke warned his peers that to allow their music to become named or categorized, would also allow it to become dated.

Like other genres of art, Jazz is challenged by contradiction. It has to be defined so people can relate to what is being discussed. But Jazz is alive and of its time, and to define it inhibits it as it continues to evolve, and expands beyond those original definitions. And just as each generation begins to acquire an understanding of the music of its period, the art form has already moved on. This evolution is sure as life and death, and is the greatness of this music we call Jazz.

If Louis Armstrong or Duke Ellington grew up as teenagers in *today's* fast moving society and culture of hip-hop, would their compositions be written in the

same manner and structure and with the same feel? No one questions their genius, but how could they not be influenced by all the factors that impact the culture and society of a generation?

Americans should be proud of the fact that this great American art form, whose
roots sprout from the African American experience, has influenced artists and musicians globally. We are in the midst of a creative period unlike any experienced
before but unfortunately, in a world that needs to define and categorize, it's up to
each individual to find his or her creative path and I hope in some way this book
will help in that journey.

This book is not about jazz and how it is defined and perceived by its many fac-
tions but in the importance of today's innovative ideas and vision as expressed by
the artists through their own voices. Art will always reflect truth and if there is one
common characteristic shared by the diverse group included here, it is a vision to
move music forward through their own creative spirit. That vision separates the
true innovators from those who fear risk and remain comfortable only in rehashing traditions of the past.

I feel tremendously grateful and fortunate to have been a part of a learning experience that I could not have acquired anywhere else or at any other time. Perhaps the most difficult task was in selecting the material for the limited amount of
space available. I deeply regret that I could not include all of the material and sincerely apologize to those that gave their time and of themselves.

In closing, I have chosen to organize this book by artist in alphabetical order
rather than by category or popularity, which in the end has absolutely nothing to
do with artistic vision. This book began out of frustration that some of the most
creative and innovative work is not accorded due respect and appreciation in its
own time. Thus I feel extremely indebted to all of the artists that have contributed
their insights into their own personal world of creativity. Through music, they
share the inner workings of the human mind and the voice of the soul. They continue to provide a vision of who we are. We only have to pay attention.

This is for them.

                                                          Lloyd Peterson

❶

FRED ANDERSON

There comes a time for every musician who chooses music as their lifelong pursuit, a dream of reaching that creative place beyond the notes of a score, beyond the world of academics, and beyond the reach of the instrument they play. It's a mysterious place that can elude even the world's greatest musicians, is rarely discussed, and is even more difficult to explain. It provides more questions than answers, and those that create from it are few. Chicago composer and saxophonist Fred Anderson is one of those few.

WHAT IS MUSIC?

Music is life and is bigger than all of us. We need to nurture it, keep the spirit going and, like anything artistic in life, it needs to be preserved. And it's difficult to put into words because each person interprets what it means according to how they feel at that particular time in their life. Some people experience it over and over and some people experience it for the first time. It's our existence but you have to listen to hear the story. It's your understanding of yourself and a language that you can learn to speak. When you are faced with difficulty, it can provide you with peace but trying to explain it is another thing completely. It provides a forecast for what's going on at that time. And it's like this life. You don't know when you are going to leave or how long you are going to stay, and then all of a sudden it's over. It is a mystery that is unexplainable and is its greatness. Music will always be.

❷

DEREK BAILEY

Guitarist Derek Bailey died on Christmas Day, 2005. Sadly, his passing has barely been acknowledged and continues to burn at my frustration and need for publishing this work. In a world where individual voices are usually scorned, Derek Bailey stood alone, secure in his accomplishments without concern for what lesser minds may have thought. Creating a musical language through his own unique and eccentric intellect, Bailey influenced several generations of improvisational musicians of every instrument.

Born in Sheffield, England, in 1930, Bailey, along with Evan Parker and Tony Oxley, established Incus Records in 1970. In 1976, he formed the group Company, which drew from the talents of various cultures of Africa, North and South America, Japan, and Europe, and in 1980 he published the very important and influential book *Improvisation*.

YOU HAVE SAID THAT THE TWO MOST STIMULATING THINGS IN PLAYING ARE INDIFFERENCE AND UNFAMILIARITY.

Yeah, that's right. When putting them together. And it's strange how stimulating indifference is. I have always noticed that the best groups are the ones with people who are not the same, who don't have too much in common. They have some things in common but perhaps the main characteristics were how they worked with each other personally. And quite often, their musical outlook is quite different and that can really produce all kinds of things and I have seen that over and over again. The first two people I played with in this kind of music were Tony Oxley and Gavin Bryars. Both are composers but nobody would put on a concert of their two compositions unless they were being provocative. They write two different types of music though they play together beautifully and they are different kinds of people but that was about the most satisfying group I have ever played with. We were all completely different. I was older than them and I had a different background but we were all different. And I think that is fruitful. I think compatibility in this area of music is completely overvalued.

DO WOMEN AND MEN CREATE DIFFERENTLY?

I think there is a difference but I wouldn't want to try and describe it because I don't know what it is. I know that it is much better to have both women and men included together within a large ensemble. And because it is better socially, it creates a much better atmosphere for making music. But then again, it's not as simple as more aggressive approaches or anything like that. For instance, there is not a more forthright bass player than Joelle Leandre. She's a terrifically strong player so it's not as simple as breaking it down into obvious masculine and feminine clichés.

THE IMPRESSION I GET FROM READING PREVIOUS INTERVIEWS IS THAT YOU LIKE DIVERSITY WITHIN ENSEMBLES IN WHAT IT CAN CREATE AND HOW YOU CAN INTERACT WITHIN THAT.

One of the people that I work intimately with is Min Xiao-Fen, who is a Chinese lady that plays the pipa, which is a Chinese flute. She is a remarkable player and until two or three years ago, I don't think she was very involved with full-scale improvisation. And one of the attractions of playing music for me is to play with different people and within their own context if I can.

I have found that the idea of regularly playing with the same people is not for me. I have done it for up to about eighteen months and that's about the maximum for me. And I think these thirty-five-year-long associations would drive me nuts. I tend to like ad-hoc situations where you get three or four people that have never played before. The best situation is what I have tried to describe as semi–ad hoc, which is somewhere between the immediate introduction to fresh playing and the later stage or just before it turns into a band. So there is a period, which can be as short as four or five days or as long as three months. There is a period of mutual exploration, and I don't mean that that's the total thing with the music but that's a strong element in it. When that's over, I think the music loses something. But you also gain the advantage of being a regular group and maybe a more presentable music, but that's not exactly what I'm into.

WHAT ABOUT SITUATIONS WHERE YOU PLAY WITH MUSICIANS FOR A PERIOD OF TIME, MOVE ON TO DIFFERENT DIRECTIONS WITH OTHER PLAYERS, AND THEN GET BACK TOGETHER AGAIN?

Nowadays, it seems that everybody plays with anybody, or anybody plays with everybody. I find that the musical relationship I have with Susie Ibarra works out quite nicely. We play about twice a year and we both play with other people and it works.

ARE YOU NOTICING A YOUNGER GROUP OF PEOPLE ATTENDING YOUR CONCERTS?

Oh yeah! The listeners from when I first started are totally different from those of today. At one time, you could only get what was a kind of fringe jazz audience and they never dug it anyway. They never really liked it and always thought we should be doing something else. Today, there is a kind of musical goulash out there and people seemed to be prepared to sit and listen. There are exceptions, but the audience is much bigger and certainly more tolerant.

ARE WE IN A CYCLE OR IS THE AUDIENCE BECOMING MORE EDUCATED?

I would expect things to change at some point; they always do. Without change, I think music would die. One of the healthiest places today seems to be Scandinavia. There are a lot of young players there and a lot of work. This might be because there is still a lot of benevolent funding arrangements, but the audiences seem to be large enough to carry us along anyway.

HOW DO YOU EXPLAIN YOUR MUSIC TO THOSE THAT ARE NOT FAMILIAR?

Well, I have always called it jazz and my background is jazz and jazz-related music. I have spent twenty years playing music that is pretty much all jazz related. But that was when most popular music was jazz related. There are certain things I could say for sure, but I don't know if I have a hard and fast definition. I think of myself as a playing musician. Writing composition and conducting doesn't appeal to me much and it never has. So it's a practical thing that has to do with playing and, now, playing is a difficult thing to describe. There is an activity called playing which is independent of the music. It can be applied to a lot of music and playing is what I'm interested in. And I find that free improvisation, or freely improvised music, gives me more scope for playing than any other type of music that I play. But I wouldn't describe what I do as jazz because I know how jealous jazz people are about their music. And anyway, there are a lot of things that I do that have no place in jazz in my view.

WOULD THIS BE BECAUSE OF THE INTERPRETATIONS THAT OTHER PEOPLE PLACE ON IT?

I don't mind if someone else calls it jazz. I don't know what I feel about that but I just don't mind. If I was to claim it was jazz, I think that most people who follow jazz would feel they were being misled.

IS THERE A FEAR THAT THE MUSIC MAY NOT BE AMERICAN ANYMORE?

Yeah, maybe. I think one of the ironic things is that a lot of the really great jazz players like Ellington and Charlie Parker insisted that their music not be called jazz. That has happened with a lot of the older, undeniably great jazz players. They have never been committed to being called a jazz player but have been happy to be called great players of something.

How would you describe the music of the last thirty years to students fifty years from now?

A lot of things have happened in the last thirty years. Things loosened up after the '60s or the late '50s. The music became less restricted. It's a difficult question because I have always been attracted to the ephemeral side of this kind of playing. I mean, I don't care if it blows away in the wind and nobody remembers it at all in fifty years. But there is something about the connection of it being freely improvised music and being ephemeral which is almost unique to this kind of playing. But it doesn't necessarily apply to jazz, particularly now where jazz can be studied almost anywhere. But I would think that the main thing that has happened in the last thirty to forty years or so, is that the music has become less restricted.

Perhaps the difficulty for jazz academics and historians is that there is so much diversity in jazz today because of the lack of restrictions you spoke of, so it becomes difficult to place your arms around and much easier to just say something isn't jazz.

Well, usually the way around that is to say it's not something, isn't it? Anybody who is in the business of defining musical styles is in trouble anyway.

The following is a quote from Cecil Taylor: "Music has to do with a lot of areas which are magical rather than logical; the great artists, rather than just getting involved with discipline, get to understand love and allow the love to take shape." How much of your music is from logic and how much from this other place that Cecil Taylor describes?

Well, I would have to say that I shrink from that description. Not that I don't think it's valid for Cecil and most things that Cecil says make a lot of sense to me. But the logic in music is very attractive to me. I like to look for logic in music in places where it's not usually found. Some interconnecting things in chaotic situations always intrigue me. But I'm not sure that if love and passion is not there; if absent, the music is worse for it.

Music may be magical for three or four people who improvise together freely. For the thing to work beautifully is in itself magical. And when it works very, very well, then that's extraordinary. It's an extraordinary experience. And I think it's inescapable to almost any kind of audience. Mind you, the occasions when it works very, very well are not all that numerous.

Is there a frustration with trying to get to that level for every performance?

If you consciously go hunting for it, you're in trouble. It's like thinking while playing—it doesn't help at all.

WHAT WAS YOUR EXPERIENCE LIKE IN PLAYING WITH PAT METHENY?

Pat is an explorative musician in a way that not all free players are. He really will go for something. I admire Pat. He doesn't have to take the chances that he takes in playing with different people. When he played with me, it was his idea and I couldn't see any advantage in him doing that. But he wanted to do it and he wants to do all kinds of things. And I think more musicians could be like that. Strangely enough, I think he is quite a bit like John Zorn. He will have a go at anything if not anything, anything that he thinks of.

Unfortunately, I think a lot of the best material from the work we did together on *Sign of Four* was left in the studio and never used. I was disappointed that they did not use any of the duo material that Pat and I did. I quite enjoyed playing duo with Pat.

IS THERE A RESPONSIBILITY THAT COMES WITH HAVING THE FREEDOM TO EXPRESS?

Freedom of expression is not a phrase that I would particularly use, at least with what I do. I suppose expression comes into it automatically but I don't examine that side of it. The responsibility I feel is when I try to freely improvise, and when I don't do that, I feel as though I'm not doing what I should be doing. Now, there are a number of elements within that and I think the main responsibility is to keep it fresh.

DO YOU HAVE YOUR OWN SET OF DISCIPLINES THAT YOU BRING TO THE TABLE WHEN YOU IMPROVISE?

Oh yeah, I have all kinds of hang-ups and I'm actually a very conventional musician. This is a large subject but the difference between playing conventional music and playing free music for me is total, and yet there are so many connections, which often feel the same. And yet when I started playing free, it was essential for me to play totally different from the way I played conventionally. I couldn't see any sense in coming into the free area, playing in the same way that I played technically in the conventional area. I bring all kinds of things to it and I don't know if it's an advantage or a disadvantage. It's not an open field for me like shutting your eyes, jumping in, and wailing away. I have always wanted more from it.

WHAT INSPIRES YOU?

I'm not sure I get much inspiration from anywhere. I get the urge to play with the absence of alternatives. It's a preferred activity and is what I like to do. I play everyday and quite a bit on some days. And people come over to my house and play with me once or twice a week. And that's in addition to working. This is just what I want to do and I feel pretty happy doing it. I don't look for something to inspire me and I don't get hit by lightning to the back of my head to inspire me. It doesn't work like that for me. It's a continuous thing and it rewards by pursuing it. I find that the more you do it, the more you get out of it.

DO YOU THINK IT'S MORE DIFFICULT FOR STUDENTS TO BE CREATIVE IN TODAY'S SOCIETY?

No I don't, and it might be easier. You can get away with murder today. Most of the young players that I know are not inhibited at all; whereas at one time, people did seem to be inhibited about free playing.

CAN YOU TALK ABOUT YOUR COMPOSITIONAL APPROACH?

Well, I don't write anything down. I occasionally make notes about the technical things if I come across a technique that seems like something I might want to pursue. As I mentioned before, I think that thinking while playing is hopeless. It doesn't help at all. I'm not sure what does help. Well, I do know what works for me. The best preparation for me before playing is sleeping. If I could sleep right up until the moment before I start playing, I would do it. But it's very difficult to find situations where you can do that. But I do try and find a short period where I can do that before I start playing. A blank slate is useful because you can then play anything.

THE SAX HAD A DIFFICULT TIME ACQUIRING RESPECT IN THE CLASSICAL COMMUNITY BECAUSE IT WAS SO CLOSELY RELATED TO JAZZ. THE GUITAR IS CLOSELY RELATED TO BLUES AND ROCK MUSIC. DOES IT RECEIVE THE RESPECT IT DESERVES WITHIN JAZZ?

I don't think there has been a great guitar player in jazz after Charlie Christian. You'll find guitar in almost all music and sometimes it's the predominant instrument though it's not usually the predominant instrument in jazz. Maybe it just hasn't had the right guys or maybe it has something to do with the instrument or the voice as it were. The guitar has had an interesting career, but it doesn't seem to produce players who have influenced other players on different instruments . . . except Christian, who did.

IT SEEMS TO BE A RELATIVELY NEW INSTRUMENT FROM THE SENSE OF NEW POSSIBILITIES.

Oh now, yes. But a lot of those things are things that I don't follow because I use more of a conventional approach. I don't use unusual tunings. Years ago, I kind of worked with altered guitars with additional strings and other things, but generally speaking, it's got to be the basic guitar for me. I wouldn't know what to do with a guitar that wasn't tuned the standard way.

IS THERE A CHANCE THAT YOUNGER MUSICIANS COULD GET TOO HUNG UP ON ELECTRONICS AND LOSE SIGHT OF FINDING THEIR OWN VOICE?

I don't know. I try to avoid criticizing other musicians. If they put up with what I do, I'll put up with what they do.

ARE YOU STILL LEARNING FROM THE MUSICIANS YOU PLAY WITH?

I have learned from everybody I have played with to some degree. That's one of the reasons I play with them. In just the last seven or eight years, I have gotten more out of playing with musicians that play removed from the area that I'm in. It's very strange but I seem to get more out of it. But yeah, I look to the musicians for whatever music we are going to make. I think of it as their music.

DOES IMPROVISATION HAVE A PARTICULAR IMPORTANCE TODAY?

Oh, I don't think it has importance. I think you could work out some philosophical or political aspect but I don't think it has much significance except for the people who dig it. It has such a limited power of communication.

DO YOU HAVE A VISION FOR THE FUTURE OF THIS MUSIC AND FOR YOURSELF PERSONALLY?

Ah yes, the future! I have avoided thinking about the future by design. At one time, when I thought about it, I felt that this music would have a very limited life. I thought it was something like cubism but then it began to have an influence on other things. But it's gotten bigger and bigger in different ways. I can't see it stopping now.

One of the attractions for me is in the work because I think of the guitar as an endless job or process. There is no end to guitar playing and the world is massively full of different guitar players. With other instruments, there seems to be about three or four different styles.

But on the guitar, you can find hundreds of different kinds of players. And the other thing which I found was weird and the attraction about free improvised music; I still think of it as being largely unexplored. I think there are things that could happen which have not been realized and there is something about its open-endedness that is attractive to me.

3

JOEY BARON

For those that believe that jazz no longer swings, they haven't heard the sweet soulfulness of drummer Joey Baron. Weaving inside and out of any style imaginable, he can open up a tune by inflecting his enthusiasm and feel while never losing his own voice, which is a part of his ingenuity.

HAVE WE BECOME A SOCIETY WITHOUT THE PATIENCE TO BE CHALLENGED, OPEN ONLY TO THINGS THAT ARE EASILY ACCESSIBLE?

For the creative musician, our job stays the same, which is to continue to create, no matter what the political or societal issues, but it's very easy to get distracted. The mechanism of the oppressive society at large is to distract people from doing what they really love.

And even though we're in an information age, I think people have always been bludgeoned with propaganda or media, which has never really been truthful. Moreover, I think people, particularly artists, have always had to make decisions and somehow stay committed to what they believe while finding a way to work and maintain their own integrity.

OUR SOCIETY TODAY APPRECIATES ART BUT SEEMS TO HAVE DIFFICULTY WITH CREATIVITY THAT IS NOT EASILY EXPLAINED, UNDERSTOOD, OR IDENTIFIABLE. IS THIS GOING TO BE A SIGNIFICANT OBSTACLE TO OVERCOME FOR CREATIVE MUSIC OR THE ARTS IN GENERAL?

Anytime you make a decision to be creative, you're immediately going against the grain of society, and we all live in an oppressive society. This is important to accept and is something that this country really hates to come to terms with. Sub-sequently, you'll be attacked because of jealousy, by people who are not standing up for themselves. The government has also attacked people who were committed to expressing themselves on their own terms; people such as Lenny Bruce, John Lennon, or Martin Luther King. We are living in a very conservative time with desperate attempts to perpetuate this myth that capitalism is working without any encouragement for creative activity. You have to really take it on yourself to be committed.

Look at the terribly oppressive behavior that comes from our American gov-ernment in how we conduct ourselves in the world, making laws we insist every-body adheres to, then changing our minds to suit our own purpose. I don't know how this happened. We have a president that wasn't originally elected—he was ap-pointed. Our policies are doing the very same things we accuse other countries of doing. It's OK for us to do it? No, it's not! It separates us further and further from each other. Not only in America but separation and isolation from each other in the whole world.

I HAPPEN TO BELIEVE THAT THIS IS ONE OF THE MOST CREATIVE TIMES IN JAZZ HIS-TORY, BUT PEOPLE ARE NOT AWARE OF THE DIVERSITY OF MUSIC AVAILABLE TO THEM. WHAT WILL TAKE TO CLOSE THIS GAP?

There are very few record companies today with fewer people getting signed, and those that do are not encouraged to create. However, I agree with you in that there is incredibly creative work going on right now. The situation is conservative and promoted in the way people program their bookings, the way they sign record artists and the way music is discussed.

IS CREATIVITY ENCOURAGED TODAY?

People have been trained and encouraged not to listen. For instance, I hear people play and exercise their incredibly developed technique but they are recit-ing rather than really getting inside the music. Technique is encouraged because everybody can get it, but making music is not necessarily based on technique and mechanics. Making music is a sense that you have to acquire; you have to listen and I don't think it's an encouraged activity today. It's completely misused regard-less of whether it's restaurants, coffee shops, department stores, or elevators. Con-sciously you are getting used to not hearing because it's all backdrops. People are "not" listening and everything is tuned out, ambient, and drone oriented. The end result is that you won't really listen. You assume that music is always an accompa-niment activity and this is the misuse of music.

HAVE WE BECOME A MORE VISUAL SOCIETY, PLACING LESS SIGNIFICANCE ON ELE-MENTS OF SOUND?

We are a consumer society and the push is to control, consume, and throw out. I think the depth of the music is really being overlooked and completely wasted.

It's not an encouraged quality but more about, "what do you have, what's your new project?" Some people can deal with that and come up with a new project every time you turn around.

However, that may not be the way that others work and if it isn't, they're completely forgotten. It's something that has really become incredibly different in the last thirty years. Bill Evans took the same material and continued to develop inside of it. If he was starting his career today, I think he would have a pretty tough time creating and getting attention for his music. People would say, "Oh yes, he's got that trio thing, let's hear something else. What else you got?" You know, it's really insulting. We're used to buying a mechanical pencil where you can't refill the lead but throw it away, and then buy a new one. This is also encouraged on a personal level and one should realize that this is always fighting at your door, and you have to say, "I want to go hear Jim Hall play *Body and Soul* or I want to hear Lee Konitz play *All the Things You Are*. He's been playing that tune for forty years but every time he plays it, it has as much value as the latest bell and whistle out on the block."

ARE JAZZ TRADITIONALISTS HAVING A DIFFICULT TIME ACCEPTING THAT A MUSIC FORM CONSIDERED "AMERICAN" NOW HAS MORE VISIBLE INTERNATIONAL AND DIVERSE ASPECTS WITHIN IT?

I don't think America has ever claimed this music as American to this day. This country hasn't addressed that issue and what's beneath is racism, which is rampant in this country. Not to say racism is not operating all over the world but in this country it's rampant. As white people, we haven't addressed the issue of racism yet and we need to do that, not for people of color but for ourselves so we can start to tear down the invisible walls that still exist today.

I think great music is human and when I put on *Kind of Blue*, which I consider a masterpiece, I don't hear anything but great art. I don't hear black, white, a political agenda and I don't hear a country. I hear something that is much bigger than all of this stuff. I hear beauty and even though you might seldom reach that point, it's the process of trying that's really important.

This subject of jazz being American or not is bullshit, and for me personally, it's not an issue. You'll find signs of how great humans are in every country and when you think about it, we are more alike than different. Capitalism completely goes against this, tries to isolate everybody and is a driving force behind everything. Everybody has been whittled down and reduced to doing something because of the money rather than because it's what they enjoy and want to do. They are not even encouraged to take the time and space to think about it.

I think it's fine to have influences from all over the world but can you make music? You're supposed to make music, not display how clever you are. I'm very happy to listen to people's opinions of what they think is behind the music, but when you sit down and listen, does it speak to you regardless of where it's coming from? People get distracted with all the information and opportunities to educate themselves.

This leaves a lot of option anxiety. It distracts and confuses people and confusion is a big part of what's going on today. You can hear it in the records and you can hear it in the music more often than I would hope for.

I THINK IT'S COMMENDABLE OF YOU TO TALK ABOUT RACISM VERY OPENLY AND TO BE SO AWARE OF THE SITUATION THOUGH YOU YOURSELF ARE NOT A PERSON OF COLOR.

Thank you. Everybody has to take this on, as there isn't a self-help book. Though I wish I had the answers, all I can do is try and model the best I can. It's a terrible situation that has separated us. White people need to deal with it amongst ourselves and not expect people of color to be our sympathetic audience. Do you know what I mean? I feel that racism is a direct hurt to white people because I don't think one is born with those ideas of treating people differently. When you stop and think about it, for that kind of human behavior to exist means only one thing, that it was beat into them or they were forced to accept that kind of behavior at some point in history. That kind of hurt is major. We have never had that perspective of healing as white people. We are the ones that are carrying around the hurt. Until we deal with it, we're not going to be able to be effective in stamping this horrible thing out. People should understand that oppression is affecting us. Since music is just a microcosm of life, it affects the music scene as well.

IF WE CAN SAY THAT ARTISTIC EXPRESSION CAN BE INFLUENCED BY OUR SOCIETY AND ENVIRONMENT, IS IT POSSIBLE THAT A NEW TYPE OF CREATIVITY MIGHT COME OUT OF ALL THE STRIFE GOING ON GLOBALLY TODAY?

New ideas are happening all the time and the term "new" is confusing. You could have somebody playing a song that's been played 500 million times, but if they're doing it in a personal way, that's new because every person is completely unique. The thing being squashed in our society is the uniqueness we're encouraged not to have. I think newness is happening as we speak and I think it will continue to happen. Therefore, I don't think it's going to be a sudden burst like "this is new." I think it's media hype for when it's convenient to write about the drug addict jazz artist, the weird silly white guy, or the angry young black man or whatever the stereotypes are.

IS IT MORE DIFFICULT FOR A STUDENT TO BE CREATIVE IN TODAY'S SOCIETY?

There is so much information with so much of it being hype that it becomes option anxiety. It's often difficult to know which way to go and very easy to be attracted to the quick easy dollar which has nothing to do with creativity. I think it's extremely difficult for a young person today. They have to understand that music schools get grants because they adhere to rules and regulations that determine the amount of time they will have taught something. It's all about money! However, that's really not the way we learn and the fact that it works at all is a miracle. However, there are great teachers working in schools. For example, Charlie Haden is working out at Cal Arts and Gary Dial, a brilliant educator, is here in New York. I'm not involved in that system firsthand, but there are great people inside of that system working to change things and that's fantastic. I think it's best to try and seek out friends and build relationships with musicians. Don't get isolated with instructional video tapes and recordings but try to build a community of friends where you get together and listen to records, talk about it and let people know what you are doing. That's the best shot that creativity has in order to go against the isolation that is all around us.

There are also a lot of people who are totally into computers and are able to compose and record music all by themselves. We have this generation of musicians that might come up with really interesting music, but in terms of playing, they don't know how to blend with other musicians. When you think about it, what's technology? Technology is just overdubbing and layering. You are not thinking about interaction. How can you be when you are working alone? Computer programs, synthesizers, and workstations are great tools and can really save a lot of time, but they should not replace the essentials of interacting with another human intelligence. That has become really obvious to me and is one of the most harmful things that I've heard in the music in the past couple decades. It's this layering thing. At times, people are playing on top of each other instead of with each other and that again boils right down to the basic thing of what I said before about listening.

DO YOU HAVE A PHILOSOPHY THAT YOU TRY TO IMPART AMONG STUDENTS OR YOUNG MUSICIANS?

Listen and think about what you are doing and have a balance. There are so many chops out there and so little music. Technique is attention getting but it's easy to get distracted. All of a sudden you do this one technique and people applaud you, which can become addictive to the point you forget about, "Gee, is this music or is this just show biz?" My philosophy is to try and listen and trust your own thinking on everything. This is still very hard for me. I still struggle with that. If you feel like you need to play a certain kind of music for a while, go do it if that's what inspires you. Go do it no matter what because the minute you start not trusting your own thinking, you are going to get into trouble.

For drummers in particular, try to understand the traditional function of being a drummer. You're a musician who plays the drums. This has been said by many different people, but somehow people still don't get it. It really means a lot to take that on and to really understand the function at least in jazz and creative music in that you're going to play music that has a symmetrical time structure to it. Your function as a drummer is to be able to hold that time. Have it feel like something and that something has to be personal. Achieving that personal touch is a long process. You just don't pick up the drums and start thinking you're God's gift to music. It's important to know what came before you.

You don't have to be an expert but at least acknowledge it and listen to it—deeply. Be aware of it because at the root of any great art there is a history. It doesn't just happen. Tony Williams didn't come out of the blue. Jack DeJohnette didn't come out of the blue and Paul Motian didn't come out of the blue. These are artists that really inspire me and there's a whole list of them. You can hear Roy Haynes, Philly Jo Jones, Jimmy Cobb, Louis Hayes, and Kenny Clarke in Tony Williams for instance. You can also hear Kenny Clarke in Elvin Jones, Sid Catlett in Elvin Jones, Elvin Jones and Tony Williams in Jack DeJohnette.

PERHAPS MORE THAN ANY OTHER DRUMMER, YOU ARE RESPONSIBLE FOR BREAK-ING DOWN THE STEREOTYPE OF WHAT THE DRUMS BRING TO THE CONTEXT OF A GROUP SETTING. YOU HAVE YOUR OWN MUSICAL VOICE YET THE DRUMS ARE SO CRIT-ICAL TO WHAT HAPPENS WITH TIME IN THE GROUP CONTEXT. BUT YOU VERY RARELY READ ABOUT HOW MUSICIANS DEAL WITH TIME.

Time is like a sphere. Imagine a bunch of spheres floating above us that are in-visible. Grab one, hold it, embrace it, but let it float a little bit. It might go up and it might go down but do that in accordance with what the music is calling for and have it interact with what your band mates are doing. Listen to the pop records from the '60s like the Otis Redding records that used the rhythm section of Booker T. and the MG's and the great Al Jackson. You'll hear things fluctuate but the feel is always there and that's great and it's human. You could clock it and say "Oh, he's off a beat here and he drags there," but you could do that with Miles Davis or to anybody. Somebody told me once that you could be dead right . . . and that really is true!

I try to think about the feeling of what's going on. When I improvise, I don't just improvise rhythms and dynamics, I'm also dealing with feels. There are ways to play four quarter notes where you can play one measure of quarter notes a certain way and you can play another measure a different way and it has a different feel. This is often completely overlooked. I don't know why but no one ever told me about that, it was just something I heard in music and it made me feel a certain way. I related to that particular feeling and it became part of my vocabulary. Sub-sequently, I learned how to invoke it by trying things out with people in context. If I'm playing the drums by myself, I'll play something and listen back and see if it feels good or does not feel good. Am I too close to it or too afraid to admit that it's good or bad? You know like, what's real here?

I don't think people can just sit down at the drums and have a killing sense of time. Time is really something that needs to be worked on. I remember hearing a story from a really fantastic drummer named Jimmy Zitano who was a Boston drummer in the '50s and '60s. He was playing a jam session with Herb Pomeroy's band and he let Tony Williams, who was a youngster at the time, sit in. Tony took a solo and was obviously breaking the bar lines. But at the time, Jimmy Zitano was thinking that Tony should be playing inside the form of the tune. Afterwards, Jimmy tried to impart some advice to the up-and-coming young guy. I can't re-member Jimmy's exact words, but basically it was something to the effect of "Damn nice ideas but you might want to pay attention to the time, the time frame." Tony looked up at him and said, "I was playing distance, I wasn't playing time." Jimmy said that totally knocked him on his ass. What a precocious remark. I wish I would have known Tony, but just to hear that story was exciting. It's a very mature understanding, and, at that point, Tony Williams was completely devouring the history of jazz drumming.

Part of making music when you are dealing with symmetrical rhythmic structures is to be able to provide a solid rhythmic base. Every musician should be able to do that, not just the drummer, and that's part of the problem. Drummers end up babysitting a lot of musicians who basically are more concentrated on soloing and playing on top of you rather than with you. So they play ideas that are rhythmically extremely rushing or dragging. As a drummer, that makes you feel like you are carrying a weight that weighs a ton and it shouldn't feel that way.

Rhythm is a part or function of every musician's responsibility. We need to address rhythm, time, and achieving a feel as well as keeping steady time. A metronome has no feel. It's not about being metronomic, but about keeping a steady pulse, and learning how many different kinds of "feel" there are. Once you are on that road, then you can start thinking about time in terms of what Tony Williams was referring to at such a young age. I think distance is important, also how time can be manipulated in terms of distance; for example, the music of Morton Feldman. I'm not a real big aficionado of that music but have been recently exposed to it. He would deal with time in how it can be manipulated in the larger sense or how musical ideas can be stretched to where they challenge one's normal perception of time, much in the way like a magic trick. When you see someone do a magic trick, on some level, it challenges your perception of what you know is reality. I think it's really important to check out people like John Cage and Morton Feldman to broaden your perception.

Rhythm is important and is crucial for music. It doesn't have to be in every piece, but I think the ability to hold time and tempo gives you more freedom. If you can't hold a tempo, or play "out" of tempo, then you are not really free. Freedom means the ability to have a lot of options available at your disposal and choosing which option you believe will make the music happen. It's OK to specialize but I wouldn't call that freedom. There are people who do that but personally, I've always enjoyed being able to experience a wide variety of music. That's the way it came to me and that's how I heard music as music. I didn't hear it as this genre. This is the country-music genre and this is the rock-and-roll-genre; music was always just music to me.

I think it is harder for a young musician today; everything so specialized, so separate. When you get right down to it, time is time. Whether you're playing a Johnny Cash song or whatever the latest pop hit is, time is time and basically on some level, I think it's important as a percussionist and drummer to be able to hold it, and generate feel. The only common thread within music is the time and I'm talking about symmetrical-based structure music. It's just crucial for drummers to really get that together.

I'M GOING TO GIVE YOU TWO CASES WHERE IT APPEARS DRUMMERS AND BASS PLAYERS CAN COME UP WITH THEIR OWN LANGUAGE WITHIN THE CONTEXT OF A LIVE

SITUATION; YOURSELF AND GREG COHEN, AND WILLIAM PARKER AND HAMID DRAKE. I UNDERSTAND THAT EVERYBODY IS WORKING WITH THE TIME, BUT YOU GUYS SEEM TO HAVE A UNIQUE RELATIONSHIP WITH IT.

I think it's about a respect thing and it's also about exactly that, a relationship. I don't have the pleasure of knowing Hamid personally so I can't speak to what's happening between him and William, but I know William and I know he is very dedicated and very personable. When he makes music, he brings that to the situation. And from everything I have heard on record and what people say about Hamid Drake, I hear a similar quality about him.

For Greg and myself, we have been playing music on and off since the mid-'70s. There is a process along with the respect I feel for him and I feel that coming back along with a closeness. That respect opens up closeness to where you can push things forward and let things happen. As far as maintaining your personal voice, that again goes back to the work of listening and thinking about what has happened and who has played your instrument before you. Devouring that, ingesting that, thinking about how "you" would do it and then taking that to each situation. The ultimate bottom line is making the music happen. When I play, I'm myself musically and when William plays, he brings himself, he's not just reading the charts and I'm sure that Hamid Drake is doing the same thing. I know he is. It's a process.

Many young people might hear this, go to their next job and try to play in a way that is completely inappropriate and have an attitude like, "Well man, that's my thing." Well, the bottom line is really the thing. The bottom line is music. If they are playing in a band they don't want to be in, then maybe they should get in a band that's a little more in the direction of what they are hearing. That's where you can let your ideas happen and develop. If you are playing in a commercial situation like a wedding, then your function is to provide background music. People don't give a shit about listening to music at a wedding. They are there to enjoy the celebration. It's not about you being paid attention to as an artist, which is fair. That's what the premise is. If you accept that kind of a job, try and make the music happen because there is music that can happen in that situation. You have to be aware enough to know you can't go in and play incredibly abstractly if somebody wants to dance an anniversary waltz. It's like going to a restaurant, ordering eggs and the chef coming out with some shit and says, "Well no, I'm just doing my thing," when all you wanted was a couple of eggs over easy. It's the same thing and a misconception because when you are young, you want to set the world on fire and do it right now. But it's a process and doing it right now never stops.

Like anything, I think the key is to really enjoy what you are doing. If you are not enjoying what you are doing, then you have to make a plan. Try things until you find something that hits your button and plan a way to move your artistic life in that direction.

MOST PEOPLE DON'T THINK OF DRUMMERS AS COMPOSERS, BUT YOU HAVE BEEN QUITE SUCCESSFUL IN THIS AREA. I WAS WONDERING ABOUT YOUR APPROACH TO

COMPOSITION. IS IT INTELLECTUAL OR INTUITIVE AND HOW MUCH IS IT STRUCTURED
VERSUS IMPROVISED?

First of all, my concept as a player is a compositional one and I don't relate as
a technically oriented player. I don't really have the kind of chops to get a football stadium up on its feet. Sometimes I wish I did, just to be able to pull things
off physically, but basically, I'm really a compositional player. I play ideas that
might not involve flashy displays of technique but create a musical story. I'll hear
certain melodies when I'm at the drums and when I can think of that, I'll sit down
and write down whatever ideas I get. That's how it's intuitive. But sometimes it's
very structured. If I want to write a ballad that has a very short form, I'll set that
up and then try and fill in the spaces. It's not just about any one thing. At times I
want to deal with rhythmic structures. Sometimes I want to have lush sounding
chords. I'll work and work until I find something that satisfies me, and then write
those down. It might be a part that isn't anything spectacular on the drums. I'm
not trying to showcase myself as a Buddy Rich, "Watch me play this blazing single stroke role." That's not what I do. I like to instigate things happening, create
music, and some things cannot necessarily be done from behind a drum set. For
instance, you can't just yell out to other players this voicing or that voicing. Writing for me is a way of getting a context I hear in my head that I would like to have
happen. I like things to happen by chance and I try to leave enough room in compositions for that to occur.

As a composer, you have to take responsibility on some level for the form foundation. If you are not doing that, it's better to say that you are improvising. You're
doing an improvised set which is just as valid.

THERE IS A HUMANISTIC QUALITY TO YOUR PLAYING AND TO ME, THAT'S A KEY PART
OF YOUR MUSICAL VOICE. WHERE IS YOUR INSPIRATION FROM OR WHAT INFLUENCES
YOUR CREATIVITY?

I have been very fortunate to have been around people that model integrity and
encourage soulfulness in different ways throughout my life. My mother and father
modeled humbleness, generosity, and a well-intentioned way of life, but things were
not perfect by any means. Music is not its own life but a small section of this bigger
thing we call life. The music that moves me comes from people who model this, and
every person has to find those types of people for themselves. Having close friends
can be influential and it doesn't matter how many, it's the quality that's inspirational.

I READ AN INTERVIEW WHERE YOU STATED: "THE AVANT-GARDE IS ABOUT LIBER-
ATING YOUR THINKING, MAKING YOUR THOUGHT PROCESSES VISIBLE."

I believe the term avant-garde was a military term identifying frontline soldiers.
I don't feel like a soldier but many people generalize the avant-garde as being free
jazz and I don't go along with that at all. For me, the term avant-garde or pushing
the envelope means "personal." What I was saying earlier about "new" isn't necessarily different, but new is really personal. If you're being personal, that's going

to be unique because nobody can think like you. No one has the same signature and same response as another individual.

I'm primarily perceived as a sideman but I'm a leader artistically and have my own projects. In my first band, I didn't want to have a band in which I was a sideman. I didn't want to have a band that was like everything I had been doing up to that point. Why do someone else's band and call it mine? Doesn't make any sense!

At that particular time in the '80s, I did a lot of thinking, listening, and observing and came up with this band, Baron Down, with Ellery Eskellin, Steve Swell, and later on Josh Roseman replacing Steve Swell. Not exactly a commercial success but that was not what I was trying to do. To me, it was a success artistically because I was writing and creating sonic space context for the way I play drums. It was very, very clear and there was no doubt about it. If people want to hear me play behind a traditional rhythm section, they can hear me do that with a various assortment of people and listen to that on records. But I made that thought visible and that's what I mean by putting your thinking out there on the chopping block and it is what a lot of people are afraid of. So many people asked me, "How come you don't have a bass player?" That's such a stupid question and I have to say, really stupid question. Do people ask the Kronos Quartet why they don't have a drummer? Did anybody go up to Arthur Rubenstein and say, "Hey, how come you don't have a bass player?" People get so numbed out into thinking that a jazz or creative group means a bass, piano, drums, or a chordal instrument, a solo instrument, and a rhythm instrument. That's what I mean by thinking and keeping alive and awake. Music is music. Time is time. If there isn't a drummer on the bandstand, does that mean that there's not going to be any time? I hope not. The avant-garde is about liberating your thinking and making your thought processes visible.

SINCE WE LAST SPOKE, THE GREAT DRUMMER ELVIN JONES PASSED AWAY. WOULD YOU MIND SHARING YOUR OWN PERSONAL THOUGHTS?

Elvin Jones's music has gotten me through some pretty hard times throughout my life. The spirit in his playing cuts right to the bone and inspires me always. Elvin was a musical giant. He was a giant human being. A brilliant man who generously and thoughtfully encouraged those around him. A true genius. There are people that perfect a style of playing *within* the parameters of music. *Elvin dealt directly with the parameter of time.* Time is the common thread that connects all musicians in any ensemble playing music with a symmetrical pulse. If one deals with this *parameter*, you automatically affect *all* who take part in making music, as well as *all* who listen to what is being played. This is such a major move forward. *Elvin did this!* His time feel literally changed the world. He raised the standard and modeled the possibilities of how deep, how swinging, and how soulful time can feel. Couple this with a mastery of dynamics, touch, and brushes; anytime you hear a really swinging drummer, you can bet that for every two beats you hear, one of them is Elvin's.

4

TIM BERNE

Fascinated by unconventional and complex ideas, saxophonist and composer Tim Berne has become a creative force, exploring all the possibilities in sound through his fearless and brilliant imagination.

You didn't start playing the sax until you were about twenty. That would take quite a bit of confidence.

I didn't really think about it. In some ways, the more I played the more secure I became. But at the beginning, it was almost easier because I was so ignorant.

Was there a point when you said, "Hey, I'm going to do this seriously"?

I was pretty serious very early. I didn't know what was going to happen, but I was definitely determined to show people like my friends and family that I wasn't just fuckin' around. That was probably my motivation at first and then it was just the passion of wanting to play music.

Are critics starting to understand your work?

I really don't concern myself with what the critics might think and I like the fact that there isn't only one way to see what I'm doing. Somebody might think it's jazz but someone else might think it's some kind of rock thing, but that's one of the reasons why I don't try to explain it because I don't want to demystify it. However, I also don't want to imply that the way I see it is the only way to see it. Part of what makes improvisation, improvisation is the spontaneous magic of playing music. A lot of it is unexplainable.

I have read interesting reviews from critics, but for the most part, they are not very informative whether they are good or bad. If someone says something really negative, I'll go "holy shit" and get totally depressed, but then I'll go out on tour or get together with friends and it will reinforce what I'm doing because these are the people who really matter. At times I'll get pissed at a good review that's totally inaccurate but it doesn't last very long because I can't waste my time with that stuff. No one likes to be criticized or told that they suck in so many words. I know deep down that what I'm doing means something to enough people and that makes it worth doing.

ONE OF THE PROBLEMS WITH DOCUMENTATION FOCUSING ON JAZZ, WHETHER IT'S IN ACADEMICS OR DONE COMMERCIALLY (SUCH AS KEN BURNS'S SERIES), IS THAT IT SPENDS MOST OF ITS TIME CONCENTRATING ON WHAT JAZZ CREATED IN THE PAST TENSE AND LITTLE ON WHAT THE MUSIC IS CREATING AT THE MOMENT. DOESN'T THIS SEEM LIKE A LOST OPPORTUNITY TO EDUCATE POTENTIAL ASPIRING JAZZ STUDENTS AND EDUCATE THEM AS TO WHAT IS AVAILABLE TO THEM?

I was discussing the Ken Burn's series the other night and though I didn't see the whole show, I thought some of the older material was pretty interesting but clearly it was very influenced by Stanley Crouch and Wynton Marsalis to give a fairly narrow view of jazz. The stuff they feel is important and wanted to cover was probably done OK. But just like I don't expect to play at Lincoln Center, I also don't expect to be on TV and don't think I'm owed that. I've chosen to do something that for the most part is not popular entertainment and I have a choice. In some ways, I'm glad as I would hate to be in the limelight and have everything I say or do scrutinized because it's pretty hard not to be misunderstood at some point. Obviously, the show didn't cover the last thirty to forty years very well, but by looking at the people whose opinions were sought, I don't think it intended to. I also wonder whether many of the people who were critical would have wanted to be the ones to say, "I think this is important and I think this isn't."

I have my own opinions and just as I find certain music that gets a lot of attention not very interesting, I also find people on the other side of the fence that are just as narrow-minded as the so-called traditionalists and that's just as bothersome. If it's good, it's good and I don't really care if it's in the tradition or not. I have my preferences but they are not really stylistic. It's just that some people sound more convincing than others playing certain kinds of music. There's good blues and bad blues and it's totally subjective. It's just like the avant-garde stuff. Just because someone is playing free doesn't necessarily mean it's creative. There are people on both sides of the fence that are defensive about things and I'm not going to rain on anyone else's parade. In the end, my world is pretty different from that world anyway. I go out and tour in obviously different venues than the guys that were covered at the end of the Burns film. And again, I wouldn't expect to be involved in that.

For me, jazz doesn't get many opportunities and the young musicians might not necessarily be able to relate to the earlier periods of jazz as a medium to play. But if they knew of the music happening today, perhaps they would want to get involved with a music that they have more of a relationship with.

I agree that there is not a lot of education that offers a complete view, but I also don't expect the government to be calling me and offering me money to do my next record. You can waste a lot of energy beating your head against that wall. I'm the kind of person that says well, "OK, I have $50, I'm going to do $50 worth of music," rather than think, "Gee, I wish I had $3,000 so I could do this big project." I try to not let these things stop me. For me, it takes a lot less effort just to go out and do shit and if I get lucky or I get a grant, fine. But I don't really seek those kinds of things. Just like I don't really seek legitimacy and I don't need it. I get it from my peers and those are the opinions that matter to me.

Do you find there is more creativity and more opportunities as a result of the numerous informational mediums available today?

It's a different world today and though some of these opportunities are good, it has also made it easier for people that may not be qualified, to make music. There are more people trying little tricks to get over and it's also affected the music in that you can record or use a computer to make a pop music record really cheap. Sometimes, I kind of wish there were less opportunities and people would just focus on the music and what they really believe in. People are evolving and looking for the next thing or the next way of doing things perhaps quicker than they need to. There are too many options. I mean, I don't want to fucking get into computers but you almost have to, to keep up.

How much does the lack of awareness in today's creative music have to do with the industry not being able to define and market it efficiently?

The best salespeople are the ones who believe in what they're selling and can convey that to others. I know people who are very successful selling "difficult" music because they like it and are able to convey that to other people through their enthusiasm. The problem I have with labels is that everybody is so fucking pessimistic and they accept this whole thing of "Yeah, the industry sucks and blah, blah, blah." It's as if they'd rather accept that than try and do something about it. If you followed us around on tour, you'd see there are quite a few people that enjoy the music and they buy records, and I was one of them twenty, thirty years ago. I don't think corporate record companies are really designed to do that, but there are people within the independent companies that have that same kind of "The industry sucks!" attitude. So you just have to find ways of reaching the really hardcore people, and there are more ways than just sending them to Tower Records. There are a million other ways.

THE FOLLOWING IS A QUOTE FROM CECIL TAYLOR: "MUSIC HAS TO DO WITH A LOT
OF AREAS WHICH ARE MAGICAL RATHER THAN LOGICAL; THE GREAT ARTISTS, RATHER
THAN JUST GETTING INVOLVED WITH DISCIPLINE, GET TO UNDERSTAND LOVE AND AL-
LOW THE LOVE TO TAKE SHAPE." HOW MUCH OF YOUR MUSIC IS FROM LOGIC AND
HOW MUCH FROM THIS OTHER PLACE THAT CECIL TAYLOR DESCRIBES?

The first lesson I ever had was with Julius Hemphill, and the first thing he
talked about was magic. Literally the first thing. He said, "I have been thinking a
lot about magic lately," and that kind of stuck with me because so much of what
we do cannot be explained. You can't analyze it and say, "Why does this happen at
this particular time?" It just doesn't make any sense but you can feel it when it's
happening. It's magic and that's the only way to describe it, really.

That's a great statement from Cecil but on the other hand, it's not just about getting up there and blowing. There are the technical aspects, which are comparable
to speaking. The greater your vocabulary the more you can say but you still have
to organize it. I don't think I necessarily have a lot of technique, but I'm good at
organizing ideas so I kind of compensate for that. Just as Miles Davis wasn't the
best trumpet player but as a musician, he was really advanced. He got the most
out of what he had and I think if he would have needed more options, he would
have found more. And to me, that's what technique is. Some people have a lot of
technique because they need a certain amount to express their ideas and that's
how I work. I'll get in a rut and then I'll say, "OK, I have to do something to expand." Some people do all that and then try to figure out what they are doing, but
for me, it was never a separate issue. I always tried to learn these things simultaneously. Cecil is probably someone that practices quite a bit but then his music is
pretty organic; you're not listening to his technique, you're listening to his music.

DOES MUSIC REFLECT ITS PERIOD OF TIME AND SHOULD IT?

It reflects the person and the period of time. I hadn't given it a lot of thought
until you asked the question but I think it's pretty hard to avoid. I'm hoping that
what I do is timeless in that you can't tell whether it's from the '80s or '90s, but
who knows. There are really great musicians and that's what happens. You listen
to something from Cecil Taylor from the '60s and you don't say, "Wow, that's from
the '60s," unless the recorded sound tells you that. But after I get through writing
for a day, I don't really think about it because I'm trying to get it out of my brain
as fast as possible so I can start the next day fresh. I don't like to dwell on it because it's so hard to do. The whys just don't really matter to me.

HAVE YOU CHECKED OUT KEN VANDERMARK AND WHAT'S BEEN HAPPENING IN
CHICAGO LATELY?

I don't really know the music that well but I know that Ken has done a lot to
make things happen. He's been very helpful to me and there is no ego. He's just
trying to get better and do stuff. But there is so much music going on that we know
nothing about. Until I started playing with Craig Taborn, I had no idea. The guy

lives a block away from me and there's all kinds of people like that. You can't really judge what's happening by what you have access to or by what's available. There are a lot of people doing great music, but unless they can get gigs or someone writes about them, you're not going to know about them. I get to meet some of these people as I travel and hear them and I think, "Holy shit, where did this guy come from?"

THE INTERNET IS HELPING TO FIND OUT ABOUT OBSCURE MUSICIANS THAT ARE DOING CREATIVE WORK.

I have seen some of that but I have also seen things on there that have pissed me off more than the critics. Talk about misinformation! I'll stumble on things written about me and I'll think, "What the fuck is he talking about?" Or I'll say something on stage and the next thing you know it's on some e-mail list. It's almost to the point where it's just as negative because everybody kind of passes the info around as if it's fact. Making factual statements that are just wrong. You have to be careful because everybody has his or her agenda and it's just someone's opinion. It's good and it's bad and sometimes I think there is too much information.

THIS IS A QUOTE FROM WILLIAM PARKER: "THEY, THE MUSIC HISTORIANS, ALWAYS SEEM TO LEAVE OUT THE CHAPTER ON CREATIVE MUSIC; THEY DON'T SEEM TO GET IT. I HAVE ALSO OBSERVED THAT SOME OF THOSE WHO LOVE MUSIC LEAST ARE SPOKESPEOPLE FOR IT. I HAVE ALWAYS SAID THAT THIS MUSIC COMES FROM LOVE, NOT TECHNIQUE. TO LOVE MUSIC IS TO UNDERSTAND IT ON ITS HIGHEST PLANE. LOVE IS THE HIGHEST INTELLECTUAL LEVEL WE CAN ATTAIN. AT THIS POINT THERE IS NOTHING TO PROVE."

I'm not sure about expecting people to understand it because I'm not sure I understand it and I do it. I mean it's a pretty weird thing to do, to get together with people and improvise in front of an audience. You know, like why do we do it? And I don't know why. It's just something that when it's going good, you get transported and that's probably what he's talking about. You get transported to this place that's kind of like being in love. It's that type of euphoria. I'm sure you can get that from other things but we happen to get it from music. And I can't really explain to people what that's like and can't simulate it in any way. I just know that when something special happens during a gig, you can see that everybody in the band is as happy as you can get. And then conversely when you have a gig where it doesn't work, or at least we don't think it did, it's the opposite, where you are totally depressed. So it means a lot to us and because it does mean a lot to us, I think it means a lot to other people that we put so much of ourselves into it. I think it's a valuable thing because I see how it touches people and how it touches me. But as far as understanding it, good luck, because I don't.

HOW OFTEN DO YOU GET THOSE NIGHTS WHEN YOU KNOW THE MUSIC IS HAPPENING?

It depends because the more we do it the higher our expectations become. And also, sometimes the shows that we think are the shit, we'll hear the tape and it's not. The nights where we're really uncomfortable are sometimes the really great gigs. There is a certain tension and we are breaking into something that we haven't done and it's hard to evaluate the music that way. I have been on tours where it happened almost every night and then others where perhaps it was half of the nights. It really depends, but everybody seems to recognize when it happens almost all of the time. You can just tell. I have been on tours of twenty gigs and maybe seventeen of them felt great but there are so many variables.

HAS OUR SOCIETY BECOME MORE AGGRESSIVE TOWARD CULTURE IN A NEGATIVE WAY?

It's hard to say because I live in New York and that's not really America. New York is like everything at once. And it depends on what you mean by culture because opera gets a lot of money here in New York and there is a wide range of what the arts are. There are the arts that are generally accepted by middle-class America or white America or upper-class America or the government grants people receive, and then there are the arts that are marginal to a lot of other people. If anything, the interest is waning I suppose. I think it's really hard to tell if people are really excited about orchestras and art because it's just something that's there and is always supported. I wonder if people are really that excited or if they have planned to go out a certain amount of time to see culture. It's part of being in a certain class of people, but as far as people being excited about art because it's art, there's not a whole lot of that in America. There are a lot of other distractions and so many other things you can do where you don't have to go out or make an effort and I think that has an effect. It's a little different in Europe. You do gigs in Italy and a lot of people come because it's art, a cultural event and they think it's important.

WHERE DOES YOUR INSPIRATION COME FROM?

Inspiration can come from anywhere. I could be on a subway and hear some weird sound and get an idea or I could see a shitty movie and get something from it or just by having an interesting conversation. It comes from almost anything except listening to music. I almost have to avoid listening to music when I'm writing for some reason. For me, inspiration is wanting to do it. It's not like I sit around and all of a sudden there is an idea and I write it down. It's really work. Sometimes it's easy but most of the time it's a conscious effort and I have to try to be inspired.

DO YOU HAVE A PHILOSOPHY THAT YOU TRY TO IMPART ON YOUNG STUDENTS OR MUSICIANS?

Everyone does everything differently and you have to recognize that or it just gets too competitive and then you'll get discouraged. And it's so easy to get caught up in what everybody else is doing in music school and find yourself practicing for nine hours because somebody else is, but it just doesn't work that way. Some people can practice an hour and it can be a hell of an hour and then some can practice for nine hours and it's a waste of time. You have to find your own way to work and also try not to bite off more than you can chew at one time. It can get pretty overwhelming and lead to frustration.

YOU PLAY WITH A NUMBER OF MUSICIANS. HOW MUCH DOES THAT AFFECT YOUR OWN CREATIVE PROCESS?

I play with different people to feed myself ideas or when I think I'm getting stale. I do it to give myself a kick in the ass and force myself to move forward. I play with a keyboard player now, which is new for me and I did it to give myself a challenge, which it did. Therefore, I get a lot of my ideas from playing with different people, so it's important.

DOES IT HELP TO PLAY WITH PEOPLE WITH DIFFERENT MUSICAL BACKGROUNDS?

The bigger the vocabulary the better, but they still have to know what to do with it and the chemistry is also important. They don't necessarily have to want to play the same things but the willingness to cooperate is important. I'm not that interested in playing with people that just want to get off on playing a good solo and then walk off the stage when they're done. I like people who get involved and put themselves into it and there is a personal connection that I look for too as we may also have to sit on a train together for twelve hours. So there is a lot more to touring than just getting up and playing.

WHERE WOULD YOU SAY YOU COME FROM MUSICALLY?

I have no idea, but rhythm is important to me just from the music I listen to. But I honestly don't know and I don't have a style as I've really never been that kind of player. There are people who hear all kinds of influences that are not there but that's fine to me in a way.

BILL EVANS SAID THAT MUSIC HAS MORE TO DO WITH FEEL. HOW MUCH OF YOUR MUSIC COMES FROM FEEL VERSUS LOGIC?

It's about feel and logic but a lot of other stuff. His music may have been about feel but it's more than that when we're playing. But certainly that's an important component but sound is pretty important too.

DO YOU FEEL PRESSURE WHEN YOU ARE SOLOING IN FRONT OF THE AUDIENCE AND YOU'RE IN THAT MOMENT?

I don't know if pressure is the right word but you put pressure on yourself to come up with something interesting. It depends on how it's going. If the audience is there and there is a lot of trust and the band has been playing a lot, then you are pretty relaxed, but there are other times when you cannot get anything to happen and you are tense. It just depends but I wouldn't say it's pressure.

DO WOMEN AND MEN CREATE DIFFERENTLY?

Well, they think differently based on my experience. (Laughs) Can you generalize that? It's doubtful. I wouldn't make too much out of it. Women and men are different so it would follow that they would think about music differently at times.

WHAT HAVE YOU LEARNED FROM THE RISKS YOU HAVE TAKEN IN YOUR CAREER?

I don't know if they are risks because what am I risking really, someone not liking it? It's not that big a deal. You know what I mean? Are you risking anything writing this book? People can choose to read it or not like it but that's not really something like risking your life. You don't think of it that way really when you are doing it. It's what I do and I'm choosing to do it. No one said you have to do this, you have to play this weird music, or else. So I don't really see it as a risk. The risk is almost in not doing it. What I've learned from it is that it's probably the only time that I have ever expressed myself clearly. Where I really don't hold back and I'm not inhibited. Whereas in dealing with people, you are kind of always holding shit back or you don't say what you mean. You are scared to say this and you don't want to hurt anybody's feelings. When you are playing, that's gone. You just play and do whatever it takes to make music happen. I like that because it really brought me out of a shell just in terms of being shy or being incommunicative or scared of my ideas or of expressing myself.

CAN YOU CONNECT TODAY'S MUSIC POLITICALLY, CULTURALLY, OR SPIRITUALLY?

I'm sure there is a way to do that and with some people more than others. I think music is a real positive force and it certainly doesn't promote violence, maybe violent reaction, but I really don't connect it with politics if I'm honest with myself.

DO YOU THINK ABOUT THE IMPORTANCE OF YOUR MUSIC MOVING FORWARD?

I want it to change but I don't know if I can define what forward is. I mean I don't think any of this stuff is new. It's just being organized in a different way. It would be pretty presumptuous to think that I'm going to do something new or progressive or advanced. I'm more interested in trying not to retrace my steps and maybe it means going forward but adding to whatever I'm doing rather than duplicating it, but it doesn't mean it's going forward. Some people may consider it going backwards in terms of my development, but I just try to get better at expressing my ideas. Just being clear with my ideas. It's pretty hard to do the same thing twice. It just gets crazy. One of my role models is Julius Hemphill and he was extreme about not playing it safe in terms of how things were going to go musically or doing projects that he knew were going to work without much effort.

HOW MUCH INFLUENCE DID JULIUS HEMPHILL HAVE ON YOU?

He was a brilliant and amazing man. Amazing vision though most of it was undocumented and he was an incredible influence. It was all about ideas and that's what it's about for me. It doesn't really matter how you get to them. The music that I'm attracted to is about ideas and not about craft, and ultimately, it's about sounds and ideas and probably a million other things and that's why I don't like to talk about it. You know what I mean by that? I mean there are guys that can solo and there are those that can get inside the music and that's why you are attracted to people like Miles or Sonny Rollins because even though they are playing an old form, they are really ripping apart the song and getting to the point, the core of it, and they are personalizing it. And that's what people are attracted to. That's what separates it from people who are very good instrumentalists.

DO YOU TAKE THE AUDIENCE INTO CONSIDERATION WHEN YOU COMPOSE OR PLAY?

The audience is an important part of the picture or part of the equation. But I never set out to do what I think the audience will like. But I know if I'm honest about what I'm doing and I'm convinced, most of the audience will be convinced. I've been in situations where the audience will hate us and I'll think, "God help us." But we are so strong in our belief in what we are doing, we don't condescend that we'll win some people over. But you just don't ever expect it with people who don't ever listen to this kind of stuff. Just because we are so into it doesn't mean that we can be condescending or try to do something that is not us because people will pick up on that and you almost always sabotage yourself that way. But the audience is important and you can feel it. When it's not going right with the audience, it really affects the music. There is no way that you cannot notice that, and you can hear it and feel it in the room. There are certain clubs in Europe where we just know the audience is there, we feel confident and end up taking a lot of chances. It really leads to some interesting stuff.

ARE THE AUDIENCES THAT MUCH DIFFERENT IN EUROPE COMPARED TO THE STATES?

Not really. The difference is that there is a lot more money for music. Subsidized stuff. There are good audiences here; it's just hard to get to them, to get the gigs. It's a bigger country, a bigger place. Travel is complicated. In Europe, you can speed around on a train. You can play a gig in Rome and take a train ten hours away and play another gig as whereas here, the cities are not that close together. There's no train service and it's just much harder.

CAN YOU EXPLAIN YOUR APPROACH TO YOUR COMPOSITIONAL PROCESS?

It's really intuitive. I just sit down and say I have to write some music. It starts there and sometimes I just sort of free-associate and just write anything as fast as possible, or I'll sit there and stare for three days and eventually something will happen. But usually you just have to try. You can't only do it when the ideas are coming; you have to spend a lot of time thinking. After that, I'm just looking for contrast and for ways to stimulate improvisation. The point of written music is to create a structure and motivate people to want to play. Give them ideas or put them in a space where they'll feel like improvising. The transition from improvisation to notate music is really important and I try to disguise what's written and what's improvised. I like to play around with that and make it seamless so it's just not, here is the tune and here is the solo and here is the tune again. If I want to have some impact, then I have to be able to write music that makes people want to play and that's what being a band leader or composer is about. You want to have some influence.

DO YOU HAVE A VISION FOR THE FUTURE OF MUSIC AND YOURSELF?

(Laughs.) I see piles of money coming, raining down from the sky.

I don't have a vision because I know that there are a million points of view and you can't really tie it all in and say OK, here's this vision. You know there's commerce music, there's so-called art music, and I don't think there is anyone that isn't playing for an audience. There isn't anyone I know that says I don't give a shit about the audience. That's all part of the picture and it's not gratifying to just sit home and play. I need the audience to really make everything work and to make it mean something. And we all think people feel it's important to have music or else we wouldn't do it.

5

PETER BROTZMANN

Very few musicians in the history of jazz or creative music have created a voice as powerful and distinct as legendary German saxophonist, Peter Brotzmann. Playing with unyielding conviction, he blows with relentless, brutal passion; an honest and innovative voice during a time of despair, devoid of creative respect and sensitivity.

HAVE WE BECOME A SOCIETY WITHOUT THE PATIENCE TO BE CHALLENGED, OPEN ONLY TO THINGS THAT ARE EASILY ACCESSIBLE?

I think it's happening worldwide and though it's nice to have information readily available, in the end, I don't think there is much time for anybody anymore. It's ridiculous and at times, people know where I'm going to perform or what I am supposed to be doing before I do. It's a shame there isn't any privacy anymore and I don't like it.

THE YOUNGER GENERATION SEEMS TO BE ABLE TO DEAL WITH ALL OF THIS IN-FORMATION BETTER THAN MOST, AND, AT THE SAME TIME, THEY SEEM TO BE LOOK-ING FOR MUSIC THAT HAS MORE DEPTH AND THAT CHALLENGES THEM AS LISTENERS.

Yes, and that might be a good thing. I like playing for younger audiences be-cause they can have certain intelligence and are often looking for something more than what is usually made available to us.

ARE THERE DIFFERENCES IN HOW MUSIC IS PERCEIVED IN EUROPE COMPARED WITH THE U.S.?

In Europe, we view music in the old European way of looking at art, and the American roots of the music are completely different and based as entertainment. But that's good because otherwise we wouldn't have all of this beautiful music. But within this music, there are common objectives between all of us. We don't do this as a way to earn money or to get famous; we do it because we have to.

COULD IT BE THAT CREATIVE MUSIC IS TOO FORWARD-THINKING FOR MOST OF SO-CIETY TODAY?

Nothing is too forward-thinking, but it might be that the music is too complex. Governments all over the world resist change and would like to keep their societies stupid. I also don't believe in all the globalization bullshit.

JAZZ HAS ALWAYS BORROWED FROM INFLUENCES OF DIFFERENT CULTURES. IS THIS POSITIVE FOR THE MUSIC?

I think there is danger with all the information we are talking about. We can learn whatever we want regardless of whether you are in Europe, Asia, or America, but I think we need to concentrate more on our own cultures. We shouldn't neglect our cultural roots. And it might be better if a Japanese musician focused on their own music rather than always listening to what's happening in New York, Chicago, or in Europe. And I think it's the same for us Europeans, and for young American musicians, I think it's more important than ever to study the roots of the blues and the gospel rather than just looking at what is popular or part of the mainstream.

IS THERE A CHANCE THAT A NEW TYPE OF CREATIVITY COULD COME OUT OF WHAT IS HAPPENING IN THE WORLD TODAY?

Though my European friends Evan Parker, Han Bennink, Derek Bailey along with myself had not yet met each other, we all started in this music in the same way during the '60s. I think this was because we viewed politics and societal changes in different but similar ways. The society you live in will influence you and the music that you play, and it happens worldwide. It has to. Look at the beautiful music that William Parker is playing in New York. He's not only trying to survive but also provide an example for kids that there is a better way to get out of the shit. And everybody does it in their own way, in their own society and community. And of course it looks different in good old Wuppertal, Germany, than it does on the Lower East Side of New York or Chicago. But in a way, improvised music is still on the lowest step of the ladder of culture; we still have to fight. But we always have and still do today. We are busy all hours of the day just to find a way to present our music, to make some money, to try and convince others and find a way to survive.

Today, I can get a good bottle of wine, live comfortably, and after forty years in this music, I don't complain, but there are a lot of younger people who cannot find possibilities to play. This is a problem because being on the road is where you learn and where you grow but this is getting lost.

ARE WE GETTING ANY CLOSER TO BRIDGING THE GAP BETWEEN OUR DIFFERENT
CULTURES?

I think the exchanging of ideas between artists was more prevalent in the '50s
and the '60s. I was able to work with different people in theater and within different genres of music and I believe the same thing was happening in the States. The
artistic community seemed to be much more open, but now everything is placed
into boxes. You even have to ask where you can work and New York is a good example of this.

Education teaches people to look for their own thing, which to me encourages
selfish behavior, but this is developing in other countries too. The real stuff happens on stage but it's happening less and less. Hopefully it will come back as there
is a need for it. There are also fewer jam sessions today though it's an honor and a
privilege when I get to play with older players such as Robert Barry and Walter
Perkins, who both came out of Chicago and were drummers with Sun Ra in their
early years. Perkins died February 15th of this year.

IS THERE A CHANCE THAT WE HAVE BECOME A MORE VISUAL SOCIETY AND PLACE
LESS IMPORTANCE ON VARIOUS ELEMENTS OF SOUND?

You cannot even go to the men's toilet in an airport today without hearing music that is nothing more than disturbing noise. And wherever you go, sound is all
around us along with advertising bombarding us from every angle, which I think
is a device to influence and control people. So yes, I think it's true; there is too
much of both.

IS IT MORE DIFFICULT FOR YOUNG MUSICIANS OR STUDENTS TO BE CREATIVE TO-
DAY?

Most of the young musicians today in both Europe and the U.S. are far more
schooled than we ever were. That may help, but if you are spending less time on
your instrument and on the road for time on the computer, then you are losing out
on what could help you. Playing and communication might be old-fashioned, but
it enhances the music. There are many different ways to work, but so many young
musicians are relying on so much technique that the personal voice and the exchange of ideas is becoming more and more rare.

IS THERE A COMMON PHILOSOPHY THAT YOU TRY TO IMPART AMONGST YOUNG MU-
SICIANS?

As musicians, we need to be honest in what we are doing and try to set the right
examples. And though my young saxophone friends like Ken Vandermark from the
U.S. and Mats Gustafsson from Sweden come from different backgrounds and
play very different from each other, they are like brothers. And when we get together, we play our asses off. But for me, it's good to get information from another
generation and I hope I can give back from the little experience that I have. In my

life, I have learned that in order to appreciate the world, you have to know what it looks like in the gutter.

I think Cecil is right but then again, we also have completely different roots. If you cannot find a way to express the secret parts of your life, you shouldn't be an artist anyway. And of course everyone will express themselves in different ways, but I think that that's what makes it interesting.

For many years now, I have tried to find out where the roots of my music and approach to playing may have come from. I was born during the war, grew up after the war, and was confronted with what my forefathers had done during the 1st and 2nd World Wars. Nobody would provide any answers so I had to look for the answers myself. I still have memories of burning towns and dead people from when my family moved from Poland to what is now West Germany. I was only a kid but those pictures are still very vivid in my mind and I still don't know.

I also received my first real shock when I was confronted with pictures out of Auschwitz and Buchenwald, from a film made by Alain Resnais and words by German Jewish writer Paul Celan. But the older generation would not talk about these things, and when they did, you couldn't always trust them. So I had to look for the answers myself, and I think this history is part of what makes my music so strong and passionate. It's the dark and secret side of my life.

When I was young, I believed that this could never happen again. I really believed that. I thought I could work and help prevent this from ever taking place again. Of course now, I can say that I was a little too young, a little too foolish, and a little naïve. But we still have the obligation to try, and it starts with respect for other human beings.

That's difficult to answer but different combinations can influence my playing. For instance, Louis Moholo will influence my playing in ways that will be different from how I would play with Han Bennink, but overall, I think my sound stays the same.

Drummers who provide the rhythmic feel have always been one of the most important parts of my music along with some bass players. They all have their own personal sense of time just as every human being walks in a different way. For example, Milford Graves moves in a completely different way than Han Bennink and they have their own separate way of playing. It's not so much in the way they count the time, but in the way they move, the way they feel. It's the same way that horn players have a different feel. Sonny Rollins is very different from Coltrane. It's a very important thing.

TENSION SEEMS TO BE A SIGNIFICANT FACTOR WITH YOUR MUSIC.

Tension is something that belongs to any kind of relationship; in both the making of art as well as in daily life. But it is not something that you can necessarily construct. It happens. You have to feel it and develop it.

ARE THERE SPECIFIC THINGS THAT YOU ARE TRYING TO DO WITH YOUR MUSIC TODAY?

I see things a little bit more concrete and I want to express my experiences and sounds more clear and make it simpler than it was twenty years ago. It's loving the horn and loving to create things together with other musicians. That's my vision and what I want to continue to do—to continue to find out the possibilities.

WHAT DO YOU ENVISION FOR THE FUTURE OF CREATIVE MUSIC?

I'm still convinced that what we learn from each other is most important and that comes from being on the road together. That's where the important lessons take place. It's getting together, taking risks and it's a process—not a product. This is important and needs to be very clear.

WHAT INSPIRES YOU?

After over thirty years, it may look and sound a little bit different, but in the end, I think my inspiration still comes from the same place. When I was a young man, I thought I could change the world. I was angry. And now, after all of these years and all that we may have done to try and make things better, it has done nothing! We are just as foolish as we have always been. But that shouldn't be resignation. We have reason to be optimistic and we must try to make a difference.

ARE YOU STILL SEARCHING?

I'm looking for more; for more musicians to work with and perhaps a bit more respect and patience. I only know that I will die in some year or tomorrow. Until then, I will blow some air through my horn until some good friend comes up on stage and tells me: "Brotzmann, come on, it's enough." It would be better if I should know when it's time.

6

REGINA CARTER

I don't think I'll ever forget Regina Carter's performance as a guest with Ray Brown's trio just days before he passed away. Like a proud father, he stood glowing with admiration while she played beautiful, rich, awe-inspiring melodies with an intensity transcending the strings of her violin.

In a period where women in mainstream jazz are considered more marketable for their looks than their talent, Regina Carter is the first violinist since Stefane Grappelli and Jean-Luc Ponty to excite the imagination of contemporary jazz listeners. Her family roots have provided her independence and strength to move her music forward, yet her passion remains and radiates from the gentleness of her soul.

YOUR RECORD *SOMETHING FOR GRACE* WAS DEDICATED TO YOUR MOTHER. HOW IMPORTANT WAS HER INFLUENCE?

My mother has been very instrumental throughout my whole life. She grew up very poor and wanted to make sure we had the opportunities that she didn't. As a retired schoolteacher, education was a very big deal to her, and it was important that we were exposed to things and had a wider viewpoint of the world.

WAS THE DIVERSITY OF MUSIC THAT YOU WERE EXPOSED TO FROM HER AS WELL?

The exposure to music came from her mother who graduated from Morris Brown University in 1915. She taught my mother how to play piano, and my mother thought that my brothers, who were much older than I, should take piano lessons. Then one day I walked up and played one of their pieces and the music teacher said that I had a gift. But at two years old, I was too young for piano lessons. However, when I was four, my mother found out about the Suzuki method, which is geared more towards really young children and enrolled me into classes. I loved it so I just kept going.

THE RECORD *AFTER A DREAM*, WHICH WAS RECORDED WITH PAGANINI'S GUARNERI "CANON" VIOLIN HAS BEEN A BREAKTHROUGH RECORD FOR YOU.

Yes, it hit number one on the jazz billboard charts but still doesn't warrant the type of support that other artists might receive. I get what I get and luckily have a good manager who knows the business and fights for me. But I don't get caught up in the business anymore and really don't let it bother me. There comes a time when you have to decide whether you want to be a star or do you want to be an artist? When I was younger, I thought I wanted to be a star and of course I would like to make star money, but I also know that I have to sell records and need to have a record deal.

For this record, I was prepared to borrow the money because having this record documented was that important to me—even if it only sold one record—because I was making history. It was a once-in-a-lifetime opportunity to be able to record with this violin so I was not going to pass that up. Therefore, "no" was not an option and I didn't really care about the consequences. The president of Verve Records said that although he wasn't on board in the beginning stages of the recording, he was taken by my passion for it and the fact that I was going to do it with or without them. I think that helped in the decision to provide the financial support.

YOUR PASSION ALWAYS COMES THROUGH IN LIVE PERFORMANCE, BUT AS FAR AS RECORDINGS GO, IT COMES THROUGH WITH THIS RECORD MORESO COMPARED WITH ANY OF YOUR PREVIOUS WORK.

When I finally had permission to play this violin, John Clayton (bassist and composer) said I should listen to music from the French Impressionist period because there are harmonic similarities, which would make for a perfect direction for me. I have heard records where musicians have taken classical pieces and tried to turn them into jazz pieces and they sounded real corny. I don't know if it's because of the period they were recorded, but these particular tunes were already so highly beautiful and rich, we really didn't have to add or change very much. It had more to do with our approach as opposed to how a classical player would approach it.

I also heard a recording that Fred Hersch was on called *Dance for a Dead Prince*, and it was so beautiful and I was like, wow! It was from this record of compositions from French Impressionist composers and I knew that's what I wanted to record. A record that would hopefully be touching and very beautiful to people and when I listened to them, that's how they felt. I also felt that the arranger, Jorge Calandrelli, did a wonderful job. It's his forte but I appreciated him spending time with the quintet so when he wrote the arrangements, he built them around us.

I HAVE ALWAYS ADMIRED YOUR WILLINGNESS AND ABILITY TO INCORPORATE OTHER
MUSICAL INFLUENCES INTO YOUR MUSIC. ARE YOU HAPPY WITH THIS RECORDING?

I love this recording and not just because of being able to use this violin, but because there was so much magic happening when we recorded the music. You
could just feel the energy in the room and many of the tunes were recorded on
first takes. It was really, really scary and we thought, "Wow, what's happening, like
what's going on here?" When that happens in the studio, it's really sad and difficult
when the session is over because I always go into a really deep depression afterwards. I've been on this high for so many days and then it's over and everyone goes
their separate ways and on to the next thing that you have to do.

THERE ARE MANY WITHIN THE INDUSTRY THAT BELIEVE IT'S VERY DIFFICULT TO
GET A FOLLOWING OF LISTENERS WITHOUT A SPECIFIC STYLE OR DIRECTION. BUT
YOU HAVE NEVER REALLY TAKEN THAT APPROACH AND HAVE BEEN ABLE TO EXPAND
YOUR AUDIENCE.

I was labeled a smooth jazz artist after my first two records and became a little
worried. After I signed with Verve, I still played some of the music from those
early records, and I remember a woman coming up to me at a concert saying she
didn't like the new music I was doing but liked this one song called *Don't Explain*.
I had actually recorded that tune on one of my earlier records with Lonnie Plaxico
and told her that if she liked that song, she should check out Billie Holiday. It's just
a different style and that she should try and be open and listen more. I appreciated her honesty and the fact that she came to check it out and people should be
open to check out new things. Musicians as well as nonmusicians—and I think it's
dangerous if you don't. I'm shocked that I have kept a lot of my following. When
I go into people's homes and look at their record collections, I have never met anyone that had all be-bop, rap or all they had was renaissance music. People listen
to a lot of different styles of music so who's to say that a CD with a few different
styles of music is going to bother them? I think it would be refreshing. It's the industry that has a hard time figuring out how to market that approach. If I were a
marketing person, I would think it would be exciting.

ARE YOU FINDING THAT PERCEPTIONS ARE CHANGING WITH REGARD TO THE VIOLIN?

Some perceptions have changed but not enough for the record companies to
start signing violinists in the same way that they sign vocalists and saxophonists; they
still don't look at violinists as being that marketable. If I'm getting press, Karen
Briggs who plays with Yanni is getting press, and someone like Mark O'Connor is
getting press and we are all successful, what's the problem here? I think people's
perceptions are changing, but not necessarily those within the industry.

IS IT POSSIBLE THAT THERE IS TOO MUCH DIVERSITY IN MUSIC TODAY FOR THE LIS-
TENER TO DIGEST?

If you look at what's being played on U.S. radio stations and what's popular on MTV, then compare it to what's being played elsewhere, it's really interesting and different. World and creative music doesn't have an outlet in the United States, unless you listen to the public radio stations. Big corporations control TV and radio and all of it is starting to crystallize as one where they play the same artists and the same tunes. Therefore, it's very difficult for independent musicians to put out their own records on smaller labels unless they can get their own distribution. We can be so closed-minded in this country and have decided what's popular, what's going to sell and that's all you are going to see or hear, which makes it so much more difficult.

DOES SOCIETY TODAY HAVE DIFFICULTY WITH CREATIVITY THAT IS NOT EASILY EXPLAINED OR UNDERSTOOD?

I think we are really lax right now in every sense of the word. We don't know who we are and have been brainwashed and have forgotten how to stand up and fight for things. This is a completely different time than say the '60s, when musicians formed their own record companies and there were outlets for the music. People knew what they wanted and they fought for it. They wouldn't stand for anything less, and today we just don't on any kind of level. I think people are being creative in the arts but people have to be willing to go out of their way to find it but we are not there yet. We are not starving for creativity and are still under the cloud.

ARE JAZZ TRADITIONALISTS HAVING A DIFFICULT TIME ACCEPTING THAT A MUSIC FORM CONSIDERED "AMERICAN" NOW HAS MORE VISIBLE INTERNATIONAL AND DIVERSE ASPECTS WITHIN IT?

It's kind of hard to say but it's always going to be an American music as that's where its roots are from. That's where it comes from but jazz has always had influences from elsewhere. Look at the music of Dizzy Gillespie with its Afro-Cuban influences. But it's a difficult question because people sometimes like to forget where things came from and I think that has happened with jazz. There was a time in this country when a lot of people didn't want to associate with this music because it was thought to be something very negative and it had a lot of very racist overtones attached to it. Many people want to erase history, especially in this country, but you can't erase the history. I don't think people are necessarily concerned with the international influences of jazz, but I do have difficulty when people try to erase the history of it.

HISTORIANS HAVE HAD DIFFICULTY WRITING OR EXPLAINING THE MUSIC OF THE LAST FORTY YEARS. HOW WILL A JAZZ HISTORIAN EXPLAIN THE LAST FORTY YEARS OF JAZZ FIFTY YEARS FROM NOW?

When I was in school learning about jazz, I learned about bop, the cool jazz scene, but after a certain era, it suddenly stopped. You were not learning about periods anymore and that's where it got into trouble. It would be better to have said

that, "Well, there is a style of music that's called smooth jazz and these are the
artists associated with it and this is why it was called that and there was this other
music going on at the same time." Previous periods are never going to die because
there are always going to be people playing that music, and because of influences
from different styles of music, new styles are going to be created. People have
stopped studying and by saying that that's not jazz or by ignoring it, is not going to
make it go away. Instead of ignoring it and fighting about it, give it a name and give
it a category so that people can learn about it. There is also a danger in this because people will say that they listen to jazz and say their favorite artist is Kenny
G but have never heard of Ella Fitzgerald or John Coltrane. They hear that music
and go, "Oh, I hate that," but it's just something they haven't heard. Or people
hear Miles or Kenny Garrett and then hear Najee and say, "That's not jazz." So I
think that all of this music and all of these styles have just been pushed under the
title of jazz and anything goes now, which is really dangerous because anyone can
call themselves a jazz artist.

A lot of young people don't even study the history of the music but call themselves jazz musicians. I have met young jazz violin players and I'll ask if they know
very easy standards and they don't know any of them. You don't have to necessarily like all of those tunes but you have to go back and study them. In no other music are you allowed to say, "I'm a classical musician and can play this piece," but
not know anything about Bach, Mozart, or Debussy. It's just unheard of. The music and the learning of the music has been disrespected.

MILES WAS CRITICIZED IN HIS LATER PERIOD FOR DOING ARRANGEMENTS OF POP
TUNES. BUT JAZZ HAS ALWAYS TAKEN FROM POP AND MADE IT ITS OWN. HAVE YOU
BEEN CRITICIZED FOR ANY OF YOUR WORK?

I've been criticized so much for everything. (Laughs.) Just spell my name right!
Come on, I mean what was *My Favorite Things*? That was not a jazz standard but
a popular tune of the day. I just don't pay attention to the criticisms. I do the music that I grew up with and I'm sure people have criticized me about that but I'm
happy and if I'm happy, it probably comes through the music and then I'm able to
touch people and that's why I play music. I remember seeing Stephane Grapelli
and Jean-Luc Ponty and it looked like they were having such a great time, and I
watched the people having a great time and the feeling that I felt and that's what
I always wanted. Watching Ray Brown and Kenny Barron and seeing the way they
are on the road and observing the things they didn't care about. And when I play
for people and they come up to me and tell me, "That piece really touched me,"
that's why I play and I can't worry about what people think of me or worry if they
think I'm selling out.

THE FOLLOWING IS A QUOTE FROM CECIL TAYLOR: "MUSIC HAS TO DO WITH A LOT
OF AREAS WHICH ARE MAGICAL RATHER THAN LOGICAL; THE GREAT ARTISTS, RATHER
THAN JUST GETTING INVOLVED WITH DISCIPLINE, GET TO UNDERSTAND LOVE AND AL-
LOW THE LOVE TO TAKE SHAPE." HOW MUCH OF YOUR MUSIC IS FROM LOGIC AND
HOW MUCH FROM THIS OTHER PLACE THAT CECIL TAYLOR DESCRIBES?

It's all from the other place because I don't really think about music. I was horrible in school and have no theory chops. I read music but I don't read chord changes, so if I play a tune that I don't know, people in the band have to play it so I can hear what it is. There isn't a real logic that I use, so I would say it's all from that other place. I'm lucky to have a band that's a family musically and I love playing with them. It's a real love on and off the stage so that when we play music, it's coming from a place strictly out of love and that's the only thing that I allow. Sometimes I wish I could be more logical because I think it's something you can learn but everybody can't necessarily get to that emotional place and transmit that through their instrument. So I feel those that can, are very lucky.

WHEN YOU COMPOSE, DO YOU ENVISION WHAT YOU WANT THE MUSIC TO DO FOR THE LISTENER OR IS IT MORE ON A PERSONAL LEVEL?

I don't compose that often but when I do, it's more on a personal level. The last piece I wrote was for a string quartet and I knew what I wanted it to be but what was coming out was something totally different, so I tried to force it. The piece was to be based on a personal photograph I had taken in Israel last year on a camel tour through the desert, but what was coming out was almost folkloric sounding. I'm not one that can just sit down and say, "Let me try this or use this idea." And because I don't have a strong theory background, I have to wait for it to come to me and it can take a long time. At times I'll just sit there and think, "OK, any day now," just waiting for some idea to drop from the sky. There can be days where nothing happens and I have to accept that.

CHARLES MINGUS SAID THAT YOU CANNOT TEACH STYLE BUT CAN TEACH SOMEONE TO APPRECIATE IT. THAT STYLE IS THE WAY YOU PLAY AND A VERY PERSONAL THING. HOW HAVE YOU REACHED YOUR OWN STYLE?

It was by listening to a lot of different people, a lot of different instruments, and a lot of different styles of music. I think we learn music the same way in which we talk, which is another way of having a conversation. You are going to hold onto a little of each person you listen to but hopefully won't pick out one person and copy them to where you sound exactly like them because then you still don't have a style but have cloned them. You already have your box voice so to speak, but what's going to come out is a culmination of everything you've listened to. It just kind of comes up and you never know what you are going to get because you have thrown all these things in. You get what you get.

IS IT MORE DIFFICULT FOR A STUDENT TO BE CREATIVE IN TODAY'S SOCIETY?

I think it's difficult to be creative today because as I said previously, we're not starving for anything fresh yet. We're not sick of what's being fed to us. So in a way, I think it's difficult to be creative because a lot of companies are looking for and want you to be the last group that was successful. The Buena Vista Social Club was a huge success but what they don't understand is that that was part of their culture, somebody went over there and made a successful film about them and that helped. They were always in Cuba and we didn't know anything about them. Yes that record is huge, but that doesn't mean by doing a Latin record you are going to be a huge success. Marketing people have to know how to market you and know whether you are going to be accepted in that world as well. Just because you do that doesn't mean you are going to be successful.

We are so passive in accepting what is being fed to us and if you are creative and come up with something entirely new, then you have to be affiliated with someone with the power, the money, and vision to expose you to the world.

WOMEN JAZZ ARTISTS DON'T SEEM TO GET THE RESPECT AS ARTISTS IN THE SAME WAY THAT MEN DO. IF IT DOES ARRIVE, IT TAKES MUCH LONGER AND MAYBE IS NOT ON A LEVEL EQUAL TO THEIR ABILITY. ALSO, THE INDUSTRY, AT LEAST WITHIN THE MAINSTREAM, SEEMS TO FOCUS ONLY ON WOMEN PIANISTS AND VOCALISTS. WHAT'S IT GOING TO TAKE TO CLOSE THIS GAP?

Just look at TV and how women are portrayed. Especially if you look at MTV where women are portrayed in a very negative light. It's very degrading how people in general look at and view women. And you're right, because women are usually singers or piano players . . . and I have to laugh because I remember before the head of A&R left Verve Records, he said that I should do a vocal record, but I'm not a singer. I would never try to do a vocal record because that's disrespectful to real singers. That's why I think people say, "Oh, I can sing, I can do that," not knowing what it really takes to be a real singer. They think they can do this, which is probably true because the industry, especially in the pop world, will pick up girls who are very cute, young, someone writes them a tune, and it becomes a big hit. It's like a factory. Unfortunately, because jazz has to compete with that, they do the same thing. They take the women and make sure they look a certain way in their photo shoots, so that they can compete and maybe cross them over to the pop world. And it's usually singers, and singers have always gotten the attention, and it's really difficult for instrumentalists whether it be women or men. If you look at the sales for jazz, you have vocalists selling upwards of 100,000 records, while the top jazz instrumentalist might be selling 25,000 to 50,000. There is such a huge gap, but I think a lot of it is because of marketing. I don't know how or if that's going to change, but if it does, it won't be anytime soon.

DO WOMEN AND MEN CREATE DIFFERENTLY OR DOES IT HAVE MORE TO DO WITH THE INDIVIDUAL?

I don't know. I've never been a man and I'm not trying to be silly. I think creating is just creating because it comes from the spirit, your soul and I don't think your soul is male or female. Creating depends on the individual as far as how they create, but I definitely think that within a band it can make a difference. I have another woman in my band and I can feel the difference because our energies are different. I have also been in a band of all women, and it just depends on what kind of energy you want around you or what kind of balance. For me, I like having one

other woman and three guys and that's the perfect balance of male–female energy
for me in that group. But as far as creating, that doesn't come from a human aspect but from somewhere else.

WHAT HAVE YOU LEARNED ABOUT YOURSELF FROM THE RISKS YOU HAVE TAKEN IN
YOUR CAREER?

Risks are really scary and very difficult for me and they don't come easy. Sometimes I think the rug gets pulled out from under my feet or sometimes situations
have become so uncomfortable and unbearable I'm forced to make a move. I've
always thought there is a right decision and a wrong decision, and one thing I have
learned is that as far as music and being creative, there isn't a right or wrong decision. There are just decisions and you live the task that comes with that decision.
If you make a decision, you have to trust it and move forward with blind faith. If
you spend too much time going down that road and looking back at what you could
have done differently, then you are going to miss all of the opportunities this world
is offering you and then it will be a mute point to have made any decision at all.
You have to follow your gut . . . and that's a very scary thing because there isn't
solid proof for anything to tell you what's going to happen. You just have to follow
that. The more I have done that, the more I have come to be confident with that.
I'm not afraid but know at some point it's going to be OK. That's what I have really learned and that's on a personal level and a musical level.

I have also tried to surround myself with really positive musicians where it's just
about playing the music, dealing with it and not get caught up in why someone else
has something or whatever. You can feel someone's attitude or what their negative
baggage is and I try to stay away from those people. I have found that when I
haven't, it's been a very unhealthy situation and it's made playing music horrendous. When I step up on stage, I want to have a great time. I want to enjoy the
music and I want to enjoy everyone around me, and there have been situations
where that hasn't been the case because there has been so much negativity. I remember thinking, "OK, I don't want to play with this person ever again and I don't
want to feel like this ever again."

WHAT IS IT ABOUT JAZZ AND THE ART FORM THAT IS IMPORTANT TO YOU?

That it's a music of the people, like a voice. It is a music that really allows one
to have freedom of speech if you will. It's a safe place to have freedom of speech.
It allows you to be creative and to take chances without having to know what the
outcome is going to be and that's really the beauty of it. When on stage, it's like
painting right there and neither you nor the audience knows what the painting is
going to end up being but it's OK.

WHAT DO YOU ENVISION THE FUTURE OF JAZZ TO BE OR FOR YOURSELF PERSONALLY?

It's my savior! (Laughs.) Jazz is the place where I can go and can take all of my
issues, whatever they may be and pull them into my instrument and work through

them or just get rid of them or just shed them. Yeah, yeah, it's my savior . . . especially from myself! (Laughs.)

Do you think there is a chance that a new type of creativity might come out of all that is going on globally today?

I think so but whether the world will hear it or be exposed to it, is another question!

Do you have a philosophy or some way of looking at life that you would be willing to share?

I feel like I'm in a period where I'm becoming more aware due to negative and sad events happening in my life. I'm becoming aware that we can't control everything and I'm a big control freak. People say, "As sad as you can be, it also lets you know that that's how happy you can also be." I guess my philosophy is to know I cannot control things but not let circumstances control me either. Continue to try and live and allow myself to feel things whether they are good, really sad or horrible and know it's OK. Come out stronger and don't let it stop me from living. Live life, don't let it stop you, and know you don't have to be a victim.

7

CHICAGO ROUNDTABLE

Peter Brotzmann, Germany; Mats Gustafsson, Sweden; Joe Mcphee, New York; Paal Nilssen-Love, Norway; Ken Vandermark, Chicago

There has never been a collection of creative musicians quite like the Peter Brotzmann Tentet. And when I recently attended my first performance in Chicago, not for a moment did I expect to be moved on so many emotional and intellectual levels.

Inspired by the writings of American poet Kenneth Patchen, Brotzmann has composed what I consider to be one of his greatest and most meaningful works, *Be Music, Night*. While integrating the improvisatory readings of Welsh performer Mike Pearson, Peter feels Patchen's work represents "[a] strong voice demanding humanity, solidarity and love. A voice—still not well known in his own country nor in the rest of the world, a voice we need to listen to, especially in our dark times."

The following morning, with the intensity of the previous night's performance of *Be Music, Night* still in the air, five of the performers of the Tentet came together for a roundtable discussion to talk music, creativity, and the many facets influencing society and culture today. But what made this occasion and discussion unique is that, for the most part, all five of these creative artists embody diversity, as they originate from different cultures. Peter Brotzmann is from Germany, Mats Gustafsson from Sweden, Paal Nilssen-Love from Norway, Joe McPhee from New York, and Ken Vandermark from Chicago.

Like their music, the discussion was driven and intense, and reflected the compassion that each of these fascinating individuals brings to their lives and their music, each and every moment.

A GROUP OF MUSICIANS FROM CHICAGO CAME TOGETHER IN THE MID-1960S AND FORMED THE ASSOCIATION FOR THE ADVANCEMENT OF CREATIVE MUSICIANS (AACM). ARE THERE PARALLELS IN WHAT ALL OF YOU ARE TRYING TO DO BUT ON AN INTERNATIONAL LEVEL?

PB: That's a question for you (Ken). I'm too old for that.

KV: The members of the AACM came from a different period and community along with a different set of politics, but I do feel a kinship with their self-determination in organizing situations where they could perform within the context of what they chose for themselves. And my understanding is that the AACM was very, very organized and while I am trying to connect with the musicians and find a way for the music to work, they were very devoted to the community in a way that was exceptional.

Part of my own personal interest is in trying to work in situations that are not just devoted to jazz, but it's also about being active in the process of trying to find the audience that is interested in the kind of music that we are doing.

PB: I first met the guys in the AACM about 1969 at a festival in Frankfurt, Germany, and from the very beginning, their primary objective was in getting work. They built up a community that was able to take care of all social aspects of life, and as Europeans we didn't have to worry about that. And I don't think the white middle-class American had to, but I'm sure that the black guy, besides getting work, had to worry about making life a little bit more comfortable and a bit more secure for all of the members of the community. That was my impression from the very beginning and it has always come back to getting work. If there is work, then all of the other questions can be resolved.

I SENSE A VERY STRONG PASSIONATE COMMITMENT AND A CERTAIN ATTITUDE TO-WARD THE MUSIC FROM ALL OF YOU WHEN YOU PERFORM. I ALSO SENSE A BOND. MU-SICIANS TALK ABOUT PLAYING AS IF THERE IS NO TOMORROW BUT YOU GUYS PLAY LIKE YOUR LIFE DEPENDS ON IT. IS THIS EVER DISCUSSED?

MG: We don't ever discuss it. (Laughs.)

PB: We do it for the moment, and the moment leads us to tomorrow. You have to do it with respect for yourself and for the guys you are working with, but you also need to develop your ideas. I'm always trying to be realistic, but without a vision for the future, it's useless to look beyond last night's concert.

MG: The commitment for the music has to be 100 percent, otherwise you might as well stay home. Even in rehearsals, people are playing their brains out. It's not something that is discussed, it's just the way it is and could not be any other way.

PB: When I was younger, I remember visiting the rehearsals of professional musicians and it seemed to be cool for them to play with only half a commitment. It was completely different. And I think for all of us sitting here, if you touch the horn, you play it with all you have. It doesn't matter whether it's a rehearsal or a performance and that's the only way for us.

MG: For me, it's so upsetting to hear contemporary jazz on recordings and hear the musicians play with only half a commitment. It doesn't even seem as if they are trying to do music.

FOR SOME, THE COMMITMENT SEEMS TO BE TOWARD THE ENTERTAINMENT ASPECT OF THE MUSIC RATHER THAN A COMMITMENT TOWARD THE MUSIC AS AN ART FORM.

MG: Yes, there is a huge difference.

KV: I think the connection that we all have in the Peter Brotzmann Tentet and with other people that we choose to work with in different forms of expression, is in the curiosity that we all have with this process. It's a search to find things with sound, and you cannot work with someone that is going to do that halfway. And it's not as if we talk about it or that it's similar to walking onto a football field and saying, "Let's get out there and play!" It's just an understood thing. It's understood that we respect each other and part of the reason is because everyone is about the music, working together, and finding out where it's going to take us.

And even with the performance last night, *Be Music, Night*, it was there from the first rehearsal all the way to the concert. It was always evolving. And I have to say that I was quite impressed with Mike Pearson because he improvised his approach to the text while interacting with the group. Every time he read the poems, it was different. I was quite surprised by that because I thought he would have a set way of reading the material and we would work around that. I think that the project was exceptional, but I don't think that the approach to the project as exceptional because that is the way we always work, all of the time.

We are talking about doing this performance again because there are so many ways that we can approach the same piece. And that flexibility and interest is the commonality between all of the different things that we do both individually and in different kinds of groups. There are just so many different possibilities to utilize the different tools that we have to constantly reinvent the thing and that commitment is just understood. It is not talked about, it is shown. It's the physical expression of being there on stage and knowing that the person next to you is with you 100 percent.

JM: For me, I feel very limited in what I can do because, contrary to what people think, I'm not a saxophone player. I mean, I play the saxophone and there are saxophonists who I highly respect who have studied the instrument and know it inside and out, but I have never had a saxophone lesson in my life. I play it because I really don't have a choice about things. I don't know what my limits are and I don't know what I cannot do. It's a possibility that leads to other things like playing with these three great saxophone players.

PB: Joe, perhaps you need more coffee.

(All laugh!)

JM: I had a chance to be in an environment which makes all of these things just outside of my reach more possible. And this whole thing about free jazz, I don't know what that means. Freedom is a work in progress and what we are doing is a work in progress. It's constantly evolving and I don't know what the next thing is going to be. I just know that I have been looking forward to the next note we are going to play since the last note we played last night,

WHAT IS THE MOST CRITICAL ASPECT OF IMPROVISATION? IS IT THE STATEMENT IT-
SELF OR IS IT HOW YOU ARRIVED AT THE STATEMENT TO BEGIN WITH?

KV: I did a tour in October of 2004 with Paul Lytton and Phil Wachsmann, and Lytton talked very specifically about his frustration with results. He felt that some of the musicians he has worked with have become more concerned with the end result as opposed to the process. He seems very much concerned with the performance and how it is connected to really looking for what might happen, and perhaps not caring quite as much as other musicians about having something musically successful.

PB: I think that after all of these years, I try to avoid the term free jazz, which I have hated from the very beginning. But I also have nothing against the result after a period of work, but that was not the process early on. I learned that it's good to have something in mind, and if you get there, it can be quite a nice feeling and then you can think about the next night or the next note. For Lytton, it might be one way of looking at it, but even if it gets you the freedom you want, you need to see what is happening and look at the process because the process is the thing. But I think it also limits your way of working, thinking, and feeling. I'm sure I would have talked about it differently twenty years ago but my feeling after all of these years of playing is that the result is not such a bad thing.

KV: I could be wrong, but I think part of what Lytton was talking about was voic-ing his frustration over certain people having a defined thing that they do and then they stop the searching process. And I would say that from my point of view, the work that you have done, Peter, is evolving all of the time, and looking for results is like seeing something that hasn't been done or moving to another place. And I think that part of what Paul is talking about is the frustration of people abandon-ing the search and maybe having an idea in mind and moving towards it, and just saying that this is the thing that I do.

PB: I don't want to give the wrong impression but maybe what annoys Paul is that a lot of younger people today already start thinking about the result, then pro-duce it, which is the way that maybe rock music is being produced. But I don't think it has a place in our music.

MG: This is completely true. It's really a slow process to get closer and closer to the result.

PB: It's a lifelong search and process of trying.

MG: Sometimes you can acquire the feeling of what Peter is talking about and maybe it's even good. But for me, it's not just about the process. That would be stupid because it would be to say that I am not interested in form, and I'm really interested in form when it comes to improvisation.

JM: I'm interested in form too and I'm looking at this because this is the way I try and see things. This is a form and look what's going on in there. (Looking at an awkward oblong water glass.) You can move it around and it can definitely form something to work towards, and I like that kind of fluidity.

PB: Yes, but that's that dialectic thing of what we call in the German language *form und inhalt.* That means the form and the content, which has to come together, and that is what all art is about in a way. It's very simple.
Paal Nilssen-Love joins the discussion.

WITH IMPROVISATION, YOU CREATE SOMETHING THAT IS VERY MUCH ALIVE AND THEN IT'S GONE. DO YOU EVER FEEL A SENSE OF LOSS AFTER PERFORMING A PIECE?

MG: For me, it's a process that is never done and it's never going to be finished. When it is done, there becomes a new starting point but the music is never done.

KV: There are times when I feel like I have failed at getting to the music, and if something in my mind isn't successful, then I would say that I do feel a sense of loss. I feel like the opportunity is gone, or there was a chance to do something and I failed. As Mats was saying, after a concert is over, I don't feel a loss—ever! The only loss I feel is when the music fails and that chance won't ever happen again.

I definitely feel as if a struggle is involved, and I think that everyone that I work with has a very strong sense of self-awareness and with that, a self-expectation about realizing something that is worthwhile. We can succeed or fail to varying degrees from night to night and for me personally, that can be painful. It's very much a reality in the process of either a live performance or in a recording situation.

There is a risk of failure involved anytime that we play, and I think that that is a central part of the process, because if the sense of taking a chance and risk gets removed, then the music becomes very much dead. It's like an ongoing process of pushing yourself to a point of where you may fail because of the need to find out what Joe said earlier, of what can't I do or what can I do. That's a very intense process.

PB: It has to be.

MG: If you are not willing to take a risk, the music will be empty and flat and then you might as well get rid of the music.

KV: It has become clearer and clearer to me that there is no separation between who you are as a person and what you play as a musician. And the way that you care about the way you live and the way you deal with the music are not separable. That means that it can be painful. Just like being alive can be painful. You just cannot separate those things. And I think that some of the most remarkable music or art that I have experienced is an intense expression of all kinds of things simultaneously because it's an expression of these people, in that time, in that moment, in a real and true way.

If you go back and listen to some of the older records with people like Theolonious Monk, they always sound new because there is so much in that music, and I think that's what we are striving to do. We want to make music that is true, that is an expression of us now, along with the things that we deal with, and that can be painful but it can also be joyful.

PB: As a kid, I was interested in boxing and I can compare that to going on stage. You have to accept the fight and you have to accept that there is a chance that you can lose, but you have to give all that you can in this special moment to win. You have to concentrate and get whatever you can, but on some nights it may not work and that can be painful, but without that actual experience, you don't have a chance to win the next time. And that's the thing.

KV: We recently played in Montreal with Sonore, which has always been a fantastic city to play in. The audience and the people that present the music there are really special. But for whatever reason, that night was a really hard night. There were a lot of things stacked against us and it was pretty rough. However, by the next day, we were already talking about wanting the next gig and what we could do better. And like Peter says, if you are in it 100 percent all the way, it's part of the thing you take on, that yeah, you are going to fail at times. And it's horrible when it happens (laughs), but it's very important because it illuminates so many things.

So I find those personal struggles within the context of the group fascinating because there are so many different things happening simultaneously from an individual and collective standpoint and how it can impact the success of the group and the music. There are so many variables and it's an amazing process. You can prepare as much as you want as individuals or as a group, but when you go on stage, you throw the dice and don't know what it's going to be. That's riveting, and whether the people that come to the performance know the music or not, it doesn't really matter because nothing else is quite the same artistically and it's an intense human experience. It's an unusual and special art form because of that, and it can be realized by anybody that is watching and listening.

JM: I don't know how you guys feel about this, but no matter how confident I might feel, if I start to analyze things while improvising, I'm in trouble. Because if I think something is not going to work, it will not work no matter what I do. It becomes an uphill struggle all of the time. It's like the centipede that tries to think of which foot comes next and then it cannot move. But if I can just realize that I don't have much control over what is going on even though I'm doing the best I can, then that's it! At the end, somebody else can analyze it.

PNL: It's a feeling and should feel as if the music is playing you.

JM: I don't give it that much credit.

(All laugh!)

PNL: You try not to become too mental about the music and give it the distance it needs. It's a very special feeling.

JM: I don't think that we could approach it any other way than like there is no tomorrow. We have to do that at the highest level we can and it's unconceivable to do it any other way.

PB: Yeah, I'm with you.

PNL: You give it 100 percent and don't want to wake up the next day thinking that you could have done it better.

HOW IMPORTANT IS HUMILITY TO THE CREATIVE PROCESS?

KV: When you care about the people you work with, you are constantly confronted with what you can and cannot do. You become aware of what your limits are and what you need to do to break through those limits and that's a humbling experience, and if it's not, then you are not really being true to yourself. It's like confronting yourself in the mirror and you have to try and assess that on some level.

DO YOU EVER GET A SENSE THAT YOUR MUSIC MAY NOT BE FOR THE PEOPLE OF THIS TIME PERIOD?

JM: No, I don't even think about such a thing. This is our time period and all the rest of it is a bunch of bullshit. I mean, it's not music for the future or the past. This is the time we have.

BUT IS THE MUSIC TOO "NOW"? SOMETIMES PEOPLE CAN MORE EASILY UNDER-STAND SOMETHING AFTER THEY HAVE HAD TIME TO ASSESS IT, IN THE SAME SENSE THAT HISTORY IS MORE READILY UNDERSTOOD WHEN IT'S LOOKED BACK UPON.

KV: Well, it definitely seems that mainstream society eventually catches up with what people are expressing that is happening today in real time.

But I also agree with what Joe says 100 percent. The music is about right now, but it usually ends up being a cliché and considered avant-garde because people are so living in the past. They are not thinking and only dealing with those things that they are told about. Theolonius Monk wasn't even accepted until the end of his life.

PB: Our music is vibrant and doesn't belong to the media cake, but that doesn't mean that we don't have our own importance and our own audiences. We just have to work to find them, but people have to work at finding us too. It's a process. I mean, do we want to be a part of that media cake? I doubt it. I don't want it any-more. I want to be left alone to work on my music and I'm able to find my audi-ence and I think that what comes later is not so interesting. But we are always able to find people to work with and even when we only see each other a couple of times a year, we try to make the best out of the situation and that's a wonderful thing.

My painter friends always say, "Oh man, why did you move to this terrible mu-sic? Look at us, we are doing big exhibitions in New York and we make money." I know some of them quite well and they are fucking millionaires or professors and I sometimes get a bit jealous.

(All laugh!) But just for two seconds. I then see what I have and that's really the best thing that you can have. It's working together and creating something together. That's a great feeling and if that works, you can be happy. It's a very good thing.

THE LATE AUTHOR EDWARD SAID SAID THAT MUSIC JUST MIGHT BE THE FINAL RE-SISTANCE TO THE ACCULTURATION AND THE COMMODIFICATION OF EVERYTHING.

MG: That applies to all art but perhaps music is more obvious. But of course, it's all about what we have been talking about. It's about sharing and searching and about all the active processes.

KV: I think that one of the problems with the kind of music we play is that it's very hard to commodify. We now live in a capitalist society which is almost everywhere on the planet today. There is an obsession with ownership of material things, but music is ephemeral. Even a recording is just an example of one thing and is not the ultimate expression; it's not the original. And with the kind of music we play, I think it's true that part of the struggle that we have in gaining more acceptance for the work we are doing is that it cannot be defined.

And from what I understand, Ornette Coleman is frustrated over the fact that he has been called a genius, yet he is not paid the commissions of someone like Elliott Carter, and that's a valid complaint. If you are going to talk about financial compensation, the kind of work that we do isn't truly defined. So it's kind of a catch-22. How do we explain what we do? In new music circles, they say we just improvise; we just make it up.

JM: It's like throwaway music; it's not important. But they should be paying us by the note.

KV: (Laughs.) That's the thing, because many will write off what we do even though they use the developments of people that are making this music.

A couple of days ago, I was talking about Paul Rutherford with Peter, and Peter was talking about how Vinko Globokar took many of the techniques that Rutherford developed in improvised music and Globokar is now this well-known composer. Some of his work is even fantastic, but Rutherford isn't getting a check for the royalties from that work.

So many of the people that are responsible for new innovations are not given the credit deserved. I'm mean, yeah, you can credit us, but it's this thing that's ephemeral in a world where that's not valued. Not to sound pretentious, but we are artists on stage making a statement that won't be that way ever again and how are you going to commodify that?

We are in a world where so much importance is placed on instant gratification. It's the realization that I have the best car, the best television set, or I have the most famous painting or blah, blah, blah. And as improvising musicians, we are doing something that is completely counter to that because it won't be the same ever again if we are doing it right. And the closest thing anyone could have is a recording. But if you talk to any of the musicians working on this music, they'll tell you that they don't even remember some of the recordings that they have made because they are already onto the next thing.

So we are in an unusual place in the world because we are doing something that ideally is a lifelong pursuit that goes on and on and on; it's always changing so we are always bucking against these people who want to commodify us and categorize us. People decided ten years ago even what kind of music I play and they don't know anything about what I do because I don't. And I have also seen it in the short amount of time I have worked with Peter. Almost after every concert someone comes up to him and talks about *Machine Gun*, but how long ago was that and what is he doing now?

For all of us, it's about what's right now. And it's difficult because any artist is really doing the same type of thing. A painting isn't the result, it's a step in the process, and that's why there isn't only one painting. So I think what Mats is saying is completely true. We are artists like any artists in trying to do the work. It's just that the work that we do doesn't have a specific place in our society because it's about live music, which is already an endangered species. The general population isn't interested in the idea of live music. They are more than happy to go to a concert and have people lip-sync. They just don't give a shit. So we are really strange. We play acoustic instruments, the old-fashioned way, and get up and play something different every night. Where is our place?

So we have to find it. Because after that is said, I think there is a place for us in society just by the nature of what we are doing. People are starving to have that experience and they don't even know it, so part of the problem is for us in finding those people. All societies hear music of some kind and that's a part of our tradition too. It's not just the jazz tradition or the improvised-music tradition; I see myself as part of the tradition, the idea of journeyman musicians playing music in society in bringing ideas through music to different places. I see a large connection to that. It's not just Coleman Hawkins, it's from all different kinds of societies.

MG: It's way, way more important now than ever because of that media cake that Peter was talking about. It's really more important than ever to have live music the way we do it.

JM: I don't know if you noticed but at the end of last night's performance, people could not move from their seats; they were stuck. They didn't know what to do and they couldn't get out of the theater and that was amazing. That's what happens and why we are very dangerous. We are dangerous politically because we are the first people that Karl Rove is going to go after and try and shut down because ideas are terribly dangerous and threaten these conservative assholes.

Max Roach once said, "It doesn't matter what people feel, they can love the music or hate it but they cannot be indifferent to it." You have to feel something and that's what we need to do, we have to have that kind of platform, have more opportunities to play. I mean, recording really doesn't interest me much. Once it's done, I have a hard time listening to anything I have done in the past.

PB: I hear you. Once it's done, I'm ready to move on.

THIS REMINDS ME OF A CONVERSATION I HAD WITH WADADA LEO SMITH, WHICH HAD TO DO WITH THE CIVIL RIGHTS MOVEMENT OF THE '60S. IT WAS BELIEVED THAT THE POLITICAL POWERS-THAT-BE FEARED FREE IMPROVISATIONAL MUSIC BECAUSE IT ELEVATED THE CONSCIOUSNESS OF THE INDIVIDUAL.

JM: Well, I'm labeled as a '60s free jazz musician and get stuck being placed into that period. But my music was very political, and it was intended to scare the shit out of people and to get people energized and to do things to whatever extent that it could be done. And though I probably don't package it in the same way, it's still the same thing. I need to do that and that's my intention.

KV: It's like what Max Roach said: If we are doing it right, you cannot be indifferent to it because we are projecting our commitment and it becomes a confrontation of what the music means right now. And this process that the audience and band face from different sides is an incredible experience. I didn't know anything about Kenneth Patchen prior to starting the work on this project, but the material was so exposed and the poetry so direct, that it was overwhelming.

And you never hear anything like this, and I think that's why people were attracted by the passion we had along with Mike's realization of the text. We are in a catastrophic time in the United States, if not globally, and just to have the music and the poetry in the air was overwhelming for people. It was beautiful in the true sense of it. And people never get that. It's a rare thing, and I think that the fact that we even can get to those things in the work that we do from time to time, it's crucial that it's there.

MG: The scary thing is that people are not even aware that they need it. They don't know how to get it and they don't know that they need to get it.

KV: You cannot even begin to describe the level of idiocy connected to this festival. That's a book in itself. Somehow some people made it to the concert, despite every effort to keep them from getting there. And I know that some of those people have heard the Tentet before and they were excited that OK, they are going to hear the band, but I don't think any of those people were prepared for what they were going to be faced with and how it was going to happen; on all of those different kinds of levels. It's like they were overwhelmed. Oh my God. . . . It wakes them up out of their stupor that they may be in whether they know it or not. There were people who thought they knew the band but didn't know, and that's the way it should be.

PNL: People come wanting to hear what they heard the band play last time and not caring about what the band is doing today.

PAAL, YOU SAID EARLIER THAT PEOPLE IN ALL OF THE ARTS ARE DOING FORWARD-THINKING WORK BUT SOMETIMES YOU ARE OUT THERE ALL ALONE. HOW DO YOU VALIDATE WHAT YOU ARE DOING?

PNL: When one is always true to oneself, then it's OK. You have your own understanding in the way you want things to go and as long as you carry it 100 percent, then it should be OK.

MG: Yeah, you cannot do much more.

KV: If I meet someone at a concert and they are happy about being there and about the music, I can recognize myself in them. You know what I mean?

I also value what my peers think. It means a lot to me. If I didn't feel as if I had a feeling of respect coming from those people that I respect, then I would know that I am doing something wrong or that I'm lying to myself about what it is that I am working on. And I think that fundamentally, you have to have that sense and if you abandon that even for a minute, then you are really going down to something that is going to lead to a dark place.

There are people who have done amazing and incredible work and then for whatever reasons, they make choices to leave their work and then they don't seem to ever find it again. It's a delicate thing—the respect for the music and the people that you work with—and once you let go of that for the sake of making more money or for the sake of being more famous, it slips away from you. Unfortunately, there are a lot of examples of that happening.

I RECENTLY HAD A CONVERSATION WITH ONE PERSON WHO WAS FROM GERMANY AND THE OTHER PERSON FROM SWITZERLAND. THE DISCUSSION CENTERED AROUND TOLERANCE AND THE DIFFERENCES BETWEEN VARIOUS CULTURES, AND ALL OF YOU COME FROM DIFFERENT CULTURES. DO YOU FIND THAT TOLERANCE DIFFERS AMONGST VARIOUS CULTURES AND DOES IT AFFECT HOW PEOPLE VIEW THE EVENTS HAPPENING IN THE WORLD TODAY?

KV: There were many of us that observed the recent election between Bush and Kerry right here. We watched it happen. And I know that speaking as an American who is frustrated with what's going on in this country, I was looking at where the votes were going on the map and began to realize that I don't understand anything about this country today. I mean the willingness to choose ignorance over tolerance; I don't even understand this place now. I look at that map and those parts of the country that were blue; they were the parts of the country that I tour in.
(All laugh!)
PB: Yeah, it's the same for me. I mean, I always meet very open and tolerant people where I play, but they are naturally torn by the nature of their education. So I never play in the South or in the Midwest and I have no chance to learn about these kinds of people and maybe I'm lucky.
(All laugh!)
However, I can say that the audiences and the people that I meet here are great. The people are curious, interested, and young. So for me, it's always a pleasure to be here. But of course, I see the other side too.
When I first began coming to the States, I spent a lot of time in Allentown, Pennsylvania. I was on the road with a bass player from South Africa and the other was Louis Moholo, who are both black. And there were these guys at a bar who shouted, "Close the door, nigger." And that was another world but I still think that this world exists, and being on the road with William Parker and Hamid Drake quite a bit, we discuss my experiences in this country with two black guys and sometimes it can give you a funny feeling.
I recently spent time with Braxton and we discussed the African American and the white situation and he said, "Segregation is going stronger than ever." And from my outside view; in the end, nothing has changed. It's still, "Fuck these guys and fuck those guys." I mean, it's a mess we are in and it's not only an American mess, it's really a global mess.
MG: It's so disgusting.
PB: Yes, and of course, it looks different in different countries. And it's quite a global thing, which has to do with the growing pre-capitalism situation that the world is in.
JM: It's economics.
MG: Its media controlled and we don't even know what is actually happening, we can only guess. It's crazy.

GLOBALIZATION SEEMS TO LEAVE VERY LITTLE, IF ANY, ROOM FOR CREATIVITY AND
INDEPENDENT THOUGHT.

MG: It becomes meaningless.

PNL: Yeah, the stronger the art part is, the stronger you're going to be to fight it.

KV: Things unfortunately go in cycles, and we are in this period now in which
this situation in Iraq, it doesn't seem unlike some of the things that were going on
during the late '60s.

PB: I had just turned on CNN and heard what they are now doing in Fallujah.
Man, is the only answer to drop 500-pound bombs on this village? I mean, can that
be an answer to anything? I feel I just don't get it.

KV: It seems that we didn't learn anything in Vietnam and now we are here again.

JM: We're going backwards.

KV: I mean, I'm completely baffled by it and I wasn't completely aware of the
first cycle and yet, here we come again. Some amazing things came out of that really powerful time and it seemed that, OK, maybe some changes could be made,
and yet here we are thirty-five years later in a similar place. In talking with Phil
Wachsmann, he said that if you had asked him in 1968 if we could be where we
are now, he couldn't have imagined it. He just couldn't believe that we had gone a
hundred years backward instead of forward.

PNL: Reelecting Bush proved it.

MG: These elections have affected people in Sweden too. I have never seen
anything like it. People were getting up at three or four o'clock in the morning to
watch the debates.

PNL: Everyone was watching in Norway also.

MG: Everyone felt so involved.

JM: I think they were hopeful that something would come out of the debates,
but I thought the debates were a big joke. They were not debates, they were
meant for entertainment.

PB: I was so disappointed because they all behaved so . . .

JM: It was all choreographed.

PB: You are right, it was not a debate. If you have to fight for something, you
have to punch from time to time. It was all so moderated and they were all so nice
to each other.

THERE HAS BEEN AN ELEMENT OF FEAR INSTILLED INTO THE AMERICAN PEOPLE
FOR SO LONG THAT BY THE TIME THEY GET TO THE VOTING BOOTH, THEY PULLED THE
TRIGGER OF FEAR.

KV: The Bush administration is using fascist techniques. It's just fascist. They in-
still fear in an uneducated population, don't tell them what's happening, and then
lie to them until it becomes the truth.

MG: It's about education.

JM: People were told to register and come out to the poll to vote, but they don't
know what they are voting for. They don't have a clue. They just go there and vote

because it's their duty but it's their duty to also know something. Then you have this onslaught of what we think of as news, CNN and the rest of that crap. That's not news. They keep repeating the same thing over and over and over. . . .

PB: I was watching a short news report and they continue to run the same thing twenty hours a day.

JM: It's indoctrination.

DURING THE NIGHT OF THE ELECTION, PEOPLE WERE STILL VOTING AFTER MID-NIGHT IN OHIO AND FLORIDA. BUT IF YOU LOOKED AT THE VOTING LINES, IT WAS OBVIOUS THE LINES WERE IN THE SUBURBS BECAUSE MOST OF THE PEOPLE WERE PEOPLE OF COLOR. AND THOSE PEOPLE VOTE WHAT PARTY? WHY WERE THERE NOT ENOUGH VOTING BOOTHS? FOR ME, IT WAS OBVIOUS THAT VOTING WAS MADE DIFFICULT IN THE HOPE THAT VOTERS WOULD BECOME FRUSTRATED WITH THE LINES AND THEN NOT VOTE. WHY WASN'T CNN OR THE MAJOR NETWORKS QUESTIONING WHY ONLY OHIO AND FLORIDA, THE TWO MOST IMPORTANT STATES IN THE ELECTION, WERE VOTING AT MIDNIGHT WHILE THE REST OF THE COUNTRY WAS FINISHED AND WAITING?

KV: Absolutely!

And I also think that people who are frustrated globally are going to act out and it's part of what you are seeing. Like Peter was saying, we are going to drop these bombs on this town, and that's the solution? There is a reason that this stuff is happening. And there needs to be an exploration. There is so much money involved and so much greed. I mean, what was our interest in Afghanistan and what is our interest in Iraq? It's oil. We are not paratrooping into other countries with more heinous dictators. There are so many political and economic things connected to Iraq that are transparent.

And I think what Paal was saying is true too. In the '60s, some amazing creative and important things happened that I think helped support the idea that something could be better and I think that that's what is going to happen now too. And I think the concert last night is an example of that kind of action because it was about the possibility of something better. There was a line in one of the poems that said, "War will fail." And we are in the middle of a war. We're planting the idea or the concept that it isn't the way to go. Even for the few hundred people that were there last night, that's a positive action in a very dark time. And I think that those kind of creative actions are going to happen out of desperation of what we are faced with right now. It's not a time to be complacent. And it's not a time to say that things are OK because they are really not. And I think that that kind of thing can read through very important action on the positive side. Because there isn't room for just shrugging your shoulders and saying, "Everything is OK."

❽

MARILYN CRISPELL

Her notes crash like waves at sea on a stormy winter's night; they gently float and slowly fall like early morning mist; yet it's the silence—the silence between the notes—which provides the haunting poetic beauty that is the music of pianist Marilyn Crispell.

Is THERE A DECREASE IN LISTENERS FOR CREATIVE MUSIC TODAY?

I think jazz is under fire—the concept of jazz. I have noticed a change in Europe since the walls came down that a certain amount of interest has seemed to move away from that arena. Whereas in the States, where it hasn't been as prevalent or understood, there seems to be more interest and open-mindedness towards it, but I could be totally wrong. But it's also very hard to be objective when you're in the inside doing it.

ARE PEOPLE LOOKING FOR THINGS THAT HAVE MORE DEPTH OR CREATIVE AND ARTISTIC VALUE?

Things do tend to move in cycles and there are always people who are more aware of things than others, and unless a global catastrophe happens, the majority of people continue with what they're doing. I don't think in general it's that easy to find out the truth about many things, and a lot of people don't bother because it's all they can do to keep their own lives together. And it's very possible that people will get tired of all the backward-looking imitation stuff and become open to something new. I know that when I play in this country, I get a very good response. Almost across the board really. I mean, I cannot think of anywhere where I haven't and there is kind of an openness and warm heartedness. I find people very receptive, and in most of the country, there's no "we've heard it all before" attitude. And people are always asking, "How come we haven't heard this music, where can we find the CDs and where can we hear more of it?" I really think it's about educating people and making the music available. If it's not available, they don't know it exists and they can't appreciate it because there is no way to hear it. I feel very lucky to be on what I consider a major label because it does allow more people to hear what I'm doing. There are also people who are not in that position, who are great musicians and do not get heard by the majority of the people here.

DOES SOCIETY TODAY HAVE DIFFICULTY WITH CREATIVITY THAT IS NOT EASILY EXPLAINED, UNDERSTOOD, OR IDENTIFIABLE?

I think we like to romanticize the past and I'm not sure human nature has changed all that much. If you look at what's happening politically, socially, and economically in the world right now, it's parallel to what's happening in the art world in general.

I think our culture is very much shaped by a corporate marketing mentality and that's part of the reason this music isn't appreciated here. Therefore, it's important for musicians to take the music into the schools to kids who are very young and still impressionable, who are still too young to know that they are not supposed to like something. I also wish there were more national touring programs combining education and concerts. More of what they do in Europe where they are really proud of their artists and try and educate young kids.

Basically, we spend money on what we think are all the important things (necessary to sustain our physical life, pay the rent, etc.) and if there is something left over, maybe something is given to the arts and that says something about our mentality. The arts are considered frivolous here, but I know someone who worked with kids in Harlem and brought a lot of kids off the street through painting activities and taking exhibitions around the country. It's given the kids a chance to express themselves and learn and receive respect, and that's just one example. People in Western culture think that only something material and tangible is worthwhile and things having to do with the spirit or the soul are not considered important. There again I'm making a separation. Everything has to do with the spirit or the soul. Everything has to do with it, including the things we think of as separate from it.

I think there is also this other phenomenon happening where this glut of information is out there which perhaps wasn't the case thirty years ago. There's an overwhelming amount of information available, so unless people are introduced to something or something catches their attention, they're probably not going to be interested. When I pick up a newspaper, unless there is a photo with something in particular that catches my attention, I'll tend to just glance through it. Or when you walk into a supermarket and there are thirty different brands of some product, you feel like walking out and not buying anything. I also think the computer age is over-whelming us and zillions of people putting out CDs or selling their own CDs on-line. It's hard to keep track, and how are you supposed to find out about anything? It almost starts to feel homogenous.

HAVE WE BECOME MORE OF A VISUAL SOCIETY AND PLACE LESS EMPHASIS ON VAR-IOUS ASPECTS OF SOUND?

I would doubt that. David Bowie said that the eyes are hungrier than the ears and that's part of what opera and the theater are all about. I don't think anything has changed or has become more visually oriented. I think we have always been visually oriented. In a certain sense, sound is a more abstract thing. You can col-lect a painting and look at it for the rest of your life, but with music, the true na-ture of sound is very ephemeral. It happens, it passes by, and then it goes out into the eaves somewhere and keeps traveling on.

When I first started playing music, I never wanted to record. I never wanted to freeze the sound. However, I have been very influenced by recorded music even though my intuitive feeling was, play it and let it go. I think more than saying that we are a visually oriented society, we're a materialistic society. So if there is some-thing that you can have and own and touch, maybe you are more likely to pay at-tention to that or spend money for that than on something that will be gone. Of course you can own a sound recording, but the music is still not as tangible as a painting. Thus the artists themselves become commodities; they are just used to make money, often in our society.

IS WHAT'S HAPPENING IN CREATIVE MUSIC TOO FORWARD-THINKING FOR SOCIETY TODAY?

Bach said that there would always be a limited number of people who could re-late to some of the best stuff ever made, and he was talking about his own music. I kind of believe that people who are meant to be drawn to anyone's music in par-ticular will find you or will hear you through word of mouth or from the radio or by accident. I think that's always the case, all of the time, and I don't think it's too forward-thinking. They say that the reflection of the time starts with visual arts and then it goes down through other arts. And I think what's happening now, and what's been happening since the late '50s, early '60s, is the deconstructed reflec-tion of what's been happening in the modern world. But I also think there is now movement to begin reconstructing and that's just something that I feel.

I don't really separate this time from other times as it's all connected. But I do think things are changing faster because of technology, and again, there are a lot of worldviews like that of the Tibetan, the Hindu and Hopi, which talk about the different cycles and ages of man of creation and destruction and supposedly we're in that downward phase of one of those cycles called "Kali Yuga." And when things go faster, and faster and faster, everything is gone and then a new cycle starts. Many people feel there is a big spiritual rebirth happening. I see a lot of that on the Internet and here in Woodstock; there are a lot of people involved in that. A change in the way people are using their minds, not just practical technological but maybe more intuitive. The feminine side is starting to emerge to balance out some of the stuff that's going on in the world, which is pretty macho stuff.

ARE TRADITIONALISTS HAVING A DIFFICULT TIME ACCEPTING THAT A MUSIC FORM CONSIDERED "AMERICAN" NOW HAS INTERNATIONAL AND DIVERSE ASPECTS WITHIN IT?

I think people want to hang on to something that has historical significance and validate themselves by doing that. There certainly is a validity to the history of jazz having its roots in blues and Black music and it would not have existed without that. But most of the history of jazz is integrated, and it has always been open to other influences and other ideas. It's about creativity and doing new revolutionary and evolutionary things, and now all of a sudden rather than being a living process of change, it's become a rigidly protected museum piece. Whenever someone has to defend or protect something that way, they are usually concerned about giving up some kind of power, rather than having the security to feel open and let things happen. To my mind, and who am I, nobody can say that jazz is this or jazz is that. But people like Wynton Marsalis and Ken Burns have been very successful in convincing other people of exactly that. As far as I'm concerned, I'm ready to say that I don't play jazz and to hell with it. I just play my music, although I consider jazz to be a primary influence on my playing.

Music is one of the most intangible of the arts as opposed to a visual art that you can see, touch, and hold. It's very ephemeral. It's there and then it's gone. It's a universal language that doesn't need words to communicate, so it's a pretty powerful medium. It has given birth to a lot of other forms and possibilities that we now call traditional jazz but were not considered traditional jazz in their own time—by the way.

I have wished for a long time that somebody would do a film called the "The Lost Decade." About the lost scene in the '60s and all the incredible creative music that happened at that time. A lot of these people are not paid attention to by the mass market, but as far as I'm concerned, it was one of the most brilliant periods of the music. I can't mention everyone's name, but people in particular who come to my mind with whom I've had personal contact are Cecil Taylor, Oliver Lake, Anthony Braxton, the Art Ensemble of Chicago, George Lewis, Sun Ra, Wadada Leo Smith, Billy Bang, Abdullah Ibrahim, Reggie Workman, Anthony Davis. . . . There are just so many and I don't know where to start or end. I also don't want to leave the impression that these people are overlooked or ignored, but in other cultures, they would be considered national treasures and I don't feel they have received the support and place they deserve.

DOES THE GLOBAL SITUATION TODAY AFFECT YOU ARTISTICALLY?

Things can get so bad that you can sometimes feel as if you are butting your head against a wall. Have you ever seen the film *My Dinner with Andre*? It's a great film and the guy who made that film, Louis Malle, talks about times like these, where it feels impossible to do anything. And rather than waste energy fighting it, he retreats to underground pockets of light.

Things do tend to turn around, but I think that because we live in a technological age with so much information available, people are overwhelmed. It's not like the old days where you'd go to the concert and were able to hear this music. Now, people can just put on a CD. And everyone is putting out CDs and you can burn them at home. People are overwhelmed by a glut of information, which I think can have an effect not only on me but also on many other performers.

I feel like being an artist is a political statement in a certain sense. Just by the very fact that you are being an individual and you are doing what you do and not bowing to big market corporate influences and are being true to your soul. You are trying to put something real out to the world and people do hear it and I know it affects them because people tell me that it does.

FOR MANY, MUSIC IS A WAY TO GET AWAY FROM ALL THE GARBAGE THAT SUR-ROUNDS US.

I think the arts feed the soul. They are a very important part of our society equal to technology and science. There is a great book called *Care of the Soul* by Thomas Moore. It's wonderful and he talks about the place of art in everyday life, not just by going out to galleries and to museums, etc. There are aesthetics and beauty in everyday life.

DO YOU CONNECT TO ANY OF YOUR MUSIC SPIRITUALLY, POLITICALLY, OR SOCIALLY?

Spiritually. It's interesting because these are all just words and music is something that happens on a very instinctive level. And though I don't necessarily work within those contexts, I do feel that it does come from a spiritual place and is very connected with that for me.

If music doesn't reach me emotionally, then I'm totally not interested in it. And there are techno wizards on their instruments who just don't get to me at all. As a friend of mine recently said after a concert, "It was brilliantly forgettable. There was nothing in it that curled around my heart and stayed there." And I thought that was a very beautiful way to put it.

CECIL TAYLOR SAID THAT "MUSIC HAS TO DO WITH A LOT OF AREAS WHICH ARE MAGICAL RATHER THAN LOGICAL; THE GREAT ARTISTS, RATHER THAN JUST GETTING INVOLVED WITH DISCIPLINE, GET TO UNDERSTAND LOVE AND ALLOW THE LOVE TO TAKE SHAPE." HOW MUCH OF YOUR MUSIC IS FROM LOGIC AND HOW MUCH FROM THIS OTHER PLACE THAT CECIL TAYLOR DESCRIBES?

You do music as a whole person, with your intellect and your heart. Everything. And I also totally relate to what Cecil says about love. And I agree with him about magic. For me, performing is like a ceremonial ritual, almost akin to a kind of Shamanism.

DO IMPROVISERS HAVE A UNIQUE ABILITY OR AWARENESS OF WHAT IS ALL AROUND
THEM?

I think everybody has that awareness.

IS IT ON A DIFFERENT LEVEL PERHAPS?

Perhaps different levels of being connected to it. Cecil Taylor gives another great
quote when asked about practicing. He said that he practices when he's walking
down the street or going shopping. In other words, his whole life is his art. He
doesn't separate them. To perceive life as art and everything in life as the teacher.
People tend to make a separation between those in the arts and other people,
and I feel that's a mistake. In many non-Western cultures, music is very much a
part of everyday life and it relates to every aspect of life. There is music for work,
healing, celebrations; there is music for everything. I guess what I'm trying to say
is that anybody can have an awareness to look at life as art in whatever it is they
do, even if it is something that is not traditionally thought of as artistic. Anything
that you do can be art if it's done with a particular kind of awareness.

DO WOMEN AND MEN CREATE DIFFERENTLY OR DOES IT HAVE MORE TO DO WITH
INDIVIDUALITY?

I think it has more to do with individuality. I have said for years that I don't believe in men's music and women's music, but I think if you are a woman, you are
obviously playing women's music. If you are a man, you are playing men's music.
We all have masculine and feminine elements and people like Bill Evans and
Keith Jarrett play some very feminine lyrical stuff and there are woman who play
some very hard-ass stuff. Women have babies and that takes incredible strength.
There is this tendency to think of women as weak and frail little flowers and men
are these big strong. . . . I mean you can fill in the words here. I don't know if we
create differently but I wouldn't think so but there are people who believe that.

WHEN YOU COMPOSE, ARE YOU ENVISIONING WHAT YOU WANT THE MUSIC TO DO
FOR THE LISTENER?

I'm trying to figure out what concept is trying to formulate itself and I try to find
a way to express it and this is on an intuitive/intellectual level. I'm thinking in terms
of what I hear and what I want to put out and not how it's going to affect somebody
or what they are going to think of it. I think you do something that is intrinsically
yours and that's your gift that you have to give. If you are trying to modify it in some
way to impress or please someone, then it's not going to be a pure expression.

WHAT DO YOU LOOK FOR FROM DRUMMERS AND BASS PLAYERS AND HOW MUCH OF
IT HAS TO DO WITH THEIR RHYTHMIC APPROACH WITH EACH OTHER?

I'm looking for people who are very versatile and have a background in traditional
jazz but can also cross lots of borders. People who are aware of more contemporary

developments in improvised music and can relate to it and not just say, "Oh, I'll play free," but can really relate to it from the heart. People who are sensitive and know how to listen. People who can relate to what I'm doing and respond in a way that makes sense and with respect.

CAN YOU EXPLAIN YOUR RELATIONSHIP WITH TIME IN THE MUSICAL SENSE?

First of all, time is a very complex thing. Anthony Braxton talks a lot about pulse feels, which is kind of like a heartbeat. You have your own rhythm and if you are playing a phrase that has a pulse feel of its own and if you are playing with "intention" within that pulse feel, for me, that has a sense of time. In fact, one of my favorite things is to play simultaneous but different things, like say the bass player and the drummer are playing the feel of a certain time. 4/4 time. I like to be able to fly on top of that and go in and out of it and come back to it. It's like they are laying down a carpet of time that I can weave complex patterns over. I think African drumming is also a concept that has very complex time. I am not a free jazzer who abhors playing in a time, 4/4 time or whatever (laughs)—contrary to what some people think.

DON'T YOU JUST HATE THE TERM "FREE JAZZ"?

I really do, and avant-garde, I hate even worse. Because most of the stuff that is happening now is not avant-garde; it's been happening since the '50s. There is very little new stuff that I'm aware of.

I WAS JUST HAVING THIS DISCUSSION WITH A FRIEND WHO OWNS A MUSIC STORE AND WE WERE TALKING ABOUT HOW TO CATEGORIZE THE SECTION WITHIN AVANT-GARDE. WHERE DOES IT START AND END? LIKE HE SAID, "DO I START WITH CHARLES MINGUS WHO WAS AVANT-GARDE WHEN HE ORIGINALLY HIT THE SCENE?"

Charlie Parker was avant-garde during his time and people didn't know what to do. They couldn't dance to it, or at least they didn't think they could. It wasn't the big-band stuff they were used to. He was an intellectual, an explorer, and was way out there. Leroi Jones (Amiri Baraka) wrote a book called *Blues People* and talks about how jazz is a process of change and how it's traditionally been a revolutionary music which always comes up from underneath and upsets the status quo. He talks about African music and music from other countries and the differences they have with the Western world, and that's really about process. He says that here, you do something and then you put it in a museum and look at it like an icon. So it becomes like archeology and becomes an archive rather than a living, changing process.

HOW HAS YOUR MUSICAL THINKING EVOLVED FROM YOUR EARLIEST COMPOSITIONS UP UNTIL NOW?

I use to be a composition major at the New England Conservatory, so I think there is a sense of form in what I do. But I think playing with Anthony Braxton had a big effect on me as far as his sense of sound and silence and also just learning from his compositional methods. I became much more aware of the importance of space and silence after playing with him. The presence of space is important in order to be able to define phrases. If you listen to Cecil Taylor for instance, you hear a lot of space between those phrases and notes. Prior to playing with Anthony, I played lots of notes, all of the time. Continuously, without much of a break. It was about total energy and kind of revving up and flying off the planet. When I first started playing, I wanted to impress everybody, which is a common feeling, kind of immature. That has changed over the years.

Previously, you were talking about the importance of sound. I would also say feeling and not just sound, but I think it's about melody and feeling and very much about energy and intensity. A lot of the stuff I have been doing with ECM is more about an inner intensity rather than an outer one. I feel there is a connection between the two states—wild energy and extreme introversion—two sides of the same coin. I do both and feel like there is an organic connection between them— an integration between them. With the ECM recordings, I like the idea of playing things so slowly that you are almost suspended in time.

I LIKE MUSIC WITH THE USE OF SPACING THAT CREATES TENSION, IT INVITES ANTICIPATION.

I agree. I'm a very intense person. I am all about intensity. (Laughs.)

HOW DO YOU CREATE TENSION IN YOUR MUSIC?

I think tension is created with unusual harmonies, melodies hanging in space, rhythmic complexities, the tension and release of melodic lines.

HOW MUCH OF YOUR COMPOSITIONAL APPROACH WOULD YOU SAY COMES FROM MUSICAL INTELLECT VERSUS INTUITION OR INSTINCT?

I think separating the two is a very Western concept. It's not like we have one body that has a mind and the other one that has intuition. It's all together in one brain. (Laughs.) There is a description of a state of mind, which is compared to the tuning of a string. It shouldn't be too loose nor too tight. It should be just right and in perfect balance. This concept is used to describe a state of mind when you are doing meditation. With all the music I've played, heard, and studied, there is a sense of composition and form. There is an intellect at work, guiding the direction, although the direction seems to be mostly dictated by intuition and then guided by intellect but not too tightly. Sometimes I'll start out with an idea to play something and it just doesn't seem to be happening, and what I usually do is just let the music go where it wants to go. But before, when I was talking about time, and I used the word "intention," I think that that's a really important word. Really, really important. Carlos Castendos talks about it. Anything you do and anything you are trying to focus on requires intention and that makes all the difference between something working or not working. I think, first of all, you need to have the intention to focus your mind in a way, which is very aware, very pointed, and very relaxed. It's almost like you are standing back and letting something happen but at the same time that sense of form, which is internalized, is guiding things. It's very difficult to describe.

IS IT POSSIBLE TO PUT INTO WORDS WHAT YOU ARE TRYING TO DO WITH YOUR MUSIC TODAY?

I would take it apart phrase by phrase and show the contour of the line and how I've worked within whatever time frame I'm using. About how one line leads to another. I would also talk about sense of form and germs of the ideas and how melodies come to me and how I work them out. Mostly, I'll have people do this on their own and I'll work with them on ideas on how to express themselves, find out what they're about, what they want, what they hear. I also try to work with intention because a lot of times people are nervous and not really into what they are doing. They'll just play something but there is no intention behind it. It's just something they can do like ironing a shirt or taking a bath or whatever. But the intention, the focus, is not there. I've even heard very skilled musicians do that.

WHAT DO YOU SEE FOR THE FUTURE OF CREATIVE MUSIC OR FOR YOURSELF PERSONALLY?

I tend to be optimistic and feel that people are creative beings. Our souls are creative and there is a hunger for that. I also think the future of jazz will always be affected by that hunger. I think the pendulum is swinging pretty far to the right but things never stay the same—they always change. It's anybody's guess what's going to happen. I mean people are still playing Bach and renaissance music hundreds of years later. Maybe they'll be playing traditional jazz a hundred years later. That's fine. The attitude that exists towards change and progression and what it's called—who cares. I just know that I was very influenced by what I would call jazz. By Coltrane, Cecil Taylor, Anthony Braxton, Ornette Coleman, Sun Ra. People who brought improvisation into contemporary Western classical music, which is an important synthesis.

DO YOU HAVE A COMMON PHILOSOPHY THAT YOU TRY TO IMPART ON YOUNG STUDENTS OR MUSICIANS?

Just to have the courage to be true to your own voice.

WHAT HAVE YOU LEARNED FROM THE RISKS YOU HAVE HAD TO TAKE?

I have done things because that's where my spirit or inner feelings led me and I have always followed my intuition that way, but I haven't particularly looked at those things as risks. I've pretty much always done what I have wanted to do and have hoped that people will like it but I haven't done anything based on what anyone might think.

WHERE DO YOU GET YOUR INSPIRATION AND WHO ARE THE PEOPLE THAT HAVE IN-
FLUENCED YOU MOST?

Everything I hear inspires me but I definitely came into this music through
Coltrane. I was inspired by Cecil and Abdullah Ibrahim and, to an extent, Paul
Bley, Keith Jarrett, Pharoah Sanders, McCoy Tyner and there are also the following European trios: the Bobo Stenson trio with Anders Jormin and Jon Chris-
tensen; the Joachim Kuhn Trio with Danile Hunair and J. F. Jenny-Clark; the
Barry Guy, Evan Parker, and Paul Lytton Trio and also Anders Jormin as a composer. Additionally, African and Indian music along with other world music also
are influences along with baroque classical stuff that I'm very, very into. Many contemporary classical composers. But Coltrane was the first and foremost inspiration
for getting into this music, period.

Playing in Anthony Braxton's Quartet was a very, very important part of my musical life and just my life actually. Working with someone who had these kind of
concepts very much influenced my sense of space in composition. The quartet was
like a family and it was good to have the opportunity to work with such incredibly
creative people. It was a very profound ten years or so of my musical life.

YOU SOUND VERY APPRECIATIVE OF THOSE AROUND YOU.

I'm trying to make more of an effort to be aware of things in a different way and
to appreciate things today because they may not be here tomorrow. To appreciate
the distinctive qualities of each person and each thing. Everybody is so involved
with themselves. They go through daily life not noticing a lot of things or don't
have the time to notice a lot of things. I think about this because my parents are
both in their late 80s and I'm very aware that I won't have them forever. In many
ways, they have been a factor in my thoughts and in my awareness. I'm very aware
of the impermanence of things and the ephemeral nature of life.

DO YOU HAVE A PHILOSOPHY OR SOME WAY OF LOOKING AT LIFE THAT YOU WOULD
BE WILLING TO SHARE?

I think that kindness, sensitivity, and awareness of the world around you are important. Life is like a dream in the sense that it's real, yet at the same time, it's compared to a reflection of the moon in the water. The reflection is there, you can see
it; you can touch the water but the reflection is really ephemeral. And the real
moon is like the basic mind, which is nonconceptual. The search for truth is important; seeing beauty in all forms—an acceptance of all of life. The beautiful, the
ugly, the sad and the happy. Don't be afraid to follow your spirit and your
dreams—don't let anything stop you.

9

JACK DEJOHNETTE

As one of the greatest drummers in the history of any musical genre, Jack De-Johnette is one of the few artists that has been able to define his own wide-ranging voice while playing within any idiom of music—a rare feat for any instrumentalist. Always at the forefront, DeJohnette was a centerpiece with Miles Davis and has become a vital voice in the innovation and growing repertoire of the Keith Jarrett Trio.

ARE TRADITIONALISTS HAVING A DIFFICULT TIME ACCEPTING THAT A MUSIC FORM CONSIDERED "AMERICAN" NOW HAS INTERNATIONAL AND DIVERSE ASPECTS WITHIN IT?

Let's keep in mind that jazz has always been a world music and has always borrowed from other types of classical and ethnic types of music from all around the world. Creative thinking jazz artists have always been open to incorporating music from other regions, so that idea is not new. There are also ways of making music including the use of electronics, synthesizers, sampling, and so forth and that's just how it's done. As far as this argument that it's not pure if it's electronic, rock, or if it's got a funk beat or whatever, I don't buy into that. If the intention behind what is going on is pure, it will come through whether it is acoustic or electronic.

There are those that believe music should be confined in a certain way with certain rules, which would define for them what jazz is. But it's all music and you either like it or you don't. Where I do find a problem is that our country is becoming more closed off and more isolated from itself and the rest of the world. In the process of doing that, the airwaves have fewer places whereby people can hear jazz. NPR stations around the country are cutting jazz programs and many stations have to deal with playlists that deal with a certain sound or type of music.

Thinking musicians, like Oliver Lake, Michael Cain, and Jerome Harris to name a few, are cutting edge and have never stopped looking for alternatives to what is available. We somehow manage to keep something going on but it's not an open or revolving-door kind of thing for the music. You have to search it out because you are not going to hear it on most jazz stations and hear something experimental unless you turn the radio on at three in the morning, which is when the more adventurous music is played.

THIS IS UNFORTUNATE BECAUSE THE ONLY LISTENERS THAT ARE GOING TO LISTEN IN AT THOSE HOURS ARE ALREADY AWARE OF THIS CREATIVE MUSIC, AND THOSE THAT ARE NOT, ARE NOT GOING TO BE CHECKING IT OUT.

If you present it in a way that it's intriguing to the listener, I think you would definitely increase the response. It's just indicative of our economy and our administration's policies towards the arts.

DOES SOCIETY TODAY HAVE DIFFICULTY WITH CREATIVITY THAT IS NOT EASILY EXPLAINED, UNDERSTOOD, OR IDENTIFIABLE AND WILL THIS BE A SIGNIFICANT OBSTACLE TO OVERCOME FOR CREATIVE MUSIC?

Within tribal societies, art, culture, and life are integrated and there isn't separation between them. In our Westernized society, there is a separation and art is looked upon as entertainment as opposed to being an integral part of daily life.

In Western society, we go to the museums or "go" to hear music, which is unlike tribal societies where art is part of that daily structure. For instance, take the drums, which don't hold the reverence that they have in tribal societies such as with Native Americans and in Africa. In Africa, the drums are very respected and incorporated into singing and dancing. It's number one and not separate from. Here, it's an art form but it's also your livelihood and business. There is downloading and file sharing going on as well as a lot of people making their own CDs. There is a lot to choose from and almost too much information. Like Chuck Berry used to say, "There is too much information." It's information overload.

HAVE WE BECOME A SOCIETY THAT NO LONGER HAS THE PATIENCE TO BE CHALLENGED AND IS ONLY OPEN TO THINGS THAT ARE EASILY ACCESSIBLE?

Yes and no. There are young people that don't buy into status quo, get in touch with each other, and form networks to create alternatives. And music is going to be kept alive through that networking. The musicians are trying to get together, help one another to present and record the music and stay in touch with one another. You have to be aware that the media is driving propaganda and is made to make people numb, keep them in fear and keep them away from getting in touch with their inner selves or their inner being. That's when you wake up and begin to challenge the status quo. But when people are in fear and worried about their jobs and the economy, they come home and only want to zone out and subliminally get fed all of this stuff.

IS CULTURE AND THE ARTS CYCLIC AND AFFECTED BY THE ECONOMY OR CAN AWARENESS AND EDUCATION HELP MAKE A DIFFERENCE?

It can if the whole of society is willing to prepare and appreciate the value of it. That's the question, but at the moment it's at a low point on the graph within our society. Education and social services are being cut which are needed to keep our culture alive, vibrant, and diversified. Consequently, it's becoming more monochromatic and one-sided rather than the rich mosaic of diversity which this country has always been about with all the people that live in it.

IS THERE A CHANCE THAT BECAUSE OF THE CURRENT GLOBAL CLIMATE THAT PEOPLE COULD FIND A NEW APPRECIATION FOR THOSE THINGS THAT HAVE MORE DEPTH OR HAVE MORE ARTISTIC AND CREATIVE VALUE?

Let's look at an artist such as Norah Jones, who came out of nowhere. Her music is pretty down to earth or pretty pure and a lot of people are looking for the real essence of something. It's going to take the whole society to wake up and start to demand that our government and agencies become accountable. That's one of the problems. No accountability in our system is one of our problems right now. There's no discipline and we citizens have to change that. Not only in music but also in everything, in all walks of our lives.

MILES WAS CRITICIZED FOR INCORPORATING POP SONGS IN HIS LATER PERIOD. BUT MILES WAS UNIQUE IN THAT REGARDLESS OF WHAT HE PLAYED, YOU ALWAYS KNEW IT WAS HIM BECAUSE OF HIS PARTICULAR VOICE, HIS SOUND. IS THERE A DIFFERENCE BETWEEN WHAT HE TRIED TO DO WITH POPULAR MUSIC AND WHAT WAS DONE IN PREVIOUS ERAS OF JAZZ?

Miles always played pop tunes so I don't think it's that different, he's always done that. The only difference was that his music was more groove oriented rather than straight-ahead jazz, and those within the jazz establishment criticized him for it. They wanted to hold jazz within a certain framework or certain era and a lot of people are starting to ask questions like you beyond that. Jazz didn't stop in the '70s or the '80s or '90s—though some within the establishment seem to think it did—but the music is alive and well.

As far as the criticism of Miles, many people are thirty to forty years behind the times. Not every one of course but twenty to thirty years from now those same people will be saying, "That's some hip shit!" Miles didn't have to prove anything. He put a lot of music out there that people are still working on.

IT HAS BEEN SAID THAT IN ORDER TO MOVE THE MUSIC FORWARD, YOU NEED TO UNDERSTAND THE MUSIC BY GOING BACKWARDS. YOU HAVE COVERED SO MUCH MUSICAL GROUND AND THE MUSIC HAS OBVIOUSLY CHANGED. IS IT ALL STILL PART OF THE BASIC FOUNDATION?

That could be and is fairly accurate. It's all in how people frame it. I can listen to Sonny Rollins *Live at the Village Vanguard* and that was done thirty, thirty-five years ago with Don Cherry and Billy Higgins. That stuff sounds so fresh. It's timeless! People tend to like to put dates on music and then call it old. Somebody can go back in time and listen to Coltrane and Sidney Bechet playing soprano and get inspired to play the soprano saxophone. It's a case of what you said in regard to looking backward to go forward.

IT SURE SEEMS THAT PEOPLE GET CAUGHT UP INTO TRYING TO DEFINE WHAT JAZZ IS BASED ON A SOUND AND THEN GET STUCK IN CERTAIN PERIODS OR ERAS.

You can't put jazz in a box and label it. Johnny Griffin once said, "Jazz is a lifestyle, you live it." You cannot go to a university and get it. I think the music changed from the time that musicians listened to the music on records and traveled to all of a sudden going into the universities. It got codified. It's great to have all this information written down, but a lot of what happens in music is there for listening with your heart as well as with your head.

YOU ALSO PLAYED WITH BILL EVANS, WHO SAID THAT MUSIC TO HIM WAS MORE ABOUT FEEL THAN LOGIC.

Bill had quite a brilliant mind but the feeling was more important to him.

SO YOU FEEL THAT MUSIC CAN COME FROM LOGIC AND FEEL?

Absolutely, absolutely. The key word is balance. You have to try and find a balance between both. It's all captivating.

BY THE WAY, I WISH YOU WOULD DO MORE WORK WITH PIANO.

I do some of that with John (Surman) but don't really consider myself a pianist. I use the piano when I think it can make a statement and it feels right to me.

I HAPPEN TO LIKE SOME OF THE FREE IMPROV THINGS YOU GUYS ARE DOING RIGHT NOW.

Making music from scratch. I hear people say that you can make something from nothing, but that's not necessarily true. The ingredients are in the players and they respond to each other. That's been one of the hallmarks of the bands that I have had over the years. To encourage musicians to improvise even though it may seem self-indulgent. And I really enjoy hearing musicians coming on, digging deep and challenging themselves to come up with fresh ideas every night so it's not boring.

THERE SEEMS TO BE A LACK OF UNDERSTANDING WITH YOUNG MUSICIANS TODAY THAT YOU NEED TO DO YOUR HOMEWORK, BUILD A SOLID FOUNDATION, AND USE THE RIGHT DISCIPLINES WHEN YOU TRY THE IMPROVISATIONAL APPROACH.

Anybody that improvises can sound as though they are playing a composition and have studied discipline. When you improvise, you are always creating a form for yourself to play from. You are creating a road map. You can play with total abandon but a sense of arrangement and order will be automatically there. If I play a drum solo, I will do it without even thinking and create a composition with a form to it. I cannot not do that. I can also just go abandon and sound like it's going crazy, but even in that, I create a form.

When John Surman and I improvise, eye contact is important. At the front of the piece, we don't know where it's going to go or where it's going to come out but somehow we trust that we are going to make something happen. That's the fun and the challenge of it because you are really exposed. It's risk taking.

JAZZ GETS VERY FEW CHANCES TO PROMOTE ITSELF AND I FELT THAT THE KEN BURNS SERIES LOST AN OPPORTUNITY TO EDUCATE YOUNG LISTENERS WITH REGARD TO WHAT'S HAPPENING IN JAZZ TODAY AND ON THOSE THAT ARE MOVING THE MUSIC FORWARD.

Let's just put it this way. I don't think Ken Burns was really qualified to do it in the first place. I may not agree with some of the decisions that were made, but they made an effort. And I think it leaves it open for someone else to follow up where he left off. Instead of spending time criticizing and arguing, there are other people like you who would like to tell the story and extend that. They should come together and put together a documentary or something like that. Talk to the people who are still involved with expanding and then make a statement about it. Music is not only used for entertainment but can be used for healing or helping to heal. I have seen a medicine man in Africa help a psychological disorder through drumming. My wife and I were invited to a healing that went on for four days that helped a man who had lost his memory get his memory back. It's called primitive or tribal. I think that's very cool.

DO THESE THINGS INFLUENCE YOUR INSPIRATION?

Oh yes, very much so. I think the creative spirit is fantastic. I think our planet is really out of balance from exploitation of our natural resources. We should be figuring out ways that we could cut down on our dependency on oil and clean up the air and toxicity in water and things such as this. We should be more concerned about those things. There are a lot of us that are concerned about this and these kinds of issues do inspire my writing. At the same time, I also love this planet and love the potential, the potential to make democracy a real incredible thing.

THAT'S A VERY HEALTHY WAY TO VIEW THINGS.

Well, there is more than one way to see things.

DO YOU HAVE A PHILOSOPHY THAT YOU TRY TO IMPART WITH YOUNG STUDENTS OR MUSICIANS?

The most important thing is to have a passion for what you are doing. When you play the music, you need to leave all the negative things behind and come with joy and give music that is uplifting to people. And also think about the spirituality, and I don't mean in religious terms but in a universal term. The heart and soul of the spirit. Always keep the joy of playing music with you, as music can be a very healing thing. It can also help bring about positive change.

DON'T YOUNG MUSICIANS STILL NEED TO GO BACK AND BUILD THEIR MUSICAL FOUNDATION BEFORE MOVING INTO DIFFERENT DIRECTIONS? ISN'T THERE A CERTAIN DISCIPLINE THAT COMES ALONG WITH PUTTING IN THE WORK?

Well, that's another question as you are talking about somebody that has their own voice, which is something that a musician has to work through. They emulate the people that they like and work through that and then find their own voice out of that. Some are fortunate to find their own voice right away. But again, that's a process of playing with a lot of different people, listening to a lot of different things, experimenting and exchanging different ideas and viewpoints. Not only musically but socially, political, and what have you.

IS IT MORE DIFFICULT FOR THE STUDENT TO BE CREATIVE IN TODAY'S SOCIETY? IS THERE A DIFFERENT SET OF CHALLENGES?

Students need to develop their own voices, although I think that is changing quite rapidly. The biggest problem that young students face today is that there are more practitioners than there is work. Think about that. So in other words, when you are in college or in a high school band, you have new groups that come out of that and then after you leave school and get out in the real world, you try to make it as a musician. But how do you see yourself as a musician? As an innovator, as a studio musician, as a producer, teaching underprivileged kids, or to just be the best musician you can be? The problem again is that there are now so many music students and not a lot of venues, but it depends on what you are looking for. The record industry is in pretty bad shape right now and if we go to war, the economic situation is going to get even worse.

DO YOU PREFER TO PLAY WITH MUSICIANS THAT COME FROM DIFFERENT MUSICAL FOUNDATIONS FROM YOUR OWN OR DO YOU PREFER THAT THEY COME FROM THE SAME PLACE?

It doesn't matter where they come from. I have a relationship with Foday Musa Suso of Gambia, Africa, that plays the kora. Foday is unusual because he's done things with Phillip Glass and the Kronos string quartet and has put the kora in another type of situation. He's coming from Africa but has been in America for twenty years and is diversified and can make that traditional instrument work in any kind of situation. Even though a musician may come from a different background, if they are open to the universality of music, then it's not confined by local standards. Recordings, the Internet, and television bring us closer together. So I don't think it matters, as music is a universal language. I can go anywhere and sit down and play with a musician, no matter what style he or she comes from.

I think it's more about who we are as individuals. There are men who have a feminine side. For instance, Miles was a Gemini and had these two sides. He had a macho side and he had this real feminine sensual side. So I think it has more to do with the individual as far as how it comes through. You have Terri Lynn Carrington, a young drummer named Kim Thompson, and Cindy Blackman for instance. They just play great and are great musicians who just happen to be women.

As difficult as it must already be to make it as a musician professionally, it would seem to be even that much more difficult for a woman.

Well, that's still an issue. I think it's improved over the years but there is a lot more room and still should be a lot more happening for women. The women are moving, but we need more of the feminine energy to balance the male testosterone energy, to lessen it.

You have taken many risks in your career. Can you talk about what you have learned about yourself by taking those risks?

I felt strongly about where I was at a time I did specific projects. I tried to be in step with what was going on and I felt strongly about the music statement and the musicians that I was playing with at that time. Therefore, I was probably perceived as going against the grain because a lot of my music wasn't considered commercial. People like Miles and Coltrane never thought about the commercial aspects about what they were doing. Miles may have thought about it later, but the idea was to place the music first and it's still that way. I just believe in that.

What influences your creativity?

It could come from playing with or listening to other creative musicians, but, then again, it could come from looking out the window at the mountains up here where I live. Or listening to someone say something that I find inspiring.

This is an amazing reality and dimension that we are all in and sometimes we forget how fascinating it is and how it all works. When you plug into that you can find a lot of inspiration for creativity and sometimes find more positive change. Sometimes it's the little things that influence or can be inspiring.

Can you connect today's environment politically, socially, or spiritually?

Most of the politically motivated music that I hear today comes from elsewhere like Europe, Africa, and Cuba just to name a few. I watch a channel called "World Link" that comes from San Raphael and New York. And I must congratulate them.

They show a lot of bands made up of world musicians that don't get played here in America. It also gives a perspective of news and documentaries that you won't find anywhere else. There are people like Baba Maal and Youssou N' Dour and there are some people here but I think you find more within poetry. To watch World Link TV which is now called Link TV, you have to have a direct TV small satellite.

ARE THERE ANY SPECIFIC INDIVIDUALS THAT HAVE INFLUENCED YOU AS AN ARTIST?

One of the major musicians that inspired me was Ahmad Jamal, who was also a big influence on Miles. In Chicago, there were quite a few musicians that helped me along. Chico Freeman's father, Von Freeman, helped me when I played piano. Richard Muhal Abrahms was very, very influential. He showed me that you could learn anything and didn't need a lot of money to do it. Muhal taught himself how to write and arrange through the library. It's all there, it's free and you only need to put in the time. He taught himself how to play clarinet, the piano, and a number of instruments. He was always encouraging and always available whenever musicians wanted to come around and was always available to play. He got us a space where we could rehearse and present what we wanted to play. He gave a lot of advice and was very inspirational. He also started and received a charter for AACM (Association for the Advancement of Creative Musicians) in Chicago. We had the AACM Orchestra, which consisted of Roscoe Mitchell, Joesoph Jarman, Malachai Favors, and myself just to name a few. That was very inspiring and has been a major influence on me as a composer, arranger, and bandleader. Pat Patrick was another person that helped me considerably and inspired me. I also worked with Eddie Harris in Chicago and told me that "you play good piano, but you are a natural drummer. Make drums your main instrument and it will be a different world for you." That turned out to be pretty true.

PAT METHENY HAS SAID THAT YOU ARE ONE OF HIS FAVORITE DRUMMERS, BUT SOME OF THAT HAS TO DO WITH YOUR BACKGROUND AS A PIANIST WHICH INFLUENCES THE WAY YOU PLAY DRUMS.

It really does influence me and I hear orchestral sounds in the cymbals. Some of those that have influenced me were Kenny Clarke, Papa Jo Jones, Art Blakey, Philly Jo Jones, Elvin Jones, Max Roach, Tony Williams, Paul Motian, and of course Roy Haynes would be number one, just to name a few. Sun Ra was very influential. I worked with him in Chicago and in New York. John Patton gave me my first job in New York and encouraged me to be the best I could be. Jackie McLean. These people all encouraged you to go for it. They were inspiring and we would inspire each other to not be afraid to try something different. And of course playing with Miles, and I also had a chance to work with Coltrane.

I DON'T THINK A LOT OF PEOPLE KNOW THAT.

I filled in for Elvin Jones with John in Chicago. After that he called me when he was putting together the band with Rashied Ali, Jimmy Garrison, Alice and Pharoah Saunders; we played the Plugged Nickel in Chicago for a week. John didn't talk about the music much but he talked through the music. He was a very spiritual being who showed you by example. He practiced all of the time and I never seen or heard of anyone play the way he did. He heard so many things and had so many ideas all at once. He inspired you to just go play things that you normally might not play.

I was also inspired by the music of Mingus and Sonny Rollins who I played with a lot and who I still play with. Musicians really didn't talk a lot about the music as it was spoken in the music and they trusted you. These are musicians that inspired and encouraged me. One of the things that Miles loved to do was just to listen to the musicians play and listen to them experiment. Coltrane was also like that and a lot of that rubbed off on me. I like musicians that think differently and have their own voices and challenge me. We challenge and inspire one another and are as creative as we can be. I try to keep musicians that stimulate me with their own voice and are inspired within themselves. That's the legacy that I try to pass on to other musicians.

CAN YOU SAY WHAT IT IS ABOUT JAZZ AND THE ART FORM THAT IS IMPORTANT TO YOU?

Always be prepared to play what you don't know!

WHAT DO YOU ENVISION FOR THE FUTURE OF CREATIVE MUSIC?

The future of creative music depends on whether the human community can wake up and decide if it wants to continue to live in strife and war, or is it willing to make the necessary choices that would help create an environment of peaceful diversified coexistence for everything and everyone on our planet.

⑩

DAVE DOUGLAS

After the completion of over sixty interviews, I have observed a direct correlation between innovation and artistic vision, on the one hand, and levels of awareness, on the other; Dave Douglas is no exception. Influenced by political and social injustices, the breadth and scope of his work is extraordinary. A visionary, his world of composition and improvisation is leading the way in an era that is one of the most dynamically creative and diverse in the history of music.

W HEN WE FIRST SPOKE, YOU MENTIONED THAT POLITICS, GLOBALIZATION, AND RACISM ALL INFLUENCE YOU. AND WHEN I LISTEN TO YOU PERFORM, I HEAR A LOVE FOR MUSIC, BUT AT TIMES I ALSO HEAR SOMEONE PLAYING AND COMPOSING OUT OF NECESSITY. IS THIS PARTLY A RESULT OF THOSE INFLUENCES?

Thank you, Lloyd. First of all I want to thank you for including me in this work and say how important I think it is. They say history is defined by those who write it, and over the past years I feel the official histories have more and more left out the living essence of creative music. It's a story that needs to be told to stay alive.

In answer to your question: Your whole life goes into the music, and if you're going to make vital, living music, you've got to deal with real issues. This is the necessity as I see it. In the moment of performance, you're not thinking about any one thing. You're trying to represent everything. Every part of your experience from birth to that moment. Musicians and artists bear witness to the world as they find it. The love that you see in great musicians when they perform is a love of reality, and the struggle to make original creative music is a struggle to truly represent and communicate that reality. This is why if you hang out with composers in a place where there is music that is full of clichés or kind of cloying, you can see that it's very hard to take. Music can lie, and it's a crime against the gods of sound. (Laughs.)

So first and foremost, that's what I do: represent reality. At least that's how I experience it, and any conditions that get in the way of trying to communicate that reality are an incredible frustration. As a composer and bandleader, I try to create the conditions for that kind of communication, no matter how strange the fight against falsity may look from the outside. If music comes out of my life, then it's impossible to separate out my disgust at the government—the sickening feeling of witnessing unjust killing in any form. Racism—especially for musicians involved in jazz—is such a naked form of evil that is hard to look away. How can you ignore these things once you've seen them?

I don't think that you can look at American music and ignore the way that so much of it has been formed by the effects of race and racism. I mean, it has created our entire history up to this day and beyond. Speaking just after this election, I realize that not much would have changed if we had gotten rid of Bush, though that would have been a good first step towards the acceptance and understanding of all people. But let's not go there. Oops, too late.

CECIL TAYLOR SAID THAT "MUSIC HAS TO DO WITH A LOT OF AREAS WHICH ARE MAGICAL RATHER THAN LOGICAL; THE GREAT ARTISTS, RATHER THAN JUST GETTING INVOLVED WITH DISCIPLINE, GET TO UNDERSTAND LOVE AND ALLOW THE LOVE TO TAKE SHAPE." FOR ME, THE MAGICAL PART IS THE MYSTERY OF MUSIC AT ITS MOST CREATIVE LEVEL. THE EPHEMERAL ASPECT OF MUSIC ALSO SEPARATES IT FROM ANY OTHER ART FORM. HOW WOULD YOU EXPLAIN THIS MAGICAL OR MYSTERIOUS PLACE AND DO YOU HAVE YOUR OWN RELATIONSHIP WITH IT?

That's a very beautiful quote from Cecil. I'm not sure you can explain the magical. It has to be experienced. We are privileged as humans to have access to that. When you go into that space, you experience life on other planes, and music can be a translation of that experience. Those levels are not more or less creative than any others, there is just more depth to them. There is a basic misunderstanding about the creative process that sees it as separate from the rest of human activity, like some sacred, unattainable ideal. This is false. There is creativity in everything we do, and the more grace, love, and passion we can put in our actions, the more fulfilled lives we will lead.

So I disagree that the ephemeral aspect of music separates it from other art forms. In fact, I believe that the mystical, fleeting aspects in music are what unite it with our everyday experience, what permit it to be understood. We're not human beings who are having a spiritual experience. We are spiritual beings having a human experience.

YOU STATED IN THE NOTES OF *STRANGE LIBERATION* THAT "THIS IS NOT A POLITICAL RECORD; BUT IT COMES WITH BOTH A LOVE FOR THIS COUNTRY AND AN UNEASY

AWARENESS OF THE CURRENT STATE OF JUSTICE, FAIRNESS, AND EQUALITY." I'M GO-
ING TO ASSUME THAT YOU FEEL UNEASY AS WE AGGRESSIVELY APPLY OUR CULTURE ON
OTHER PARTS OF THE WORLD.

Unfortunately, it's not our culture that we are applying around the world. We
are applying our military strength with an eye to naked economic domination. And
yes, I think that's unfortunate, to understate matters.

Our culture is the greatest asset that we have, and I wish that we were more
willing to recognize that and share it proudly throughout the world. And I mean
the whole complex mass that is American culture, coming as it does with the horrible heritage of slavery and genocide, as well as the wonderful legacy of freedom
and individualism.

IN THE SLEEVE NOTES OF *STRANGE LIBERATION* YOU HAVE A QUOTE FROM MARTIN
LUTHER KING THAT READS, "A TIME COMES WHEN SILENCE IS BETRAYAL, WE MUST
SPEAK WITH ALL THE HUMILITY THAT IS APPROPRIATE TO OUR LIMITED VISION, BUT
WE MUST SPEAK." THOSE WORDS SEEM VERY APPROPRIATE, YET WE LIVE IN A TIME
AND SOCIETY WHERE SPEAKING OUT SEEMS TO QUESTION ONE'S PATRIOTISM OR LOVE
FOR COUNTRY. HOW DID WE GET TO THIS PLACE?

I think we're much better in that regard than we were even a year ago. It became clear that the best way we could support our people in uniform was to bring
them home. But ultimately, you can't let the ebb and flow of politics determine
what you have to say.

Musicians are the real patriots in America: Thelonious Monk is as much an American and maybe more so than Charles Lindbergh. A country that gives us Anthony
Braxton and Henry Threadgill and Charles Ives and Charlie Parker and Harry
Partch is worth fighting for. I really feel that the censorship is not as much of a problem today. There is a recognition that we are all in this together, even if many of the
petty squabbles remain in our discourse. But it's the killing that's got to stop.

Creative music sometimes makes people uncomfortable because it speaks of realities they'd be more comfortable not dealing with. I make a point of saying something about the world during every show because I think that people should just
be thinking about it. I don't expect everyone to agree with me and I do get angry
e-mails from people who were in the audiences at my shows. But I always make it
a point to write back and say thanks for expressing yourself, even if we disagree.
That's what this country should be about: having a real conversation.

But for us to sit here and enjoy a glass of wine in a beautiful club and play our
music and pretend that people are not being killed in our name, that I think is the
ultimate hypocrisy. And I find that once I respond to these people, the reaction is
very warm and genuine and understanding. So I do think that the potential for
communication is there but takes a willingness to reach out from all sides.

I HAD A ROUNDTABLE DISCUSSION RECENTLY THAT INCLUDED MATS GUSTAFSSON
FROM SWEDEN, PETER BROTZMANN FROM GERMANY, AND PAAL NILSSEN-LOVE

FROM NORWAY. IN THAT DISCUSSION, THEY TALKED ABOUT THE INTEREST FROM THE
PEOPLE OF THOSE COUNTRIES IN OUR RECENT ELECTION THAT THEY HAD NEVER
SEEN BEFORE. PEOPLE WERE STAYING UP TILL THREE OR FOUR IN THE MORNING TO
WATCH THE DEBATES. DO YOU EVER GET THE SENSE THAT PERHAPS OUR SOCIETY JUST
DOES NOT HAVE A GRASP, OR IS TOO FAR REMOVED FROM THE IMPACT THAT U.S. IN-
VOLVEMENT IN THE MIDDLE EAST HAS ON THE REST OF THE WORLD?

Look, fifty-nine million people voted for John Kerry. If we could interest fifty-
nine million in instrumental jazz records we'd be doing pretty well. Many of the
sixty million who voted for Bush saw Kerry as a typical politician, which he is, and
were turned off. Bush is certainly not a typical politician, but perhaps that's another discussion.

I absolutely think that we in the U.S.A. are too far removed from the rest of the
world. It's a luxury that we have as an enormous land mass—to be isolated, to not
need to learn languages or learn about other cultures.

But I also think that most Americans are very involved with the issues. It's just
that there are many, many other things going on and the Middle East is not the
only thing on the horizon in this country. People here have many concerns and
many ways of dealing with them. The saddest part is that we are killing a lot of people and, unfortunately, that information is not available to everyone.

So I don't think you can blame people in this country for not knowing. If you
read USA Today and watched ABC News every day, what do you think your opinion would be? And most people don't even read newspapers. They don't have time
because they are working two and three jobs trying to support a family. This is a
problem with much deeper roots, and it would take a revolution in cultural education to even begin to address it.

IN THAT ROUNDTABLE DISCUSSION, WE ALSO TALKED ABOUT HOW FEAR WAS IM-
POSED ON THE AMERICAN PEOPLE AND LED MANY TO VOTE A CERTAIN WAY.

I'm surprised we're not talking about music. I mean, the characters you've gath-
ered in this book are among the most courageous people on earth. They've put
their lives on the line for their music, often at great personal sacrifice. I still believe in music as a healing force: against fear, against prejudice, against lies.

When it comes to the 2004 election I don't really know what happened, but in
my heart of hearts I would like to believe there was fraud and that Kerry really did
win. But we don't have enough information to really know what happened and
how and why. We just have to work towards what we believe in. Perhaps some day
the truth of what this administration is up to will emerge. We have to participate
in making that happen, too.

DID THE IMPACT OF 9/11 AFFECT YOU ARTISTICALLY? IF I REMEMBER CORRECTLY,
YOU WERE DOING REHEARSALS IN NEW YORK AND I THINK SCHEDULED TO PERFORM
WITNESS FOR THE FIRST TIME WHEN THE EVENTS OCCURRED.

You probably know from the piece Just Say This that it had a huge impact on
me. It took a long time to write that piece because I just felt like there was no real

way to comment musically on such a horrific event. And the piece was more in re-action to the feelings that I got down at Ground Zero than anything else—the hor-ror of it. That seemed to be the only way not to take advantage of the emotion, which seemed to be the mainstream version of dealing with 9/11.

It was ironic that *Witness*, an album of strong social statement, was released a few weeks before that event. Ironic because I created the album in the pre-9/11 world, and it was perceived entirely in the post-9/11. I didn't have a problem with that, I felt that it held up. But it certainly made the atmosphere more difficult for that project. It made the folks at RCA quite nervous, which meant there was sud-denly less support. It also meant that interviews in that period were rarely about music. And I felt as if I had to stand up for what I believed on the bandstand. That probably had a positive effect on me.

YOU HAVE TALKED ABOUT GLOBALIZATION, WHICH SEEMS TO LEAVE VERY LITTLE, IF ANY, ROOM FOR CREATIVITY AND INDEPENDENT THOUGHT.

The McDonald's-style globalization—maximized profits, minimized individual-ity—leaves very little room for creativity and independent thought. It is increas-ingly difficult to break through the tedious drone of our media, and that is sad for the arts. But I now believe that niche cultures have, in a sense, a greater possibil-ity to succeed and grow. I think that jazz and improvised music is a kind of niche culture and within that, there are many, many thousands of people who are fasci-nated by what's going on. Perhaps in defense against the mass amnesia, we are more urgently involved with the things we think are special.

I'm a little frustrated that many people trying to sell jazz culture, in particular, the corporate culture at Lincoln Center, have a vision of jazz becoming part of the mainstream globalized McDonald's world of what sells. This is not an elite music, it is music played for and by everyone. Its very purpose—the immediacy of im-provisation—is designed to cut through all that. It is unique.

I do admire the wonderful new space along with all the fundraising, and I don't think that you can fault them for that, but I do think that the ability to be flexible about creating truly original music suffers; new things and new developments have to happen elsewhere. When the tickets and the environment are so expensive, it tends to create a barrier.

In the history of music, it's very rare that an institution has been able to be at the forefront of the latest developments of the music. This is normal and to be ex-pected. Unfortunately, sometimes the PR campaign of jazz at Lincoln Center be-comes very negative. They want to define themselves negatively. Jazz is not this, it's not that, it's only swing and the blues, narrowly defined. These are the old argu-ments that we are all familiar with, and I think that European artists who have been informed by jazz feel a kind of anger and antipathy towards that. But I also sense that they have more freedom to just do their own thing and not concern themselves with it. Kind of turns the tables on the old "burdened by history" trope, doesn't it?

The discussion is much more difficult for American musicians like myself who are continuing to do new things because it's like the discussion we had a moment ago about patriotism. We are Americans and we love this country, we believe in it. Our heroes are Charlie Parker, Thelonious Monk, Henry Threadgill, Julius Hemphill, Anthony Braxton, and Bill Frisell, and yet there is this attempt to write some of those figures and the pure work that they made out of the history books. These are missing chapters in our history and I think that's a big problem for us. And it is certainly related to globalization. I see the narrowing of an acceptable, marketable vision of creative music as an effect of a global marketing ploy.

I DID NOTICE THAT YOU ARE SCHEDULED TO PLAY AT THE LINCOLN CENTER. I WAS QUITE SURPRISED.

I was surprised, too. I was invited a few years ago right after the Ken Burns thing, and I just said no. I was just so angry and I didn't want any part of it. Then the offer came along again, and they really seem to want to present the music the way it should be presented. They have been very gracious, very generous, and committed to putting on a concert with my quintet. So it won't be a fashion show (at least with me up there), just a music concert. I'm gratified to see it happen this way.

YOU ARE ONE OF THE FEW ARTISTS TODAY THAT IS INNOVATIVE BUT ALSO APPEALS TO LISTENERS OF MANY DIFFERENT GENRES. YOU JUST MIGHT BE IN A POSITION TO INFLUENCE LISTENERS TO CHECK OUT SOME OF THE MORE INNOVATIVE ART FORMS.

I'm not convinced that you can convince listeners to listen to anything. They find their way to it. I make records in a lot of different ways and some of them are more popular than others. But I feel like listeners take what they need, and leave what they don't need. I don't think any artist can change that.

My real job is just to make music, and music is a part of a larger cultural conversation. And what people say about it is also important, so I just feel that if I continue to present things which interest me and which I am excited about and which I feel haven't been done before, the communication will naturally happen.

HOW HAVE YOUR MUSICAL PHILOSOPHIES OR CONCEPTS EVOLVED FROM YOUR EARLIEST WORK TO THE PRESENT?

I feel I've been given a unique gift in the ability to follow my passions. Early on my excitement about Freddie Hubbard, Woody Shaw, Clifford Brown, and Bill Hardman led me to a real study of the trumpet. The early composition work I did in twelve-tone theory, odd meters, and intense improvisation strategies has continued to inform my work. But I feel all of that is now more in the service of a musical idea. What hasn't changed is my desire to create in community with other players. Hopefully I get better at that over time.

THE LATE AUTHOR EDWARD SAID HAS SAID THAT MUSIC JUST MIGHT BE THE FINAL RESISTANCE TO THE ACCULTURATION AND THE COMMODIFICATION OF EVERYTHING.

I think that the arts in general speak that subtle language which can serve as an area of truth and resistance. And I think that what he is saying is that in music, one can have this experience that transcends words, and that it isn't specifically an argument on any issue, yet it validates the human spirit. Though I may be misunderstanding his point.

That same experience exists in dance for example, and if you look more broadly, in architecture too. Then I started thinking about the poets. The spaces engendered by poetry can also transcend words. And if you are going to say poetry, why not literature? And then why not essays? And if in essays, why not in walking down the street?

The magic of resistance resides in all things. It's up to us to find it and activate it. Music holds a special place for me because I am a musician, but the mystery is everywhere.

BILL FRISELL GAVE AN INTERESTING ANSWER WHEN ASKED ABOUT WHAT HE LOOKS FOR IN THOSE HE COLLABORATES WITH MUSICALLY. THAT HE PREFERS TO PLAY WITH THOSE THAT ARE NOT PREJUDICED. WHAT I THINK HE WAS SAYING IS HE PREFERS TO PLAY WITH INDIVIDUALS THAT HAVE NO PREJUDICES AGAINST ANY FORM OF MUSIC. THEY ARE COMPLETELY OPEN AND ACCEPTING TO ANY DIRECTION THE MUSIC MAY TAKE. IS THAT A FACTOR FOR YOU AS WELL?

I'm sure Bill meant more than that. Bill has a way with words, despite appearances. Of course I would agree that playing music is most enjoyable with those who are unprejudiced. I would also add that it's important to continue the struggle to overcome our own prejudices.

YOU LIVED IN BARCELONA FOR A SHORT WHILE WHEN YOU WERE PRETTY YOUNG. DID THAT HAVE AN INFLUENCE ON HOW YOU VIEW THINGS AND ON YOUR APPROACH TO MUSIC?

Absolutely. First of all, there was a level of freedom. I was around a lot of adults who were doing interesting things in a way that I had never seen before. I also ran into a group of musicians who were a little older than me, who were listening to modern American music and turned me onto all of these things that I had never even heard of. And they just assumed that I knew everything about it because I was American.

I would say that I learned more about my own culture from living in Barcelona than I did about theirs. Because of the fascination with American culture in Spain, I became aware of many things about my own country. That was immensely important for me, and maybe that was also a way of learning about their culture. They were able to appreciate what was going on here that was really not being made available to me.

IN ADDITION TO LIVING IN BARCELONA, YOU HAVE HAD THE OPPORTUNITY TO TRAVEL VERY EXTENSIVELY OUTSIDE THE U.S. MUSIC OBVIOUSLY CAN BRING PEOPLE TOGETHER, BUT, OVERALL, ARE WE CLOSING THE GAP BETWEEN OUR DIFFERENT CULTURES OR SHOULD WE EVEN WANT TO?

There's a false choice: between identifying difference and closing the gap. I think we do both at the same time. Everywhere you go, local cultures are starting to have more significance for people. In the same way that I am talking about American music suddenly being important to me; if you go to Barcelona, you'll find that people are really into Catalan culture and expressing their regional differences. However, what I find is that they are doing so in a very universal kind of way. They are drawing universal lessons from these distinct ways of looking at things. So you get these fantastic musical groups from a small corner of Italy where they are developing their regional music but speaking in a more universal language.

What we used to call the composer, which is a guy sitting by himself in a room with a huge piece of paper, drawing these little dots on the page—I think that most musicians at this point admit that a composer can be any kind of musician working in any kind of medium. When we hear a contemporary classical composer today, you often hear a lot of music informed by jazz and rock and experimental music, electronics, and all kinds of things. You also hear jazz musicians who are influenced by contemporary classical music or folk music or electronica or what have you. So in a sense, musical language is becoming more universal but also more individualized at the same time.

IN THE SLEEVE NOTES OF THE RECORD *WITNESS* YOU WROTE, "I BELIEVE THAT AWARENESS IS ONE KEY TO ESCAPING FROM THE MADNESS." DOES THE FORWARD-THINKING ARTIST HAVE A UNIQUE ABILITY OR AWARENESS OF WHAT SURROUNDS THEM OR IS IT JUST A MATTER OF CARING?

I don't think awareness is a unique ability; I think that everyone can live consciously. First, it's a matter of curiosity and, second, it's a matter of caring. It's hard to know what to do; I mean, look at the crises in Africa these days. It's horrible. When you read about the situation in Fallujah and Najaf, especially after our election, which seemed to validate the destruction of civilians. What do you do? Just stay involved, stay aware, and know when things are going on and use whatever work you are doing to further the goals of ending injustice. Accept the suffering as you go about your work, but try to be a positive force for change.

DOES THE ARTIST HAVE A RESPONSIBILITY TO SOCIETY?

As a citizen of the world there is a responsibility. It has nothing to do with being an artist or not. I just think that if everybody took a moment to look around and see what their impact was, we wouldn't have a lot of these problems. It's as simple as that. That doesn't mean that you have to have a Ph.D. in social theory. It just means that you know the car that you drive and where you shop and where you put your trash—the little decisions that you make everyday—are part of what happens around the globe.

YOUR MUSICAL DIRECTION HAS BEEN TREMENDOUSLY DIVERSE. WHEN YOU FIRST REALIZED THAT YOU WANTED TO CREATE MUSICALLY, WAS YOUR VISION AS DIVERSE AS WHAT YOUR WORK HAS BECOME?

I have learned something new with each new project, so I hope my vision and understanding of music keeps expanding. When I was starting out as a bandleader, I had models that I looked to of people who had multiple groups and were doing different kinds of music like Lester Bowie, Paul Motian, Tim Berne, John Zorn, Don Byron, Steve Coleman, Henry Threadgill, Joe Lovano, and the Art Ensemble of Chicago. These are people who play in many modalities in the search for a personal statement. I also found Misha Mengelberg and the ICP at a certain point.

And later on I found out about Mary Lou Williams, who was also a musician of myriad visions. I had grown up being much more of a mainstream jazz type musician—thinking that I would play with Art Blakey and the Jazz Messengers. My big hero was Woody Shaw as trumpet player and composer. He is still an enormous hero for me. But of course Miles Davis also held an enormous importance for me. His work, over the course of a career, was much more broad and posed many more questions about what elements could be included in improvised music. For me and my friends, rather than thinking about that transformation over fifty years, we swallowed all that music at the same time. There was an enormous feeling that all those musics should and could coexist. Listening to Ornette's electric stuff, and Weather Report, and Fred Frith, and Gilberto Gil, and Steve Lacy, and Joni Mitchell, and Anton Webern—that has been the late twentieth-century experience. How can you separate those musics, and more important, why would you want to?

Also, the recorded legacy of music involved a lot of studio manipulation, something I was not aware of coming up. I grew up thinking everything had been played just so. And that was what I emulated in my music—creating those kinds of quick cuts and transitions that were actually by-products of the recording studio.

Coming from that perspective, I was trying to cram everything that I was hearing into one project and I struggled with that for a lot of years. That's one of the reasons I didn't get a record made until I was thirty. I just couldn't focus in on one thing—I couldn't settle on a way to say one thing without negating everything else.

At a certain point I realized that I didn't have to say everything in one space. I felt satisfied saying one thing that could hint at everything. I'm not sure if listeners were able to hear that—everyone hears something different anyway—but I got to where I was able at least to put a musical concept forward and feel OK with it. It began with different sets of musical ideas with different sets of musicians.

I learned a lot from the musicians I worked with: Mark Feldman, Mark Dresser, Erik Friedlander, Michael Sarin, Jim Black, Brad Shepik, James Genus, Uri Caine, Joey Baron, Greg Cohen, Guy Klucevsek, Ikue Mori, Chris Speed, Josh Roseman, Clarence Penn, Chris Potter, Greg Tardy, Susie Ibarra. These people showed me more than they know about how to compose. And how not to compose.

At the root of all these projects were the same ideas: that each musician should have room to say their own thing. That this is a music that develops in community. And that the music has to remain fresh in each performance, inviting in the intensity and immediacy of human experience.

WHAT DRIVES YOU?

It's the ideas that drive me. The ideas are the easy and fun part and I get them all the time. I jot them all down but the following through is 90 percent of the work. So I get all these ideas and I could let them all fall by the wayside and do nothing or I could sit down (laughs) and make a schedule for myself and figure out how to get it done.

The music doesn't exist until you actually do it. And even though I'm a composer who writes on paper, I still feel like the piece isn't real until the sound is in the air. So a lot of it is about creating the situation, to let these ideas of communicating that reality come to life. And you want to get to that real place when the work comes to fruition. That takes a lot of work. It takes work to make sure the thing doesn't end up being just an idea. It's got to have blood and guts, and you've got to fight to put them there. For music to matter, it's got to deal on the level of things that matter: love, survival, truth.

How important is humility to the creative process?

I can only speak about my own creative process, and even in that case I'm not sure how much of it I really understand. So much of the creation is magical and intuitive. My feeling is that a lack of humility tramples on that mystical essence. You must be ready for anything and ready to accept anything and assess it honestly. That means failure as well. If you can't recognize failure, then how can you remedy it? And you have to be very humble to truly be in the moment.

Has your life in jazz so far been everything that you thought it would be?

(Laughs.) I don't know if I have a life in jazz. I have a life in music, no doubt. Jazz is such a conflicted word at this point, but I don't have any other word for what I do. When a layperson asks what kind of music I play I say jazz, and that feels natural. It seems to easily encompass so many kinds of music making. I think that's one of the great things about it, in fact. When I hear people try to put jazz into a very small box, I get really upset because I have a personal feeling for the word and what it means. But there are many people who would like to see a kind of badge of authenticity, a limit to what can be referred to as jazz. Maybe this whole ridiculous argument is just the narcissism of small differences. I don't know.

This music did not come out of my culture, and I could see someone who's very involved with the cultural background and significance of jazz music being upset by any success had by someone like me. On the other hand, I believe that the masterpieces are a gift to humanity as a whole, and if music has anything to say to humans, it says it to all humans. All great music is worth being learned and valued by anybody. And an artist's job is to take legacies and lessons and transmute them into something new.

Also, quite simply, any individual should be able and allowed to play any music they want to play. An individual should be able to define themselves however they want to as long as it doesn't infringe on anyone else's right to do the same.

There's no easy answer here, if there is one at all. And maybe this boils down to arguments about who gets the gigs and who gets the press. How poignant. That's why I laugh when you ask about my life in jazz. You're trying to get me into more trouble, aren't you?

As for my life, it continues to evolve. I am happy to be involved with music every day. I am happy to wear a lot of hats within this music world. But I don't think I ever thought about what it would be like and I still don't. It just keeps growing as I keep following the music. I truly feel that in that sense I am floating. Not a directionless floating, but going where the music takes me with as much honesty and truth as I can.

It's not easy; it will never be easy. At one point, I hoped that it would some day be easy to sit around and just do my music. I prayed for many years that I would have enough success to be able to make a living and focus exclusively on creative music. And now I have been doing that for over a decade, and it hasn't gotten any easier, Lloyd. (Laughs.) I don't mean the life part of it but the work itself. The writing of a new piece; it's just as much of a struggle as the last. I feel like my best ideas still flow effortlessly, but it takes so much work to get to the point to where they are flowing effortlessly that you can't really say that it's effortless. You know, I'll sit in a room for two weeks trying to write with no results and then one day, I'll just write a whole long thing. But I don't think that I would have written it without the two weeks of struggle. To be honest, I don't think anything gets achieved without great agony. But the result is a sort of effortless effort.

HAMID DRAKE

He creates from an ancient wisdom transcending time and place, light and dark-ness, color and form, through a spirituality that he communicates from the warmth and depth of his soul. It's a place where diverse rhythmic patterns are born and re-born night after night, inspiring all those who listen, who feel, and are open to the possibilities of a living and evolving, creative universe.

IS SPIRITUALITY REFLECTIVE OF ONE'S COLOR, ETHNIC BACKGROUND, OR DOES IT EXIST ON A DIFFERENT LEVEL?

There is a place in music that transcends name and form, which encompasses race and color. But we have grown up with certain conditions and that has con-tributed to our view of life and expression.

I was listening to a conversation Amir Baraka had with a few Italian journalists while I was in Rome and they were asking how Albert Ayler developed his sound and Amiri said, "Well, if you really want to know how it came about, you have to go back to the church that Albert came from. He learned how to play by playing hymns and gospels in the church." What you play is also a reflection of where you come from, and being a person of color is naturally going to be a part of it. That's going to be an expression of it. It's from the church and black community but you also want to reach a place where you transcend name and form. Where your art becomes universal so that it can have an effect upon others regardless of name, form, creed, or color.

Once you reach a certain place, you are getting into the mysticism of sound and music. The mysticism is that which creates the bond in the heart of people. It has a psychological influence. It's just like listening to Indian music, which is definitely a product of that particular culture and climate. There is something in it that affects the spirit and the heart of the body and the being. It gives it a universal quality. The Indian term Raga means to color or paint the mind with sound, and paint is paint no matter where it comes from.

But it's also about intention. If you have vast intentions, it will lead you to vast results. So I would hope that people playing various forms of music today will have vast intentions no matter what the style is. Even if you limit it to particular style, your intentions can still be vast. But the style is just the framework that you work with, the frame of reference that you have.

ARE YOU AWARE OF THE STRENGTH THAT MUSIC HAS IN PERFORMANCE?

Music has a very strong healing potential. Albert Ayler said that music is the healing force of the universe, and I would also say that vibrations are not limited to just what we might conceptually call music. There are many traditions that believe in spiritual attainment by the aid of music, and I think music has caused people to take interest in other cultures.

There is a man by the name of Hazrat Inayat Kahn who brought the Sufi methods to the West in 1910 from India and wrote a book called *The Mysticism of Sound and Music*. He said, "Life is a symphony and the action of every person in this life is the playing of his particular part in the music." So, he is giving up the idea that the music is more than just plucking strings and breathing through a tube. Music is the grand symphony that all human beings are taking part in.

HOW DO YOU EXPLAIN THE CREATIVE SPIRIT TO YOUNGER STUDENTS OF THIS ART FORM?

One of the secrets of the great tradition is that if one truly perceives and understands it, it can help one find their own voice, their own uniqueness. We don't need another Coltrane. He did his thing and no one can do it like him, and we don't need another Art Blakey, Pepper Adams, Art Pepper, Bird, Beethoven, Mozart, Buddha, Christ, or Krishna. Everyone has their own uniqueness and we do need people like Hamid, Lloyd, and Fred Anderson and all of these other people to bring forth their uniqueness.

The great teachers were great examples because they went through their lives and struggles to express what they feel. And we are struggling to be able to express our uniqueness. So I will tell them to study and try to find their own voice, their own unique thing.

Don Cherry told me something very important; he said, "Style can be the death of creativity." Especially if it limits you to hearing things from one narrow, limited perspective to where you are judging one thing over the other. He was talking about having a more expansive view. Having an understanding of them all will help you from being limited and prejudiced regarding all aspects of the tradition. Only when the clouds come into the sky does the sky appear to have obscurations, but they are clouds that are just passing. It doesn't mean that one has to play all styles but be as versatile as possible and not be limited or inhibited by any singular style.

Some aspects might even seem contradictory to others. Free music might seem contradictory to mainstream music and vice versa, but it's really not. It's just another mode of expression, just another way of expressing the same note. And who am I or any one person to say that person doesn't have the right to explore. The intention is what's important.

ARE WE BECOMING MORE ACCEPTING AND TOLERANT OF OTHER CULTURES?

I think we are becoming more aware of them, but I'm not sure about being more tolerant. If we were tolerant and accepting, we would be in a place where we were more readily available to recognize the unity within all this diversity. But our actions tend to show us that we have a long way to go.

DOES OUR SOCIETY LACK THE PATIENCE TO BE CHALLENGED AND ONLY OPEN TO THINGS THAT ARE EASILY ACCESSIBLE AND UNDERSTOOD?

I think most people have a tendency to be interested in other things; it's just that it's hard in today's world to find out about something without having it prejudged for you because of the massiveness of the media. We need to recognize that there is a consciousness of something that is flowing through life and is breathing and living life. If we can adapt the perspective that there is some type of unity with life, then maybe we'll be able to be more tolerant of those things that appear to be outwardly different. Nothing is as it appears, but we continue to prejudge people and cultures because of appearance, which is unfair. We have to go beneath the surface and we'll find that the one element that we all have in common is suffering. Our understanding has to grow.

ARE YOU STILL GOING THROUGH A PROCESS OF SELF-DISCOVERY?

Oh yeah! I'm an unfinished product. (Laughs.) There are all these different qualities to explore and then it becomes like an alchemist process. The more you discover, the more you learn there is to discover.

WHAT IS BEAUTY TO YOU?

Beauty is one of the dimensions of love. It's the expression of integrity, commitment, and vast intentions. It's the vibration when it comes together but it is also very broad because people interpret beauty differently. What may be beautiful from one person may not be to another. We can say that a tree is beautiful but we may not know the essence of that tree. Beauty just happens to be one of the expressed forms of that which is mysterious.

THE FOLLOWING IS A QUOTE FROM CECIL TAYLOR: "MUSIC HAS TO DO WITH A LOT OF AREAS WHICH ARE MAGICAL RATHER THAN LOGICAL; THE GREAT ARTISTS, RATHER THAN JUST GETTING INVOLVED WITH DISCIPLINE, GET TO UNDERSTAND LOVE AND ALLOW THE LOVE TO TAKE SHAPE." HOW MUCH OF YOUR MUSIC IS FROM LOGIC AND HOW MUCH FROM THIS OTHER PLACE THAT CECIL TAYLOR DESCRIBES?

I think that Cecil is absolutely correct. The practicing of your discipline can take on a logic and hopefully you'll go beyond the place where you can transcend self. Then it becomes magical and becomes a play of the elements. And through the play of the elements, many things are created, but one of the great forces that is motivating the whole thing of course is love which also allows us to enter into the magical play of the mystery. This is a place without definition, without boundaries. It's unlimited.

YOU HAVE A WIDE ARRAY OF VARIOUS RHYTHMIC FEELS WITHIN YOUR PLAYING. HOW MUCH OF IT DERIVES FROM DIFFERENT ETHNIC CULTURAL INFLUENCES?

I have and still have a great relationship with my friend Adam Rudolph. We originally met at Frank's Drum Shop in Chicago when we were both fourteen years old, and Adam encouraged me to investigate other percussive traditions and to start studying congas. Our relationship just blossomed and blossomed and we started sharing a lot of information and records. His contribution to my understanding of various musical traditions of the world is unbounded. I owe a lot to Adam.

I was also fortunate to begin studying tablas with a man by the name of Paul Arman (Papaiah) who is from Hyderabad, India. I would even sometimes stay at his house with him and his wife, who is from Canada. He exposed me to this whole world of Indian classical music when I was about eighteen. And after studying with him for a few years, he began taking me to parties, which included Indian doctors and lawyers, and he would play sitar and I would accompany him on tabla. The Indian people were really amazed to see someone from the West studying and playing one of India's traditional instruments.

Paul exposed me to this whole other world of culture and music that had a profound affect on me at a very young age. I am forever indebted to him. That was perhaps the first time that I received a small inkling of what the guru disciple relationship was like in the Indian music tradition of a whole culture. A seed was planted and that seed through various other experiences grew into something greater which changed my own approach to playing.

CAN YOU EXPLAIN YOUR RELATIONSHIP WITH TIME IN A MUSICAL SENSE?

I have to give a lot of credit to Fred Anderson. He encouraged me to listen to a particular drummer and how he approached improvised music and, in particular, how he played the head to composition. His name was Ed Blackwell. (Laughs.) And after listening to Blackwell, that changed my whole approach to jazz drumming.

The way Blackwell played the head, freed the drummer. He played the rhythmic structure that the other instruments were playing melodically. And after playing this way for a period of time, my body relationship even began to change with the music. It gave me a sense of melody and rhythm that was different than what I had before. The drums did not have to be limited to a rhythmic support.

I also started to incorporate African, Indian, and Latin musical influences and began hearing subtle aspects of the rhythm and melody and the way they were flowing. It didn't mean that I had to play exactly what they were playing, but I could play an aspect or my own interpretation of it. That helped me to reinterpret what the horn players were doing and find my own voice.

WHAT HAS FRED ANDERSON MEANT TO THE HISTORY OF THE CHICAGO CREATIVE MUSIC SCENE?

Fred Anderson's influence has been phenomenal. He is a great humanitarian while continuing to perpetuate the music but has also been a tremendous influence and inspiration for younger musicians. He has always provided a place for musicians to be able to present their music, which is important, and of course today, he has the Velvet Lounge. He is a great player with a huge dedication and his knowledge of the saxophone is enormous. He's an amazing disciplinarian in the way he fine-tunes himself through practice from his love and passion he has for the music. He has also been an inspiration for those that are interested in what we call "the great tradition." The great tradition encompasses all styles of playing within not only the form we call jazz, but all of the things that have contributed towards the formation of the thing we call jazz.

WHAT HAS HE MEANT TO YOU PERSONALLY?

Fred is not only a great musical figure to me but he's someone that I have a remembrance of from when I was a small child. He has not only influenced my musical perspective but also my humanity. My family lived with Fred's family in Evanston, Illinois, and we eventually moved across the street. Though Fred is my elder, we were born in the same town of Monroe, Louisiana. Thus, Fred and his wife Bernice were very close and very good friends with my parents.

Fred has also always been like a musical guru for me, and it pleases my heart a thousand fold to see Fred given his due. Many people have heard about Fred but have never seen him. To see Fred perform is a beautiful thing. It brings joy to my heart to see him receive love and appreciation.

YOU OBVIOUSLY HAVE VERY STRONG VALUES.

I'm very fortunate at this time in my life to have two wonderful Buddhist teachers who are from the U.S. I feel very fortunate and it's important to follow the tradition of your compassion. I have also had the great fortune to be able to travel and be exposed to many different cultures and points of view. When you travel, you see that suffering abounds everywhere, and that does a couple things for you. It can help draw your heart to compassion and loving-kindness for others and for yourself and it starts to make you reflect upon human life.

Human life is really precious so what am I going to do with mine? How can I relieve my own suffering so that I may be able to help others in some way? There are so many things going on in the world today and it's amazing how humanity suffers on various levels from all of the different wars. Right now, we are talking about what is going on in Iraq but people forget that two or three years ago, a million people were slaughtered in Rwanda. A million people! And now, it just goes across the news like it's some small event. And we are talking about Iraq, oil, and building a government, but a million people were slaughtered!

WHAT MAKES YOUR RELATIONSHIP WITH WILLIAM PARKER UNIQUE AND WHAT DOES IT MEAN TO YOU PERSONALLY?

It's the love that William and I have for each other as brothers and human beings and the respect that we have for each other's playing and for each other's humanity.

William is a remarkable human being and has a strong sense of compassion for others. He has a wide interest in musical forms from many, many different cultures and an ability to play a lot of different instruments, which I respect. He will go out at two in the morning and drive his car where people cannot hear him and practice his various flutes. He is amazing! Let alone what he has done for the bass. He has such a wide range of playing with many different people.

We have a relationship of trust, and music is our particular function or particular mode of expression. The music and the various people that we have played with have gotten us to this point. It's the musical expression of our relationship. Like they say in the hood, "We got each other's back." There is this conversation going on all of the time.

WITH SOME DRUMMER AND BASS PLAYER COLLABORATIONS, YOU CAN SOMETIMES TELL WITHIN SECONDS THAT IT'S NOT HAPPENING. THERE IS TOO MUCH WEIGHT IN THE MUSIC. BUT WITH WILLIAM AND YOU, IT DOESN'T SEEM TO MATTER WHAT THE DIRECTION IS, YOU ALWAYS SEEM TO COMMUNICATE VERY EASILY. IT ALWAYS WORKS AND SOUNDS FRESH. WHAT MAKES IT HAPPEN?

First of all, it's of mutual respect. We both take the lead and supporting roles but sometimes it happens simultaneously. William may play a phrase, I'll respond to that phrase, and then he reacts to my phrase and so on. It goes back and forth and is that place where you forget about self and is where the mystery comes in. I cannot necessarily logically define it, other than to say that it's a relationship of love and respect. That's the core foundation and if it's there, then naturally you are going to listen to the other person and support what they do and this whole other entity is born. It's two souls, two beings, united in that moment. From the unity of those particular two entities, a third entity is brought into being. And that third subtle entity is the mystery of the creative process.

It's also special to play William's compositions, which can be in any style. After a while, you can start gravitating towards the subtle essence of a composition, which, in a sense, becomes your composition. William gives the basic outline but then you get inside the composition and then the composition becomes your unique expression and that can be from the group point too. That's what Ornette and Coltrane did with their greatest groups. Coltrane wrote these great compositions and the people that he was working with at the time were able to get into the subtle essence of the composition, so it became the group composition and the individual's composition at the same time.

WHAT IS IMPORTANT ABOUT THIS ART FORM TO YOU?

It can help one find their unique voice and their own process of creativity. The great teacher Rajneesh Osho defines creativity as "unleashing the forces within." This music definitely has that capacity to do that. He also called it the "fragrance of freedom." But creativity has a process too. We are the canvas but we have to prepare the canvas and there are a lot of other things that go within that. Hopefully you get to a place where the music transcends name and form. To unleash your own creative forces that are latent within you and find your own unique voice.

⑫

BILL FRISELL

If there is a given within the music of guitarist Bill Frisell, it's the honest approach in every note he composes and plays. There are no compromises. His magical world of creativity incorporates yet transcends all styles and genres of music, and as one of today's most original and innovative composers, he has created a unique and distinct voice that has developed into his own personal musical language.

Without perhaps trying to do so, Frisell creates the greatest support yet for the argument that jazz doesn't have to be stylized, compartmentalized, or labeled. There is a seamless quality to his compositional approach that weaves between various cultures, generations, and styles within his art form. Bill prefers not to speak about his music but to let it unfold and thereby challenge listeners to find their own interpretation, their own relationship with the music. Within the depths and at the heart of his creative process, he stays true to the jazz approach, yet on the surface, there lies a musical diversity from many generations of Americana to the music of South America, Europe, and Africa. A brilliant guitarist, one hears influences from Jim Hall to Hendrix, but to focus on his technical proficiency would be to deny his compositional genius as a painter of sound.

HAS IT BECOME MORE DIFFICULT TO STAY TRUE AND HONEST WITH YOUR OWN CREATIVE PROCESS AS YOU HAVE BECOME MORE SUCCESSFUL?

It's kind of a double edge with a lot more of everything, but it can go both ways. There's a lot more distraction but then there are a lot more opportunities to do exactly what I want to do. It's weird when people start noticing you. There are more reviews, more is written, and people start talking about you like what we're doing now. It's not about what the music is really. I remember the very first time I did an interview, I was just petrified. It was for a French magazine and the guy was a real nice guy but I could hardly talk and didn't know what to say. I was terrified. I have done thousands of interviews but I still have difficulty verbalizing. I guess what I'm trying to say is that there is this whole other area of activity and I feel I have to be careful as this whole business thing can kind of take over.

I'd also like to think I'm not influenced by what people say either negative or positive, but I can't really help noticing what someone says. I'm the only one that really knows what's going on with my music and I try to not let what someone says influence me too much but I'm sure it does. And there was definitely something pure thirty years ago when I was sitting in my little apartment practicing with hardly any gigs and nobody knowing who I was. It was just the music and nothing else. That's changed for sure.

YOU HAVE BEEN WITH LEE TOWNSEND OF SONGLINE/TONEFIELD PRODUCTIONS FOR QUITE AWHILE, WHICH IS KIND OF UNUSUAL WITHIN THE INDUSTRY TODAY. THAT SUPPORT HAS TO HAVE HAD A LOT OF INFLUENCE IN THE CREATIVE FREEDOM YOU HAVE BEEN ALLOWED.

Well, definitely, and I know my situation is really rare. Lee is my manager but he also produces a lot of my albums so he has this sort of double function, but I think of him as my friend perhaps before all that other stuff. I have also been with Nonesuch Records since I first came to Seattle, which was about 1988. There are so few artists that are able to stay with the same record company anymore. People get signed and then get dropped or the label goes under. It's so rare that you can have any kind of consistency and it's fortunate that I don't have to worry about it because it can really affect the music, but I also know that it could all fall apart any second. There is probably some guy in a tower with a cigar that gets to say, "Let's get rid of those guys." Nonesuch is just a small part of whatever the company is and I don't even know what it is anymore. Warner, Time Warner? I guess what I'm trying to say is that I don't take it for granted because you never know.

WHEN PEOPLE HEAR YOUR NAME, THEY DON'T THINK IN TERMS OF A STYLE OR CAT-EGORY ANYMORE, THEY JUST THINK OF THE FRISELL SOUND. WOULD IT BE A MORE POSITIVE APPROACH IF THE INDUSTRY WOULD MARKET THE MUSIC BASED AROUND THE INDIVIDUAL ARTIST RATHER THAN SPECIFIC STYLES OR LABELS?

Boy, I wish it was that way because it feels uncomfortable to be boxed in or la-beled and perhaps I have gotten out of it a little bit but I still feel excluded. I feel as if a small victory has been made if someone from another area gets to hear my music. It's frustrating that if it can be one thing that it can't be another, and it doesn't make any sense because hardly any music is just one thing.

Pulse magazine had those desert island discs where people were asked to select ten records they would bring to an island. I don't know if it's a reflection of how people have been conditioned, but one person would list ten Rolling Stone

records and the next guy would list ten polka records. It was weird. I couldn't believe how narrow some of the listening was. If I had to go to an island and only had
ten picks, I would want to listen to different flavors of music and that would seem
the most logical thing to do. But we have had it pounded into us and it just doesn't
make any sense to me at all.

THERE SEEMS TO BE A YOUNGER CROWD OPEN TO BEING CHALLENGED AND
CHECKING OUT CREATIVE MUSIC TODAY.

A couple of weeks ago I was playing with Paul Motian and Joe Lovano at the Village Vangaurd and I noticed the age span of the audience. There were little kids
with their parents, students, and there was a gentleman that must have been
ninety years old sitting in the front row. It was incredible and really cool. There
were all kinds of people and I felt that what I was seeing had nothing to do with
what the big machinery puts on us. It seemed like a whole bunch of people that
just wanted to listen and it was as simple as that.

HAVE WE BECOME A SOCIETY WITHOUT THE PATIENCE TO BE CHALLENGED?

I'm really starting to think the volume of information we receive and the speed it
comes at you is overrated. It's not necessarily good. I'm constantly running around
from one place to another, and more and more I'm feeling how important it is to
stick with one thing. As I get older, it takes me longer to absorb things in a deep way,
and I feel that that's what I need to do for the music to really come out in a true way.
Subsequently, before the information gets processed, it has to seep way down in me
to get absorbed and taken in. I just can't take it in and spit it back out. Part of the
reason I came to Seattle was because I wanted to be in a place unlike New York
where I would soak up as much information as I could. I needed to slow down and
not be in a place where I was constantly bombarded and be able to meditate on what
was in there and try to figure out what my own thing was. There was a documentary
on Warren Zevon who recently died where he said, and I don't know if this is from
him or if he is quoting someone else, "We buy books because we think we are buying the time to read them." I don't know if that does anything for you but it's what I
do and what I think a lot of people do. I sometimes think back to the period I was
in college and was living in a house with a bunch of friends. We would sit around
hour after hour listening to music, and I just don't get a chance to do that much anymore. It's getting harder and harder to get into stuff in a real deep way.

IS IT MORE DIFFICULT FOR A STUDENT TO BE CREATIVE IN TODAY'S SOCIETY?

It's always been difficult, but perhaps it's worse now than it's ever been. But I'm
also not sure if it's not the same pattern happening over and over. The people that
are doing something different always have to struggle against the easy way somehow. I know it's hard but I'm just not sure if it's more difficult now or just the same
pattern going around in a circle.

Do you have a philosophy that you try to impart among students or young musicians?

You have to really love what you're doing and just keep trying, stay persistent and keep at it. Every time I have done something with any kind of ulterior motive other than just for the music, I've always gotten into trouble. I have always tried not to sacrifice any part of the music and kept my focus on what I'm getting out of it musically and I think that's where people get into trouble. They start looking for something other than the music, whether it's for money, girls, or trying to get famous. You start running after something you'll never figure out because you can never figure out what people want you to do. You have to do what you want to do and believe in that and that's all you can do really. I know there are pressures and it's not easy, but it's just a disaster if you start running around trying to figure out what somebody else thinks is right.

Do traditionalists have a difficult time accepting that a music form considered "American" now has more international and diverse aspects within it?

I think it's always been there and it was the same when Charlie Parker came along. Dixieland musicians wanted everything to stay the same and would put his music down. Additionally, it seems that retro traditionalist stuff has become where all the money and power is and perhaps that wasn't the case before. But there have always been people that would resist progress but I'm not sure because I wasn't around in the '40s to experience that. But I do think history keeps repeating itself.

Are we spending too much time documenting the past with little regard for the present?

I feel there is more information now than there ever was. In the late '60s, there was Berklee in Boston but there really wasn't a school where you could get a major in jazz. Of course it's like you said, it's all based on the past. Though there wasn't an Internet, you could find places to hang out and it was an obscure way of uncovering information. It was difficult to find tunes or written music, and if you could find the records, you still had to transcribe the material. There is so much available now, though perhaps not right on the cutting edge. With computers, you can now find out about some guy doing something in Turkey or Mexico and communicate with them instantly where before, you had to go to that place and find those people. However, there's something to be said about actually being with a person where you can slow things down and try to learn directly from a person rather than getting it from a book or computer. That's something that's kind of scary because it's really a different thing to sit with somebody and know what they smell like and everything else. It's really different than figuring it out from a CD or a book.

I read a quote that was attributed to you that reads, "Rather than as a style, I see jazz as a way of thinking, a way of attacking music." Could you expand on those thoughts?

In the '60s, jazz was this constantly living evolving thing and when you went out and bought the new Miles record, you would see the whole history, the whole map of everything moving ahead. You'd buy a new record and that was part of what it was. You'd learn about the history but it hadn't stagnated or solidified into this one thing. Part of the deal was that if you played jazz, it was understood that you had to understand the history but were supposed to figure out a way to move it ahead. So you would think about the process and copy people but you would try to imagine what these musicians were thinking or look at what they did from record to record or how did they get from this point to that point. What rules did they break or what happened that made things move and then I would try to imagine what could I do to take this and find my own thing with it. That was part of the struggle and still is for me. It seems that in the last few years, priorities have become mixed up and turned into this thing. OK, jazz is this and to do it correctly, you have to wear a suit, look a certain way, and have to follow all these rules and stay within certain parameters. That's just not what it's about for me. So people ask, "Is what you're playing now jazz?" I mean, I don't know what it is I'm playing, it's just music. But I still feel as if it's coming more from jazz than anything else, even if it doesn't sound like it. Even if it sounds more country and western or whatever kind of style it sounds like. I still think the inner workings come more from jazz than anywhere else.

IS IT POSSIBLE THAT BECAUSE NO ONE HAS HEARD A JAZZ MUSICIAN PULL FROM THE COUNTRY AND WESTERN GENRE THAT THEY CANNOT RELATE IT TO JAZZ?

It's all happened before. Sonny Rollins made that record *Way Out West* and I used to listen a lot to Gary Burton's music who made a record called *Tennessee Firebird* in the '60s, which is the exact thing that I did. So it's not like I did anything new. I shouldn't take credit for that.

FOR ME, IT'S KIND OF ALL WHAT HAPPENED TO THE SAXOPHONE WHEN IT WAS INTRODUCED TO CLASSICAL MUSIC. IT WASN'T RESPECTED BY THE CLASSICAL COMMUNITY BECAUSE THE SOUND OF THE SAX WAS SO CLOSELY RELATED TO JAZZ.

Right, and it has nothing to do with the outside sheen of the thing. You have to listen through or past the edge of it.

AND THE GUITAR IS SO CLOSELY RELATED TO SO MANY OTHER THINGS.

Yeah, just the sound of the guitar can't help but bring to mind other things. It's so easy for it to resonate or associate it with all the pop music or non-jazz stuff.

KARLHEINZ STOCKHAUSEN SAID THE ARTIST HAS LONG BEEN REGARDED AS THE INDIVIDUAL WHO REFLECTED THE SPIRIT OF THEIR TIME. THAT THERE HAVE ALWAYS BEEN DIFFERENT KINDS OF ARTISTS: THOSE THAT ARE A MIRROR OF THEIR TIME, AND THE VERY FEW WHO HAVE VISIONARY POWER. IS IT POSSIBLE THAT WHAT'S HAPPENING IN CREATIVE MUSIC IS TOO DIVERSE AND FORWARD-THINKING FOR MUCH OF OUR SOCIETY?

There are so many variables in what you just asked. There are visionary people or people who have somehow found their own way into the future, but there are also people rehashing things which have already been done. I think it's hard to know when you are in the midst of a particular time period, and sometimes you don't even know what's happening until the dust clears years later. When most really great music was happening, many people didn't even realize it was happening. Just think of all the Monk, Ornette, or Coltrane records and what people were saying when they first heard this music, and it really wasn't the fault of the industry. Some people got it and some people didn't.

I can sometimes get discouraged and think, "Wow, there's no music happening," and it may seem the only music that really gets me going is old stuff, but then there's always somebody doing something somewhere. They might be hiding under a rock somewhere but I think because we are human, it's always kind of going to be underground. There's always something percolating and I still have enough faith in people that something is going to turn up.

HOW MUSICIANS DEAL WITH TIME AND THEIR RELATIONSHIP TO IT DOESN'T SEEM TO GET DISCUSSED THAT OFTEN. YOUR APPROACH IS UNIQUE IN THAT IT CONJURES UP INTENSITY REGARDLESS OF TEMPO, THERE IS A PARTICULAR TENSION.

I have always felt that the way musicians play is also the way they talk. I like space and silence in music and it's such an important part of the music of my favorite musicians like Miles and Monk. I think about it a lot, but in the end, it sort of comes down to your physical body which dictates how you do it. Upon hearing a note, a phrase, or some kind of sound, players and listeners need time to figure out what they just heard. You just can't cram everything all together. It's more of an organic unconscious thing which is what happens when you play anyway. You do all this thinking and studying but when you start to play, you have to shake off all that intellectual stuff. What hopefully comes out is from a deeper place.

REGARDLESS OF WHETHER YOU ARE IN A THREE- OR EIGHT-PIECE BAND, THE MUSIC HAS A TENSION CREATED BY YOUR SENSE OF TIME. IT SEEMS TO CREATE ITS OWN ENERGY.

Everybody has their own feel for where they place notes. One person is right on it or another person is real even or behind or ahead of the beat. There are as many ways to do it as there are people. It's another thing that's really hard to talk about or describe and another one of those unspoken things with the people I play with. When everyone is playing together and feeling it in the same way or sometimes not feeling it in the same way, there can be a relationship that works. One person can be pulling and the other could be pushing but they are not doing it the same way and it can cause a certain momentum or tension to happen.

YOUR APPROACH TO MELODY SEEMS UNIQUE IN THAT YOU BREAK IT DOWN PIECE
BY PIECE UNTIL YOU ARE DISSECTING THE ELEMENTS OF SOUND WITHIN THE CON-
TEXT OF MELODY. CAN YOU EXPLAIN THAT PROCESS?

When I first started getting into jazz, I studied what was going on with the music theoretically and would look at things more in a mathematical way. I would look
at the chords and learn what the chord tones were, what the scales were. But
somewhere along the way, I tried to understand all the inner workings of the
melody. If the melody isn't there, then it really doesn't mean anything. It's also
where it gets harder to explain. With every song, I'm trying to internalize the
melody so strong that that's the backbone for everything that I am playing no matter how abstract it becomes. Sometimes I'll just play the melody over and over
again and try to vary it slightly. It's really coming from that, like trying to make the
melody the thing that's generating all the variations rather than some kind of theoretical mathematical approach.

COULD YOU EXPLAIN WHAT YOU MEAN BY INTERNALIZING THE MELODY?

It's playing and hearing the melody and not playing anything but the melody until it starts going on inside your body, even without thinking about it. But the older
I get, the longer it seems to take to learn new things and get it to the point where
it's really deep down in there somehow.

CECIL TAYLOR SAID THAT "MUSIC HAS TO DO WITH A LOT OF AREAS WHICH ARE
MAGICAL RATHER THAN LOGICAL; THE GREAT ARTISTS, RATHER THAN JUST GETTING
INVOLVED WITH DISCIPLINE, GET TO UNDERSTAND LOVE AND ALLOW THE LOVE TO
TAKE SHAPE." HOW MUCH OF YOUR MUSIC IS FROM LOGIC AND HOW MUCH FROM THIS
OTHER PLACE THAT CECIL TAYLOR DESCRIBES?

Well, I'm hoping it's coming from that place that he's talking about. That's what
I'm trying to get at but, like he said, there's all that stuff like discipline. For me,
music is kind of a magic thing. When it's really happening, I'm trying to figure out
what it is though I can't really describe it. But the real depth comes when you get
caught up in this ocean of music and get swept away.

HOW MUCH OF YOUR COMPOSITIONAL APPROACH WOULD YOU SAY COMES FROM
MUSICAL INTELLECT VERSUS INTUITION OR INSTINCT?

It can come from both, though ideally when writing, I won't even think about
it. I may not know what to do at first and will start with an intellectual exercise that
will get me going and lead into a place where I don't know where I'm headed. It's
the same way when I'm playing. The best stuff seems to come when things are not
figured out, but it can be such a mixture.

I'll write and accumulate a lot of little things and if I have the time, I'll write
everyday. Those little things will add up but are not fully formed but come from
musical thoughts floating by. When it's time for a project to be done, it becomes a

little more intellectual in that I'll take these bits and try to stick them together and try to actually see what they are. See if it will work or maybe add things to it or harmonize something in a certain way but the raw material always seems to come from a more mysterious place.

THIS IS A QUOTE FROM MILES DAVIS: "YOU HAVE TO PICK OUT THE MOST IMPORTANT NOTE THAT FERTILIZES THE SOUND. IT MAKES THE SOUND GROW. IT'S LIKE PUTTING LEMON ON FISH OR VEGETABLES. IT BRINGS OUT THE FLAVOR. YOUR SOUND IS LIKE YOUR SWEAT." ARE YOU GETTING CLOSER TO THE SOUND THAT YOU HEAR OR DOES IT KEEP CHANGING?

Every time I try to play a note, I just can't quite seem to get it. I move closer but can never really get it and it's a constant struggle all of the time. But music has always felt like that. I used to think that there would be a time when it would just become good or that everything would feel wonderful all the time. But that's not in the nature and there's always this infinite way to go. But if there weren't, there wouldn't be any reason to play anymore. It would be boring. But it can also be frustrating, and it took me awhile to learn what that feeling was. It would seem that it could kind of flip people out to where they would quit playing and never really get there.

YOU PLAY WITH A DIVERSITY OF MUSICIANS AND ARE GETTING READY TO COLLABORATE WITH SAM YAHEL AND BRIAN BLADE. WHAT GOES INTO CONSIDERATION WHEN DETERMINING WHOM YOU WANT TO PLAY WITH?

I don't know how I choose people to play with, but so much of it has to do with the person and the feel I get from being around them. Of course I want to play with great musicians, but there has to be a feeling. I can usually tell before we have played a note if it's going to feel good when we play, just by what it feels like standing next to them.

I met and played with Sam through Brian a couple of years ago. We played only one song for a benefit concert and it felt so good and I have been trying to figure out a way of how we could get together again. And Brian is one of those guys that is so open, giving, and everything he plays just makes you feel good. He's just one of my favorite musicians and you can tell how much he loves it.

YOU HAVE DONE TWO PROJECTS IN COLLABORATION WITH VISUAL ARTISTS. THE PROJECTS WERE BASED ON THE WORKS OF GERHARD RICHTER AND JIM WOODRING. IS THERE A RELATIONSHIP IN YOUR MUSIC TO WHAT YOU SEE VISUALLY?

I tried to let the paintings dictate or determine the structure of what I was writing, but I also tried to take into account Richter's way of working. I have never met him but I viewed a documentary on him and read a lot of the things he had to say and he seemed to struggle with a lot of the same things that a musician does. A lot of his paintings are done with a lot of improvisation and he struggles to know when to stop or the moment you know it's there. If you go too far then you've lost it. When we recorded the music, we did it all live and it was just one take from beginning to end, and that was definitely influenced by thinking about the way he painted rather than going back to mix or fix things.

With Jim Woodring, I was writing for the images but I also felt we had this common unexplainable thing and really understood each other and the music would happen in a very abstract way in the same way that his paintings do. I guess it's different because we're close friends but just comparing those individual things; there is a different feel because of that.

WHERE DOES YOUR INSPIRATION COME FROM OR WHAT INFLUENCES YOUR CREATIVITY?

It's still from music and musicians, but I guess I'm becoming more aware that it can come from anywhere. Looking out the window, going for a walk, or just feeling a certain way. It could be from just about anywhere. It's just being a human really. Music is just a reflection of whatever we are as people. If I stay wound up in a room and am thinking about nothing but notes and chords, after a while it really doesn't mean anything.

WHAT HAVE YOU HAVE LEARNED ABOUT YOURSELF THROUGHOUT YOUR CAREER?

I just feel—so lucky. Like I won the lottery and I'm being allowed to do all of this stuff. That's what's amazing to me. When I was younger, I always dreamed about being able to record and have gigs and now it's actually happening and it sometimes just seems too good to be true. I don't really know what I've learned because with music, it's never ending and in so many ways, it still feels like the first time I tried to play.

IS IT POSSIBLE TO PUT INTO WORDS WHAT YOU ARE TRYING TO DO WITH YOUR MUSIC?

I don't know because music is the only way I have of expressing myself. That's how I communicate what I need to communicate. I need to have people listening and it's nice to sit around the house and play my guitar, but when you're playing for people, that's what I love. I still don't know that there is anything describable in what I'm trying to say.

I feel lucky to be able to play music in front of people, but it can seem so selfish. I'm doing it for myself but I need people there too. It doesn't make any sense if the people are not listening or getting something out of it, but I also know that you cannot try to figure out what people want to hear. All I can do is what I want to do. I just put it out there and hope that they are willing to listen. I think musicians get into trouble when they try to figure out what someone else is going to like, which can turn into a disaster.

WHAT DO YOU ENVISION THE FUTURE OF JAZZ AND FOR YOURSELF PERSONALLY?

I can get kind of bummed out with everything getting computerized and compartmentalized. Everything's getting squeezed out and I can get discouraged but then I'm actually pretty optimistic. There is always somebody doing something interesting and this kind of music has always been a little bit underground. You have to look around for it a little bit, but I think that's just part of the deal. You start to think it's not there and can get discouraged but then if you look, there is someone in some basement figuring something out, trying to do something. I think the future is going to be fine.

LAST THOUGHTS?

Music is so cool and so powerful. I wish everybody could play music. Like my friend Danny Barnes says, "Music is good." It's a good thing. I just feel so lucky to get to do this all of the time.

⓭

FRED FRITH

Originally from England, guitarist Fred Frith is currently the professor of composition at Mills College in Oakland, California. Attacking music with adventurous experimental curiosity, his progressive and complex methods have opened new pathways into undiscovered worlds of sound and improvisation.

FOR THOSE WHO WANT TO CATEGORIZE AND DEFINE MUSIC, HOW WOULD YOU DESCRIBE YOUR MUSIC?

I would hopefully try to avoid it. There isn't a single category, for a start. I play in a very loud power trio called Massacre, a duo using homemade instruments called Normal, an improvising trio called Maybe Monday, and a guitar quartet playing only composed music. I write film soundtracks and dance scores, string quartets and ensemble pieces, and am currently finishing work for orchestra and electric guitar. Idiomatically I have much more to do with rock than anything else and don't consider what I do to have much in common with jazz, and most of my composing techniques are derived from working in the recording studio. If there's a label for that, let me know. . . .

OUR SOCIETY TODAY SEEMS TO HAVE DIFFICULTY WITH CREATIVITY THAT IS NOT EASILY EXPLAINED, UNDERSTOOD, OR IDENTIFIABLE. WILL THIS BE A SIGNIFICANT OBSTACLE TO OVERCOME FOR CREATIVE MUSIC?

We are in an era of unprecedented commodification and corporate control, even by previous capitalist standards. Culture in the USA has suffered enormously as a result. On the other hand I'm encouraged by the extent to which my students seek out information and empower themselves with it. I think we are entering a period where the disjunction between what is "officially" viewed as successful and what is going on at street level has never been more extreme. This is actually quite exciting.

ARE TRADITIONALISTS HAVING A DIFFICULT TIME ACCEPTING THAT A MUSIC FORM CONSIDERED "AMERICAN" NOW HAS INTERNATIONAL AND DIVERSE ASPECTS WITHIN IT?

Jazz has always included diverse cultural music styles, from its very inception. That's what the music *is*. This has continued throughout its history—listen to Sun Ra's pop singles, Dizzy Gillespie's Cuban music, the Brazilian influence of the '50s and '60s, Ornette with North African drummers, Coltrane and Indian music, Indo-Jazz Fusion from 1966—jazz musicians have always sought to include what they hear. Some, like Miles, were castigated for it, but the music has been defined by continuous attempts to reinvent and recontextualize it. The idea of the music as "American" is already problematic, and in the end I feel that those who wish to define the music as exclusively belonging to the black community which invented and developed it, and those who want to define it as American classical music, whatever the color of the players, are both misunderstanding the way culture works.

Jazz's spectacular and unprecedented achievement is that it has permeated every culture in the world. Jazz of every stripe is played everywhere, just as Western classical music is played everywhere, but it happened much more quickly and it is much more universal in its appeal. You can hear Dutch musicians play New Orleans music in a tradition which in Holland goes back well over fifty years. The most passionate and inspiring big band jazz I've ever heard was played by Czech musicians. In the '70s, groups like Brotherhood of Breath mixed South African and British musicians to lift the roof off; bebop is played in every city in France and has been taught in the state-run music school system since years before the same was true in the USA. The music has become a part of normal life outside the States and probably has a greater and more diverse listenership than it does here, where radio coverage of jazz is minimal, where major labels have all but abandoned jazz except for the rerelease of winners like Kind of Blue, and where the issue of acknowledgment and ownership has taken over the debate at the expense of creating genuinely new forms in the music itself. That is also unprecedented. We'll see what happens.

But the biggest selling jazz magazine is in Japan, and the biggest audiences for jazz are European and Japanese. Why should it be surprising that these audiences have nurtured their own versions of the music, just as America nurtured its own versions of the Western classical tradition? What is surprising is only that Americans, far from feeling pride that the music has grown and expanded so far, are locked in a debate about who the music belongs to. This debate is rooted in the shameless exploitation of black artists by white artists and entrepreneurs, an economic fact of life throughout the history of jazz. You can't discuss the history of the music without addressing that fact. But meanwhile, the train keeps rolling. I mean, where is the center of gravity of jazz now? It sure isn't the Lincoln Center.

MANY JAZZ JOURNALISTS HAVE A DIFFICULT TIME IDENTIFYING OR EXPRESSING THE SIGNIFICANCE OF JAZZ PRODUCED DURING THE LAST FORTY-YEAR PERIOD. SOME ARE NOT EVEN WILLING TO ATTEMPT THIS, AND THERE ARE EVEN THOSE WHO SEEM TO MAKE AN EFFORT TO DIMINISH ANY SUCCESS WHEN IDENTIFIED. WHY DO YOU THINK THIS IS, AND HOW WOULD YOU GO ABOUT DESCRIBING WHAT JAZZ HAS BROUGHT TO THE ARTS OVER THE LAST FORTY-YEAR PERIOD?

I think the problem is rooted in the same cultural debate that I already outlined. You are less likely to find this unwillingness among European or Japanese jazz journalists, for the simple reason that they are exposed to a lot more new jazz than their American counterparts. As long as cultural debate in the USA is overshadowed by slavery, which I think is the single most burning issue that I experience here, this is unlikely to change. I think anyone who's followed the history of jazz since the '60s would identify AACM in Chicago or BAG in St. Louis as vital elements in the evolution of the music. Names like Richard Muhal Abrams, George Russell, Anthony Braxton, Anthony Davis, Yusef Lateef, David Murray, Butch Morris, George Lewis, Leo Smith, Geri Allen, Henry Threadgill, Oliver Lake, and many others indicate the innovative vitality of the music in this last era within the African American community; yet none of these players and composers is acknowledged as important by the media establishment as far as I'm aware, let alone by the conservative musical forces that dominate the media at the present time. There is no support for them from major labels anymore, and journalists do tend to have an exaggerated respect for what corporations are giving them—they don't tend to explore much outside of what they're being told by media publicists.

And this list doesn't even attempt to look at what's happening musically outside of that community, which is a huge amount. . . . The fact is that free jazz, which is now disparaged, has had a major impact on rock culture through bands like Sonic Youth and countless others. And that the community which really cherishes the achievements of all the musicians mentioned above is no longer necessarily American, and that means for some American writers that it simply doesn't count, since Americans of every color tend to have an America-centric view of the world, especially when it comes to culture. I mean, Bjork was hip enough to ask Oliver Lake to play on one of her songs years ago, but the equivalent of a Bjork in the States wouldn't even know who Oliver Lake was. . . .

JAZZ HAS ALWAYS BORROWED FROM THE POPULAR MUSIC OF CERTAIN PERIODS. WHAT MAKES TODAY DIFFERENT? AS MILES DAVIS CAME INTO HIS LATER PERIOD, HE BEGAN TO PLAY POP SONGS OF THE DAY WITH HIS OWN ARRANGEMENTS; MANY CRITICIZED HIM FOR THIS APPROACH.

There is no difference. It's just about power and money and a conservative idea of a tradition. They attacked Miles because they couldn't deal with the fact that he was successful on his terms and not theirs.

IN FIFTY YEARS, WHAT WILL A JAZZ HISTORIAN WHO TEACHES STUDENTS SAY ABOUT THIS PERIOD?

They will point to the turmoil, the racial polarization, the attempt to preempt the music for specific political and cultural agendas, the fact that jazz ceased to be a useful term in reference to creative improvisational music, the globalization of experimental culture, the fragmentation of the record industry, and the fantastic explosion of improvised music in non-American cultures. For a start. . . .

ARE YOU SEEING AN INCREASE IN LISTENERS FOR CREATIVE MUSIC?

There is a constant increase in listeners for creative music, particularly among those who don't want to be told what is right and wrong but to judge by what they hear. People who think this is a tiny ghetto of fanatics are simply thirty years out of date. I think part of what motivated jazz conservatives is precisely the awareness that there's a huge audience for new improvised music, and that that music isn't necessarily jazz. They're right—it isn't, and it doesn't pretend to be. But it's born out of the real experiences of real people, and it speaks to an audience on that level, so it's alive. Is jazz alive in that sense, any more than classical music is? We can preserve and appreciate it, and learn from it, but classic bebop is no longer about contemporary life any more than Mozart is.

WHO DO YOU FIND ARE THE LISTENERS OF YOUR MUSIC?

I think it's hugely diverse. People who are awake and interested.

DO YOU BELIEVE THAT CREATIVE MUSIC WOULD RECEIVE MORE ATTENTION IF THERE WERE GREATER AWARENESS THROUGH MORE RADIO AIRPLAY?

Radio is a catastrophe in this country and it's about to get worse. You can hear so much more interesting music on radio outside of the States that any claim the U.S. has to being the center of this music is absurd.

WHAT ARE YOU TRYING TO DO WITH YOUR MUSIC TODAY?

To paraphrase Francis Bacon, the painter: "to make images as accurately off my nervous system as I can."

THE FOLLOWING IS A QUOTE FROM CECIL TAYLOR: "MUSIC HAS TO DO WITH A LOT OF AREAS WHICH ARE MAGICAL RATHER THAN LOGICAL; THE GREAT ARTISTS, RATHER THAN JUST GETTING INVOLVED WITH DISCIPLINE, GET TO UNDERSTAND LOVE AND AL-LOW THE LOVE TO TAKE SHAPE." HOW MUCH OF YOUR MUSIC IS FROM LOGIC AND HOW MUCH FROM THIS OTHER PLACE THAT CECIL TAYLOR DESCRIBES?

Logic is for when I'm considering what I might like to do. Love is for when I'm doing it.

IS JAZZ A THING OR AN APPROACH OR PROCESS TO MAKING MUSIC?

I'm not sure if at that point the word ceases to have much useful meaning. Clearly you can't talk about jazz without dealing with its very strong cultural identity in the African American community. On the other hand, even within that community there's a divide between the conservationists and the radicals; both sides of that divide would insist on the music's belonging to them. I have never seen the scene as polarized as it is right now.

IN MY OPINION, ONE OF THE PROBLEMS WITH THE PURIST ATTITUDE IS THAT WORK FOCUSING ON JAZZ (SUCH AS KEN BURNS'S DOCUMENTARY) DOES NOT PROVIDE IN-FORMATION ABOUT THE MUSIC BEING COMPOSED AND PLAYED TODAY AND ABOUT THE MUSICIANS WHO ARE MAKING IT HAPPEN. DOESN'T THIS SEEM SHORTSIGHTED, PER-HAPS A LOST OPPORTUNITY TO EDUCATE POTENTIAL ASPIRING JAZZ STUDENTS?

It was more of a calumny than that. It sanctimoniously justified the exclusion of artists on the grounds that it was too soon to judge their importance, but then dwelt on a musician who is a fabulous player, but hardly a seminal figure in any overview of the history of the music. That alone did the credibility of the work a great deal of damage.

IF THE PERFECT CREATIVE SITUATION IS COMPLETE FREEDOM, SHOULD THIS CRE-ATIVE PROCESS HAVE INTENT? ISN'T THERE RESPONSIBILITY, WITH ITS OWN SET OF DISCIPLINES AND CONSIDERATIONS THAT COMES WITH FREEDOM?

I disagree with the premise; I think it's meaningless. There is no perfect creative situation, since most interesting work comes about in response to who we are and where and how we live, regardless of how "free" or "not free" we may be. Doing this work involves responsibility and intent, discipline and care whatever our situation. . . .

WHERE DOES YOUR INSPIRATION COME FROM, AND HAS IT CHANGED OVER TIME?

I ask questions and try to answer them.

DO YOU HAVE A PHILOSOPHY THAT YOU TRY TO IMPART AMONG STUDENTS OR YOUNG MUSICIANS?

Don't waste your time.

YOU HAVE PLAYED IN A NUMBER OF DIVERSE SETTINGS WITH MANY DIFFERENT MU-SICIANS. HOW DOES THIS INFLUENCE OR CHANGE THE CREATIVE PROCESS OR THE RE-SULT OF THE MUSIC BEING PERFORMED OR COMPOSED?

I believe that music is fundamentally characterized by being a collective activity. I welcome and embrace that. Every project has its own identity, and its own problems and rewards, but without partners it means nothing. Even solo performances are social events with a collaborative aspect to them.

IT'S ONLY MY PERCEPTION, BUT WOMEN JAZZ ARTISTS DON'T SEEM TO GET THE RE-SPECT AS ARTISTS IN THE SAME WAY THAT MEN DO. IF IT DOES ARRIVE, IT TAKES MUCH LONGER AND MAYBE IS NOT ON A LEVEL EQUAL TO THEIR ABILITY. WHAT WILL IT TAKE TO CLOSE THIS GAP?

Women artists of any discipline are in the same position. It has changed hugely due to the activism and collective strength of extraordinary women; I don't believe that it will truly change until men are not only aware of it, but prepared to relinquish or share power. This is not happening. When Marsalis was asked why there were no women in the Lincoln Center band, he reputedly said, to paraphrase, when a woman can play like Charlie Parker then maybe there'll be a woman in the band. If he applied the same criteria to the men, there wouldn't be a band at all! It's an indication of what women in jazz are up against. But, interestingly, when you stop calling improvisation "jazz," women are present in much greater numbers (Ikue Mori, Zeena Parkins, Joelle Leandre, Irene Schweizer, Christine Wodraszka, Maggie Nichols, Anne-Marie Roelofs, Shelley Hirsch, Dorothea Schurch, and on and on). Why?

DO WOMEN AND MEN CREATE DIFFERENTLY, OR DOES IT HAVE MORE TO DO WITH THE INDIVIDUAL?

I'm sure both are true. In the former case I wouldn't exaggerate it, however. I've played with scores of women and men improvisers over the years, and I've detected all kinds of playing styles in both genders—aggressive, retiring, sensitive, boorish, playful, humorless, virtuosic, primitive, whatever. Dana Reason is writing her doctoral thesis on this subject, I believe, and I'd be most curious to read it.

AND FINALLY, DO YOU HAVE A PHILOSOPHY OR SOME WAY OF LOOKING AT LIFE THAT YOU WOULD LIKE TO SHARE?

If you aren't having fun making music, do something else.

14

ANNIE GOSFIELD

From the sounds of satellites drifting in space to the sounds of factories of Nuremburg, Germany, Annie Gosfield blurs the lines between conventional music and noise. She has written chamber, electronic, and large-scale compositions as well as music for dance, but her ability to explore and find beauty in every corner of the sound universe is ingenious.

MANY OF THE PEOPLE WHO ARE INTERESTED IN AND OPEN TO NEW IDEAS IN MUSIC WERE INFLUENCED BY VARIOUS FORMS OF MUSIC AT A VERY YOUNG AGE. DOES LISTENING HAVE TO DO WITH A DIFFERENT MINDSET?

I was born in 1960, the youngest of four children in a musical family, which gave me a ringside seat to watch music (and society) change. I grew up in an environment where people felt that they could change the world, so as I started writing music, anything seemed possible. I was exposed to an enormous variety of music, which encouraged me to be open-minded, to avoid purist notions about genre, and to have respect for all kinds of music.

After studying composition in college I played in bands and free-improvisation ensembles in the punk clubs of Los Angeles. The spirit of defiance was contagious and taught me to have a thick skin, to not fear rejection, and to always write exactly what I want. I learned a great deal about working with different musicians' strengths and weaknesses, and I try to maintain that same collaborative spirit when writing for others.

WHAT DOES ARTISTIC FREEDOM MEAN TO YOU AND IS IT ENCOURAGED BY SOCIETY TODAY?

I feel enormous responsibility to maintain artistic freedom as I witness personal freedoms being stripped away by our government. I always felt that part of any artist's job description was to speak out, and as arts funding shrinks and becomes more corporate, it becomes even more critical to maintain artistic freedom and integrity. Artistic freedom has always been ingrained in my compositional process: I don't censor my music or write anything in order to please somebody else. Although it's very important for me to write for individual performers, my ultimate goal is to create the music that best reflects my own artistic vision. I am striving for music that can be beautifully interpreted and performed by a musician, I'm not striving just to please a musician with what I've written.

Within the new music community there seems to be a growing preoccupation with popularity and success. The shift in focus from art to commerce tends to discourage artistic freedom. For me, one liberating aspect of being a composer has been the fact that huge sales have never been a concern, which has allowed me to write exactly what I want and freed me from the pressures of the marketplace. Tzadik is a perfect example of an independent label that operates outside of the usual music industry practices, and John Zorn has created a model that proves that it is possible to treat an artist fairly, support his or her artistic vision, and even remain financially solvent.

IS THERE A PHILOSOPHY INVOLVED WITH YOUR WORK?

If there is any one message that I want to convey to the listener, it is to pay attention to all sounds, without dividing the world into separate categories of music and noise. My compositions often explore the inherent beauty of nonmusical sounds and are inspired by diverse sources such as machines, destroyed pianos, warped 78 records, and detuned radios. I use traditional notation, improvisation, and extended techniques, while emphasizing the unique qualities of each performer. I have always been captivated by sounds that aren't considered music, and any barrier between music and noise has always seemed artificial. Incorporating these sounds in my music is as natural as choosing a pitch set or creating a rhythmic figure. It simply means working with a broader palette of sounds and a deeper pool of influences.

I try to tap into each musician's knowledge and personal experience, while drawing them into my own compositional orbit and pushing them just a little further. Traditional notation allows me to put music in a neutral context, so each performer can approach it without preconceived notions of style or genre. It's a way of subverting the form from the inside: The notes on paper are a familiar language, but the sounds that are produced push the music beyond the familiar.

I don't like music that sounds as if it's been created in a vacuum. I am the product of my environment and the sounds that accompany it, as much as I am the product of my education and every note of music that I have absorbed since childhood. I don't live in a sterile concert hall, and my music has, in a sense, picked up the grime, grit, and noise of this city around me.

In recent work I've been considering the great struggle negotiating the fine line between music and noise. Simple as it sounds, it is always a challenge to work with melody, rhythm, and emotion while developing new sounds. I sift through the influences of everyday life, striving to create music that is unified and whole, always looking for the one perfect solution that completes each individual piece. I look forward to a lifetime's work of learning the idiomatic oddities of every instrument, balancing relative density and texture, while breathing life into it all.

⑮

MATS GUSTAFSSON

Some of the most progressive music being created today is coming from Europe. Is it jazz, improvisation, or avant-garde—does it matter? What is and should remain critically important, as it should be for any composer, is that this group of individual players is expanding upon the music of the past, in this time, in their own unique way.

Swedish saxophonist Mats Gustafsson is one of those very important and remarkable players. With a massive sound that can be staggering, Gustafsson has become an improvisational force and will continue to be a major influence on the future of creative music.

LET'S START WITH YOUR MUSICAL BACKGROUND.

I was born and raised in Umea, Sweden, which had a wonderful jazz club that held weekly concerts. And even though we were located far up north, they were able to bring in really great music. I was only fourteen and still recall Steve Lacy and George Lewis as well as great Swedish musicians such as Per-Henrik Wallin and Power Noise Trio, Lokomotiv Konkret, so I was exposed to jazz and free-improvised music early on. And for me, I thought this high level of music should be available in every town in Europe and, for that matter, everywhere in the world, but I was mistaken of course.

I was also fortunate to have Kjell Nordeson to play with and to be able to try new ways of improvisation. We were probably very naive but very open to ideas in trying new things together and it was great to be able to do that. I then moved to Stockholm at a time when I needed more input as I think we all do all of the time.

But I was really disappointed upon arriving in Stockholm and finding out that there wasn't even one jazz club with the same quality of music that the club in Umea had.

WHEN DID YOU FIRST REALIZE THAT YOU WANTED TO PLAY MUSIC?

I started playing the flute at the age of seven, but after seeing Sonny Rollins at the yearly jazz festival, it killed my dreams of wanting to be a good flute player. (Laughs.) It was his tone and his sound, and at fifteen, I just needed to play the tenor sax and there was no other consideration. After that, I was in a local record store that was just a gold mine which was owned by a man named Stanley, and I had the most shocking listening experience from a record that I ever, ever had and that was hearing Peter Brotzmann's record, *Machine Gun*. That changed every-thing—that record made me see the connections between my roots in punk rock and the content and mechanics of free jazz.

THERE IS A LOT OF CREATIVITY COMING OUT OF SWEDEN TODAY. WHAT'S HAP-PENING?

I don't think it's just a coincidence. It's a series of events that have happened over time which have influenced the music scene in Sweden right now. And this mechanism of creativity has been happening in different places all over the world and I saw it exploding in Chicago during the mid-'90s and it's still going on today. It's a result of small groups of many generations of musicians, producers, and record labels starting their activity at the same place and at the same time. It's now happening in Oslo and Stockholm. So right now, there is enormous activity going on which I am very happy about because I don't need to travel as much in order to reach creativity. It's just amazing to be a part of such a process.

WAS THERE A NETWORK OF MUSICIANS THAT ORIGINALLY CAME TOGETHER IN OSLO AND STOCKHOLM THAT SUPPORTED EACH OTHER?

Oh yes! I can talk about Stockholm because the pipeline to Oslo is a pretty new thing. Norway was very active in the '60s when it came to free and contemporary jazz, then things flattened out for some time. But Norway has only had real heavy action going on for the last six or seven years. However, in Stockholm, it's a little bit different. When I moved to Stockholm from Lapland in the mid-'80s, it took some time but I was really well taken care of by musicians like Dror Feiler and, a little bit later, Raymond Strid and Sten Sandell, who formed the group Gush in 1988. So I was really lucky to meet people to work with because I was still very young and inexperienced and there was already a scene for improvised music in Sweden at that time. The scenes in Norway and Sweden are now very much linked together.

IS THIS ONE OF THE STRONGER PERIODS FOR MUSIC IN STOCKHOLM RIGHT NOW?

Yes, but it's not like we're in heaven because we still have to fight for it all of the time. There are very few places to work, but a lot of really great musicians and artists. Today's younger generation of people from the ages of twenty and twenty-five have a much wider reference base when it comes to other kinds of music. And a lot of musicians don't necessarily come from the jazz scene. Many come directly from electronic, noise, or rock scenes as well as from the jazz scene. Their interests and listening habits are much more interesting and I think that that is very promising.

Additionally, there is also a new audience and a very positive feel right now amongst the musicians. Many more people now seem to be referring to free improvisation or free music, which I think is good. People such as Peter Brotzmann, Evan Parker, and Derek Bailey are being referred to as much as Miles or Coltrane, so I think it's positive.

DO YOU FIND THIS INTEREST GROWING WHEN YOU PLAY INTERNATIONALLY?

Yes, and I think the reasons are important. I have a very strong belief that the giving, sharing, and interaction in improvisation creates a big demand for a high level of communication between people. It's a very honest approach and there is a need for this because the world and Western society is falling apart right now. There is a high level of stress and the way of communication is so commercialized. To fight all of this back is actually one of the strongest driving forces for doing this music. This music can be a trigger for a chain of events that can lead people to think about things that matter, perhaps influence them, and for me, it's a significant reason for doing the music. You could say that the music is about resistance on a lot of different levels and, for me, maybe resistance is the key word in the process of making music or art.

BUT HOW WOULD YOU DESCRIBE YOUR MUSIC TO SOMEONE THAT IS UNFAMILIAR WITH YOUR WORK?

You know, no one should ever describe their own music because it always gives the wrong emphasis to the music; music should be experienced with an open mind. You should always try to digest music in a way that is as open as possible. So I have a problem with trying to describe my own music (laughs) because I don't think you should. People should try and find out for themselves. I really believe that the search itself is an important part of the experience. It's one of the most important ingredients. You cannot just sit in front of the TV or computer and believe that the information will come to you. You have to be active and look for the information yourself.

DO YOU THINK YOUNG AUDIENCES FEEL CHALLENGED BY THE MUSIC SUCH AS WHAT YOU AND KEN VANDERMARK ARE DOING TODAY?

For me, it's really not that important who's doing it, only that it's being done. It's been unreal to find someone like Ken to work with. He is a musical brother and we share the history of the music together. And I think he is one of the most important voices of the last ten years anywhere on the planet. Not just because of his music, but also because of his engagement with the music of others. Ken is the most unselfish musician I have met and when he gets shit from different communities, it makes me furious. And, unfortunately, it's always about jealousy on such a low level. And the way that Ken was using his MacArthur money to realize other people's projects and records and not just his own, it's just fantastic.

DO FREE-IMPROVISATIONAL MUSICIANS CONSIDER THEIR MUSIC AS PART OF JAZZ?

It's a matter of defining jazz, which people have been trying to do since jazz was born. (Laughs.) I mean, I'm a jazz freak and I do think of myself as a jazz musician though a lot of people would disagree because they don't think that what I do has anything to do with jazz outside of playing the saxophone. But I could put it like this. To me, jazz has always dealt with resistance and this has been the case throughout the entire history of jazz. It has to do with the times and the society along with political movements up to perhaps the '70s. There was a natural chain of development from the very start of ragtime, big band, swing, bebop, hard bop, free jazz, fusion, and free improvisation. The music developed in a very interesting and dynamic way and then suddenly in the '70s and '80s, jazz didn't deal with resistance anymore and was trying to copy what was done before. For me, jazz was no longer what it was. It just became cheap entertainment.

I believe that what we have right now is very, very creative and it has to do with improvisation and resistance and that's the need of jazz. OK, now I'm defining jazz, but for me, that's what it's about. There are many types of jazz being created today that many players would not call jazz at all. And one of the most noncreative forms of music right now is actually this so-called bebop movement with Marsalis and onward because, for me, jazz is not about trying to copy something from the past. I can understand why people follow this, but it's not my cup of tea and it has nothing to do with resistance and very little to do with a personal language and almost nothing to do with improvisation.

So for me, I'm simply interested in trying to find situations where I need to improvise. I try to place myself into situations where I am forced to improvise because there is a lot of resistance in the music or in the situation. And that's what jazz was about in the past and what it's still about today. I'm not trying to say that I'm even playing jazz, but I am trying to find situations where I am being challenged. I don't want to place myself into situations where everything is very fluently happening because it's not interesting. It's much more interesting to be in a situation where you really have to struggle a little bit.

Also importantly is that people will sometimes misunderstand you because there is really fantastic traditional jazz still being created but it all has to do with one thing. If someone puts their own personal stamp on the music or if you can hear someone's voice behind what's going on, then it's cool—then it's jazz. Maybe it's traditional, but if it's improvised, then it's great! I just don't like to be misunderstood that if I think someone is trying to play bebop, that it's stupid. It's just not what it's about; it's about the personal voice.

ARE TRADITIONALISTS HAVING A DIFFICULT TIME ACCEPTING THAT A MUSIC FORM
CONSIDERED "AMERICAN" NOW HAS MORE VISIBLE INTERNATIONAL AND DIVERSE AS-
PECTS WITHIN IT?

I think there are a lot of hang-ups when it comes to the discussion of jazz being
strictly American or whatever. Jazz is definitely American from the start, but we all
live on this planet together and there is a lot of great, great, great jazz being made
all over the planet. It's not just in Europe or the U.S. because there is fantastic shit
being made in Japan and also in Africa. If you look at the very roots of jazz from the
very beginning, it bounced back in the '50s and '60s. There are really great and
strange mixes of jazz which includes many various genres of music. There is great
shit happening everywhere! And, in a way, I don't think jazz belongs to anyone. I
don't care if you are Italian, Argentinean, or if you come from Boston, as long as you
do something good and as long as you want to share what you are doing with others.

THE FOLLOWING IS A QUOTE FROM CECIL TAYLOR: "MUSIC HAS TO DO WITH A LOT
OF AREAS WHICH ARE MAGICAL RATHER THAN LOGICAL; THE GREAT ARTISTS, RATHER
THAN JUST GETTING INVOLVED WITH DISCIPLINE, GET TO UNDERSTAND LOVE AND AL-
LOW THE LOVE TO TAKE SHAPE." HOW MUCH OF YOUR MUSIC IS FROM LOGIC AND
HOW MUCH FROM THIS OTHER PLACE THAT CECIL TAYLOR DESCRIBES?

I agree completely because it really doesn't have to be logic at all. It has to do
with other levels of consciousness, which could also be defined as love. But true
greatness comes from within. You know what I'm saying? You cannot "hear" Albert Ayler without feeling it or without being conscious of what's inside of you.

It's also the illogical decisions and contrasts that are the most interesting, and
the logical decisions are never that interesting because they already belong to the
history and tradition. It's much more interesting to find the conflicts.

But music works best for me when I'm improvising and not thinking at all. I'm
empty and just play. And basically, the music is playing me. It is a very emotional-
based music with a very spiritual content. There is also very good logical music,
but I think the best of that has already been made.

DOES IT HELP TO PLAY WITH VARIOUS MUSICIANS THAT COME FROM DIFFERENT
MUSICAL REFERENCE POINTS THAN YOUR OWN?

In order to develop yourself along with your music, you have to play with new
musicians to get new input; otherwise, your music will never expand or grow. On
the other hand, it's also important to develop your working relationships with the
people you have spent a lot of time playing with and, of course, some of them will
come from the same reference points as yourself. But that's the beauty of improvising. It's the mix of the two.

It's the different backgrounds and those references will come out of the music
and out of the different personalities that you are dealing with. It's also about talking with different people about the philosophic and political aesthetic, which is
very creative because you get so much new information and all of this can go into

your brain as well as your heart. I'm carrying it with me all of the time and I can bring it out when I play. So yes, it's extremely important to play with musicians that have different backgrounds and reference points but it's also important to play with people that are similar to yourself. You have to find new people to play with all of the time or you can become stagnant.

There is also the situation of not playing with someone for awhile and then getting back together again. People change and you can share this change together and I think that's what makes improvisation so unique and so beautiful. It's the sharing of different experiences, different backgrounds, different traditions, and different cultures. Everything is there in the music and you can get so much out of it. I really love this way of communicating, this way of making music together. It's so beautiful to share.

I HAD A CHANCE TO SEE RAYMOND STRID PERFORM FOR FIVE NIGHTS OVER A VERY SHORT PERIOD OF TIME AT THE VANCOUVER JAZZ FESTIVAL, AND IT WAS VERY OBVIOUS THAT HIS MUSICAL VOICE WAS INFLUENCING THE OTHER PLAYERS AND WHAT WAS HAPPENING ON STAGE EACH AND EVERY NIGHT.

Yeah, he is one of the people that took care of me when I moved to Stockholm, so I owe him so much. He is probably the one person that I have played with the most on this planet. He is the best and one of his strengths is that he can play in any kind of context and he will put his personal input on each situation. Sometimes he can be passive and, at other times, quite a bit more active or aggressive. He's a great improviser in dealing with different musical contexts and never losing his own identity, and that's what it's about.

WHAT INSPIRES YOU?

There are many influences that have occurred within my lifetime but my family is fundamental in order for me to be creative. They rock! And literature and art have been the main sources of information that I cannot live without but of course the more obvious is music.

ARE THERE SPECIFIC PEOPLE WITHIN THE ARTS OR LITERATURE THAT HAVE TOUCHED YOU?

I can tell you that it's usually more of an emotional or spiritual thing that sets something off. Antoni Tapies, a Catalan painter, is a favorite of mine. The writer Paul Auster is becoming a real favorite who is so much about flow and improvising in how he is expressing himself. He writes a lot about chance situations, and I don't think that I have ever read anyone that could put emotion into words so effectively. I would say that he has probably been as important to me as Albert Ayler was at the beginning of my exploration in his music. Auster makes you think and it becomes a unique communication between the author and the reader.

IS IT MORE DIFFICULT FOR STUDENTS TO BE CREATIVE IN TODAY'S INFORMATION SOCIETY?

I think it depends on the way you look at it because there can be a danger with easy access to information. But I believe in the process of looking for stuff because that in itself is a very creative process. Music has to be developed in a slow way in order to go deeper into yourself and to be able to digest it and continue to try it again and again and again. The struggle in finding out and discovering new things is good, but it's a very problematic thing right now. The speed in which information comes at us from all directions is just insane. There isn't any way that you can deal with the amount of information and the amount of CDs coming at you. If you are interested in free-improvised music, there is no way you can afford to buy all new CDs; there is just too much.

It's also great to be active when you are looking for stuff, but if you are not aware of what's available in free-improvised music, abstract painting, or sound poetry, there is only a very small chance that you would get exposed to it because there is so much other information available. Commercialism is just so much stronger now than it was twenty to thirty years ago so independency is going to have its problems in getting through. Thus, there are just not many ways to cut through this massive amount of information. You can reach the people that are already "in it" so to speak, but it's really difficult to reach people who are unaware of this music and where the unexpected meeting with the music could even actually change their lives, or at least expose them to something different and alternative.

Is THERE A COMMON MESSAGE THAT YOU TRY TO IMPART WITH OTHER MUSIC STU-DENTS?

I think you can point to the doors that need to be opened, but people need to find the key to open the doors for themselves. And it's not that I don't want to share because I love to share when people are interested, but I believe in the process, and it has to take time because most of what is really creative needs time to go deep inside of you.

It's also an interesting question because I think it's best to play together, to hang out together and basically talk about everything, which doesn't need to be only about music. It's about sharing your life and the music together, which cannot be taught in school. And you can learn about improvisation much quicker by playing and sharing with many other people. Of course you can learn the history and the tradition, along with the technical aspects, in school, which is good, but when it comes to creating your own language, you have to get out there and find out for yourself.

Is THERE A RESPONSIBILITY THAT COMES WITH THE FREEDOM TO EXPRESS WITHIN IMPROVISATION?

I don't think anyone is really free within improvisation. Small children can be free because they have no reference point or any knowledge about traditions. As an improviser, you can be free to choose where you want to go with the music, but that decision has to be intuitive. You have to be able to empty yourself and open yourself up. You also have a backpack that carries all of your reference points and all of your experiences, which is not only music, it's everything! But you also have to have the technique in order to reach your luggage and be able to respond to what someone else is saying musically at the very moment it happens. The technique is the tool.

Another way to put it is that you have to be aware of what you have played, only after you have done it. Then you can move on. You don't really intellectualize or analyze while improvisation is happening. It's a flow of energy and events and you have to be able to go with it or against it. For me, if I start to analyze what is actually going on, I should probably just shut up. In fact, if I catch myself thinking about the music, I tend to take a step backwards and become silent and will enter the music again when the analyzing or thoughts disappear.

It's a little bit of a complicated scenario but a very interesting process. There are a lot of paradoxes built in because in playing free, you have to have really good technique, but then some people believe that you are not really free if you have technique. However, it's about being free to choose the direction in the music, in every instance, and for me, that's what musical freedom is all about. Responsibility for me is to continue doing this until I just drop dead.

How much does it have to do with risk?

A huge bunch! It's one of the most important keys to this music. Because if you are not willing to take a risk, you'll never find out what the possibilities are. You have to take it one step forward and try to make a statement, though that statement might get you kicked off the stage (laughs), but you have to take that risk of saying who you are. It's really one of the biggest keys and that goes for the listeners too. You just can't listen to the same kind of music every day and every week. You have to receive some kind of new input from other forms of music in order to appreciate the music you love the most. It doesn't make much sense to listen to the same record or music over and over again.

What are you trying to do with your music today?

The reasons why I play this music have to do with politics, resistance, as well as the music itself, as with many other things that are important to my life. I'm continuing to explore mechanisms and the relationships between music, resistance, and the ideologies, but also trying to find possibilities in changing the way people look at music, life, and society. It's all connected. Everything is connected but you have to be willing to take risks in order to receive the connection.

Again, the musical answer is really difficult because I don't know where my music will take me. I might be working with completely different people in a year than who I am working with right now or I may be still working with the same people because there is so much to explore together. I wouldn't be doing this music if I knew where it would take me.

Do you have a sense of where music is going in the future?

The world is in such a negative balance right now, but chaotic situations can bring people together. I think we can look forward to more cross-pollination of new voices in dealing with the tradition in different ways, and I think there will be new tools for the music that will change the mechanisms. But the most important part of jazz is that there will always be independent personal voices that will appear and have something powerful to say on another musical level that we haven't heard before. And thank Tor and Odin, it will always be like this in jazz.

BARRY GUY

As mentioned previously, some of today's most creative and innovative music is being composed and performed in Europe. This is partly due to the process of incorporating various approaches from the history of jazz, along with the rich diversity of traditional European musical influences. Importantly, it's also a direct reflection of the respect jazz has received on a global level, and one of the pioneers of this artistic direction is the very brilliant bassist and composer Barry Guy.

HOW DID YOU FIRST BECOME INVOLVED WITH CREATIVE MUSIC?

I began with compositional studies in London at a very fine art school called Goldsmiths College, which had of course many other disciplines available to the students, music included, but its art department was legendary. I had met Bernhard Living, a classmate who was an alto player and lived in my area. We began playing standards and blues at workingmen's club performances where drunken guys would lurch towards us and try to sing along. But Bernhard also had a great interest in the American avant-garde of the '50s. Not only in music, but also in the dance collaborations with Merce Cunningham and John Cage and the paintings of Jackson Pollock and Mark Rothko. This young lad had an enormous appetite for any of the new things in the arts. He turned me on to Charles Mingus and convinced me to take compositional classes where we basically talked about compositional procedures and ideas. We were pretty much perceived as the lunatic fringe because most people were trying to do reruns of Beethoven and things along that line. But our interest was not only in John Cage and company, but also in the visual arts, jazz, and contemporary music in general.

At the end of the school year, we had to write a composition and since I was already interested in improvisation, I wrote a piece called *Perceptions*, which was written for nine players. The middle section had a cadenza for alto saxophone and trombone. And though the alto piece was intended for Bernie, he ended up conducting, but I had also met a trombone player by the name of Paul Rutherford who used to lurk in the local pubs when he wasn't playing. So I found him and bought him a beer and asked if he would like to come along, and he pulled in Trevor Watts to play the alto part. Within about two weeks, I was invited to play at the Little Theater Club by John Stevens and this was pretty much engineered by Paul and Trevor. So that's where it all started, but, at the same time, I was still working at Ronnie Scott's old place a couple nights a week as part of the rhythm section. Additionally, I was also working with local conventional modern jazz-type bands, so the Little Theater Club and freely improvised music seemed like a huge hurdle to overcome because it was all very mysterious to me at the very beginning.

It required me to get into the psyche of the band members to fully understand what the intentions were. But this was interesting for me because it had a lot of aspects of contemporary musical sonorities. They used highly experimental sounds which I had been studying and trying to understand. Subsequently, the philosophy of a freer scenario and of allowing sounds to form themselves in space was essential to me because it demanded a high degree of cooperation and humility between the musicians. Not to say that there were not moments of tension and argument about direction and motivation, but that's all part of the process of learning.

I also wanted to improve my bass technique so I enrolled into the Guildhall School of Music and Drama for four years. I wanted to learn how to play the bass properly and understand different music, but I had a pluralistic attitude towards music anyway. Thus, everything was a great discovery for me.

ARE ESTABLISHMENTS LIKE THE LITTLE THEATER CLUB STILL AVAILABLE FOR THE MUSICIANS TODAY?

The Little Theater Club was a unique institution, which had a lot to do with the goodwill of the management. They held plays and after those evening performances, we would move in at about 10:00 and the lady that ran it would stay up as long as we were there. Those kinds of things are very rare. It has always been difficult to establish a regular venue for more esoteric musics, and today's younger musicians have the same problems, perhaps more acutely so these days. Often you need a single person to get the ball rolling. The drummer John Stevens was a tireless advocate for opening up opportunities for playing.

I DON'T THINK THAT YOUR WORK WITH THE LONDON JAZZ COMPOSERS ORCHESTRA WILL BE FULLY REALIZED FOR QUITE SOME TIME. WHERE DID THE IMPETUS COME FROM?

I suppose the initial impulse came from the total joy that I had in playing and getting to know quite a large selection of musicians that came into London. Some left and some stayed but it was always a changing scenario. There were also those that became part of more established ensembles, which included people like Derek Bailey, Evan Parker, Paul Lytton, Trevor Watts, John Stevens, and Paul Rutherford. Then there was Howard Riley with whom I played for several years and of course great times with Louis Moholo and Mike Osborne at the Peanuts Club. I was having the time of my life playing with all of these people and decided I wanted to bring as many of these musicians together as I could under one umbrella. So I wrote the piece *Ode*, which was meant as a one-off project of large-group music. I wanted to bring together pure joy and exuberance in an environment of discovery.

I also found this huge sound addictive and it's reflective of my compositional studies, which I did at Guildhall. It gave me a chance to work with a big ensemble, which I enjoyed, although I can't say it was easy because everybody had a different attitude towards improvisation and written music. But it also became a self-fulfilling prophecy because once it started rolling, I couldn't stop it. I could express all of my musical attitudes without having to worry about satisfying a symphony or chamber orchestra, in which I had played and written for in the past. It was a completely different music.

With the LJCO, there was this huge open landscape of improvisation and composed elements that became possible. One could work on the symphonic scale without having too many of the obstacles you would have with a normal symphony orchestra. So for me, it was like an open book and I suppose that's pretty much how it has been all of these years.

After the release of *Ode*, I became increasingly interested in compositional procedure and soundscapes, and as I began to implement structural ideas that I was becoming more and more interested in, I began to alienate some of the players. They began losing interest as the music became more abstract and similar to contemporary music. So, after a discussion with some of the players, we agreed that there should be more compositional involvement from the players themselves. This included Howard Riley, Tony Oxley, Paul Rutherford, Kenny Wheeler, Phil Wachsmann, and I know I'm leaving some people out. Additionally, this also included the conductor, Buxton Orr, who was my compositional professor and also conducted the band along with adding a couple of compositions. Also, Bernard Rands, a friend of mine and composer who is now a professor at Harvard, wrote a piece and we also picked up a piece from Krystof Penderecki, which was originally written for the Globe Unity Orchestra. So in a way, the band had a focus of material that was different from my own and it alerted me to some of the problems I was providing for the musicians.

Obviously, other people in the band will have different resolutions in their approach with composed and improvised music and this made me rethink things. I also became very involved with baroque music for many years performing with John Eliot Gardiner's Monteverdi Orchestra, Christopher Hogwood's Academy of Ancient Music, and Roger Norrington's Kent Opera Company and the London Classical Players. Additionally, I held the city of London Surfonia principal bass

chair while playing chamber music. This deviation meant less involvement in improvised music, but eventually I came back to the music with a refreshed spirit and
attitude and even a different way of writing. It was Evan Parker, by the way, that
suggested I renew my association with the improvising community which he perceived was slipping away.

This also opened up the scenario a little bit with less conducting and more
group decision making, and I also used a less abstract way of writing for the orchestra. And ever since those first days, I have been trying to simplify the compositional procedure so the players have a friendlier association with the score or my
ambitions. So in a way, it was like reinventing the wheel. Every time I write a piece
I have to ask, "Well, what happened to the last one; what worked? What do I want
to achieve by writing the next piece?" There is always this question of why, why,
why? In the end, this caucus of work and selection of pieces that have been committed to CD reflect some kind of progress.

YOU RECENTLY COMPLETED A TRIO RECORDING WITH MARILYN CRISPELL AND
PAUL LYTTON CALLED ODYSSEY THAT YOU MUST BE QUITE PLEASED WITH. A LOT OF
YOUR MUSIC IS MORE DENSE, BUT THE APPROACH WITH THIS RECORD REMINDS ME
OF THE SPACING THAT BILL EVANS USED IN A LOT OF HIS WORK. THE SOUND OF YOUR
BASS IS QUITE RICH AND THE MUSIC HAS THE FEEL OF THREE DISTINCT INDIVIDUAL
VOICES PAINTING ON THE SAME CANVAS IN A VERY POETIC WAY. IT'S QUITE A MOVING
RECORD.

Bill Evans is also a great favorite of mine. The trio with Scott Lafarro and Paul
Motion had such poise and invention along with an ease in which they made the
music and the way they communicated. This was a major influence on me. I think
you'll find a similar spirit in the playing of Marilyn Crispell, who has been a revelation to me. She is one of those pianists who allows the bass player to fit inside
the music rather than being a kind of add-on. It's also in the way she voices and
the way the lines come together. For me, it's a great pleasure to consider musical
directions and avenues together because I know damn well that she will find the
innermost core of the music and really bring something out.

Paul Lytton is a musician that I have worked with for many, many years and in
particular with the Evan Parker Trio. And he is quite unpredictable in many respects. There is something so understated about his playing on the record
Odyssey. Whenever he makes a mark like a painter would on canvas, it's in the
right place and in the right color. He even likes the album, which is miraculous because he doesn't tend to like anything he plays. Lytton is brilliant.

I think the album is unusual because it has a different space in which we all operate against a more conventional piano trio. And I like the fact that we can move
between the poetic and against almost romantic sound to quite abstract scenarios.
So, in that sense, it's a very complete trio and very rewarding.

You mentioned my bass sound. The instrument I used was a new five-string bass
that was made by Roger Dawson who runs with my fantasies in what basses can
sound like. I'm interested in getting sonority from the bass and require all the ex-

tended sounds to mean something. I need the instrument to act fast and I need it to be almost like an athlete; the wood needs to work at the right speed. I'm not one that is interested in acquiring the more conventional bass or heavier sound. I'm trying to find a flexible instrument that is capable of dealing with all of my sound-world fantasies and, importantly, all of the extensions that I use on the instrument all have to have a reason for being there. So I need an instrument that can deal with everything and Roger has done a remarkable job.

BILL EVANS SAID THAT MUSIC IS MUCH MORE ABOUT FEEL. HOW MUCH OF WHAT YOU COMPOSE WOULD YOU SAY COMES FROM FEEL COMPARED TO LOGIC?

It's hard for me to answer precisely because I have an internal energy that leads me when I compose or improvise, telling me what's right. And I think if you consider all of the principles we have been talking about, and you are blessed with good technique playing the notes and placing them in the right place and communicate, then that's the feel for me. That's the energy and the forward motion of wanting to do something and researching. Of course logic comes into it because we have all been through our instrumental processes and performances, which build up over the years. How we physically get around the instrument and how the instrument can speak. We also know we can communicate, so it's just a matter of putting it all together and hoping at the other end that we create something that has sort of a harmonious result that seems appropriate to our energies and our philosophies.

DO YOU HAVE A VISION FOR YOUR WORK GOING INTO THE FUTURE?

The vision is continuity and invention.

Let me give you an example: The trio with Marilyn and Paul has just completed a new album (*ITHACA*) which reflects on the architecture of Daniel Libeskind and Zaha Hadid. I have tried to portray space and encounters derived from the work of these architects. The continuity resides in the very special way in which the trio works together, and the invention comes through opening up the conduits of structure and intention.

SO, IN A WAY, YOU ARE FINDING WAYS TO STAY CLOSE TO ARCHITECTURE OF WHICH YOU HAVE HAD A LOT OF INTEREST.

I worked for three years with an architect in London before finally going to music college where I needed the years to figure out what I wanted to do. And these three years gave me breathing space to not only get involved with improvised music but it also gave me time to find out what was really essential to my life. And, of course, music eventually took over, but architecture is still a major force and a major interest in my life.

IN A SENSE, JAZZ HAS ALWAYS REFLECTED THE TIME IT'S FROM. ARE TRADITIONAL-ISTS HAVING A DIFFICULT TIME ACCEPTING THAT A MUSIC CONSIDERED "AMERICAN" NOW HAS INTERNATIONAL AND DIVERSE ASPECTS WITHIN IT?

Difficult word isn't it. Every single person who is acquainted with jazz has a different interpretation of what it is and what it should be. As non-Americans, we know the history of jazz, that it's African American music which grew out of the horrors of the slave trading of the last century and early this century. You are quite right when you say that jazz is a kind of barometer of the age. It changes its weather patterns as different attitudes arrive in different instances from all over the world. If you take jazz from its first utterances to where it is now, it is absolutely obvious that it is a world music or can be considered a world music. You have people in Japan, Australia, America, Britain, Norway, Russia, or almost in any country that you want to talk about playing music with a relationship that can be construed as jazz or from the music of jazz.

I suppose in some ways, some Americans may feel as if their baby has been hijacked and I can understand that attitude. There was a point when we decided not to use the word jazz in the work we were doing because of the problem of how the music was perceived. So I have mixed feelings about it. I prefer not to call it jazz, but "improvised music" as a genre often derails the listener because of some of the baggage that has been associated with it in the past. There have been horrors of activity loosely residing under the umbrella of improvised music. The word "jazz" is in fact a very, very difficult term to drop but it's also a very difficult word to work with. It's a contentious word but I tend to think of jazz as a philosophy of freedom, openness, and world global communication. It's a great social music to bring people together. I think importantly under that banner of the word "jazz," there is a sensibility, understanding, humility, and a willingness to work together in groups, which in this day and age seems to be the thing we are lacking most in the world. If jazz has any currency, it's an ability to focus people's energy on a singular purpose and ideas to create. I guess we will continue to use it in a loose way.

ARE YOU SEEING AN INCREASE OF LISTENERS FOR THIS MUSIC?

It's kind of a roller coaster but there seems to be an amazing audience in America right now for improvised music. Peter Brotzmann, Mats Gustafsson, and Evan Parker are enjoying huge successes there. When I brought the London Jazz Composers Orchestra to Vancouver and Victoriaville, the audiences were stunning. Perhaps it's similar to when Mingus first came to Ronnie Scott's in London. To see the man actually doing it was just mind-blowing for young and impressionable musicians. The LJCO's reputation preceded us through recordings, so the audience was ready for the live band.

But I also think audiences vary according to what's happening politically and socially. For instance, a lot of the initiatives supporting music over the last few years are being threatened and it's pretty much happening everywhere. I think the festivals are running on the last drops of gas and certainly, as the years go by, the more one gets more depressed about seeing how much money goes towards arms and such activities. It's always culture that gets hit first and, consequently, you lose audiences. All of these initiatives that have been set up by people with great enthusiasm and good creative ideas are all left to wither. I think it comes and goes with the economy and politics. Both are bad these days so the arts go first.

We do get a lot of feedback from all over the world from people that enjoy the records, and it's great to know that the folks are out there, so it's not totally bleak but one does fear for the future for this type of music. And I suppose all we can do is keep going with what seems to be a very unpromising future, but as long as we can stay alive and keep playing the music, it's a privilege to have that as a way of life. If you can put over the joy of the expression of making music and the power behind the way in which you make the music, that's a great thing in itself but the opportunities are getting less. And I guess I have been lucky enough to have been around for quite a long while now. There are people that are aware of the music and I get asked to do things, but it's much harder for the younger players. I might be wrong but I think there is a problem there, but there are some good young musicians around who will push.

DO YOU THINK WE ARE CURRENTLY IN A PERIOD THAT HAS DIFFICULTY WITH FORWARD THINKING AND CREATIVITY?

I think there is a sense of that because it's this whole thing to do with globalizing, marketing, and big-money thinking. A lot of it conforms to plans and structures, which are theoretically put together, and it seems that there is no place for the creative arts within this system. But the trouble is that it takes huge resources to keep this whole thing or machine turning. If you look back in history, you'll find defining moments where certain aspects of the art are flowered because of particular political singular activity. For instance, the baroque period was supported by the aristocracy and if you became a composer; you would be accountable to the count or duke and would produce the music for the needs of the kingdom. The church also supported composer-musicians. Now it's the marketplace with all of the associated vagaries.

This kind of thing comes and goes according to world situations. But now with the ability to move with the information around this tiny planet of ours so quickly, the idea of creativity doesn't really get in there because it's all to do with boxes and business, and I think we are in a very strange period right now and I'm not quite sure how it's all going to resolve itself.

There is also uneasiness in the world in general, and it's tricky living with it and fully understanding it. And even though lots of information is being passed around, quite a lot of it is false. It's very difficult to sift through everything, but we must. In some sort of way, when you get these unstable periods, sometimes arts can work in a creative way because it goes underground and people have to find ways and reasons for doing things despite the big monopolies. Sometimes something can come out of it. But creativity in general is not seen by the majority as a useful adjunct to their lives.

THE FOLLOWING IS A QUOTE FROM CECIL TAYLOR: "MUSIC HAS TO DO WITH A LOT OF AREAS WHICH ARE MAGICAL RATHER THAN LOGICAL; THE GREAT ARTISTS, RATHER THAN JUST GETTING INVOLVED WITH DISCIPLINE, GET TO UNDERSTAND LOVE AND ALLOW THE LOVE TO TAKE SHAPE." HOW MUCH OF YOUR MUSIC IS FROM LOGIC AND HOW MUCH FROM THIS OTHER PLACE THAT CECIL TAYLOR DESCRIBES?

Well, I think he is quite right and I pretty much agree with everything he says. By approaching music in that way, it doesn't necessarily mean that if you are working on a more structured piece that it doesn't negate the possibility of approaching it from another direction. Certainly from every aspect and every note that I want to play, it has a lot to do with communication. I think Cecil has formulated it in the right way and I'm very sympathetic with that attitude.

IS THERE A COMMON PHILOSOPHY THAT YOU TRY TO IMPART ON YOUNG MUSICIANS?

I try to get across openness and kindness and try to get them to understand that if you are going to get involved in creative music, you have to open yourself up completely and have some humility as well as developing your particular talents.

And I'm all for an equitable society. When I run my bands, everybody gets paid the same. There isn't this idea of a big star and everyone else picks up the crumbs. The American system is a bit like that where there is a star and everyone else is a sideman. I like to think of everybody as equal because to be quite honest, if I didn't, my conscience would tell me to just pack up and do something else. And I know that in the London Jazz Composers Orchestra, that music wouldn't work unless I treated everybody exactly the same. I do that with respect and also in terms of financial payments. In fact, only one person doesn't get paid and that's me, but the music is the prize for doing it.

I also tell students to look out for somebody else before yourself. For me, it's been a good philosophy because it means that I can pay attention to the details of the human condition and how people interface with the music or come together in the music. This has worked all my life and the music sounds much better for it.

IS THERE A CERTAIN LEVEL OF HUMILITY REQUIRED TO CREATE AT A HIGH LEVEL?

Well, I think at the end of the day you feel a lot better for it because rather than shouting or intimidating people, it's a clearer and more interesting way of getting results to allow the combined spirits to blossom. But I have also worked for an orchestra maestro who could be a pig but we made brilliant music under his direction. It's one way of producing results but I don't prefer that and I think it depends upon how you were brought up.

When I was a little kid after the Second World War and food was still relatively hard to come by, we had had one particular fish dinner and my mother put the food out on the plate and I said to her, "Look, I don't have enough, I want yours as well." This was a very interesting moment because she said, "Well, you can have it if you want, but it means that I won't have anything." The penny dropped right there. It was just a small thing but it has been with me all of my life. It's the act of taking without thought. Now, before doing anything, I like to think of the consequences in humanitarian terms of the actions, and it's the same with music. My greatest ambition is to make music in a very, very humanitarian way. An organic way so that it grows naturally without tension, and to be honest, I think that's also the best way to get through life.

WOMEN DON'T SEEM TO GET THE SAME RESPECT AS ARTISTS IN THE SAME WAY
THAT MEN DO. IT CAN TAKE MUCH LONGER AND MAY NOT ARRIVE ON A LEVEL EQUAL
TO THEIR ABILITY. IS THIS A PROBLEM FOR WOMEN GLOBALLY?

I think so and why should this be? It's a strange conundrum, isn't it? I have tried
to promote the idea of using women in my bands but to tell you the truth, the London Jazz Composers Orchestra has no women in it. I guess it has to do with circumstance. Within jazz and improvised music, I happened to find male associates
that made the right sounds for my ears. However, I have tried to redress the balance by writing music for Marilyn Crispell, Irene Schwitzer, and Maggie Nichols
as guests of the orchestra. Marilyn was also the founder member/pianist of the
Barry Guy New Orchestra. For me, the sounds become before gender.

But you're right; it's a fact that women have had a pretty bad deal over the years.
I really haven't used women that much but I do when I can. I use Marilyn because
I like the way she uses her strength, causing a huge storm on the piano, and yet,
on the other hand, she can be as delicate and beautiful as a butterfly. And I think
that's an amazing attribute for a pianist to have and to refer to all of these different types of articulations. She is a beautifully schooled pianist and it has been a
great thrill for me to play with someone so great.

I try to do a lot of homework before embarking upon a piece, identifying what
the strengths of the individuals are. For instance, in the BGNO (Barry Guy New
Orchestra), I realized that Marilyn could, with her flexibility, allow me the chance
to write some sensitive ballad-like material for her which would at times, in the
"Inscape–Tableaux" piece, completely refocus the musical dialogue. A little like
filmmaking in that I wished to pull the listener quickly from the big open shot to
a scene with something really special and intimate.

When I wrote for the New Orchestra Workshop in Vancouver, I had a list of the
players and their preferences. I wanted to know their musical strengths as individuals so I asked for background material on everybody—who they had played
with and what kind of ensembles, etc. So that was all part of the information
process of building up a portfolio of knowledge of people and I find that terribly
important. Whenever I do a project, I like to enter into the people themselves. Get
behind the intentions of how people like to play. So that's a part of the broader picture and it's very important for structural realizations.

I BELIEVE THAT YOUR FRIEND AND PARTNER, MAYA HOMBURGER, MANAGES THE
LJCO ALONG WITH THE RECORD LABEL MAYA RECORDINGS. I UNDERSTAND THAT
SHE IS QUITE RESPECTED AS A VIOLINIST. CAN YOU TALK ABOUT YOUR WORK TO-
GETHER?

Yes. We do as much as we are allowed to. Maya is a baroque violinist but originally started out as a modern violinist. She played in the Camerata Berne Chamber
Orchestra for many years and then decided the interpretations that they were doing
of Bach and Vivaldi and the other early baroque composers was not the way that it
should be played. So she auditioned and accepted a job with John Eliot Gardiner's

English Baroque Soloists as the second violin leader. She now occasionally leads the orchestra for special projects and otherwise pursues a career playing solo and chamber music concerts. We work as a duo also, which is delightful since we manage to play music from the baroque period through to contemporary compositions.

Maya has also taken a great interest in improvising since coming into contact with many of my colleagues. Her management skills are exemplary, and, as well as the musical side of things, she project managed a house we built in Ireland to our design. It was a roller coaster two and a half years but we survived to tell the tale. We have a great time together.

THERE IS A QUOTE FROM CLASSICAL VIOLINIST YEHUDI MENUHIN THAT READS, "IMPROVISATION IS NOT THE EXPRESSION OF ACCIDENT BUT RATHER OF THE ACCUMULATED YEARNINGS, DREAMS, AND WISDOM OF OUR VERY SOUL."

He was a great man, great thinker, and great humanitarian. He had the combined weight of humanity on his shoulders and he somehow managed to deal with it and come across as the most balanced and pure person. It's a shame that he is not around now. I would like to pass on a few of his ideas to some of the politicians that are upsetting the world at the moment. Unlike some of the world's "famous" composers, Menuhin had the insight to understand that improvisation was not the "unstable chemistry" proffered by them.

ARE YOU PERSONALLY AFFECTED BY THE EVENTS HAPPENING IN THE WORLD RIGHT NOW?

It's frightful and I don't know how they are getting away with it. It's something that seems to be beyond our ability to stop. Even if 95 percent of the people of the United States said, "Don't do it," they would still do what they are doing. Somehow the political and military complexes have an agenda all of their own, which somehow leaves everybody else behind. It may be too late, but I'm just hoping that there will be a resolve in Europe by some of the countries of the United Nations to really put a stop to this nonsense, this big adventure. You get the feeling that when you get that amount of money committed to the effort, nobody wants to back off. It's all about political face now. And the ramifications could completely destabilize the global economies. It doesn't seem logical or reasonable to pursue their adventures in Iraq with the knowledge that this could be the case. Perhaps there really is a tendency amongst these people to promote a mass suicide of the world for their ideological ends. The right-wing "moral" agenda mixed with a compliant media is a frighteningly ugly and powerful force. We must be aware of the awful civilian casualties that will accrue from these terrorizing activities.

IT'S DEPRESSING AND FOR SOME OF US WITH THE U.S., ALSO EMBARRASSING.

It's embarrassing for us within England as well.

DO YOU HAVE A PERSONAL PHILOSOPHY OR WAY OF LOOKING AT LIFE?

We have masses of beauty available to every one of us. It's keeping our eyes open, our ears open, and our hearts open to receive ideas. It doesn't matter whether it's coming from architecture, paintings, sculptures, music, or from the written word; it's all part of a great mystery in how all of these things develop and can bring us great joy. These things can inform us, and if we allow ourselves to stay open to receive and understand the beauties of the world, then I think the world will be a much better place.

①

DAVE HOLLAND

He is one of the very few composers that has been able to stay true to his own creative vision regardless of the changes and cycles felt by the music industry. Hired by Miles at the age of twenty-one, bassist Dave Holland has crossed genres throughout his career while always being able to resonate with the listener on emotional levels. As a bandleader, he emphasizes the importance of individuality, along with the significance of music existing on multiple levels. A graceful and eloquent man, Dave Holland has never compromised his bold and ingenious musical voice.

SOCIETY HAS ALWAYS HAD DIFFICULTY ASSESSING NEW ART FORMS DURING ITS OWN TIME AND THE BAND THAT YOU WERE IN WITH MILES DAVIS, WAYNE SHORTER, JACK DEJOHNETTE, AND CHICK COREA FROM 1968 TO 1971 IS A PERFECT EXAMPLE. THOUGH ONLY TWENTY-ONE YEARS OF AGE AT THE TIME, WERE YOU AWARE THAT SOMETHING SPECIAL WAS HAPPENING?

I knew that Miles was a very, very special artist, so when he asked me to join his band, it was an extraordinary opportunity. Of course something special was happening, but I would say that something special was happening around Miles most of the time. But the first experience that I actually had with the quintet included Miles, Herbie, Wayne, and Tony Williams. And it wasn't as if the band was put together in one day and we were playing the music of *Bitches Brew* the next. There was a gradual transition. When I joined, the band was playing a broad history of Miles's music from *Round Midnight, Stella By Starlight* to some of the more recent things like *Nefertiti* and a few of the songs that Wayne Shorter had written for the group. Wayne and Tony had been in the band for quite awhile and Tony left about six months later. So there was a gradual development and as with any working band, the music was developing from gig to gig. New material was being introduced which developed into new directions within the general flow of the music and that's kind of how the new development happened.

IT ALSO SEEMED THAT THOUGH THERE WERE OTHER BANDS MOVING IN A MORE ELECTRIC DIRECTION DURING THIS TIME PERIOD, THIS PARTICULAR BAND OPENED THE DOORS AND LIFTED THE WEIGHT THAT SEEMED TO PREVENT COMPOSERS FROM STEPPING AWAY FROM PREVIOUS TRADITIONS AND WAYS OF COMPOSING. IT PROVIDED A NEWFOUND FREEDOM FOR OTHER MUSICIANS TO MOVE IN NEW DIRECTIONS. WAS MILES AWARE OF THIS AS IT WAS HAPPENING?

I think Miles was interested in changing the sound of the group and one of the ways he wanted to do that very early on was by introducing the electric piano, which happened just before I joined the band with the record *Miles in the Sky*. But as the electric piano gained more presence, it needed the characteristic of the electric bass to support the music, which was one of the reasons why I volunteered to play that instrument. I had played the electric bass when I was thirteen so it wasn't strange, and the atmosphere in those days was quite open in terms of the interaction between jazz musicians and more contemporary popular artists such as Jimi Hendrix, who was involved in a number of different types of projects. Also, the Cream with Eric Clapton was doing very extended improvisations along with the cross-pollination of contemporary music and the more improvised world from jazz musicians. But we must remember that it's all coming from the same roots, which is built on the blues and African American music.

MILES WAS RECOGNIZED FOR HIS ABILITY TO DISCOVER NEW TALENT BUT PERHAPS EVEN MORE CRITICAL WAS HIS ABILITY TO UNDERSTAND THE MENTAL FRAMEWORK OF EACH INDIVIDUAL. COULD THEIR CREATIVITY MOVE FORWARD WITHOUT BEING HELD BACK BY MUSICAL PARADIGMS OF THE TRADITION WE JUST SPOKE OF? WITHOUT THIS COLLECTIVE CREATIVE THOUGHT PROCESS FROM ALL MEMBERS, I DON'T BELIEVE *BITCHES BREW* HAPPENS, AT LEAST NOT IN THE SAME WAY. HOW IMPORTANT IS THIS MINDSET TO CHANGE AND INNOVATION?

I wouldn't agree that jazz stayed within the same tradition. What about the innovations that were happening with the late '50s with Ornette Coleman, Cecil Taylor, Coltrane, and the introduction to more open forms of the music?

BUT WHAT ABOUT AS FAR AS THE INTRODUCTION OF ELECTRIC MUSIC?

I'm not necessarily disagreeing with your premise but only trying to expand on it. Horace Silver introduced a crossover of soul jazz concepts, which was using rhythm and blues beats in jazz, and there was evidence of that quite early on. I think where we are differing is that you are looking for a lightning bolt moment and I think the music tends to develop more gradually and this was certainly the case with Miles and the music with the early quintet. The seeds of many different things were being planted early on, but that's not to say that Miles didn't put them together in a unique and special way as there is genius in extracting from the things that are around you and making something new. So the introduction of electric instruments was there in many forms of music already but Miles put it together in a very personal and special way. His work was that of an incredibly creative and visionary musician.

CHEMISTRY IS ALSO AN ASPECT THAT SEEMS TO BE UNDERAPPRECIATED. GROUPS OF INDIVIDUALS JUST DON'T SEEM TO STAY TOGETHER THAT LONG TODAY, YET YOU HAVE HAD SOME SUCCESS IN THIS AREA. HOW SIGNIFICANT IS CHEMISTRY TO WHAT YOU ARE TRYING TO CREATE WITH YOUR MUSIC AND BAND SOUND?

It's essential. One of the things that I value in music is the collective aspect along with the strength of the statement from the individual. It's the ability to create a personalized statement along with serving the collective vision of the group at the same time. It's communication. And I think that that's been a characteristic of this music in so many different ways going back to the early days of Louis Armstrong, King Oliver, and the great musicians from that period. That was also a big part of Duke Ellington's music. It's the collective aspect and the integration of the soloists in written music. And of course Mingus also took great steps in that direction, so I think it's evident. In the '40s, there was a lot of focus on the individual soloists so the collective aspects were not as prevalent in a lot of those groups. The collective was going on but it was more a series of solos. Thus, you didn't often get collective improvisation going on other than from the soloists within the rhythm section.

COMPOSING IS ONE OF YOUR GREATEST STRENGTHS, BUT IMPROVISATION SEEMS TO BE A CRITICAL ASPECT OF THE DYNAMICS THAT BRINGS TOGETHER THE RELATIONSHIP OF YOUR COMPOSITIONS AND THE EMOTIONAL INVOLVEMENT OF THOSE YOU COLLABORATE WITH TOGETHER. HOW IMPORTANT IS THIS TO WHAT YOU WANT TO HEAR FROM YOUR COMPOSITIONS?

The compositions are there to serve the improvisers and I think that Miles is a good example of this. There isn't a greater example of minimalism than the music he wrote for *Kind of Blue*. The written material doesn't add up to a lot of notes or a large amount of composed material, yet the composed material was ideal in terms of being a direction and framework for the improvisers to work with. That's a signature of a lot of Miles's music. He was able to find compositional context for the music that was just enough to give framework and direction for the improvisation and, at the same time, give a lot of room for new things to happen. And that's certainly a part of what I have been doing. The balance between form and freedom in the music is important for one to consider and of course there are lots of ways to do that.

IS IT POSSIBLE THAT A NEW TYPE OF CREATIVITY MIGHT COME OUT OF THE GLOBAL EVENTS HAPPENING IN THE WORLD TODAY?

Creativity is happening every day on various levels. The world is demanding us to be creative at every moment so we don't have to only look for creativity on a large scale or only in a musical way. How are we going to maintain the values and positive upward moving energy in the face of so much adversity and opposition? This puts demands on people and, of course, artists are people. Their work is going to reflect their experience in the world, and I don't think that tragedy or opposition is necessarily the only motivator. It certainly focuses your energy and can crystallize your thoughts in a way that can make you want to make your statement.

The tragedy of 9/11 can be taken as an example from my own personal life. I was in New York finishing up the music for the *Monterey Suite*, which was commissioned by the Monterey Jazz Festival, when this terrible event happened. We boarded an empty plane wondering if anybody was going to have the courage to come to the concert and we ended up with 8,000 people. This was probably one of the most memorable experiences I have ever had because of the context that it was in. It was the meaning and the significance of asserting your will and determination in the face of adversity and the commitment that it gave you, and I think that it was a shared experience by a lot of people.

So THERE WAS AN UNSPOKEN COLLECTIVE UNITY AMONGST EVERYONE?

It was more than unspoken. I spoke with all of the band members with concerns about flying and concerns about their families. It was a moment to stand up and be counted. You have to decide how you are going to react to these kinds of events and bear down and try to enjoy the positive or crawl away and hide somewhere.

THERE IS A VERY POSITIVE QUOTE FROM YOU THAT READS: "ONE SEES THE SAME EMOTIONS IN THE AUDIENCE NO MATTER WHERE YOU GO SO YOU REALIZE QUITE QUICKLY UNDERNEATH OUR BASIC CULTURAL DIFFERENCES AND REFERENCE POINTS THAT THERE'S AN ESSENCE OF HUMANITY THAT RESONATES EVERYWHERE." DO YOU BELIEVE WE ARE CLOSING THE GAP BETWEEN OUR VARIOUS GLOBAL CULTURES?

Beneath all of our cultural differences, people want to love, laugh, have a family, have food on the table, and experience their lives in very similar and basic ways. It's expressed differently in various cultural forms all over the world and I'm afraid that I'm sometimes not always the best at absorbing common cultures. I just arrived back from Shanghai and was struck with how much more Westernized it has become since I was last there eight years ago. I guess to some degree, it's an inevitable globalization culture. However, the old and the new exist there together. Even with all of our differences and similarities, when you look into somebody's eyes, you see the very same humanity that you see in everyone else's eyes.

DOES THE ARTIST HAVE A UNIQUE AWARENESS LEVEL OF WHAT SURROUNDS THEM?

Certainly being involved as an artist often leads you to self-examination, and sometimes by understanding yourself more clearly, you get to understand the world around you. But I wouldn't say that in a general way. There are many examples in history of artists who were absolute catastrophes and certainly didn't show very good insight into human relationships or current events, and I don't think that being an artist automatically increases your awareness and sensitivity to the people around you. I suppose, in the end, it's all up to the individual in what they are reaching for and what their values are.

IS THERE A ROLE AND RESPONSIBILITY THAT THE ARTIST HAS WITHIN SOCIETY?

I do feel that the artist has a responsibility. Usually a person becomes an artist because they have been born with an inherent talent, which is a gift, and if you have been fortunate to have that happen, then I think you carry the responsibility to nurture and take care of it.

The function of the artist within society is certainly to show something beyond the reality we experience from a day-to-day level, and the language of art is one that can be very precise and also be very neutral. It demands the observer or the listener to be creative and that's one of the things that art gives to people. It's the ability to stretch their own creative experience as the observer and to go beyond.

If you look at a painting, which might express something in a different way than what you have experienced before, the demand is on you to get involved in that experience and to interpret it for yourself. And I think that music is the same way. In that sense, music serves a very important function in stimulating new ideas, new perceptions, new concepts, and new ways of looking at things. It's finding new ways of reexamining the common feelings that are familiar to all of us but perhaps framing them in different ways.

YOUR MUSICAL DIRECTION HAS BEEN TREMENDOUSLY DIVERSE. WHEN YOU FIRST REALIZED THAT YOU WANTED TO CREATE MUSICALLY, WAS YOUR VISION AS DIVERSE AS WHAT YOUR WORK HAS BECOME?

It's interesting that you should say that. I can see from one perspective that the work is very diverse but from a personal perspective, there is a center to it. Even though it manifests in many different settings, there are some central concepts that carry through.

I have always enjoyed a lot of different kinds of music from when I was a very young kid. We had one of those old radios where you could spin the dial and check out different things so I have always liked different kinds of music and have always been intrigued by things that I have never heard before. I had a curiosity about things in relationship to music. Additionally, categories have never been that important to me in how they are divided up and boxed. To me, it has more to do with the integrity and what's behind the music and that's what I look for.

I have also enjoyed being able to experience many perspectives, which is one of the advantages of being a bass player. You have an opportunity to function in a lot of different settings and find ways in how the bass can enhance whatever music you are involved with. That's something that is stimulating to me, to be able to deal with that as a creative question.

WHAT IS IT THAT DRIVES YOU?

It's hard to say specifically but the love of music is at the bottom of it. It's been a part of my life from my earliest memories and is as important to me as breathing. So it's hard to separate music from all the other things that I have done every day since I was four years old.

I guess what drives me is an interest and curiosity of wanting to become a better musician and find a more clear and relevant way to express myself. Not just recreating worlds that I have already experienced, but to find new ways of approaching things along with setting new challenges, to expand the boundaries and find new and better ways of expressing my feelings. In the end, it's how you have expressed yourself. Have you really connected with everybody on stage and made something special happen with each other and has it reached the audience. When that happens, it's one of the most wonderful feelings that you can have as an artist.

HAS YOUR LIFE IN JAZZ SO FAR BEEN EVERYTHING THAT YOU THOUGHT IT WOULD BE?

I try not to have those kinds of expectations. Obviously you set goals for yourself, but I don't have goals where I say, "What if this doesn't happen, is that the end of it?" (Laughs.) I just try to take things one day at a time in terms of what my expectations are. Coltrane once said, "If I could play one new idea every day for a year, I would end up with 365 new ideas and that would be fine. That would be progress." In other words, it's one step at a time, which is very much what I am trying to do.

My life in music has gone beyond what I ever expected, beyond what I had ever dreamed of. I don't take opportunities for granted and don't expect a particular thing to happen. I have had modest expectations in terms of possibilities and try to work and let the music be the thing. When I was a young man, I wrote something on a piece of paper when I was going through a very difficult creative period. I wrote, "You take care of it and it will take care of you." And that's a little bit of a mantra for me. The world changes, opportunities change, and all you can do is take care of the music in an honest way and have it come from your heart and I think you'll be taken care of.

18

SUSIE IBARRA

Susie Ibarra is known best behind the drum kit, but perhaps her greatest talent is her diverse compositional brilliance and her understanding of sound. With fire, wisdom, and grace, she explores traditional and contemporary music cultures, painting colors of poetic sounds through her deep and vast world of improvisation.

The creative process, as I am finding out, is a lifetime endeavor, if it is to evolve. Heartfelt inspiration and pure intention for a piece of music is a gift that can be revealed from various circumstances. As a result, expressing music in improvisational or compositional forms provides a large palette to draw from.

Sometimes the music is very immediate for me, and sometimes it is a reflection or meditation on a piece that may take a long time to see its fruition. In both forms, I look for the best way to communicate and create great music with the other musicians involved. It is a process of understanding and learning language to express and create art together.

In addition, collaborative art, with multimedia, also expands the possibilities and palette of artistic expression. It allows the work to be much larger and more vast than originally intended. Also, an audience experiencing a performance, and their interpretation, brings breath and depth to one's work.

I am also able to draw upon vocabulary and musicality that is known language, and I also find myself naturally gravitating by coincidence to new sounds, extended techniques, to express music. It can be overwhelming, exciting, and also comforting to know that I am in an ongoing process of understanding and expressing musical language. As an improviser and performer, I have only more recently, in the last five or six years, begun to focus on composition. At this moment, and probably for a while, I'll be working on putting onto page what I hear in my ear. I'm hopeful that at a certain moment, some secrets will reveal themselves.

19

EYVIND KANG

I have had the opportunity to have several conversations with violinist Eyvind Kang and always stepped away amazed at the level of his sensitivity and creative intelligence. At the same time, I'm not sure that I have ever met anyone with the ability to appreciate music on so many different levels and in so many different forms. Not surprisingly, the broad spectrum of his compositional universe reflects these very diverse and perspacious traits.

LETTER TO VIOLINISTS

A tradition says that our instrument was invented by Sappho, poetess of antiquity, who thought to draw a bow of horsehairs across the strings of Thrice Greatest Hermes' lyre. Among the few fragments that remain of her poems, these lines, "I took my lyre / come now / heavenly tortoise shell / become a speaking instrument," are loved by violinists, for they show that the very motion of drawing bow across string is above all an act of poetry. Therefore we say that the fact of violin playing is conditioned on the poem and its attendant Muses.

The symbolism of bow on string gives us our vertical and horizontal dimensions of violin playing. Violinist Michael White teaches that these dimensions, crossing as they do on the very point of contact, create an "X-factor," a kind of crossroads from which may emerge still other dimensions. What happens in geometry, the necessity of the sphere from the circle, circle from line, line from point, also hap-

pens in violin playing. The place where the bow touches the string is a place of
zero dimensions. From there, we create a sound capable of infinite variation.

Pythagoras is said to have done some interesting research related to the vertical
dimension of our instrument. Where we put down our fingers to shorten the
length of the string, we make changes in the pitch of the sound, by means of the
inverse relation of the string's length to that of the frequency of its vibration. A
very pure relation, expressible in the simplest numerical terms by inverting the ratio of one to find the ratio of the other, as if the length of string and frequency of
its vibration were mirror images. From this we get the concept of "notes," which
are abstractions of the pure numerical relations. In Sanskrit these places are called
svara, which literally means that which shines *sva*, from within itself *ra*. The impression these make on the mind of the violinist, a subtle perception of the glowing or shining of the notes intoned in relation to one another, which emerges from
within itself as the pitches emerge from within themselves.

Giordano Bruno writes, "If two lyres or cithers are tuned in the same way, and
if a string of only one of them is plucked, its sound is not only consonant with the
string of the other, but it will generate the same motion in the other." According
to Aristotle, this would be because atoms in the air are moved to vibrate by the
motion of the first string, fly into the other and mechanically cause it to vibrate in
turn. But as Thomaso Campanella rightly asks, "How can we account for the fact
that, when the other string is not tuned to the same pitch, or one of immediate
consonance, that it will fail to vibrate?"

Violinists are confronted with this question every time we play, because there
are generally four strings on our instrument, and these tend to vibrate sympathet-
ically to the pitch we are playing on another string. Not only could the open strings
respond simultaneously to our notes, but also the very memory of another note in
our minds. Even the possibility of a future note might be intoned this way.
Whether there is or isn't such sympathetic vibration, we would still assume this is
a matter of effecting those relations of number as seem to shine from within themselves, by means of changing the length of the vibrating string with the left hand.

For us the left hand path arises from the vibrating string considered as a whole,
with attendant *svaras* whose shining we perceive, approach, and touch. There's a
Tantric image of Siva and Sakti in the passion of intercourse, Siva standing still,
Sakti facing him, mounted on him at the waist, flailing her many arms. She is the
motion of the left hand towards, in and around the *svara*, she is all fingering, shift-
ing, bending, and vibration of the note. Siva is the aspect of a note glimpsed in the
manifestation of overtones and difference tones which emerge from the *svara* in
its geometric relations to the open string.

Look down the vertical string, gaze into the infinity of pitches there. Johannes
Kepler suggests visualizing this as a circle and inscribing other geometric forms
into it. We imagine a triangle which touches the circle in three places. Taking one
of these points as the beginning or end of the string, we bring the circle back into
a straight line, and we find that each of the two remaining points lies exactly on
the places where we would play our second harmonic. To do the same procedure

with a square, pentagram, six-pointed star, etc., yields subsequent harmonics. We should realize that all these harmonics sound together in each pitch, which shows that there are inner aspects to every sound, correspondent to different kinds of shapes that could be put into a circle. This also suggests a geometrical basis for intonation that the exact position of each note could be chosen according to the positions of harmonics in another note.

In this respect, the forms symbolizing the seven chakras can be compared to notes. Physically speaking, harmonics are literally vortices of energy on the string, for instead of vibrating vertically, like the rest of the string, they vibrate in and around themselves. In the second, third, fourth, and fifth harmonics, the most easily audible, we find a triad over two octaves, a complete tonality, a musical entity which brings us the possibility of movements, of melody and phrases. In the central image of Tantric practice, Kundalini, visualized as a snake coiled up in the root chakra, awakens and ascends the spinal column, activating the other chakras as it reaches them; this could be compared to a musical phrase, awakened by the possibility of a single note shining from within itself, which ascends through, and activates the possibility of, another note. The idea of music is thus opened to violinists. But we must beware, where our instrument is concerned, we hereby enter a realm unconditioned on any other idea, least of all the generalized positions of the seven notes of the diatonic scale and the twelve notes of the chromatic scale, for those are mechanical constructs, and, as we have begun to see, our instrument is essentially mystical.

Looking into the architecture of the instrument, we perceive a communication between realms, animal, vegetable, and mineral. For example, our strings are usually made of a long thin strip of metal, wound around a gut core, with the exception of the high E, which is essentially a thin metal wire. In these alloys we see the fact of alchemy, of metals transmuted to their most resonant state. But we also have to wonder why it is that such a beastly and sacrificial material as a cat's guts are used as the core. I think it would be worth inquiring into the subject as a whole, to draw correspondences between animal parts and musical instruments in general. Here we only note the fact that, in a certain sense, instruments wouldn't be possible without animals. Even if they could be made using other materials—which they can— it's still possible that the idea of the instrument wouldn't exist without the idea of the animal. Thus we say that the spirit of the animal is present in the sound of the instrument. Bruno speaks of a drum made of a wolf skin, communicating through its sound, the essence of a wolf, to other drums made of sheepskins, who become frightened. In violins, the cat essence within the sound of the vibrating string shows us another connection to the tradition that is named for Hermes Thrice Greatest, for it is often said that our "Hermes" was none other than "Thoth," god of the early Egyptians, for whom no animal was as sacred as the cat.

Before turning our attention towards the bow and horsehairs which activate the string, we consider the question of rosin. In the act of rubbing rosin of a tree over the hair of a horse's tail, we notice that it improves the grip of bow on string and helps to produce a clearer and brighter sound. A mechanical explanation is that, by its stickiness, the rosin will cause tiny spikes on the horse's hair to stand out, and these in turn will pluck the strings in quick succession as they glide along—a beautiful hypotheses, but lacking in subtlety, avoiding consideration of the inner meaning of the act and the talismanic nature of the materials. What exactly is rosin? George Berkeley speaks of "an exceedingly fine and subtle spirit, whose immediate vehicle is an exceeding thin and volatile oil; which is itself detained in a grosser or more viscid resin or balsam, lodged in proper cells in the bark and seeds, and most abounding in autumn or winter, after the crude juices have been thoroughly concocted, ripened, and impregnated with solar light." This describes a chemical arrangement in nature, through which we may approach and know an inner aspect of a tree's vital energy. According to Paracelsus, every kind of plant life is essentially bonded to a certain star in the universe, specific to each species, by which the plant may know when to blossom and to perform its other essential functions. This star quality of a plant is known as its "quintessence." By this theory, doctors work with the quintessence of a plant when they prescribe medicines to their patients. In the same way, we work with the fine and subtle spirit of the tree, as it is "detained" in the rosin, when we apply it to the horsehair. In turn, the spirit of the horse who has provided this hair is present in the most active part of the bow. To be sure, a luthier of resource might choose to string a bow with another material; each can work in its own way to produce musical sounds, which shows that a mechanical explanation of the utility of horsehair will not suffice to explain why it is that the horse is clearly chosen to be the animal invoked in the act of bowing. Nor does this seem odd to violinists. One of the oldest bowed string instruments, the *moorin xuur* of Mongolia, in addition to using horsehair for strings as well as bow, is literally carved at the scroll into the likeness of a horse's head. Apparently it is designed this way in connection with its function as a shamanic instrument, bringing the spirit of "horseness" to a ceremony.

All around Central Asia, different types of violins, involving the use of horsehair, are bonded to the conception of the horse as a supernatural creature. It does not follow that these violinists are shaman, but that they are actuators of the shaman's horse spirits, which may be their vehicles to go around between realms. Indigenous stories tell of flying, magical horses who go between heaven and earth. In different religions and mythologies, we encounter magical horses, unicorns, winged horses, eight-legged horses; all of these are a part of the physical memory of our instrument.

In a word, talismanic forms of horse, cat, are combined in a geometry based on the crossing of the bow and string, in the composition of the violin. In the act of bowing or plucking, the string is set into vibration which corresponds to the position and movements of the left hand. This vibration is transferred through the bridge, belly, and through the sound post, called "anima," from where it spreads to the back plate, along the ribs, and throughout the body of the instrument, resonating every part there and projecting itself out again, through the sound openings shaped as an "f," into the air outside. Within the shape of the violin's body the sound of a note, as we hear it, is created. The timbre of a sound, consisting, we are told, of emphases within its harmonic content, is mostly determined here, because each frequency vibrates along a certain wavelength, which resonates within a place of the same proportion in the shape of the instrument. The curve of the ribs, the arching of the front and back plates, which approximates the number of the golden section, phi, the two ellipses of slightly different sizes, separated and again joined together by the inward arcs of the ribs, the two chambers of the violin's body, which emphasize different overtones throughout the range of each of the four strings, and which combine them again in the air outside; each of these give us the infinite degrees of possible resonance we need to play any note.

That the body of our instrument is said to resemble a human body, especially a female form, is not surprising to violinists, because as the comingling of a sperm and an egg in the womb of the mother creates an embryo, so we create, by drawing bow across string, an embryo of sound in the body of the violin. By virtue of its particular shape, it gives birth, so to speak, to the sound we hear. Again, we consider the devotion of Sappho and her many followers to the goddess Aphrodite and to the Muses. "I took my lyre / come now / heavenly tortoise shell / become a speaking instrument." Accepting the tradition that, with these words, the poetess created our instrument, we believe, in a way, that its shape has emerged as a kind of honoring of the form of the Goddess. Concerning the emanation of sound from the violin's body, let neither a listener nor a violinist exclude the possibilities of the mystical, which is to say virginal, birth, for this would allow that the creative principle, like music itself, be unconditioned on any other concept, neither sperm nor egg, bow nor string, nor any causal relation.

On the other hand, it's possible that the shape of the violin is created by its sound, since the effect of harmonious combinations of notes on matter is to cause it to assume organic forms, as shown by Swiss scientist Hans Jenny in his "Cymatic" demonstrations. In one of these beautiful experiments concerning the effects of sound vibrations on matter, it is revealed that the harmonious combination of multiple pitches on silicon particles cause them to come together in specific forms in three dimensions, one of which resembles the tiny skin cells of a newborn baby, a sort of donut whose cylindrical walls rotate ever inward. If this is possible, why couldn't these cell forms, evoked by a continuous harmonization of the same tones, assume the characteristics of actual flesh cells and eventually form a fully grown body? One might say that violinists intuit this possibility with each note, in their awareness of the consciousness of pitches, for whatever has a consciousness might also have a body, though it may be in a different dimension. And why wouldn't this body, formed by a sound, as a golem is said to be formed from the intoned Hebrew letters of the sacred text, have been known to the old masters of violin making, such as Nicolo Amati and his ancestor Andrea?

Once in a while I have mentioned these kind of things to violinists and suffered outbursts like the following: "On the contrary, our instrument is a material, inanimate object. The mysteries you talk about are among the many mistakes of history, which have been committed to the detriment of violinists. Our instrument is a prisoner in a golden cage, on account of these kind of elitist prejudices. For example, the way you look around, trying to understand different traditions, and then seize upon a meaning for every aspect of the instrument is a form of imperialism. Think hard: there is no absolute truth to the violin, no universal explanation of its idiosyncrasies—if there were, how could one account for the many techniques which violinists use? Some play sitting down, with the scroll resting on their ankles, some hold it from their shoulders, others from the inside of the elbow, some rest it upright on the knee; there is no right or wrong way. There are no notes which are absolutely in tune, or out of tune. There is no one correct design for the instrument. Look around, each violin is different. You have no right to speak for violinists, or to tell us how to conceive of our instrument. In fact, music and philosophy exists wherever there are people; there is no single tradition, there is no connecting thread between all ways of violin playing. Our instrument is simply a song of going and returning, over the ages, according to the mistakes of history. By bringing up all the same misconceptions, totally worn out by academia and pedagogy, that all our traditions came from ancient Egypt, Greece, etc., ad nauseam, you threaten the sovereignty of any independent way of violin playing."

In Haiti, there is a repertoire of religious songs that open with the exclamation, "honor!" to which it is replied, "respect!" Therefore, I will conclude all these considerations by mentioning the names of some violinists whom I honor and respect, some of whom I have heard in person, some only on recordings, some of whom I've actually met and talked to about violin playing. Each of these in their way manifest the inner world of the instrument through their playing and give one the sense of dimensions within dimensions of sound. I must admit that my knowledge of violinists is not very broad. Then again, as Heraclitus said, "One man is worth ten thousand to me, if he be best." Dr. N. Rajam, Michael White, Alice Pierrot, Polly Bradfield, Stuff Smith, Lakjo Felix, Tommy Peoples, A. Kanyakumari, T. N. Krishnan, Fitz Kreisler, Kosugi, Tony Conrad. In terms of the perfection of the left-hand path; complete elucidation of pitches and tonal entities in many dimensions; total presence in the moments of stillness before bowing, which are bonded with the exact rhythmic warp of the phrases; the energy and power coming out from the friction between horsehair and string; the full tonal realization of the violin as body, where the violin is cup and violinist is cupbearer, as Sappho writes of Hermes, "who took up the / wine jug and poured / wine for the gods"; the sense that sounds expand the realm possibility and actuality; and the intense effect of their music on the heart, these violinists are altogether beyond my scope to describe. Furthermore, there is a vast universe of violinists unknown, or known only to a closed circle of people, which, in another way, is the essence of the instrument's legacy in musicians: to remain occulted, hidden, concealed, unknown, anonymous—traditional aspects of the characteristic deportment of violinists. For these types of violinists, I reserve my humblest gratitude.

(20)

STEVE LACY

Like for many others, hearing about Steve Lacy's death from cancer caught me off guard. I found myself rethinking whether it would be appropriate to include within the book, the letter I had received from Steve in January 2003. I was disturbed when I originally read his letter because one of the primary incentives for publishing the work, was partly for the very reasons he argues. But six weeks prior to his passing, I decided his words were too important not to include and through his agent, requested and received Steve's permission.

Steve Lacy's presence will be greatly missed. As one of the early pioneers of the soprano saxophone, Steve approached music as though life depended on it. A benefactor of the MacArthur Fellowship, he spent half his professional years in Italy and France with his wife Irene Aebi, returning to the United States in 2002, where he taught at the New England Conservatory of Music in Boston.

His letter reflects his struggle, his passion, along with his frustration with those who tried and failed to describe what obviously meant so much.

DEAR MR. PETERSON,
JAZZ IS ALREADY HOT MUSIC; IT DOESN'T
WANT TO BE 'GRILLED'. ANALYSIS IS LIKE KILLING
BUTTERFLIES, SO AS TO CLASSIFY THEM, IN FORMALDEHYDE.
WE RESIST! "IF YOU HAVE TO ASK WHAT IT IS,
DON'T MESS WITH IT" (FATS WALLER).
JAZZ IS A LANGUAGE, A WAY OF LIFE, A
GLORIOUS HISTORY. HOW CAN YOU SAY WHICH WAY IT
(AS IF IT WAS AN 'IT') IS GOING, OR EVEN, THE NATURE
OF THE JAZZ OF OUR TIME. DON'T BE RIDICULOUS, HAVE YOU
HEARD EVERYBODY?, OR EVEN, ANYBODY, ENOUGH TIMES?
PERSONALLY, IN THE MUSIC I MAKE, I'M NOT TRYING TO EXPRESS
ANYTHING, I DON'T BELIEVE I'M THAT IMPORTANT, I THINK
THE WORK (THE MUSIC) IS OF FAR GREATER INTEREST - OTHERWISE,
IT WOULDN'T BE WORTH DOING.
NOBODY ASKED US TO PLAY LIKE THIS. WE ALL HAVE TO
STRUGGLE TO MAKE A LIVING AT IT. WE PLAY WHAT & HOW
WE WANT TO PLAY, + ONLY THAT, DURING A LIFETIME.
NOW, HOW ARE YOU GOING TO QUANTIFY & QUALIFY THAT?
WHAT IS THE PRICE OF FREEDOM?

Steve Lacy

JAN. 7, 2003

Figure 20.1.

㉑

GEORGE LEWIS

As an improviser, educator, and explorer of musical expression, George Lewis has become one of the significant contributors toward the respect and recognition jazz is finally receiving as one of America's most notable and distinguished cultural achievements.

WAS THE AACM ESTABLISHED OUT OF A COMMON INTEREST AMONGST PEERS OR OUT OF A FEELING OF NECESSITY?

My impression was that it was more a question of necessity—but then, what was the necessity? The people that formed the AACM seemed to be extremely diverse, from Melvin Jackson, who made the record *Funky Skull*, to Betty Dupree, who played with Earth, Wind and Fire, and to the people that we now recognize as being a part of the AACM. At a certain point, the idea was to try and find a way to support the activities of the creative musicians. You can tell that from the purposes [paraphrases from the AACM set of nine purposes]—providing an atmosphere for the creative musicians, making a workshop, forming a place for people to get free musical training, and so on. Those ideas were formed pretty much from the beginning.

As far as I can see, people needed to have venues surrounding their work—whatever their work was. The work was really diverse. Having listened to tapes of the meetings, no one spent any time at all arguing about the stuff people thought they were arguing about. The standard histories of the AACM say that it was designed to promote free jazz. No one ever talked about anything like that.

They seemed to be pretty concerned with whatever their music was, and I really don't think they had a simple definition of what it was. And whatever it was, people felt that they were not in control of the venues and the circumstances surrounding the production of the music, and so that made it difficult to do certain things that you wanted to do. So the necessity really was to assert control.

WAS THERE A MUTUAL SEARCH FOR WISDOM AND SPIRITUALITY?

No, I don't think so, because the people were too diverse. Everyone had their own idea of what that meant, so you couldn't really say that. I would imagine that if you spoke to another member—but that was exactly the thing about the AACM. People came together as a collective to support whatever individuals wanted to do. If individuals were concerned with issues of spirituality, then you would support that, but there were people who weren't that concerned with it. Basically, you couldn't say that there was any mutual anything, other than that they should support each other in whatever their explorations happened to be.

SO IT APPEARS THE MEMBERSHIP WAS HUGELY DIVERSE IN MANY ASPECTS OF INDIVIDUALITY AND CREATIVITY.

That's the thing, because individuality usually means competition, cutting each other's throats, or something. But it was mainly a matter of, well, what is it you would like to do, and how can we sustain and support that—even if only morally, by working for your concert, to do what needed to be done to promote your music and to make sure that it gets a hearing, that your work receives a hearing. These were the important things, and there were also certain people who were noted for being more concerned with issues of the spiritual than others. But in terms of an overall, generally agreed upon quest, no.

DURING THE CIVIL RIGHTS MOVEMENT OF THE '60S, IT HAS BEEN SAID THAT THE POLITICAL POWERS-THAT-BE FEARED FREE IMPROVISATIONAL MUSIC BECAUSE IT ELEVATED THE CONSCIOUSNESS OF THE INDIVIDUAL. WERE YOU AND THE OTHER MEMBERS OF THE AACM AWARE OF THIS PHENOMENON?

So, in order to answer that, I would have to assume that that was a real phenomenon that people believed in? (Laughs.)
I think that there were people who really believed that powerful social structures were "afraid" of black music or certain kinds of African American music. But I'm not sure that that's something that I could really sustain. In a certain way, I think there is a kind of flattery associated with that, the idea that someone in Washington, J. Edgar Hoover, is quaking in his boots at what you are doing with your saxophone. But at the same time, it was obvious that great pains were taken to infiltrate a lot of these organizations, to try to cause problems for them in various ways—economic censorship of various kinds, political censorship when necessary, or termination with extreme prejudice in some cases. There are always rumors.

In the end, oppositionality could certainly be inferred from the seeming refusal of many of the artists to embrace whatever the mainstream modes of thought were supposed to be at that time—or not even a refusal of anything, but simply embracing oneself, one's colleagues and community, and to connect one's musical expression with the community in some way. This didn't necessarily mean to find out what the community thinks is interesting and then to produce more of it. Since you come from the community, your work is already rooted. This just showed how diverse and mobile the community of artists could really be. So if there's any fear there, it might be fear of that sense of diversity—that the music could range from Minnie Riperton to the Art Ensemble of Chicago. Rather than some particular music that everyone's supposed to be afraid of, I think it's the composite nature of creativity that's the scary thing.

DID THE MUSIC OF THE AACM REFLECT THE STRUGGLE OF AFRICAN OR BLACK AMERICANS DURING THE TIME OF THE CIVIL RIGHTS MOVEMENT?

The simple answer is "of course," and the problem with that is that no one ever goes past the simple answer. I suggest that if someone really wants an answer to that question, they watch the DVD of the movie *Medium Cool* by Haskell Wexler. It was a cinema verité documentary about the 1968 Democratic Convention, and the story, which was done with actors, was filmed within and around the intricacies of the event itself. The actors were placed in the middle of these real events as they were unfolding.

The DVD included commentary by Wexler and his associates, and they're talking about a scene in which Studs Terkel had promised them that they would be introduced to "Real Black Militants."

So I was wondering who these people would be, and when I got to that part of the movie I found that the "Real Black Militants" turned out to be Muhal Richard Abrams; Jeff Donaldson, one of the founders of the Africobra art movement; John Jackson, who was a trumpeter with the AACM; and several other people who were associated with the more progressive African American art scenes of the mid-1960s. These scenes were definitely concerned with community uplift, and certainly in the case of Muhal, spiritual uplift as well.

It was interesting to me that Wexler and the others had no idea who these people were, even today. So for them, these were Real Black Militants from the community who had these amazing powers of performance. And the reality was that these were people who had been performing and acting in the visual and performance world longer than the filmmakers themselves.

They were improvising their parts right while the movie was going on. The filmmakers were astonished at their ability to improvise, but that was what they had been doing anyway. That was the nature of their art—involved improvisation and performance. But it also involved a real sense of community rootedness and involvement.

Every music is reflective of the situation that you find yourself in, but the idea that it has to be continually framed as reflective of one thing is the oversimplification that people really don't like. A lot of these musicians were trying to express the diversity of their experiences. And when you see a group as diverse as the AACM, the civil rights movement and its struggles were just one part of a very complex reality. I think that the easy assignment of this music as a kind of simplistic reflection of the tenor of the times that's with compatible something you might read in a history book—well, too much has been collapsed onto that sign.

I HAVE ALSO HEARD AACM MEMBERS SAY THAT THEY FELT THERE WAS A RELATIONSHIP WITH THE MUSIC AND THE MESSAGES THAT WERE BEING EXPRESSED BY BLACK LEADERS OF THAT TIME.

I feel that this was only one of the things that was reflected, and you would have to really talk about the total diversity of the messages. What I don't like is the collapsing onto the same signs, because it gets to be a kind of cliché. It might be comfortable for people who really want to be remembered as having been identified with all that ferment, but in fact there was no monolithic direction to the so-called civil rights movement. There was just a great deal of debate—over dress, culture, political direction, and debates over how expressive culture could be manifested in support of objectives that no one even agreed on. So if the music was reflective of a particular debate and reflective of some monolithic set of black leaders, well, which black leader was it? Was it Whitney Young or was it Stokely Carmichael? Martin Luther King or Ron Karenga? I mean, no single music could be reflective of all those leaders, but it could be reflective of the debate and the ferment of the period.

I thought the music reflected the sense of possibility and the possibility of change. People really felt that social change was around the corner and could be achieved, and I think the music certainly reflected that, along with the audacity and fearlessness of it. It was the willingness to take risks—to take chances. And one of the biggest chances was in making silence in the midst of all that screaming. In a certain sense, it was the ability to create unstable silences and incorporate that into the music. It seemed to be a statement of possibilities. That would be my retrospective take on it.

As a person who came up with the AACM in the early '70s, I saw all of this, and I felt that I was buffeted by all of those winds. You could see the number of ways and different directions that young persons from Chicago could think of themselves as manifesting African American culture. But African American culture wasn't the only culture to be manifested. You lived in the world and it was a complex world, and you had to situate yourself in that world. It wasn't just the South Side of Chicago, and whether you wore a dashiki or not. There was a lot going on, and these were cosmopolitan artists in an increasingly globalized and decolonized world. So for me, that was the sense that I drew from that period, thinking retrospectively about how one negotiates the call for identity. In other words, identity seemed to be a major issue that was in question and the push seemed to be whether one would adopt a monolithic identity or a multiply mediated identity.

The AACM seemed to opt for the latter. People were saying that the music reflected the diversity of the black experience and that experience was potentially infinite. So for the people within the AACM who started the phrase "Great Black Music," that slogan seemed to be a statement of the diversity of diaspora, rather than another way to say "jazz," as some people have said, a serious misreading.

DID THE IMPROVISATION OF THIS PERIOD PROVIDE YOU WITH A SENSE OF RELEASE, SAY IN A GOSPEL SENSE?

My first experience with any of that music was on recordings. We were listening to them in high school. I remember being very baffled by *Ascension*. I just couldn't figure it out. But then a simpler music came my way. That was the second Coltrane "Village Vanguard" record, which I could understand more easily. (Laughs.) But I don't think even that was able to prepare me for people like Fred Anderson or the Art Ensemble of Chicago. I was a little bit nonplussed. I wasn't quite sure what I should do. Maybe I even fainted, listening to it. So if that could be called a form of release, so be it.

My period of greatest learning about this music was being a participant rather than being a listener first and then thinking, wow, I'd like to do this. Taking part in it helped me to understand it. I still remember the power of it, that energy, kind of hitting me at a certain point. And it may be that the experiences of the people who are listening to it and the people who are doing it are similar, but diverge at certain points.

DID THE MEMBERS OF THE AACM FEEL AS IF THEIR AWARENESS LEVEL WAS UNIQUE?

I think that any time that a group of people comes together around a set of goals that they all share, they develop a group concept of themselves. I think [AACM] people took pains to not separate themselves from "the masses," so-called ordinary people. That would have really defeated the purpose, to create a new elite around a group of issues that no one could understand but them. That was more what people heard about bebop—you know, the glasses and the in-group talk. I'm not sure how much of that was reflective of an elite stance, as it's been portrayed.

I think that people were really trying to do a music that reflected their own experience. And in the end, when you look at the audiences that came to this music, they were extremely diverse, so that meant that the interaction between audiences and the musicians also produced more diversity, produced more points of view. So that kind of kept a check on the building of an elite consensus that was disconnected from what was going on outside.

You are also talking about the idea of somehow considering yourself to be a child of destiny, and I think that there was probably a little bit of that. But there really was no real, objective reason for that. It was just what people were encouraged to believe in what they were doing. It was that belief that was the sustaining force, and that's what is meant by creating an atmosphere—an atmosphere in which possibilities could be imagined and beliefs could be sustained and nurtured.

THERE IS AN ENERGY AND POWER FROM THE MUSIC OF THE AACM THAT I BELIEVE
WILL KEEP THE MUSIC TIMELESS. PEOPLE JUST NOW SEEM TO BE BECOMING MORE
AWARE OF THIS WORK. WAS THE MUSIC TOO FAR AHEAD OF ITS TIME WHEN IT WAS
COMPOSED OR TOO COMPLEX, OR IS THIS JUST THE SITUATION WITH ANY FORWARD-
THINKING WORK?

When someone's music, or a variety of approaches to music, suddenly touches
a number of people, that's the time when it was supposed to do that. In a way, it's
its own self-fulfilling prophecy. Particularly in certain corners of the jazz community, people seem terribly exercised about whether they're reaching mass audiences, and I think most of them have no idea how stochastic those processes really are. At a certain point, you start to see that there are two million identical
products and one person gets selected. It's been shown to be practically random,
so in a sense one can choose on the basis of whether a particular person who becomes famous had a better deodorant than the other person.

So it's better to skip all the talk of timelessness, and then you find yourself asking questions, like, What was the time this music was in? Who was the audience?
What was their interest in it? Instead of tying the whole experience and story of
the music to some kind of demographic number.

I think there is a stronger message there, and I think the message has to do with
the possibilities for mobility and diversity that the music symbolizes. I think people got that from it, and I think there's still a place for that.

The idea that we don't know what it's going to be is critical. If we know what it's
going to be, maybe we shouldn't even bother doing it, because in a way, we've already done it. This sense of surprise and portent to the music seemed to be important as an experience, even prior to hearing a note. It's just the expectation
level, that now, these people have come here to present us with something that
they don't think we've heard before. That's what we're coming to get, to perform
this mind melt with this other part of the community which is trying to present us
with these ideas that they feel are new.

IN OUR SOCIETY TODAY, WE "GO" TO HEAR MUSIC OR "GO" TO LISTEN TO MUSIC.
BUT IN MANY AFRICAN SOCIETIES, MUSIC IS A PART OF EVERYTHING IN EVERYDAY
LIFE. IS THERE A CHANCE THAT AT SOME POINT OVER THE GENERATIONS WE BECAME
A MORE VISUAL KIND OF SOCIETY AND PLACED LESS SIGNIFICANCE ON VARIOUS ELE-
MENTS OF SOUND?

It's hard to escape that impression. Whether it's called logocentricity, or visual
hegemony, or whatever, there is a sense of power of the visual. If you look at new
media technologies, the largest impressions are always from the visual technologies, and the sonic technologies seem to be rated second.

Music is a part of everyday life here too. In most places, music is a part of everyday life, so I don't think that separation between traditional societies and so-called
advanced societies really works for me. A more salient distinction could be the extent to which music becomes separated from the other senses. In other words,

somehow the visual aspect gets separated from the sound, and we're expected to go to concerts but not to intermedia spectacles.

This is where you come across groups like the Art Ensemble of Chicago. Those who only read the press release that said "Great Black Music" and didn't actually look at the visual iconography of the group didn't get the Asian references or the Native American references but collapsed it all onto the textually signifier "black." So that kind of logocentricity actually gets right into the way in which the music is received. It's a kind of lazy logocentricity on the part of some commentators, and an easy one. If you don't like the idea of "Great Black Music"—it's overly black nationalist, or racist, or whatever—then it's easy to simply go with the phrase as something that you have problems with.

But when you start looking at the sounds, you start to say, boy, this Great Black Music has to be pretty diverse stuff, whatever it is. You've got people doing Buddhist chants in the middle of it. What does that mean? I guess what it means is the idea of a people who are looking outward, rather than navel-gazing. It's really a globalizing riff.

THE CREATIVITY OF THE AACM ARRIVED AT A TIME OF THE CIVIL RIGHTS MOVEMENT. BUT WE ARE NOW AT A DIFFERENT TYPE OF CROSSROADS, WHICH IS MORE GLOBAL IN NATURE. IS IT POSSIBLE THAT A NEW CREATIVITY MIGHT COME OUT OF THE CONFLICT AND STRIFE THAT IS HAPPENING GLOBALLY TODAY?

The first thing to consider is that the AACM will be forty years old in 2005. It was conceived in a formal way, it had elections, officers, a governance structure, and a business structure. It wasn't just a band. It was a group of people that came together to form an institution, and the institution still exists while going through generations of change.

We have seen waves of creativity from this group of people. And now, there are much younger people than me, like Nicole Mitchell [flute], Savoir Faire [violin], Chad Taylor [drums], Maia Axe [multi-instrumental performer], and if there is really any utility to something like the AACM, it should be able to nurture that kind of creativity. Those people aren't going to sound like the old people; they are going to be different. There'll be a lot of discontinuity. We can't depend on linear progression anymore.

Their history will be totally different, but the idea of the AACM, as a kind of magic, secret, and empowering word that stands for a range of possibilities that gets invoked from using the word, is something that will endure.

But in the more general sense, if you're talking about the possibility of a new creativity arising, I don't really see any creativity deficit right now. I see lots of interesting things going on. There is plenty to learn from, and if we are lucky, we get to see as much of it as we can before we kick off.

I CERTAINLY AGREE AND ESPECIALLY WITH THE WORLD BECOMING SMALLER, PERHAPS WE ARE IN THE MOST CREATIVE PERIOD OF OUR HISTORY.

One hopes so, but globalization brings discontents as well.

Interviewing the AACM musicians who went to Paris, they saw things that they never could have seen in Chicago or New York. They were at a point when the technologies of travel were just becoming powerful enough so that people could assimilate these new experiences which are now taken for granted.

But this is where I begin to depart from the antiessentialists. I feel that there is an essence of creativity that is a human birthright that doesn't go away and that we are all basically born with. It's not just the province of a few superpeople. I feel that when people are listening to music, they can do it because of the sense of empathy that allows them to respond to the creativity of other people by feeling their own creativity. In other words, those neurons start firing and those experiences, those bodily feelings, start to resonate with the creativity that's coming from outside, because they've got it within them.

The challenge is for more and more people to recognize the importance of that birthright. It's different from saying that everyone is an artist, because there are lots of people who are not artists who are creative, and creativity is not just one tiny thing. But you don't want to commodify it to be the province of an official artist who gets written about in newspapers and all of that. We want to be able to recognize the ubiquity of creativity as a means of recognizing its crucial nature to our experience as human beings on this planet, and maybe on the next planet. (Laughs.)

DOES THE SITUATION IN THE WORLD TODAY AFFECT YOUR COMPOSITIONS?

Composing what?

NOT SO MUCH YOUR TEACHINGS BUT YOUR MUSICAL COMPOSITIONS AND, BY THE WAY, MANY OF US WISH YOU WOULD COMPOSE MORE.

Well, I really don't make those distinctions anymore, it's all creativity for me and I don't really care where it comes from. (Laughs.) I don't have any political statements to make, if that's what you mean. The only statement I feel like making, I do it in sound and in what I am trying to do here [Columbia University].

To say that one is affected by events in the world is, at this point, kind of a truism, so I really wouldn't want to indulge myself in that. There are certain things that I would like to see happen, but those things may be things that will be bounced off of other horrible things.

If I were to really apply myself seriously to the business of political or economic analysis, I would have to go into it with the same fervor and the same level of integrity and commitment that I now try to apply to musical and historical endeavors. And if I'm not prepared to do that, then it becomes somebody just shooting off his mouth and I already do enough of that. (Laughs.)

I'm trying to avoid the glib statement of universal peace. It's easy to say those things when you are sitting in the belly of the beast, the world's largest, and arguably most rapacious, imperialist power, and you have this big job as a tenured holder of an endowed chair within that institution. You're differentially enabled and disabled, and you are implicated perhaps in some fairly major crimes, to coincide with some of the successes that you might have personally achieved.

The thing that amazes me is that the people who are given to these glib statements seem to have no idea of the extent of which they are implicated in the very things that they are trying to critique. At a certain point, all you can really say is that you are trying to uphold some values that will be of benefit to people.

I don't want to be the person who makes a litmus test for other people as to how committed they should be to some struggle that I think I'm committed to. In the end, people are going to be situated differently and that means that there is going to be someone who has a more focused notion of what everyone should be doing.

But that was the thing about the AACM, that the people who had focused ideas about what other people should be doing normally left the organization, because no one paid attention to them. (Laughs.) This isn't to say that people couldn't be seduced into unified action, but the idea of a prescriptive reality that everyone was somehow going to be subject to seemed not to work for those people, and it doesn't really work for me.

ONE OF THE PROBLEMS WITH DOCUMENTATION FOCUSING ON JAZZ, SUCH AS KEN BURNS'S SERIES, IS THAT IT SPENDS MOST OF ITS TIME CONCENTRATING ON WHAT JAZZ CREATED IN THE PAST AND LITTLE ON WHAT THE MUSIC IS CREATING AT THE MOMENT. DOESN'T THIS SEEM SHORTSIGHTED?

I have to admit that I don't think at all about jazz education, but I will venture this as a start. There is no history of jazz anymore; in fact, there's no history of anything else. These linear histories disappeared a long time ago, and it seems to me that if disservices are being done, it's simply in the ideologically driven nature of those holes in the official accounts. The power that those official accounts are trying to grab for themselves becomes very apparent in the end.

But I do not expect Ken Burns to be able to portray an entire history, though I do think that someone from the communities that I hold dear will be able to step forward and do it. I have no doubt of that. And that history may not be the history of jazz. It may be the history of something else.

What ends up really being true is that if those communities do not take it upon themselves to create those histories and nurture them, then there's not much that can be done for them. Far be it from me to sit around critiquing a TV show that I didn't even watch. There were a lot of things that I had to do and I was sort of in the midst of creating my own history.

I thought the parts that I did watch were fascinating, and I think that in the end, the amount of information was the best thing. We don't want to necessarily say, well, this shouldn't have been done, because you get out of it what you need to get out of it. And then the holes that are left indicate places where more work has to be done. And the inability or disinclination of certain people to do that work isn't really my concern. I'm concerned with my own ability to realize those things and I think that's kind of an AACM trait. It's an autodidactic trait, a trait of self-determination and self-help. It's not waiting around for the corporate culture to recognize you.

ARE MUSIC ACADEMIC PROGRAMS MOVING IN THE RIGHT DIRECTION AND WHAT WOULD YOU LIKE TO SEE IMPROVED?

I don't have any critique of academic music. First of all, it's impossible to critique it because it's too diverse. Academic this, academic that—it's meaningless. Like any kind of broad brush, it's just too thin, with too many holes. Now, that having been said, there are several things to recognize about academia. The first is that academia as a composite institution is extremely well entrenched and unlikely to go away. What that means is that if you need a lever and a place to stand, academia gives you the place, but you have to bring your own lever, and if you can get your own lever going, then you might be able to produce something.

What I discovered was that people whose books I have been reading for years, and whose ideas I had been studying and assimilating, had no idea at all about the issues that animated the creative communities that I was a part of. But at the same time, the ideas that emerged from those communities seemed perfectly compatible with a lot of the ideas that I had seen and was studying. So it seemed that my role was one of creating and nurturing new kinds of dialogue where I could both learn from and contribute to some of the debates surrounding critical issues affecting the planet. Many of these debates are taking place in the academic domain and those that don't believe that are maybe out of that loop. There are certain things that they are not reading or haven't seen. But if you see it from both sides, you will also see the holes on both sides of academic and nonacademic pursuits.

My wish is to foreshorten that distance, so that we don't have the binary any more of "you're in or you're out," "town and gown," "academic and reality," these kinds of things. People who talk about academia as if it's not the real world have no idea how much money passes through academia everyday, and that money is extremely real. They know it when it's time to get a gig but they only see a pittance of that. The fact is that if you just step back and think about any large university system as a multibillion-dollar corporation that has a huge impact on the local, regional, and national economies, you start to get a sense that the lack of reality is on the side of people that claim there's nothing there.

So in the end, as a power center, academia is still extremely important and internationally situated. It's both a barrier to and producer of change, and some of those changes haven't been so pleasant, but some of them have been arguably for the better.

The biggest contribution that I think can be made to the future of musical academia is to multiculturalize and hybridize it and make it more responsive to interdisciplinarity, in the sense of an increased awareness of its own borders and the need to expand those borders or even erase them.

I think it was John Cage who said that performing was one thing, composing is another, and listening is a third—what can they ever have to do with one another? Well, the obvious answer is improvisation, which is about composing, performing, and listening, but that's an answer that he would have been expected to miss. But perhaps the larger issue is that the differences between those things need not be absolute and, in fact, are not absolute at all.

And even if we leave improvisation out of the picture, it seems obvious that we need creative people who embody or nurture all of those activities while looking at historical creative scholarship as being something that can contribute to the state of the art in fruitful ways. So for those performers or composers who are sort of afraid of becoming too involved in academic pursuits, what I find is that it's those perspectives that academia needs the most. The people that are producing sounds are the people who are uniquely equipped to provide those perspectives. Interactivity in general is what produces new perspectives. What produces the boring stuff is hiding out in specialized corners.

IN THE LAST FEW YEARS, WE HAVE LOST TWO KEY CONTRIBUTORS FROM THE ART ENSEMBLE AND THE AACM, LESTER BOWIE AND MALACHAI FAVORS. WOULD YOU MIND TALKING ABOUT WHAT MADE EACH OF THEM UNIQUE IN THEIR OWN WAY?

If you look at the Art Ensemble as a collective, it's like the AACM in microcosm. Being a collective, it's harder to understand its importance than if we heroicize a particular individual within the AACM. We say, this person is the smart one, and now this person is so smart that we don't have to really say that they're part of the AACM anymore. The Art Ensemble always connected themselves with the AACM. They refused to let themselves be separated from the collective because they were a collective themselves, and all decisions were taken collectively.

I know this because when Lester left the group for a moment to do some other work, they asked me to be a part of it. So I got to see at firsthand how the thing was organized, the intense nature of the rehearsals and the work.

If I may be permitted a speculation, Malachi and Lester were two of the major proponents of the idea that the AACM and the Art Ensemble were best thought of being collective. So, at great cost to their own possibilities, perhaps, they held that collective up as being of equal status with any stardom that they might have been able to achieve. They saw larger value systems there that the Art Ensemble could exemplify. That's what I learned from their work. They were incredibly nurturing to young people like me, and very welcoming. You know, I miss these guys. They helped me to find out who I was as a person, and they indulged all of my youthful arrogance. Artists shouldn't expect that; you're being a jerk and they just take it in stride: "Maybe he'll grow out of it."

The Art Ensemble represents five different manifestations of an Afrodiasporic culture. Each one of the people is an individual but somehow they fit into this collective.

Our society is driven by so many dislocations of race and class, different kinds of mobilities and ideologies, and, in the end, that got into the composite community that the Art Ensemble and the AACM helped to bring into being. So when you saw people genuinely moved by the passing of Malachi, this great musician, you began to see that a lot of that stuff really didn't amount to all that much. It wasn't like a distraction, but something that had to be worked through to get to the point where you understood the nature of what had been lost. You know, to see Chuck Nessa in tears made me really think.

So in writing a book about the AACM, you began to see that you had to talk about everyone in the community who was a part of it. It wasn't just that there was one group of people in the community who did this great thing. It was more that this community—the people that wrote about it, the people that played it, the people who went to the concerts—they all produced it, and hopefully they all got something out of it that was unique, and they all felt the loss at the passing of these members.

Roscoe once said in an article that, "Well, we made it possible for George Lewis and all these other people so that they didn't have to sleep on floors." Well, it's true. (Laughs.) That was pretty obvious and you had to recognize that. And so basically, I look at that as being an incredible gift to myself and others, and I don't know if I can ever pay them back. It's like your parents; there is no easy way. You just owe it and that's it.

Fred Anderson, Seattle Earshot Jazz Festival, October 2001.
Photo by Daniel Sheehan

Dave Holland, Brussels, Belgium, November 1992.
Photo by Jacky Lepage

Misha Mengelberg and George Lewis, Guelph, Ontario, September 2000.
Photo by Frank Rubolino

Jason Moran, Bowery Ballroom, New York, January 2004.
Photo by Peter Gannushkin

Greg Osby, Gand, Belgium, July 2002.
Photo by Jacky Lepage

Dave Douglas, Tonic, New York, September 2003.
Photo by Peter Gannushkin

William Parker, Vision Festival, New York, May 2003.
Photo by Peter Gannushkin

Hamid Drake, Salzburg, Germany, November 2002.
Photo by Peter Gannushkin

Bill Frisell, Gand, Belgium, July 2002.
Photo by Jacky Lepage

Pat Metheny, Vancouver, British Columbia, February 2005.
Photo by Lloyd Peterson

Peter Brotzmann, Vision Festival, New York, June 2005.
Photo by Peter Gannushkin

David S. Ware, Vision Festival, New York, May 2003.
Photo by Peter Gannushkin

David Murray, Liege, Belgium, May 1998.
Photo by Jacky Lepage

John Zorn.
Photo by John Zorn

Joey Baron, Brussels, Belgium, November 1991.
Photo by Jacky Lepage

Jack DeJohnette, Seattle Earshot Jazz Festival, October 2000.
Photo by Daniel Sheehan

Marilyn Crispell, Tonic, New York, December 2004.
Photo by Peter Gannushkin

Chicago Roundtable: Peter Brotzmann, Paal Nilssen-Love, Ken Vandermark,
Mats Gustafsson, and Joe McPhee, November 2004.
Photo by Lloyd Peterson

Barry Guy, 2004.
Photo by Francesca Pfeffer

Evan Parker and Steve Lacy, Gand, Belgium, April 2002.
Photo by Jacky Lepage

Ken Vandermark, Vancouver, British Columbia, December 2004.
Photo by Lloyd Peterson

Wadada Leo Smith, Vancouver, British Columbia, 1999.
Photo by Laurence Svirchev

The Thing: Paal Nilssen-Love, Ingebrigt Haker-Flaten, and Mats Gustafsson,
Lisbon, Portugal, 2004.
Photo by Laurence Svirchev

Susie Ibarra, date unknown.
Photo by Claudio Casanova

Brad Mehldau, Liege, Belgium, May 1999.
Photo by Jacky Lepage

Joshua Redman, Seattle Earshot Jazz Festival, October 2003.
Photo by Daniel Sheehan

Regina Carter, Lugano Jazz Festival, Switzerland.
Photo by Tasic Dragan

22

PAT MARTINO

Pat Martino stormed onto the jazz scene at fifteen, already demonstrating advanced technical proficiency rarely seen or heard. Suffering a potential life-threatening brain aneurysm at the age of thirty-two, Martino came out of surgery barely recognizing his parents, without any recollection of his guitar or career. After long, disciplined, and intense study, he was able to capture his past, with a renewed spirit and passion for music, and his life.

WHERE DOES YOUR HUMBLENESS COME FROM?

I think more than anything, it comes from an appreciation and enjoyment of my life. And wherever it is taking place along with other individuals is my life itself. I really respect each of those moments and the interaction that takes place under those conditions.

DOES IT INSPIRE YOUR COMPOSITIONS?

Absolutely. I give very little thought to anything but to the moment itself, with the music itself. And I appreciate it when it happens, but it's not always as consistent as I would like it to be. But I think that that is just human nature and a very healthy reminder.

IT ALSO MEANS A LOT TO THE AUDIENCE AS WELL.

It's the interaction with other people that are present in what seems to make a third point of view in what becomes one large, unified holistic event. In that context, it transcends across itself and it spreads out into many other implications.

THE GUITAR, IN PAST HISTORY, SEEMED TO HAVE DIFFICULTY IN BEING ACCEPTED WITHIN JAZZ. HAS THIS BEEN A CHALLENGE FOR YOU?

I think so, yeah. Under specific circumstances, it has really come to the forefront, especially when in collaboration with an organ, a Hammond B3. There are tendencies to lean toward the guitar as secondary to most of the instruments in jazz until a few years back with the evolution of fusion music, which I think had quite an impact.

ARE YOU FINDING THE AUDIENCES MORE IN TUNE TO WHAT YOU ARE DOING TODAY COMPARED TO WHEN YOU FIRST STARTED PROFESSIONALLY?

That's hard to say. The comment that I just made was specifically with regard to that particular idiom. But in general, I think that the guitar is one of the most popular instruments. It's a very intimate instrument, not only linear but also harmonically. But idiomatically, yeah, I think it has been secondary to the keyboard because generally the music has been constructed based upon the rules and regulations of the piano.

JAZZ ATTENDANCE HAS FALLEN OFF RECENTLY. IS IT BECAUSE OF A LACK OF INTEREST, IS IT ECONOMICS, OR ARE WE JUST GOING THROUGH A CYCLE?

That's a very interesting question. It's not only economics but it's also the expansion of technology and the availability of global participation. We don't necessarily have to be mobile to interact socially with others anymore. We have the Internet and e-mail at our disposal and, of course, the media. There are so many more things that make it a little bit more comfortable to remain stationary, and I think that that's a drastic change in terms of interaction with the arts. There are now different options and different alternatives for quite a number of folks. So I think that this does have quite a significant impact on all of the arts.

AS A RESULT, HAVE WE LOST OUR INTEREST IN BEING CHALLENGED?

A person can now sit at their desk and enjoy themselves intimately and privately. There isn't a need to participate in other forms of art when they can be part of the performance itself. You also have these exceptional individuals that are a little bit more in tune to the human experience and how profoundly music affects the health and well-being of not only themselves but also other things that are surrounded by those conditions.

IN THE '60S, MANY DIVERSE CULTURAL ELEMENTS BECAME MORE VISIBLE IN JAZZ. IS THE MUSIC INDUSTRY HAVING A DIFFICULT TIME MARKETING THE DIVERSE CULTURES THAT ARE MORE PREVALENT IN MUSIC TODAY?

I think that one of the major differences between now and the '60s was that a majority of the performing environments were a little bit smaller in terms of intimacy as opposed to festivals and large concert halls where the artists are at a distance from the audience. The audience becomes separated so there is a loss of intimacy. So quite a few things that have altered the experience itself, especially for the youngest players who are now involved in learning and trying to understand the authenticity of jazz in terms of the past, compared to the present, and where that seems to be moving into the future.

DO YOU THINK STUDENTS HAVE A DIFFERENT SET OF CHALLENGES TODAY?

I think the most challenging of all is the precision of perception itself, with today's reality which is quite different than it was in the past. And when that's hampered by a desire on behalf of any individual, the authenticity in the craft itself has to be able to obtain that accuracy extended from the culture that surrounded it in the past. And that is a very difficult if not impossible thing to do.

There are so many things that have a great deal to do with the world around us, including the music that is taking place at a place or point within it, but authenticity with regard to idiomatic concern in terms of the art of jazz and its evolutions from the past, present, and future through these things, has a great deal to do with the world. And as much as one would like to know more about a specific performance, a solo within that performance, by an artist at that time period, the more difficult it is, due to the fact that as a viewer, we don't have the opportunity to be present at the time that it took place. So a transcription of a solo, as an example, would be a very difficult thing to achieve authenticity with, when the conditions that surrounded that original moment are no longer available. It's difficult to see the temperature of the room, the condition of the instrument, the environment where it took place and was recorded in. A good example is a session I did in the early '70s with Paul Chambers and Richard "Groove" Holmes. When Paul brought his bass in, it was January so it was very cold, the instrument exploded due to the change of temperature coming into Rudy Van Gelder's studio, but there just so happened to be another bass there at that time. It was an older bass covered with dust and they changed the strings for Paul and we went on and recorded that particular project.

Now a student of contra bass who may try to transcribe what Paul played could never be aware of the difference in his playing that affected the event itself. So these are realities that I am referring to with regard to the precision of authenticity in terms of a witness or a view of what it would seem to have been unless you were there yourself. You would have never known the true nature of that. So I think that there is a major difference in all types of description and all types of determination which comes from a more set time, than a real time.

IS THIS A CREATIVE TIME FOR JAZZ?

Absolutely. But it is taking place on a larger spectrum due to the nature of our times which also includes the availability or lack of financial support. In the '60s, jazz was taking place from city to city in the U.S. in rooms that were tuned into that form of music. But it began to shift and expand more and more, it began to move in a broader context; so now it's global with worldwide festivals. Most of the artists who are functioning within this global industry are forced to be subject to this, so it's a little disappointing compared to a few years back when it was flourishing in small areas.

WHAT WOULD YOU TELL STUDENTS FIFTY YEARS FROM NOW ABOUT JAZZ OF THE LAST SEVERAL DECADES?

It's my opinion only and not to be taken to the forefront of importance, but the metamorphosis of the arts, especially with music, is that it has transcended this point in time comparative to the last few decades. It's transcending to a point where it's coming closer to a more general context of what spontaneity really is. It has, for quite sometime now, begun to interface itself with other idiomatic forms of the art. You now have classical music and jazz splitting their radio time as opposed to twenty-hour hours of jazz or twenty-four hours of classical. A breakdown of the entire method of communication is taking place and jazz is being affected by that. And for the authenticity of the meaning of the word "jazz" itself, which is based upon formulas of spontaneity, it then has to be a broader context in the way we think in terms of entertainment itself. We have become broader because of the expansion of our exposure to different cultures as well worldwide.

So I think that teaching in the sense of jazz is no longer confined to a small type of entertaining music. Now it's becoming a system of perspective, and I think that it's extremely more valuable in this context than it ever was.

SO IT'S BECOME MORE OF A PROCESS?

Yes, it's closer to a process of expansion of one's perspectives than it is a process of focusing attention upon an entertaining distractive form of enjoyment from its surroundings.

HAS THIS CHANGED THE WAY YOU COMPOSE OR THE WAY YOU LOOK AT MUSIC?

Absolutely, absolutely; very much in that we have all these other tools and the ability and opportunity to utilize them. Jazz itself can be seen as a tool, to be used successfully within specific environments and specific markets, and when that becomes second nature to any individual, that person is no longer forced to have to focus attention upon that as a priority. It then becomes a functional tool to be used with plausible grace and ability under any circumstance. It becomes second nature to the individual who has obtained that. Very much like a bicycle. When a person begins to learn that vehicle, whether it's a bicycle or an automobile, learning the machine itself is of most importance prior to enjoying it as much as the one who doesn't know how to use it. So it's separate from the entire event, until it becomes absorbed into the individual who experienced it. When that takes place, then the tool is as easy to use as a fork that is used at dinner. And one never thinks of using it with ability, primarily because one is more interested in what it was designed to do.

In that particular place, jazz can also become that utensil for the individual that has enough experience with it, or any other form of art. And then it's the individual's decision as to what that particular blessing will give them the ability to obtain, and that's what interest becomes available for that individual. So it may seem that jazz is what that interest may be in, but it really isn't, jazz is part of the household, it's part of the home that the individual has movement within. And that's an ongoing reality; it's always changing.

So I think that teaching music in that context begins to transcend entertainment, it transcends a product that can be sold strictly for the industrial branch of its use. It then becomes a mode of perception for an individual to begin to see the application for the same reasons that make it a masterful procedure which can be applied to other ways of working, to other ways of thinking and other ways of viewing life.

IS THERE A COMMON PHILOSOPHY THAT YOU TRY TO IMPART ON YOUNG STUDENTS?

The most common thing is *now*, wherever they are and whomever they are with. That is the greatest observation that can take place, the greatest participation to take place. The greatest moment is that moment, now. And I think that there is nothing more realistic than that.

HOW DO YOU TEACH SOMEONE HOW TO RAISE THEIR AWARENESS LEVEL?

That is such a difficult question to answer and I wouldn't know where to begin. I can refer to quite a number of considerations that make all the sense in the world, but when you are dealing with youngsters who are aggressively hungry for new experiences, the experience itself is more important than what it contains, and what it contains would be just as painful as it is joyful. And they will see the polarities of these conditions in every moment, and where they turn to in terms of perceiving that gap in a valid healthy way is contingent upon a third viewpoint which is not subject to the good or bad of what they may select. Whether it's difficult or easy, whether it's sad or happy, whether it's major or minor, and whether it's dark or light. You are always going to see the two-sided oppositions; you are always going to see disappointment and the success and the lack of success. And they are going to seek one more than the other, and until they reach a point where they can view both of them in operation at all times, from a third point of view, then all of the things that they are witnessing are not realistic. So that's what makes it very difficult to answer a question like that.

THE FOLLOWING IS A QUOTE FROM CECIL TAYLOR: "MUSIC HAS TO DO WITH A LOT OF AREAS WHICH ARE MAGICAL RATHER THAN LOGICAL; THE GREAT ARTISTS, RATHER THAN JUST GETTING INVOLVED WITH DISCIPLINE, GET TO UNDERSTAND LOVE AND ALLOW THE LOVE TO TAKE SHAPE." HOW MUCH OF YOUR MUSIC IS FROM LOGIC AND HOW MUCH FROM THIS OTHER PLACE THAT CECIL TAYLOR DESCRIBES?

All of the music itself initially comes from love. Like any other thing that em-
anates into a real-time manifestation of itself. In other words, the composition
aside from the process. The process itself is the love of the process, the creative
process. The creation itself is indeed with love, love of whatever it may be that is
being created. A person could love a terrible thing and that's why it is being created because love is that terrible. At the same token, love is working in every way
so that the ideas that you shared as the quote coming from Cecil, due to the fact
that once the creativity manifests itself as an end result, it then becomes two-
dimensional, primarily because the process has reached its finality. So yes, all of
the music initially came from the process itself. And what is witnessed afterwards
is finality with the product itself. But it is really not what the love really was. It is
the only thing that can be viewed from another viewpoint. It's a second issue, it's
a different issue. And that's why it's important, in my case, to again point to the importance of it being reduced to a tool. It's the end result, the finale that becomes
the tool that becomes a utensil to be used as a smaller object in a larger frame of
reference. And that frame of reference references social interaction.

AND YOUR INSPIRATION?

My inspiration comes from love itself. It comes from all of the things that I
have always loved—about music, about playfulness and childishness. Of course,
to be able to maintain that childishness and the love of it is such a challenge in
this place. I can be blunt and remember a time, publicly remember a time, when
my playfulness and childishness was a necessity to being interrupted by my
parental duties. My parents would say, "Stop playing and do your homework."
And I would have to do so because, primarily, it was my responsibility as their
child to take their advice and do so. But there came a time when it became necessary for me to go back to what I enjoyed the most by comparison of the result
of looking for that enjoyment in what they said had to be done. I didn't see it in
there. So, I went back to what really stimulated me intuitively and that was the
love of what I was doing and why I loved doing it. And I think it's the same thing
today; that has maintained its continuity. Because of the hard struggle in allowing
it to exist without being hampered by expectations in a more adult-dimensional
framework.

YOU HAVE PLAYED WITH A NUMBER OF VARIOUS MUSICIANS. HOW DOES THAT
CHANGE THE PROCESS OF THE MUSIC THAT IS BEING PLAYED ON STAGE?

Of course it's extremely effective. It's effective in many ways that have very abstract meanings when it comes to the craft of music and the expectations between
the musicians in relationships. To be as simplistic as possible, I find that the most
valuable facets of these forms of interactions with other artists is from the results
in the sense of caring and respect for each other. The value of the human experience and to be in tune with and in awe of each other instead of being competitive
toward one another. These forms to me are secondary to the destination that it

brings about. This has a great deal to do with it. Primarily because it frees one of being judgmental about the product itself.

SO IT'S NOT ONLY ABOUT THE FOUNDATION OF WHERE THE MUSICIAN COMES FROM MUSICALLY BUT ABOUT WHO THEY ARE AS A FELLOW HUMAN BEING.

It's not really who they are, it's what they are. They are my life. Whoever I am with is my life. I find it valuable and rewarding, magically rewarding and blessed in itself. To be able to participate in my life sensitively with others. Let me put it to you this way. I used to think that a bandleader was a successful adult who learned all the secrets and had control of quite a number of people. And as a sideman, I came to understand how insensitive certain individuals are as leaders with regard to such things as accommodations, transportation, timing, and how much work they had to provide on behalf of others. At times, there were musicians who were incompetent but were included because there were less costs. These things came about to me in terms of true experience and, of course, I share that with the music. I didn't even realize the substantial implications that led to growing up as a human being. So this had a lot to do with it prior to, as well in, performance. When I am in the midst of other artists, not only the performers in terms of the instruments that are being played that are making the audio aspect of the event but also the other people that are there with other facets of that moment. It's impossible. You can understand what would cause Cecil to say something like that under the circumstances.

WHAT HAVE YOU LEARNED FROM THE RISKS YOU HAVE TAKEN IN YOUR CAREER?

The most valuable things that I have learned from the process, which is still taking place, is that it's still just as difficult to understand the difference between now and the beginning of this. The difference now is that whatsoever should be a challenge from the music itself and the conditions that surround it ultimately result in a reaffirmation that comes from understanding the necessity for endurance, patience, compassion. All of these things that lead to a more virtuosic success, lead closer to virtuosity, in a sense of second nature when it comes to implementation of the art itself. The end result comes in a better way of deeper enjoyment of life itself and a greater appreciation as well as a respect for the blessings of it.

CAN YOU CONNECT TODAY'S MUSIC POLITICALLY, SOCIALLY, OR SPIRITUALLY?

Politically, I find it impossible. Primarily because I never had any interest in politics. Socially, I find it extremely rewarding. Primarily because it has global access due to computers, and feedback available on the Internet, and social interaction within that context as well as a more real-time display of the same implications that take place after the performance in the midst of touring.

WHEN YOU COMPOSE, DO YOU ENVISION WHAT YOU WANT YOUR MUSIC TO DO FOR THE LISTENER?

It has nothing to do with it. At times, the composition takes place outside of music itself and what happens is usually an expression of it, sometimes feeling. A good example: I was having coffee with another pianist by the name of Ron Thomas and we were talking about musical terms and the conversation was so interesting. In fact it was Ron Thomas that introduced me to Karlheinz Stockhausen and Elliott Carter, and, at the same time, I was introducing Ron to John Coltrane, Miles, and others. We were sitting there at the table and talking about a 7 sharp, 9 chord, and in the process of that, I picked up the guitar and played with the voicing of it and started moving it around to show him how it worked on the guitar and suddenly out of that movement came a composition. And that composition became "The Great Stream," which went on an album sometime after that. The composition came out as it appeared as maybe forty seconds after this long, enjoyable conversation. So sometimes that is what causes a composition. It's not thinking of the music at all. It's the virtual interaction and the 7 sharp, 9 chord was just the topic that allowed us to integrally interact as people. So sometimes the composition comes from something that has nothing to do with the music itself.

That's just one way it takes place. Another way is the variable ways of music of reducing any specific type of formula such as a mode, play a mode such as a lydiam, ionian, dorian, mixolydian, or any of these by taking a mode and taking it outside of music by extracting it from music itself. And taking it and freeing it and leaving it with another tool and extracting that tool from something that you are not going to use in that way anymore. Like the alphabet, A, B, C, D, E, F, G is the ionian mode of music, it's the first seven letters of the alphabet. And by taking A, B, C, D, E, F, G as tones and not as letters and then repeating it for the next seven letters from "H" on and the next seven letters and then the last five letters and you now have an A-minor alphabet. And then you can take the word Coltrane and you have C, A, E are the tones for "Col" and then F, G, A, G, E for "trane" and that's another way and you have a melody. By using one system to expand another so that if I'm outdoors and I have to be interrupted by other responsibilities and I do feel like composing music, I'm no longer distracted from my internal interests. Then I can see the music in lots of places—from cars to the middle of streets, in the words that I hear people saying, so I sometimes compose like that too.

WHAT IS IT ABOUT JAZZ AND THE ART FORM THAT IS IMPORTANT TO YOU?

The opportunity that results from it in the way that it brings me closer to other people. Meeting new people all of the time. It exposes you to other interests and other people with other identities. Different experiences with different social interactions.

WHAT DO YOU SEE FOR THE FUTURE OF JAZZ AND YOURSELF PERSONALLY?

I really can't answer that to be honest because idiomatically, my appetite and my enjoyment of different flavors have broadened to such a degree that it's very difficult for me to refer to jazz specifically as an interesting idiom. I enjoy whatever I hear and where I'm at in the moment. And I find that to be so spontaneous that that's what the meaning of jazz has become to me.

ARE YOU PLEASED WITH WHERE YOU ARE TODAY?

Oh yeah, absolutely. But I'm not pleased with the necessity that's taking place worldwide. Whether it's necessary or isn't is another story but personally, yes I am. I'm very fulfilled.

DO YOU HAVE A WAY OF LOOKING AT LIFE THAT YOU WOULD BE WILLING TO SHARE?

Whatever comes before you is exactly what you need, it's your life. And this has to be valued as such and you have to focus on that as such. I remember when someone or something would come before me that required a responsibility and I would dislike it very much because I wanted to do something else at that moment. And I would try to avoid such responsibility and also decisions would sometimes be difficult within the same context. And under those conditions, it would cause me not to make those decisions and procrastinate until it became so painful that a decision had to be made. And that's how I learned the importance of being more decisive. Well, initially it was the decision itself that stood right before me and I would need to walk all the way around it to look at it from another angle and avoid it as much as possible in the process. So whatever comes before me is the most powerful blessing that there is—it's the ability to participate in my own life.

❷❸

CHRISTIAN MCBRIDE

He has taken the bass out of the box and opened the possibilities for future generations of players. With his wide open and fearless attitude, Christian McBride can lay down a groove with more rhythmic feel and melodic soul than the lords of funk ever imagined.

IN 1998, YOU PARTICIPATED IN PRESIDENT CLINTON'S TOWN HALL MEETING, "RACISM AND PERFORMING ARTS." WHAT EXACTLY WAS DISCUSSED?

The discussion consisted of the different ways that racism plays a part in the performing Arts—inside racism, outside racism, ageism, sexism, etc. In general, race always plays a part, particularly in American culture. There is always a race card being played somewhere for some reason. The jazz industry is now like any other industry. It's money driven, image driven, and it's a bad driven! There is just as much ageism in jazz as there is racism. For example, it's not hip to give someone in their seventies or eighties a major label contract in jazz. Roy Haynes is one of the last surviving musicians on this earth who actually was part of the bebop revolution and is playing stronger than ever, and he's recording for a small European label. Maybe that's a blessing in disguise because at least he doesn't have the pressure of being forced into something he doesn't want to do, but still, the majors won't give him any consideration. Why? Because he is considered old. Hank Jones is another of the last surviving musicians of the bebop revolution. I don't know if he has recorded a CD for a major label in the last twenty-five or thirty years. Maybe he has, I don't know. Of course I'm extra sensitive to this because I was a part of what they called the "young lion revolution" where musicians of my generation were getting major label contracts strictly because we were young and were known as the disciples of Wynton Marsalis, who, of course, is the fountainhead of what the layperson associates with young jazz musicians. But now that's past. Guys like Roy Hargrove, Joshua Redman, and myself are not quite as young so they cannot play the "young lion" card anymore. So now, the whole focus is on singers. Unless you sing, you really don't have a chance in hell. And it's funny to watch how all of these things just arbitrarily change. About ten years ago, most labels were not even thinking about young singers. It was all about instrumentalists. For instance, Verve was one of the few labels, particularly in the early '90s, that didn't try to hold onto the young lions game. They were signing Joe Henderson, Abbey Lincoln, Betty Carter, Marlena Shaw and trying to revive their careers because they had their roster balanced with a lot of young artists, old artists, black artists, white artists, and South African artists. Now, Verve isn't really a jazz label anymore.

Diana Krall is a really great friend of mine. I love her. But she is about the closest thing to hardcore jazz they have on Verve. If you listen to Diana's records, they are good, they are swingin' and there are some great songs, but it's not what you would call hardcore. They have Diana, Lizz Wright, Will Downing, and this new guy, Jamie Cullum. They have singers galore. And as I mentioned, these are all people who are friends of mine and I wish the very best for them. But it's amazing how many people there are that don't receive what they deserve and racism plays a part in this. It has nothing to do with their artistry. For example, whenever producers want a record that is very heavily based on rhythm, they'll probably call someone who is black. But if they want something a little more ethereal and not so rhythm based, they'll call a white player. Where does this come from?

Herbie Hancock is one of the few musicians who is great at doing everything. If you want a funky keyboard player or someone who can play outside or a little avant-garde, you can also call Herbie Hancock. But he can also play spacey, thought-driven music as well. I just don't feel that musicians receive credit for being diverse, and I think it's a color issue. If a producer wants someone for what is perceived to be "thinking" type of music, John Pattitucci might get that call before I get that call. Maybe I'm wrong, but I've always felt this. Black players are perceived strictly as feel-good, rhythm players and white players usually as "sensitive" and "thinking" players. That shouldn't be the case but it's been a part of American culture for the last one hundred years in jazz.

The subject of women in the performing arts was also discussed. How many people consider women real key figures in composing and improvising? They are usually relegated to playing the piano.

Vocals and piano.

Yes. But of course there have been a lot of great female jazz drummers and bass players. Vi Redd was a funky alto sax player and vocalist from Chicago who sounded like Sonny Stitt. Even though Mary Lou Williams played piano, she was two-fisted and could give anybody a run for their money. And Maria Schnieder is incredible. She is so incredible. I absolutely love her music and I had the oppor-

tunity to work with her a couple of months ago and she is one of the few serious
protégés of Gil Evans, a direct protégé of Gil Evans and Bob Brookmeyer. All of
that comes through in her writing, but if some big mainstream producer needs an
arranger, they are probably not going to think of Maria Schnieder. Why? Beats me.

YOU ARE ONLY THIRTY-TWO YEARS OLD BUT HAVE ALREADY BEEN ON OVER 200
CDS. IS THERE A COMMON PHILOSOPHY THAT YOU TRY TO IMPART WITH YOUNG MU-
SICIANS?

Yeah, I always tell them to remember, "Absolutely no one likes working with an
asshole!" Do the job you've been asked to do, and do it right. When it comes to
money, get paid, but don't ever nickel-and-dime people. I also tell young musicians that following your heart always wins out in the end, but it's something very
difficult for young musicians to understand. It might take a little time but you have
to have patience and not compromise your philosophies to keep up with the game.
Stay true to yourself, and in the long run, you'll always win.

When I first arrived in New York, my goal was to play with every single musician I possibly could regardless of style and cover the entire spectrum. I wanted
to spend time with Wynton Marsalis, Lester Bowie, Oscar Peterson, Elvin Jones,
Neal Peart (laughs), Bernard Purdie, and with Cecil Taylor. I wanted to do it all
and believed that it could only make me a better musician. It helps define your
goals, your personality, and helps you build and form the road for yourself. I also
found it interesting that many of the young musicians that I came up with tried to
stay close to Wynton Marsalis and allow him to be their only influence. Consequently, they ended up talking like him, dressing like him, and acting like him.
Miles Davis was also a strong presence and influence but was always interested in
encouraging guys not to stay in the same place—to not get complacent, and
though they might not necessarily agree with him, that was cool too. Miles wasn't
going to say something like, "Ah well, you screwed up, you didn't follow my philosophy. Therefore you are not doing the right thing." I find that a lot of the people who have become really close to Wynton are scared to break with his doctrine.
"You have to do what I do or you are not considered one of my boys anymore." It's
very much a cult-like atmosphere. At least it used to be when I hung around him.
I don't know if it's still like that.

YOUR INFLUENCES CROSS MANY GENRES OF MUSIC AND I KNOW YOU ARE A BIG AD-
MIRER OF JAMES BROWN AND HAVE WORKED WITH STING. WHEN YOU WERE COMING
UP ON THE SCENE AS A YOUNG "JAZZ" MUSICIAN, DID YOU HAVE TO ASK YOURSELF
WHETHER IT WOULD BE OK TO INCLUDE THESE OTHER INFLUENCES? DID YOU HAVE
TO CROSS THAT BRIDGE?

Yes I did, and to be honest, there is one genre that I have never liked, and that's
smooth jazz. I would like to think that I can be influenced by everything, but I
would say that 99 percent of smooth jazz does not influence me. But it has helped
me to realize what I did *not* want to do! One of the great things but also one of the

dangerous things about jazz is that it's a very tightly knit family. When I first arrived in New York and started hanging out at Bradley's, the Village Gate, Birdland,
and started playing with the really true hardcore heavyweight jazz greats, guys like
John Hicks, Gary Bartz, George Coleman, James Williams, Victor Lewis, and
Bobby Watson, I felt so proud that I was being included as a member of this small
family. Of course, a strong family is going to be very protective of their fellow family members, too. But a time came along when I had the opportunity to participate
in pop and R&B gigs and there was a moment when I had to ask, "What is the family going to think about this? Will I be disowned, and will they not like me anymore?" I was made to understand that you don't moonlight with pop stars. One of
the first pop gigs that I had, outside of the jazz world, was playing with Bruce
Hornsby in 1994.

BRUCE HORNSBY HAS A WONDERFUL APPROACH TO MUSIC.

Yeah, and for someone that is a pop artist or considered to be a pop artist, he's
very jazzy. Today, playing with Bruce wouldn't be much of a stretch, but at the
time, "Oh man, you're playing with Bruce Hornsby? Didn't he play with the
Grateful Dead? Are you kidding? Why are you playing with him?" I also performed on a record by pianist Michael Wolff in 1994. Michael was the musical director for the Arsenio Hall show, which had just gone off the air at the time. Being the musical director of a talk show, no one really knew Michael as a really
serious jazz pianist, along with the mentality and prejudice that says L.A. musicians are not good jazz players. But people forget that Michael Wolff's first major
gig was with Cannonball Adderley in 1975. He was Cannonball's last pianist. During the session I did with Michael, Tony Williams played drums and I was going
to do the session just on that alone. But someone who shall remain nameless
scolded me for doing this record. He said, "Why are you playing with Michael
Wolff? You should be playing with Kenny Barron, Cedar Walton, or somebody like
that. You don't need to be playing with Michael Wolff." I said, "Come on now, let's
not be stupid. One, I'm getting paid. Two, I'm getting to play with Tony Williams.
And three, Michael is a really good player. OK, so he might not be a Kenny Barron or a Cedar Walton, but who are you to judge!?" I started thinking, "Wow, this
is really heavy." And I guess there is a point when you have to make a decision that
says, "I'm OK with playing and being influenced by other styles of music and if
'The Family' doesn't like it, I'm sorry, they are just going to do what they have to
do. I cannot be held back like this. I have to leave the house; I'm 18 years old!"
(Laughs.) Nevertheless, because the jazz community is a tight-knit family, it becomes awkward when someone breaks out, and there are older family members
who may not have received the credit they deserve.

IT HAS ALWAYS INTRIGUED ME THAT THE VERY THING THAT IS THE STRENGTH OF
THIS ART FORM ALSO HOLDS IT BACK.

Absolutely.

THE FOLLOWING IS A QUOTE FROM CECIL TAYLOR: "MUSIC HAS TO DO WITH A LOT OF AREAS WHICH ARE MAGICAL RATHER THAN LOGICAL; THE GREAT ARTISTS, RATHER THAN JUST GETTING INVOLVED WITH DISCIPLINE, GET TO UNDERSTAND LOVE AND ALLOW THE LOVE TO TAKE SHAPE." HOW MUCH OF YOUR MUSIC IS FROM LOGIC AND HOW MUCH FROM THIS OTHER PLACE THAT CECIL TAYLOR DESCRIBES?

I agree completely and that's why I want to play and hang with Cecil Taylor. What makes music special is the unexplainable area of magic. And sadly, there are many musicians who will tell you that it doesn't exist and that you have to make the magic happen. But you cannot plan magic. It's like love. Can you really plan falling in love? Love and music are very much the same thing—it's harmony. Finding the perfect mate is like finding the perfect chord. It's a chord you really like to play and once that chord starts to grow on you, you understand the sound of the chord and you voice it another way, which is the same thing with love. When you have dated someone for a long time and leave the puppy-love stage, you have to go on to something else. And the strength of that love helps you get to that level without any problems. It's the same thing with a memorable musical experience— it's magical.

The most memorable musical situations that I have ever been involved in were unplanned. And with my own bands, I like to leave a lot of space for magic to happen. It's fine if it doesn't happen, but nine times out of ten, there is going to be at least one moment that's going to feel really, really good to the audience and myself. One of my favorite bands of all time for that particular reason was Weather Report. Weather Report was one of the only really great improvisational groups that was modern but still traditional in their approach. They used electronic instruments, but there was a lot of strong grooves with room for improvisation. With Joe Zawinul and Wayne Shorter at the helm, you couldn't go wrong. If Weather Report was to happen now, they would probably be called a world music group. This is one of the few North American groups that became popular who were openly influenced by music from Africa, South America, Central America, and always had a lot of things going on simultaneously while keeping their roots connected in traditional jazz. That's why I always loved Weather Report so much and have always tried to adapt that concept to my band. It's open for a lot of magic to happen.

CAN YOU DISCUSS YOUR RELATIONSHIP WITH TIME IN THE MUSICAL SENSE?

I knew that playing with as many musicians as possible would stretch my relationship with time. Victor Lewis, Billy Hart, Joe Chambers, Carl Allen, Kenny Washington, and Lewis Nash all have different concepts of how to play time. Elvin Jones and Jack DeJohnette play loose and around the time. Kenny Washington and Jeff Hamilton underline the time. Bernard Purdie and Steve Gadd are strict and funky with their time. Idris Muhammad is very funky, but is looser with time. He's got that New Orleans thing happening. I have heard people say that I play on the beat as opposed to playing behind or on top of the beat, but it all depends on what song you're playing and on the situation. More often than not, playing on the beat is going to be where people feel the pulse the best. I'm not sure where that comes from and I'm not sure why it's like that but for the most part, I tend to be a guy that prefers to play right on the beat—right on the pulse. But depending on whom you are playing with, sometimes you have to switch up and make adjustments. Sometimes I have to be a little bit on the edge, and that's OK, too. If I play with a drummer who likes to play a little bit behind the beat or likes to settle in a certain type of time, I may push that drummer, and this is where musicianship comes into play because the drummer now has to make a decision on whether to push with me. But I may pull back and then we'll lock. That stuff happens in one to four beats and is very quick. There is always an unspoken language going on between the bassist and the drummer where you make adjustments to really lock. Once that happens, you understand what it is and stay there.

ARE THERE PARTICULAR TYPES OF DRUMMERS THAT YOU PREFER TO PLAY WITH?

I have always liked to play with drummers who play on top, who push a little bit and have that little bit of tension where it's just a smidgeon faster than how you counted it off. Just to kind of give it that New York edge, and I find that most of the really great jazz drummers play like that. It's one of the reasons why I like Terreon Gully, who plays drums in my band. He's not very exact but plays around the time. He doesn't play exactly on the beat but plays all three—he plays behind the beat, on the beat, and on top of the beat, all at the same time. It's very dangerous but that's what I like about it. He's a very dangerous drummer—kind of like driving an SUV coming around the corner at ninety miles an hour. But Terreon is also very original. Sometimes you crash but the fun part is recovering. These are the kind of drummers that I like playing with. And every time I play with Jack DeJohnette, I feel like I'm walking on a minefield!

CAN YOU DESCRIBE YOUR APPROACH AND WHAT YOU ARE ATTEMPTING TO DO AS A BASSIST WITHIN THE CONTEXT OF THE MUSIC?

The bass is such an important instrument for the sound and for the aura of the song. Depending on whom I'm playing with and depending on the situation, I can take certain liberties and give the music a little lift. I always felt great bass players not only play the right bass notes within the composition but also go the extra step to bring that little extra thing to it. Ron Carter is one of my biggest heroes at not only covering color in the rhythm, but at coloring the harmony. If you give Ron Carter an F-major chord, of course he is going to play F but he could play G, A, C or whatever note to give it that little jolt, and everyone in the band will wonder, "What was that?" I have tried to take that concept and be very subtle because it's still the bass and the instrument that everyone is leaning on for support. You have to pick your spots but that's part of the beauty of being a really true musician.

YOU PLAYED WITH FREDDIE HUBBARD FOR A WHILE, AND I FEEL DEEPLY THAT HE
HAS NEVER RECEIVED HIS DUE FOR WHAT HE HAS BROUGHT TO THIS MUSIC. DO YOU
MIND EXPRESSING YOUR THOUGHTS ABOUT HIM?

Freddie Hubbard is the most influential trumpet player of the last thirty years.
Miles had a greater influence on jazz as a whole, but Freddie has been a greater
influence on the trumpet. He was one of the few trumpet players who could play
the instrument like a saxophone and one of the few trumpet players to play with
the two tenor legends of their time, John Coltrane and Sonny Rollins. He took the
concept of playing sheets of sound and applying fast arpeggios and jagged lines to
the trumpet, and once that happened, Freddie took off on a plane all his own. For
many of us that were around Freddie a lot, we understand that a part of the reason he hasn't received his just due is somewhat by his own doing. It was his
lifestyle. I think about Freddie almost everyday and I feel really lucky to have
played in his band when his chops were still strong. I caught the tail end of his
greatness and I cherish that. All of Freddie's peers are gone—Lee Morgan, Woody
Shaw, Blue Mitchell. Donald Byrd is still alive, but really doesn't play much anymore. Freddie is the only one, and the fact that he is still alive and cannot quite
produce like he used to is heartbreaking to us. All of us who love Freddie and
know how important he is to the history of this music say silent prayers every day,
"Come on Freddie, practice! Get your lips strong so you can come out here and
claim your throne. It's waiting for you and nobody will ever take it from you."

I UNDERSTAND HE IS HAVING TROUBLE WITH HIS LIP MUSCLES SO IT MAKES IT DIF-
FICULT FOR HIM TO PLAY.

Yes, but it can be fixed. We all make excuses for why Freddie is not out here,
but the truth of the matter is, if he really wanted to, he could. But I guess it must
be very difficult for a man in his mid-sixties who worked so hard his whole life to
become the world's greatest trumpet player on earth and now cannot do it anymore. He's just not inspired to work that hard and get back to that point, which I
can understand. Nevertheless, it's sad because nobody can do what he does.

WHAT WERE YOUR EXPERIENCES LIKE WITH RAY BROWN?

Ron Carter, Paul Chambers, and Ray Brown are my three acoustic bass heroes,
but Ray Brown provided the most influence. Everything about Ray Brown is of the
highest level. His technique, his sound, his notes and his time . . . everything about
the man. When I finally met Ray, it was a student–mentor, father–son relationship
right away. Out of all the great jazz musicians I have had a chance to associate with,
Ray Brown was by far the most poignant relationship I've ever had with an elder
statesman of the music. We talked about a lot of things, which didn't always have
to do with music. One of my greatest moments as a human being was when Ray
and I tossed a baseball around after a summer festival. Ray was my man and he
mentored a lot of musicians. And talk about someone who did not get his just due!

People talk about Art Blakey and Betty Carter, who were responsible for bringing up all of these younger musicians onto the scene, but because Ray Brown waited till later in his career to do that, it has kind of slipped by everybody. There's that subliminal ageism from the jazz press again. But Ray Brown was responsible for getting a lot of younger musicians the opportunity to shine in a way that wasn't usual for them in other situations.

YOU HAVE ALSO SPENT TIME WITH PAT METHENY.

I first played with Pat while touring with Joshua Redman and Billy Higgins in 1993. Pat is one of the very few people to attain one common goal that all jazz musicians desire, and that's creating their own sound. There have only been a handful of people in jazz during the last thirty years that have really developed their own sound, and when you hear Pat Metheny, you know it's Pat Metheny. He is the only person that I can think of today who has done that. He hits one little line, and you know that sound, that flow, and know it's absolutely Metheny. And the Pat Metheny Group is one of the most influential groups of all time and sounds like no other. Pat is also the biggest superstar that nobody knows. He has influenced so many people and sells out concerts all over the world, but you hardly ever see him on television or on the cover of pop magazines. He has had the highest level of commercial and artistic success imaginable. Yet he is still a low-key major superstar and has done it without compromising. Pat Metheny's music has never, ever been commercial and I think the fact that he has been able to become such an icon at both artistic and commercial levels without doing anything to sell his soul is absolutely amazing.

THERE WAS A MAGAZINE THAT HAD ASKED PAT TO DO A COVER STORY BUT PAT REFUSED UNTIL THEY RAN A COVER STORY ON A BLACK JAZZ MUSICIAN.

Pat is a very serious humanitarian. He is always looking out for the musicians and the music and has always done it his own way. He is very quiet about it, though one of the famous "blasts" in the history of music was from Pat when he went off on Kenny G in that famous interview. But he will tell you himself that he didn't think it would get as much press as it did and was only intended for one person to hear, but it leaked out.

WHAT HAVE YOU LEARNED FROM THE RISKS THAT YOU HAVE TAKEN?

I have learned that there are more musicians than I ever realized who are equally just as inspired but are afraid to take the risks. I am also amazed that there are so many people in America that are so easily influenced away from their individuality. It's difficult to feel like you are welcome to stretch out and do what you are not used to doing.

DO YOU HAVE A VISION FOR WHERE YOU WANT YOUR MUSIC TO GO IN THE FUTURE?

I'm really trying to take all the many different layers of sound going on in my brain and compose a complete sound. I have played with a lot of great musicians, and when I write music and tour with my band, those inspirations come out on a lot of different levels.

WHAT IS IT ABOUT MUSIC THAT IS IMPORTANT TO YOU?

Music is the sonic mirror of life and means different things to different people. True musicians and true creative people in general have a very clear head and open ear, and I think one of the things about pop music or media-driven pop music is that people are buying ready-made mirrors. But real, true, unadulterated improvisational music is similar to a mirror because when you look in that mirror, you have no choice but to see yourself. When people listen to media-driven pop music, they cannot see themselves. If you listen to John Coltrane, Duke Ellington, Charlie Parker, or Cecil Taylor, there are no lines drawn for you, you have to create your own lines. That's what is so great about jazz.

(24)

BRAD MEHLDAU

HAVE WE LOST OUR PATIENCE AND DESIRE TO BE CHALLENGED?

One negative tendency I've noticed is a tendency to fetishize information in it-self, as an end. I'll give an example. One of the worst gigs I ever did was a "show-case" for the launch of some company that was releasing some gadget—I think it was the MP-3 player or something similar, something you hold in your hand that can store all this music. It was the height of the dot-com boom, and it was at some chic place in Manhattan, with all these loud twenty-something people getting juiced and talking over each other. A couple of guys were rabidly explaining to me about how great this thing was, about how it was going to change how we experi-ence music. Anyhow, some guy made an announcement about how their company was on the forefront of this technology, "We're kicking ass," rah-rah. . . . And then he got all serious and said, "We have a very important artist here tonight who's go-ing to share his music with you," and tried to make some kind of segue from the product launch into my performance, something about "It's these kind of artists who you're going to be able to hear in a different way in the future. . . ." Really cheesy stuff. It was quiet as I sat down, for about fifteen seconds, and then within about twenty seconds of the first tune I played, the din was even louder than be-fore I had begun playing—they had to talk louder to hear themselves over the pi-ano, I guess. Anyhow, what was so depressing was that these people were suppos-edly excited about what this gadget could do for their music experience, but they weren't interested in actually listening to music. It was all about acquiring music, cataloguing it, collecting it, having it. That's fetishism, and I've noticed it in a lot of different contexts in terms of how people view music insofar as it's information at their disposal.

Having said that, I don't know if American society as a whole is much worse off on the whole than it was. Mass culture has always catered to the short attention span. But each individual still has choices—what he or she wants to listen to, etc.—even though there's a certain amount of coercion involved. There's also another side to this high-speed information culture: If you know what you want, if you are able to educate yourself and discern your own tastes, you have an incredible freedom to roam through an endlessly available amount of information, which can't be a bad thing in itself. It comes down to the individual.

OUR SOCIETY TODAY APPRECIATES ART BUT SEEMS TO HAVE DIFFICULTY WITH CREATIVITY THAT IS NOT EASILY EXPLAINED, UNDERSTOOD, OR IDENTIFIABLE. DO YOU THINK THIS IS A SIGNIFICANT OBSTACLE TO OVERCOME FOR CREATIVE MUSIC OR THE ARTS IN GENERAL?

Yes, I think a little of what you're driving at is related to what you mentioned previously about information. In every age, it seems, we try to find tropes to explain the creative process. In various periods, creativity has been seen in a divine, quasi-religious light, or seen as a fiction, something to be "deconstructed" as a conceit of the artist. If the big trope of our epoch is "information," our age is certainly less hospitable to the notion of creativity than say, Europe was in the nineteenth century. "Information" is ultimately a bunch of ones and zeros, and it does not tell us about the process of creation; it points to the result. Information becomes the object, a thing in itself that is viewed in its own realm, and to the extent that it's not us and the Other, it becomes deified, a godlike presence. The whole thing is very antihumanistic. We become viewers, receivers—consumers—of information versus seeing ourselves as potential creators of something. A godlike presence should involve mystery. There should be awe and even fear—how does that greatness exist, what is the nature of it? The cult of creativity, however dated it may be, packs a powerful punch, because it identifies the mystery within us, not outside of us: When we create something, we're playing at being gods, poking around the edges of the sublime. When we deify information, though, we're relinquishing that status, placing the sublime outside of ourselves completely.

But it's a form of atavism to call for some return to a more humanistic viewpoint—you can't change the tide. I don't think any of it spells trouble for creativity in music or the arts in general, because art still has the ability to critique society, by its definition. An artist has the luxury of using the very aspect of society that he or she is critiquing as material for his or her artwork. The result is about the same as it ever was in terms of output: You get a lot of crap, and the occasional stroke of genius, where someone illuminates something about our world to us.

IN A SENSE, JAZZ HAS ALWAYS REFLECTED THE TIME IT'S FROM. AGAIN, WITH SO MUCH INFORMATION AVAILABLE TODAY, MANY DIVERSE CULTURAL MUSIC STYLES ARE MORE VISIBLE IN JAZZ COMPOSITION. ARE JAZZ PURISTS HAVING A DIFFICULT TIME ACCEPTING THAT A MUSIC FORM CONSIDERED "AMERICAN" NOW HAS MORE VISIBLE INTERNATIONAL AND DIVERSE ASPECTS WITHIN IT?

The ill will starts when people trade on the term "jazz." When I started doing the festival circuit, around 1990, I noticed that each year there would be a different genre to appear—you'd have acid jazz, Klezmer music, DJs, etc. Not to belittle or question the validity that surrounds these kinds of music, but merely to show what I mean by trading on jazz, I've observed a common byline in the media that surrounds these different genres. It's like, "This is the new music that's going to release us from a narrow definition of jazz." The implication is that jazz isn't hip enough in its own right, that it needs fresh blood, and aren't we the listeners lucky that we're going to get pulled out of the cobwebs? But this sentiment is full of bad faith: Why is this music appearing on a jazz festival then, when the whole subtext is that it's too hip for jazz? In fact you could argue that often it's the opposite case—often musicians trade on the allure of jazz as a term to get over, simultaneously thumbing their nose at jazz. That's a drag.

Jazz is often a trope that signifies freedom from the shackles of category. But it also has a strong identity in its own right. When Wynton Marsalis says something like, "You have to address the blues in this music," or swing, or what not, I get from that: You're making a choice to call your music jazz. You don't have to, after all—you can just say, "I just play music; no labels." But if you do call it jazz, then people will have a broad set of associations with the term. Now, you can play the relativism game and say, well, my associations are different than yours. That's bad logic though—if you constantly keep everything in the conditional brackets of relativism, than you short-circuit the viability of your own (presumably more open) definition of jazz ahead of time. Eventually you have to have some sort of loose identity. It's not that hard; you just do it in big brush strokes. You can base the identity on the inception of jazz and go from there. Or, even more simple, you don't raise the question of identity in the first place. It only gets raised when someone has a bad faith about the music—when they're thinking too much about how something's jazz or how they're not jazz, and imposing that on you.

I look at jazz as American in the same way that I look at classical music as European: There were certain factors that made that music originate from a certain time and place. The culture of that time and place has passed, and the music is now shared and created internationally, but that initial culture still informs the music. It would be absurd to think that there's not something inherently American in the spirit of jazz; it would be equally absurd to say that it must speak as a music at all times in some authentically American voice—whatever that would be. Jazz is like a very generous family with a big house that has lots of guests from all over. Every so often, a visitor is particularly illuminating and affects the viewpoint of jazz permanently, leaving something behind in that house that will stay there forever. But that just doesn't happen that often—most visits just aren't that illuminating. Maybe a sort of pragmatic purism is to say, look, not everything can be great and earth shattering and instantly important.

THERE IS MORE AND MORE INFORMATION FOR EACH GENERATION TO DIGEST, AND THE CHALLENGE BECOMES GREATER FOR STUDENTS OF THIS MUSIC TO COMPREHEND.

IT TAKES MORE TIME. IN ONE SENSE, THE GROWTH PERIOD IS MUCH LONGER, BUT AT THE SAME TIME, THERE IS ALL THIS INFORMATION TO PULL FROM THAT HAS NEVER BEEN THERE BEFORE.

That's why most people specialize—they focus on a few periods and delve more deeply into them. I read somewhere that Hegel was the last philosopher who could still give a full account of the whole history of human thought in his writing—at least Occidental thought, like starting from the Greeks—and that after him, there was just too much information, so people had to stop trying to go for that metaview.

I DON'T THINK WE COULD EVER COME UP WITH A GOOD DEFINITION OF WHAT JAZZ IS NOR DO I WANT TO TRY. HOWEVER, I DO BELIEVE IT HAS MORE TO DO WITH THE PROCESS OF CREATION RATHER THAN RE-CREATION. ONE OF THE PROBLEMS WITH DOCUMENTATION FOCUSING ON JAZZ, SUCH AS KEN BURNS'S SERIES, IS THAT IT SPENDS MOST OF ITS TIME CONCENTRATING ON WHAT JAZZ CREATED IN THE PAST AND SPENDS LITTLE OR NO TIME ON WHAT THE MUSIC IS CREATING AT THE MOMENT, WHICH, TO ME, IS THE ESSENCE OF THIS GREAT MUSIC WE CALL JAZZ. VERY LITTLE INFORMATION IS USUALLY BROUGHT UP ABOUT THE MUSIC BEING COMPOSED AND PLAYED TODAY AND ABOUT THE MUSICIANS WHO ARE MAKING IT HAPPEN. DOESN'T THIS SEEM SHORTSIGHTED, PERHAPS A LOST OPPORTUNITY TO EDUCATE POTENTIAL ASPIRING JAZZ STUDENTS AND EDUCATE PEOPLE TO WHAT JAZZ IS REALLY ABOUT AND WHAT IS AVAILABLE TO THEM?

The only argument for that shortsightedness in regard to the series' view of everything after the 1960s is that not enough time has passed to judge whether the music since then is canonical. But it's not a good enough argument, because the series should have taken into account the undeniable aesthetic impact of jazz since then, the real pleasure and joy that so many people have received from jazz created in the last thirty years. As for ignoring what's happening here and now, it would have been better to have completely ignored the scene now, because what they actually did was give a small nod to a handful of arbitrary musicians. It was like Ken Burns asked someone, "Who's happening now?" and that someone thought about it for a minute and then rattled off some names. Then they flashed still photos of those musicians and the whole thing took about five minutes. It was embarrassing to watch, the last segment of that series.

THE FOLLOWING IS A QUOTE FROM CECIL TAYLOR: "MUSIC HAS TO DO WITH A LOT OF AREAS WHICH ARE MAGICAL RATHER THAN LOGICAL; THE GREAT ARTISTS, RATHER THAN JUST GETTING INVOLVED WITH DISCIPLINE, GET TO UNDERSTAND LOVE AND AL- LOW THE LOVE TO TAKE SHAPE." HOW MUCH OF YOUR MUSIC IS FROM LOGIC AND HOW MUCH FROM THIS OTHER PLACE THAT CECIL TAYLOR DESCRIBES?

There is an undeniable magic that takes place when it's working, but there's also an intellectual process at play; the two work together.

WHEN WRITING COMPOSITIONS, DO YOU ENVISION WHAT IT IS YOU WANT YOUR MU-
SIC TO DO FOR THE LISTENER OR IS THAT EVEN A FACTOR?

I go about writing something that will hopefully be satisfying by my own lights,
with the idealistic belief that my aesthetic will find communion with at least one
listener. I create for myself and hope that someone else will relate.

HOW MUSICIANS DEAL WITH TIME AND THEIR RELATIONSHIP TO IT DOES NOT GET
DISCUSSED THAT OFTEN VERY OPENLY. CAN YOU DISCUSS YOUR APPROACH WITH TIME
AND HOW MUCH IT IS INFLUENCED BY THE RELATIONSHIP BETWEEN THE OTHER MU-
SICIANS WITHIN THE GROUP?

Part of the reason that time doesn't get discussed that often is because it becomes very esoteric in the context of word-language, and difficult to explain. Our
approach to time in my trio can get complex, but the way it's been developed has
been a largely intuitive process. We all influence each other, but Jorge Rossy
(drummer) has definitely had a strong influence on me from the gate. When we
started playing together about ten years ago, he got me into playing in odd meters
like 7/4, and we worked out a lot of stuff together.

DRUMMERS AND BASS PLAYERS CAN COME UP WITH THEIR OWN LANGUAGE WITHIN
THE CONTEXT OF WHAT'S HAPPENING IN A LIVE SITUATION. WHAT DO YOU LOOK FOR
FROM DRUMMERS AND BASS PLAYERS AND HOW MUCH OF IT HAS TO DO WITH THEIR
RHYTHMIC APPROACH WITH EACH OTHER?

I look for a good feeling of swing and forward motion. A drummer can be creative and sensitive, but if the feel is wrong it's like a weight on your shoulders, and
it makes the process of playing together a chore, a real drag. You can tell whether
the feeling is good within seconds. With bass players I look for the same good feeling. Also important for me with bass is a good sound and good intonation. I prefer
bass players who generate the sound out of the wood of the instrument itself more
than the amp. I want some attack on the notes, which usually means having the action higher versus low. That's just my preference.

MILES DAVIS HAS SAID THAT THE RIGHT NOTES CAN FERTILIZE THE SOUND OF A
COMPOSITION, THAT IT CAN MAKE THE SOUND GROW. MUCH LIKE ADDING LEMON TO
FISH OR VEGETABLES THAT BRING OUT THE FLAVOR. THAT IT'S YOUR SWEAT. WITH
MANY OF YOUR COMPOSITIONS, YOU SEEM TO EMPHASIZE WHERE AND HOW YOU USE
SOUND TEXTURES AND COLORS. CAN YOU DESCRIBE THAT PROCESS, YOUR APPROACH,
AND WHAT YOU ARE ATTEMPTING TO DO WITHIN THE CONTEXT OF THE MUSIC?

I've written a lot of tunes over the last several years that have been at least
somewhat with Jorge Rossy (drums) and Larry Grenadier (bass) in mind, and that
has to do with what you call their "sound texture"—it's an important aspect of the
whole thing for sure. The tunes kind of build off and develop out of each other. I
hear an approach, for example, that Jorge takes on a tune, and I have that in my

head as I'm writing something new; it becomes a starting point for something else. Jorge's very adept at creating a drum texture that complements the composition, and adds something to it. It probably has to do with the fact that he plays piano and has a strong knowledge of harmony—for him a subtle thing like voice-leading within a chord may suggest a different cymbal, a drier approach, hand drumming, what have you.

CHARLES MINGUS SAID THAT YOU CANNOT TEACH STYLE BUT CAN TEACH SOMEONE TO APPRECIATE IT, THAT STYLE IS THE WAY YOU PLAY AND A VERY PERSONAL THING. HOW HAVE YOU REACHED YOUR OWN PERSONAL STYLE?

That's a nice quote. I started to feel like I was developing my own style in my early to mid twenties. Your style is your attempt to express the music you love most dearly in an honest fashion, in your own idiosyncratic way. There are a few steps to that process. First, you are a fan of a body of music, you fall in love with it emotionally, and it seeps into your consciousness and is a memory for the rest of your life, informing everything you hear and play. You are unconsciously building a personal canon. Then you imitate examples of that canon, but they are as of yet separate and not distilled, so they don't speak with the authority of your own identity. Then at a certain point, your canon solidifies into a whole, and your voice becomes an amalgamation of the most central musical experiences you've had. I think this notion of distilled experience is important. Being exposed to music, particularly earlier in life, leaves an imprint on your memory that is strong in the same way that other "primary" experiences are: love, loss, pain, sexual, what have you. A raw, emotional experience of music that is powerful indelibly marks your understanding of all other music that follows, including the music you set out to play. When you start to have your own style, it's not so much that you become a new player, but more that you discover who you've truly always been, and are merely able to put an authentic voice to it.

25

MYRA MELFORD

Currently the assistant professor of improvisation and jazz at the University of California–Berkeley, pianist Myra Melford's compositional diversity is influenced by her studies with Don Pullen and Henry Threadgill and by her nine-month residency in Calcutta, India. A complex and dynamic improviser, Melford paints images in sound, melding rhythmic textures with her diverse and virtuosic musical sensibilities.

How would you describe your music to a classroom of students?

Words are clearly not the best way to handle it because words can be misunderstood and people have different points of reference. So if I were not able to play my music for them, I would explain that I have been working on creating my own style and approach to composing and improvising that's been informed by many different kinds of music, including jazz.

My introduction to improvisation was through learning to play the blues in the Chicago style. I studied classical music as a child with Erwin Helfer, a great jazz, blues, and boogie-woogie player. Along with the classical repertoire, which included a lot of Bartok, Kabalevsky, and other twentieth-century music, he would have me imitate or make up my own answers to his phrases while playing over the blues changes. When I began to study jazz in college, I quickly became interested in how improvisation is approached in many of the world's cultures and have been investigating that music ever since. Like many artists working in the genre of creative improvised music, I've been influenced by the diversity of the music I've heard. Maybe not inspired by everything, but I have been able to pick and choose

what is most interesting to me. I think we are living in a time now where everything is available to hear no matter where you live, and we've moved into this period of the globalization of music that, if handled with awareness and respect, is
opening the way for all kinds of interesting cross-pollination or "hybridization."
This of course is nothing new; it's been this way for as long as people and music
have traveled. But with recordings, the travel part isn't even necessary. Though I
found through living and studying Hindustani music in Calcutta, there's something
very powerful about listening to and learning about a particular music while im-
mersing oneself in the culture that produces it.

IS IT PERHAPS POSSIBLE THAT THERE IS TOO MUCH DIVERSITY IN MUSIC FOR THE
LISTENER TODAY?

I wouldn't say that. I think the problem is that for a number of years now, at
least in our society here in the U.S. and to some extent within Europe, the emphasis has been on what sells. And that approach is now also reaching Third World
countries. So we now have the lowest common denominator of accessibility in the
music and people haven't been educated to listen to anything that takes much of
their own attention or input. They want to hear a certain kind of dance music or
certain beat, and most of what they are interested in is pretty banal or violent, depending upon the music. We're at the point where what people heard growing up
was fairly watered-down pop music, and the younger generation today doesn't
have a point of reference for anything more stimulating or more demanding. This
is not to say, however, that there isn't great popular music, but rather that the majority of the population will settle for much less.

I think this is less true in Europe, where people grow up with a broader musical education and enjoy a greater commitment from the government, which sup-
ports a diversity of cultural institutions. Thus, people have a far greater ability to
listen to many kinds of music and learn to appreciate it. The problem we have is
that the more creative or adventurous music is marginalized, except for what's provided on college and public radio stations, which the majority of the population
doesn't listen to. And because of the current economic climate, there's less willingness on the part of the recording industry to take chances on releasing creative
music versus what will sell. But you have to separate what the market can bear and
what people need to do to express themselves and what other people need to hear
to enrich their lives. And taking that into consideration, I don't think that there
could be too much diversity. I think the challenge is to find new ways of using the
current technology to create a different kind of marketplace for the arts. And also,
of course, to get our priorities and values straight, as a global society.

HAVE WE BECOME A SOCIETY WITHOUT THE PATIENCE TO BE CHALLENGED?

I was just having a rehearsal yesterday with some friends and we are all in our
forties now. We came into this music by being inspired by people like Ornette Coleman and the artists in the Association for the Advancement of Creative Musicians,

and we never questioned whether this was the right thing to do or not. We weren't looking at it from the standpoint of "How are we going to make a living?" We looked at it as, "I can't imagine a greater life than trying to develop my artistic vision and my own voice to the greatest extent that I can." People like Ornette inspired me and so enriched my life that I'd like to try and offer that to my world, my community, as well as to future generations. And I don't know how many people are choosing this life for this reason today. There is a lot more thought going into "How am I really going to make a living and what's really hip?" It's so much more about money and an MTV or Hollywood sensibility today. Again, I don't mean to cast a negative slant on the need to be practical and support oneself or to put down the quality of some of the work coming out on MTV and in Hollywood, but rather to question the values and intentions behind how and why music is created.

I would like to think that people from my generation are going to stick with it and keep doing what we set out to do from the beginning, but it's really difficult if you are having trouble making a living or you feel that, "Wow, there is nobody to put out my music right now." In addition to fewer gigs and less pay, how am I going to live and still do this music that I believe in? So we, like the music business, need to adapt to the times as well. And I don't know how many younger generations are going for that sort of purist approach to creative music and how many are being swayed by what's going to sell. So I think it's a little hard to tell right now, but I do think there are some generational differences. And I'd like to think that there is a way to stay committed to what you believe and make music that people want to hear, and there are people who are doing that, and that's what keeps me going.

DOES SOCIETY TODAY HAVE DIFFICULTY WITH CREATIVITY THAT'S NOT EASILY UNDERSTOOD?

So much is driven by the global economy and global politics right now. There are problems with education across the board in this country, certainly when it comes to cuts in funding for arts education and lack of support for cultural institutions that provide necessary education and enrichment. So much emphasis today is on training for a place in the job market, and even in some of the most privileged schools, there are severe cutbacks in these kinds of arts programs. And it takes education to be able to appreciate this music or any kind of art that requires some involvement on the part of the audience, whether intellectual understanding or just patience or the ability to open your ears and eyes and get inside another person's world and imagination. And I think that's what we're lacking as a society, to a great extent. We need the fostering of young people to appreciate this music. And it is a generational thing to the extent that each generation is affected by its economic, political, and cultural milieu. Hopefully things will turn around again. The economy may bounce back in a few years and we may start putting more money into the arts. I believe people want and need music and art that's truly stimulating and challenging and inspiring. Great art stimulates the imagination and opens the way for all kinds of creative solutions to the problems in the world, and it also nourishes the soul.

Is THERE A CHANCE THAT BECAUSE OF THE CURRENT GLOBAL CLIMATE THAT PEO-
PLE COULD FIND A NEW APPRECIATION FOR THOSE THINGS THAT HAVE MORE DEPTH
OR HAVE MORE ARTISTIC AND CREATIVE VALUE?

I think so. Perhaps a greater majority of people will start looking for something
that is more meaningful. I'm of two minds. When people are facing difficult times,
sometimes it creates a certain kind of soul-searching and will lead people to look
for and find answers within art and creativity. But then you can also have the flip
side of that, where people go for a much more superficial, easily digestible entertainment that helps to distract from the problems but doesn't necessarily nurture
or heal. And I suppose it can go either way, and it probably will go both ways at
the same time. It's just a question of what will capture a greater majority of society or the public's imagination.

Do YOU HAVE A PERSONAL PHILOSOPHY THAT YOU TRY TO IMPART TO YOUNG MUSI-
CIANS OR STUDENTS?

I'm a great advocate of trying to speak to and discover one's own truth, and I
think this is the greatest thing that we can offer. It's great to have gifted artists who
offer something to society by doing something very well, but what's really enriching to me is when artists have something original to say. That's what I try to encourage in young people. To recognize, nurture, and offer their own gift and greatness to the world.

IT'S UNFORTUNATE THAT THE NEXT QUESTION IS EVEN A SUBJECT BUT THAT'S THE
REALITY OF IT. AND MAYBE IT APPLIES MORE TO THE MAINSTREAM, BUT WOMEN JAZZ
ARTISTS DON'T SEEM TO GET THE RESPECT AS ARTISTS IN THE SAME WAY THAT MEN
DO. Do WOMEN ARTISTS HAVE TO DEAL WITH THIS ISSUE WITHIN CREATIVE MUSIC?

I do think it's a little different because creative music is really part of a larger alternative or substratum of our society. When people are marginalized, either for
their race, their sex, their class, nationality, religion, or whatever, coupled with
some sort of creative vision, I think you tend to have a more inclusive perspective
on the world, not to say that biases and blindness don't exist, but, largely, I have
found that within the creative music community, there is less sexism and less
racism and there's more of a "let's see what we have in common and what we can
do to help each other, to support each other," rather than trying to defend ourselves or compete against each other.

IN THE BOOK ARCANA PRODUCED BY JOHN ZORN, YOU WROTE A CHAPTER ON THE
IMPORTANCE OF THE INTUITIVE AS WELL AS THE INTELLECTUAL PROCESS, AND I
FOUND WHAT YOU SAID VERY INTRIGUING. YOU SAID, "WHAT'S CRUCIAL IS THE CON-
NECTION BETWEEN THE LANGUAGE OF THE HUMAN HEART AND THE ACT OR PURPOSE
OF CREATION." CAN YOU DESCRIBE IN MORE DETAIL WHAT THAT MEANS TO YOU?

This is something that continues to be a really important motivation for me and
what fuels me to continue to keep developing as an artist. I can be interested in

intellectual concepts and look to the intellect to seek fresh ideas and sounds by ex-
posing myself to other art or by using my intellect to devise sounds and combinations of notes that I may not otherwise conjure up. But if I don't internalize them
and reinterpret them through my heart and make them my own, they remain
meaningless.

When I'm referring to the heart, I'm talking about joining whatever outside influences I'm exposed to into my own essence, down into the deepest part of my self,
and have them then come out of me into the world. Over time, you start touching
on infinity so there is really no end to that process. It's just going deeper and deeper
and accessing a more profound heart of myself that I think is in everybody. When
I can come from that, then it's touching that in other people. To me, that's the greatest thing that art can do. It brings us back to our own truth, our own selves.

YOU ALSO MENTIONED THAT YOU EXPLORED FREE AND STRUCTURED IMPROVISA-
TIONS, EXPERIMENTING WITH DIFFERENT FRAMEWORKS AND TRYING TO CREATE AN
INVISIBLE SEAM BETWEEN WHAT WAS NOTATED AND IMPROVISED. CAN YOU EXPLAIN
FURTHER?

It's looking at the basic building blocks, the materials of music, and finding new
ways of assembling the basic elements of texture, tone quality, rhythm, melody,
harmony, and so on. Being an improviser, I'm developing the capacity to be able
to compose something on the spot as opposed to taking time to rework something
and perform it. There are two ways of exploring something. There's the spontaneous exploration of an idea and there's applying intellect and looking at all the
permutations and figuring out what I can do with this material to develop it when
I look at it over time rather than in the moment. Once I have these two different
perspectives and have this development of material, then I look at how I can create a spontaneous, or very alive, immediate experience of this material that draws
on both. It draws on the written material and the intellectual processes (or homework), but makes it immediate and this is what I'm trying to do.

WHEN YOU COMPOSE, DO YOU ENVISION WHAT YOU WANT THE MUSIC TO DO FOR
THE LISTENER?

I want the listener to experience something wonderful within themselves. To
connect with a sense of well-being, a sense of peace or a wave of love, some insight,
or just to be comforted or inspired. That's what I'm looking for, and it's not so much
that I have a vision for the sound itself because that becomes secondary. The first
thing I want is for someone to experience themselves. Therefore, my understanding is that I have to experience "that" myself while I'm creating—to touch into that
energy and bring it out into the open—creating that space with music and with
sound so that other people can have that experience. How I do that becomes the
next level. What materials, what sounds, what instruments, what energy, and so on.

WHAT INSPIRES YOU?

People who tap into "that," who play or create from that connection to the heart. It doesn't matter what style or how simple or complex an outward form it takes. No matter how simple something appears, if it comes from the heart, it has some kind of complexity and a depth belying its simplicity, it's anything but superficial. And likewise, a work of art that takes the highest level of intellect and intelligence to create can also have that ability to communicate from the heart, if that's the intention of the creator. Additionally, there is my own search for truth that is probably the biggest thing that underlies how I gather inspiration from the mystic poets like Rumi, the Hindu saints, or the great Zen masters. All of that inspires me. Because, as much as I feel as though I have to create music, that's secondary to feeling that I have to find the way into that which gives meaning to being alive.

YOU HAVE WORKED WITH A DIVERSITY OF MUSICIANS. WHAT HAVE YOU LEARNED FROM THOSE EXPERIENCES?

I have learned something from everyone I have worked with. More from some than others, but I'm certainly open to the possibility that I can learn from anyone that I work with. I learn a tremendous amount from my students. Teaching music is an interesting thing because so much of my own development has been largely self-directed. I didn't undergo a standard musical education, in the conventional sense. I put together my own program at Evergreen State College in Olympia, Washington, and spent a year at Cornish College of the Arts in Seattle. I considered going to the New England Conservatory in Boston, but I eventually decided that the artists I was most interested in were in New York and thought I might as well go there and study with them rather than stay in school. I went on to work, study, and then perform with a lot of people that I have admired such as Butch Morris, Henry Threadgill, Leroy Jenkins, and Joseph Jarman. And, of course, I learned from the members of my own ensembles. I'm trying to bring this same awareness and approach into my classroom at the university, to encourage an environment where everyone can learn from each other, no matter what level they've reached.

DO YOU MIND DISCUSSING WHAT HAVE YOU LEARNED FROM THE RISKS THAT YOU HAVE HAD TO TAKE?

I just want to preface this by saying that I never really felt I had a choice about what to do with my life. As much as I would have liked to do something other than music at times, I just couldn't. What I'm getting at is that I didn't see choosing music as my career as "taking a risk," but I can look back at it this way. On the one hand, I was so clear and had such drive and need on a soul level to do what I'm doing that I didn't even consider the financial implications of the choices I was making. I also didn't consider making "more commercial" music, which came up over and over again, because it just never seemed to be a compelling reason to do music to me.

So I really didn't have any choice, as my task seems to be to grapple with life through the pursuit of music. I could say that music is a form of yoga for me in that way. To create music that was really meaningful to me.

I guess you could say I took a risk but I didn't see it that way. On the other hand, I do take risks all the time by getting up to play music for an audience that's still "in progress." And I also experiment with new things, knowing the audience may be waiting to hear what I did that last time they heard me. Those are the kinds of risks that I am conscious of taking because that's what I need to do to grow as a musician. And certainly I take the risk of doing what feels right to me, rather than trying to second guess what other people will like, though I do hope they'll get something positive from my music.

DO YOU HAVE A PHILOSOPHY OR SOME WAY OF LOOKING AT LIFE THAT YOU WOULD BE WILLING TO SHARE? I HAVE A FEELING IT'S THE SAME WAY THAT YOU LOOK AT MUSIC.

Exactly, exactly. There is no difference, no separation from what I'm trying to do with my music and what I feel is the greatest thing I can go for in this lifetime, which, as I said, is to realize who I really am and to be able to be fully present in the moment. That's what improvisation in music is all about—being fully present in the present moment, and to experience the love that I have within myself and share that, rather than all the other crazy stuff that is going on in the world today. Music is my path to the truth I'm looking for, and I'm very fortunate to have that. I really am.

26

PAT METHENY

There may not be another contemporary composer whose music better reflects the time in which we live, yet remains so misunderstood. Imitators may have watered and smoothed down his rich, complex, and innovative art form, but the creative genius of Pat Metheny lies deep beneath the surface, a place of heartfelt passion and beauty, of melodic depth and spirit.

But that's not all that is important about Metheny. He is a humanitarian and a significant supporter of the arts and once refused to do a feature story for a jazz magazine until they had published a cover story on an African American musician. His understanding of the creative process is extraordinary, and though he is one of the few musicians that can be identified with a specific sound, his explorations as an artist are without boundaries. As is the case with most forward-thinking work, it may be years before the essence of his art form is fully understood.

OUR CULTURE TODAY APPRECIATES ART BUT SEEMS TO HAVE DIFFICULTY WITH CREATIVITY THAT IS NOT EASILY EXPLAINED, UNDERSTOOD, OR IDENTIFIABLE. HAVE WE BECOME A SOCIETY WITHOUT THE PATIENCE TO BE CHALLENGED, OPEN ONLY TO THINGS THAT ARE EASILY ACCESSIBLE?

As much as I am concerned with the general downward spiral of culture that we all seem to be aware of and experiencing at the moment, I also think it is important to remember that there probably never has been a true "golden era" where everyone everywhere was hip to the best stuff that was available to them. I think throughout history the very best in art was most likely appreciated by a minority of the general population, either because of limitations forced by economic access or because of general lack of interest resulting from limited educational opportunities. My feeling is that we are still at a fairly early stage in our evolution. It may be hundreds of years before we reach a point where everyone has the kind of listening skills to really appreciate the level of music and art represented by a musician at the level of Johann Sebastian Bach or John Coltrane or Charlie Parker. But the value of their music exists regardless of the cultural context that it is perceived in—that is really important to remember.

WITH ALL THE INFORMATION AVAILABLE TODAY, CULTURAL MUSIC INFLUENCES ARE BECOMING MORE VISIBLE IN JAZZ COMPOSITION. ARE WE HAVING A DIFFICULT TIME ACCEPTING THAT A MUSIC FORM CONSIDERED "AMERICAN" NOW HAS INTERNATIONAL AND DIVERSE ASPECTS WITHIN IT?

To me, I have always had some misgivings about the whole idea of emphasizing the Americanness of jazz to the point of exclusivity. While, as Americans, we should be proud of its heritage as a key component of American culture, the nationalistic celebration of it being something that *must* represent its American roots can also limit the incredible implications of what the form offers, and therefore in fact somewhat diminishes its glory. To me, the form demands a kind of deep representation of each individual's personal reality. One of the many things that makes jazz unique is how well suited it is to absorb material and styles and infinite shades of human achievement so well.

THERE ALSO APPEARS TO BE A YOUNGER CROWD, OPEN TO BEING CHALLENGED AND CHECKING OUT NEW MUSIC TODAY. COULD IT BE THAT WE ARE AT A CULTURAL LOW POINT AND PEOPLE ARE STARTING TO LOOK FOR THINGS THAT HAVE MORE DEPTH OR CREATIVE AND ARTISTIC VALUE?

Young people seem to be especially well suited to explore. I really believe that there is a period in most musicians' lives where they grow at a much faster rate, and I think that that is true of listeners too. It doesn't have to be when you are young, but it often is. I think throughout history you would find a large youth movement interested and surrounding the development of the best stuff in jazz.

IF SOCIETAL EVENTS CAN INFLUENCE THE CREATIVE PROCESS, IS IT POSSIBLE THAT A NEW TYPE OF CREATIVITY MIGHT COME OUT OF THE STRIFE AND TURMOIL HAPPENING IN THE WORLD TODAY, AND DOES IT AFFECT YOU AND YOUR WORK?

Everything that happens around you affects you as a musician. However, it may not happen in an overt way. For myself, I often think of the whole thing of being an improvising musician as being kind of like a reporter—you talk about the things that are going on inside and around you. But I think each person's response to the events of their time are very personal and unique. One of the great things about jazz, and in fact any kind of instrumental music, is the poetry that it offers. There are ways of discussing things in the syntax of sound that just cannot be expressed any other way.

MANY MUSICIANS HAVE TALKED ABOUT HOW 9/11 AFFECTED THEM WHEN IT HAP-
PENED. SOME WERE NOT ABLE TO DO ANYTHING CREATIVE FOR MONTHS, YET, FOR
OTHERS, GETTING BACK TO MUSIC WAS THE ONLY WAY TO MOVE FORWARD. WHAT IM-
PACT DID IT HAVE ON YOU PERSONALLY AND AS AN ARTIST?

Since I live in New York, it was a local thing for me. We all had direct contact
with the event one way or another. I made a record around that time called *One
Quiet Night* that was a solo guitar record. I actually didn't even realize I was making the record; it was just kind of personal playing. I can't say for sure that it was
in response to the events, but somewhere there seemed some connections.

YOU HAVE HAD THE OPPORTUNITY TO TRAVEL VERY EXTENSIVELY AND ALSO LIVE
AND EXPERIENCE LIFE OUTSIDE THE U.S. ARE WE CLOSING THE GAP BETWEEN OUR
DIFFERENT CULTURES AND WHAT IT WILL TAKE TO BRING US CLOSER TOGETHER, OR
COULD THAT ALSO CLOUD OUR DIFFERENCES IN WAYS THAT WILL NOT NECESSARILY
APPRECIATE OUR CULTURAL DIFFERENCES?

This is the biggest cliché in the world, but thirty-some years of touring around
the world has really proven this to me—people are really much more alike everywhere than they are different. People are naturally proud of their own heritage
and the things that make them unique. But, personally I am much more interested
in the ways that everywhere you go, there are so many things going on that are exactly the same between people, and especially the way they listen to music. That
ultimately gives me a lot of hope.

DOES THE FORWARD-THINKING ARTIST HAVE A UNIQUE ABILITY OR AWARENESS OF
WHAT SURROUNDS THEM AND IS THERE A RESPONSIBILITY WITH THAT AWARENESS?

I think a good refrigerator repairman has an awareness of things that you or I
can scarcely imagine. Same with a little kid. Everyone has a sense of things going
on around them that they filter through their needs and desires at that point in
their life. I can only speak for myself as a musician, and for me, as my awareness
of musical things has increased, it has enhanced my perception of every other
thing in my life. And gladly, I can say vice versa. Somehow it all goes together.

YOU HAVE SPOKEN ABOUT THE POSITIVE INFLUENCE MUSIC HAS ON YOUNG CHILDREN,
AND THERE ARE MORE STUDIES THAT HAVE SUPPORTED THIS ANALOGY. WHAT DO YOU
KNOW ABOUT IT AND WHAT IS IT ABOUT MUSIC THAT PROVIDES THIS LIFE AND ENERGY?

I think music occupies a unique spot in humanity. It is unlike anything else, and
therefore difficult to measure. But I think somewhere in almost everyone, music
is kind of a necessity. I have often thought of music as a kind of vapor that occupies that same frequency of human response as those other unquantifiables that
we all seem to need—love and faith.

ONE OF THE PROBLEMS WITH DOCUMENTATION FOCUSING ON JAZZ, SUCH AS KEN
BURNS'S SERIES, IS THAT IT SPENDS MOST OF ITS TIME CONCENTRATING ON WHAT JAZZ

CREATED IN THE PAST TENSE AND LITTLE ON WHAT THE MUSIC IS CREATING AT THE MOMENT, WHICH IS THE ESSENCE OF THIS GREAT MUSIC WE CALL JAZZ. DOESN'T THIS SEEM SHORTSIGHTED, PERHAPS A LOST OPPORTUNITY TO EDUCATE POTENTIAL ASPIR- ING JAZZ STUDENTS AND EDUCATE PEOPLE TO WHAT JAZZ IS REALLY ABOUT AND WHAT IS AVAILABLE TO THEM?

Jazz is such an infinitely interesting topic that there would be dozens of ways to describe it in the form of a documentary film. "Lost opportunity" would be an apt description in this case.

CECIL TAYLOR SAID THAT "MUSIC HAS TO DO WITH A LOT OF AREAS WHICH ARE MAGICAL RATHER THAN LOGICAL; THE GREAT ARTISTS, RATHER THAN JUST GETTING INVOLVED WITH DISCIPLINE, GET TO UNDERSTAND LOVE AND ALLOW THE LOVE TO TAKE SHAPE." HOW MUCH OF YOUR MUSIC IS FROM LOGIC AND HOW MUCH FROM THIS OTHER PLACE THAT CECIL TAYLOR DESCRIBES?

I love his description. The "magic" factor, the qualities that are unquantifiable are the most interesting and least discussed when it comes to jazz. But I feel that, in fact, those qualities are largely intangible and there is a reason why they resist textual or verbal contexts, a reason why so much writing about jazz is so superflu- ous. The mystery of the process itself remains one of its great appeals.

I THINK THAT COMPOSING IS ONE OF YOUR GREATEST STRENGTHS, BUT IMPROVISA- TION SEEMS A CRITICAL ASPECT OF THE DYNAMIC THAT BRINGS TOGETHER THE RE- LATIONSHIP OF YOUR COMPOSITIONS AND THE EMOTIONAL INVOLVEMENT OF THOSE YOU COLLABORATE WITH TOGETHER. CAN YOU DISCUSS YOUR APPROACH OF BRING- ING THESE ASPECTS TOGETHER?

They are similar tasks that happen at wildly different temperatures. The heat of the moment causes a result that differs from the coolness of time to consider. How- ever, they feed each other and seem to bask in the relief that one offers another. The performance aspect, whether as an improviser or when playing the written parts of the music, is so largely affected by the audience and the general environ- ment of it all that you can't separate that from the equation either. All in all, the whole idea is to tell a story—to form a narrative and to try to offer something to others that you yourself have found to be true or meaningful or even just that you think it sounds good. The skills that come with learning about improvising greatly enhance the composition process for me, and the inverse is also the case.

IT APPEARS THAT TIME, SPACE, AND INTENSITY ARE SIGNIFICANT ELEMENTS THAT MAKE UP YOUR COMPOSITIONAL FORM AND ARE ALWAYS CONSIDERED WITHIN YOUR OWN PERSONAL VOCABULARY WITHIN THE GROUP COMPOSITIONS. CAN YOU EXPLAIN HOW THESE ASPECTS ARE DEVELOPED?

I have often talked about how I thought the geography of where I grew up af- fected me aesthetically. There was a lot of space out there—you could really see things far away, and see things from a distance in perspective with each other. But I left the Midwest when I was eighteen and have lived in fairly intense urban settings ever since. But that reserve of quiet is always there for me—that first eighteen years in Lee's Summit, Mo., really added up to a base for me that I feel that everything else came out of. I think as I have learned more about music and how it works over the years, I naturally gravitated at different periods towards different ways of deploying things. There have been periods where I have very intentionally played lots and lots of notes, and others where it has been quite sparse and full of space. I like to be able to invent a way of playing or writing that seems to be appropriate and resonant (for me) in each setting, something that seems to reflect where I am at that particular moment.

CAN YOU DISCUSS YOUR PERSONAL RELATIONSHIP WITH TIME?

Well, time . . . that is a big one, maybe the main one. To me, the way each musician ultimately sounds is about how they perceive time and how well they are able to listen and live within the time. And I mean that on the most micro level and the most macro level. To play great swing time with a rhythm section is still a rare quality that within jazz is only achieved by the very best players. But then, if that feeling of time is not informed by the spirit of the larger sense of time (the things that make 2005 different from 1958), the feeling of it is noticeably less compelling somehow. To me, when I think of someone like Roy Haynes—his "time" is his own. He owns it, every nanosecond of it. And he can offer it in connection with a personal history that gives it weight, or he can offer as a human being that is equally conversant and interested in the things that make *this* moment in time unique. That would be the model for me, to be able to render the sound of time in a way that reminds everyone just how precious—and vital—it all is.

MILES DAVIS HAS SAID THAT "THE RIGHT NOTES CAN FERTILIZE THE SOUND OF A COMPOSITION THAT IT CAN MAKE THE SOUND GROW; MUCH LIKE ADDING LEMON TO FISH OR VEGETABLES THAT BRING OUT THE FLAVOR. THAT IT'S YOUR SWEAT." YOU WORK A LOT WITH DENSITY WHILE ADDING VARIOUS COLORS AND TEXTURES TO YOUR GROUP COMPOSITIONS. CAN YOU DESCRIBE THAT PROCESS OR WHAT YOU ARE ATTEMPTING TO DO WITHIN THE CONTEXT OF THE MUSIC?

Another great quote. I think that we all become musicians because we love music. For me, I try to follow that love in a very devoted and serious way. The stuff I really love becomes potential for me. Why do I love *that*? What is it that I love about *that*? Those questions, as a fan, mean one thing—but the thing that separates musicians from being fans is that I feel that we all naturally want to play the things we love. Involved in that learning process is, in fact, an enormous amount of sweat. That sweat represents *you*—your spirit, your soul, all the things that make you unique. The mix of a musician with a sound that they love, that they are pursuing and aspiring to, is a recipe for a certain kind of intensity. When this intensity gets applied to a spontaneous act such as improvisation, in the right hands, with the right material and the right kindred spirits, the result can be basically the highest level of human achievement manifest (i.e., the Coltrane quartet, the Miles quintet of the '60s). The goal for me would be to try to manifest into sound the things that I love, the things that I have found to be worthwhile and valuable through a lifetime of pursuit of this stuff.

A NUMBER OF YEARS AGO, YOU SPOKE ABOUT HEARING A SOUND THAT YOU WERE TRYING TO REACH BUT THAT IT KEPT MOVING AWAY AS YOU GOT CLOSER. ARE YOU FI-NALLY GETTING ANY CLOSER TO THAT SOUND AND ARE YOU ABLE TO ENJOY YOUR ARTISTIC ACCOMPLISHMENTS?

It is way more fun for me now than when I first started. When I first started making records, I had only been playing for a few years. Now, with lots more experience, I am able to much more faithfully reproduce the ideas in my head directly through the instrument or the pen. There is a real pleasure in that growth that I do appreciate. However, music is really hard. And everything you learn does in fact open up vistas of previously unseen possibility. But that is a big part of what makes it such a fascinating and rewarding zone to devote one's life to. As far as enjoying my own artistic accomplishments, I am one of those guys who always wishes it had been better. I am naturally pretty critical, but not in a negative way. I always just think I could have done better. Actually, I think we all could almost always do better! So, so far I have never had the luxury of basking in any sense of accomplishment; I am always working on trying to make the next thing better if I could.

YOUR MUSICAL DIRECTION HAS BEEN TREMENDOUSLY DIVERSE. WHEN YOU FIRST REALIZED THAT YOU WANTED TO CREATE MUSICALLY, WAS YOUR VISION AND MUSICAL PHILOSOPHY AS DIVERSE AS WHAT YOUR WORK HAS BECOME? HOW HAS IT CHANGED?

Pretty early on I had a strong sense of what kinds of things I wanted to do. It seemed to me that that there were huge areas that I was interested in that were fertile zones for study and research. The "diversity" of it is something that gets talked about a lot, but for me it is all of a piece. It is all music that I love and feel close to. I have always just wanted to represent myself honestly as a musician. To edit out huge areas of interest in the name of stylistic "purity" (an impossibility anyway when it comes to jazz) would have not be a good course for me, since musical honestly is at the top of the list for me as a fan and hopefully as a player. As time has gone on, there are some things that have changed, but mostly the general approach to it all has remained constant. The main difference is that I can get to much more stuff more consistently now than I could when I first started out.

JAZZ CAN REQUIRE MUSICIANS TO TAKE A NUMBER OF RISKS IN THEIR CAREERS AND YOU HAVE TAKEN MANY. WHAT HAVE YOU LEARNED ABOUT BOTH MUSIC AND YOURSELF?

Risk taking is at the core of it all. And those risks may be subtle ones that fall well below the radar of other people's perceptions or they may be overt career ones like what you are talking about. For me, I have always been pretty stubborn about wanting to sound a certain way and play a certain way that would allow me access to the maximum amount of stuff that I love about music in general. It is hard to see such a rather inclusive view of music as being that risky or radical, but in fact the general urge to dismantle the stratifications that rule the status quo ultimately do bear out to be controversial at the minimum to some folks, outright blasphemous to others. What I have learned is that all you really know is what you love—and that can be the only compass that one should use to guide oneself. As soon as you give the aesthetic reins of power to an audience, other musicians, a critic, the guy sitting in the third row, your girlfriend, your boss—you have crossed a line that is difficult to recover from. This is not to say that you remain stubborn and isolated in your "vision" because your vision has to be pliable and malleable to the reality of the conditions that you are actively participating in at a given moment (i.e., it always sounds crappy to quote "Donna Lee" on a country and western gig that you may be doing to pay the rent). To me, the goal would be to render an honest musical response the opportunities that each moment in sound offers that is effective at making that music sound the best that it possibly can sound. Is there a risk in that? Yes, in the reconciliation of your own personal aesthetic with the specific realities of what is actually going on right then on the bandstand around you. The risk is *always* there, along with the opportunities.

DO YOU HAVE A COMMON PHILOSOPHY THAT YOU TRY TO IMPART AMONG STUDENTS OR YOUNG MUSICIANS?

Yes, to be yourself.

WHAT IS IT ABOUT JAZZ AND THE ART FORM THAT IS IMPORTANT TO YOU?

It is one of the greatest aesthetic inventions of all time for its inclusiveness. It is a form that asks each participant to bring the qualities to the table that makes them unique. I would be on the left wing of jazz that would use the widest possible umbrella to embrace all of the different subsets of players that would like to find a common ground under the jazz banner. And to me, this is one of jazz's greatest assets, and it has always been a puzzle to me to see the enormous efforts made to keep people out and to constantly form new definitions (that always place the definer themselves at the center of the universe of their own definition of it) that become less inviting to not only players but listeners as well.

YOU HAVE THE REPUTATION OF BEING ONE OF THE HARDEST-DRIVING ARTISTS TODAY WITH MORE PROJECTS GOING ON AT ANY GIVEN TIME THAN MOST ARTISTS TARGET IN A GIVEN YEAR. WHAT DRIVES YOU?

I love music and I love working on music. Every second that I get to spend practicing or writing or playing is really like a gift to me. I feel that the thing of getting to go around and play gigs and play with great musicians is an incredible privilege. I feel incredibly lucky to have led the life that I have been able to lead.

HAS YOUR LIFE IN JAZZ SO FAR BEEN EVERYTHING THAT YOU THOUGHT IT WOULD BE?

Maybe ten thousand times more. I never dreamed that learning about and understanding music would offer the kinds of insights into so many other areas.

DO YOU HAVE A PHILOSOPHY OR SOME WAY OF LOOKING AT LIFE THAT YOU WOULD BE WILLING TO SHARE?

There was a line from a small film that I worked on a few years ago that I thought really summed it up: "It is always worth the trouble." Whatever you offer, if you make it the best you have, you will always get some great stuff in return, even if it takes a while. I always try to make each moment, each encounter, each gig, each meeting with someone, special—because this is it. It is not in preparation for something else. Use the time you have to do something you love.

27

JASON MORAN

With maturity and wisdom beyond his years, pianist Jason Moran ingeniously explores complex rhythmic shapes and colors of every genre while never compromising his musical personality and artistic vision.

I ADMIRE YOUR FEARLESSNESS IN INCORPORATING ALL OF YOUR MUSICAL INFLU-
ENCES AND DOING IT WITH CONVICTION. WHERE DID YOU GET YOUR CONFIDENCE?

My parents are very confident people and they instilled that into my two brothers and myself. And they never denied us anything so we never had to seek out things from the street, from neighbors, or from strangers. We were also very content to be at home with each other, and with that kind of upbringing, you can take it for granted, but as you get older, you begin to recognize what kind of effect your parents can have on you. So I have come to realize that all of my blessings have come by way of my parents. They really took care of me and then threw me out into the world so that I could go on to swim.

MY BROTHER RECENTLY DEALT WITH LEUKEMIA AND I JUST LEARNED THAT YOUR
MOTHER RECENTLY PASSED AWAY FROM THE SAME DISEASE. DO YOU MIND SPEAKING
ABOUT HER INFLUENCE?

People who are brave enough to deal with cancer always put things in perspective.
My appreciation for the performing and fine arts came from the house. And all of the music from the most recent CD was recorded after a visit to see my mother in Houston, and I had also never recorded a CD in the way in which this one was

done. Additionally, *Same Mother* was supposed to be very to the point, which is how my family and the people of Houston are. There is something very blunt about music and about musicians, whether they are singing in prisons or in the church choir. It's a blunt expression that blues, gospel, and jazz has given African Americans and it can't be taken lightly because it's one of the outlets where you can really tell your own story.

So the music took on an entirely different character. There were pieces that were written in a totally different style that required a demand from the musicians in an unobvious way. It was stripped down to get to the roots and not be ashamed to express that.

CAN YOU EXPLAIN HOW GROWING UP AS A BLACK OR AFRICAN AMERICAN IN OUR SOCIETY HAS INFLUENCED YOUR MUSIC?

I think that every person, no matter who they are, has struggled; whether it's with their culture, their family, or their health. Everybody is faced with equal amounts of stress. I think that most of the time, people take everything for granted and they take their health for granted. So with respect to being a person of color, you really find out a lot about stereotypes and what happens to you when you go to Berlin, Istanbul, or Ireland. They are all different experiences within themselves.

But in America, most black people have stories of experiencing blatant racism. You see it when you turn on the television or read the paper and you see it when you walk out of your house. Most musicians and most African Americans that I come into contact with speak about race just as much as what they are going to eat for dinner. It's a subject that is still at the forefront of a lot of our minds, especially in the arts.

But no one has it worse that anyone else, and it's just a sad fact of life that you have to deal with it in America. But through the music, I have always felt that in order to express, you just have to deal with yourself as much as you possibly can.

HOW MUCH OF YOUR MUSIC IS FROM EXPERIMENTATION?

Hopefully every night that I perform is experimentation to some degree. Sometimes we know that that's not the case, but there is a fair degree of experimentation that happens onstage that no one else knows about except for maybe my wife, and things have to make it past her before they make it to the stage. She's an extremely tough critic, extremely tough. So whatever I intend to do has to be fairly raw before it reaches the other band members, and that's part of the process.

I also don't consider anything that I play original because I know where it all came from. I know that if I play this certain thing, that that's Jaki Byard or this is Herbie Nichols, Andrew Hill, Art Tatum, Earl Hines, or Willie "the Lion" Smith. Those thoughts are going through my mind when I perform, and that's really a part of what Jaki Byard was about and what he was teaching when I was studying with him. He had a way of tricking you into learning a bunch of traditional stuff while mixing a lot of elements that would not usually be considered appropriate for bebop, straight ahead, or stride piano, and from that, you would come up with a new mixture.

BUT YOU SEEM TO KNOW EXACTLY WHAT YOU WANT TO DO.

Oh, it's very definitely precise, but I wish I were more precise. I'm struggling right now with not being clear enough with my musical intentions. I want to get rid of some of the vague areas of my playing and my presentation of music onstage. I'm striving for preciseness.

BUT DOESN'T BEING TOO PRECISE LIMIT YOUR VIEW?

I've been researching this conceptual artist, Adrian Piper, who works with gender/racial issues in her artwork, and when I saw her exhibition, it was so direct that it punctured my soul. I had never seen anything so direct in my life. The experience of walking through her retrospective just shattered all of my thoughts about music and chord changes, so I'm currently on this road to try and be clearer with my message. I think *Same Mother* is a step in that direction.

HAVE WE BECOME A SOCIETY WITHOUT THE PATIENCE TO BE CHALLENGED?

I don't think we could be further from art as a society, but art has rarely been highly respected or extremely popular; at least not during my lifetime. It definitely breeds a different kind of person but I don't think it's a fault or a gift. Countries in Europe have a rich history, but America's history is shorter and forming an identity is going to take some time. Jazz is a young music and hip-hop is even younger. We are on our way! (Laughs.)

IS THERE A CORRELATION BETWEEN HIP-HOP AND JAZZ?

Well, early hip-hop songs sampled Art Blakey, Horace Silver, Wayne Henderson, and Wayne Shorter. So for me, it's that simple but that's the music that I grew up with. So when I hear Wu-Tang, I recognize Thelonious Monk and Duke Ellington. I think that some of it is still based on jazz, but as a music that is a vital expression of culture, it couldn't be more parallel with jazz. It's an expression of mostly urban African Americans, which was the same for jazz. Musicians get together and talk and learn more about harmony and learn how to put it all together and then you get movement and that's what's happening now.

ARE WE AT A CULTURAL LOW POINT WHERE PEOPLE ARE STARTING TO LOOK FOR THINGS THAT HAVE MORE DEPTH OR CREATIVE AND ARTISTIC VALUE?

Maybe, but I don't consider the world at a low point because I think the world has always been at a pretty ignorant level. But on the flip side is all the positive aspects of life that are either ignored or taken for granted. There has always been death and destruction all around the world, all of the time. There has never been a utopian earth, so I don't think we are at a low point. When you don't have a farm or supermarket to go to for food, that's a low point.

JUST HOW INFLUENTIAL IS THE MEDIA?

It's a dominant factor around the world, and I think the younger people are checking out different music because there is a lot happening in other forms of music. There are a lot of younger jazz musicians such as my friend Tarus Mateen who played on Lauren Hill and Christine Aguilera's latest records and has played with a lot of hip-hop groups. Right now in my age range, there is a lot of back and forth between hip-hop, R&B, and jazz.

I also think there is a rebirth of bands using instruments onstage, where it wasn't such a big thing in the late '80s and '90s. You saw musicians backing up singers, but now people are playing instruments again and playing them in front of the MTV crowd. And I think that has a lot to do with younger people coming out to the clubs and is influencing a lot of younger musicians to study music. Columbia now requires every student that enters its grounds to study jazz history for two weeks.

So as a whole, the music may be getting a bit more respect and a bit more exposure to a certain age group. And younger musicians like myself try to make sure younger people know who these musicians are because those are your friends and you want your friends to come and see you play. (Laughs.)

ARE THE GLOBAL EVENTS HAPPENING TODAY HAVING AN EFFECT ON YOU?

In the real global sense, no. In the immediate sense of living uptown, next to the projects and witnessing that world as a global subculture of America, yes. It's very informative of the music I'm playing. But outside of my immediate world, I would have to say no. I may use certain influences but it may be more subconscious.

If you travel and take your part of the world with you, whether that's Texas or Harlem, people are usually blown away by it. It's like going to a baseball game. You watch it on TV, which is one thing, but you have to deal with commercials, whereas you can go to Yankee Stadium and sit in the outfield for eight dollars and the guy that is yelling next to you might actually be more interesting than the game itself.

The audience experience is usually greatly affected by the music they hear in that one hour span of time or however long it is. And what they hear and see along with the interaction they may have with us after or before a concert can open their minds.

It used to be that if you were from Texas, people assumed that you must be a cowboy. But today, they may assume that you like George Bush. You know, just letting people know that there are other people in Texas besides him has been great! (Laughs.)

ARE WE BEGINNING TO CLOSE THE GAP BETWEEN OUR CULTURAL DIFFERENCES?

I think we are, but I live in New York so my perception is way off. You end up mingling with a wide variety of people, whereas growing up in Houston, there were a lot of different ethnic groups, Indian, Mexican, Vietnamese, and Chinese but everybody was really separated from each other. We didn't go to Indian or Vietnamese restaurants until I got to New York. So there are really basic things about examining other people's cultures that wasn't the average part of your day in Texas. You didn't go to the city and try to mix in with everyone else. So New York throws me way off, but you can tell when people have never seen a black person before. You can just tell. When you are in Italy and a little kid that is eight or nine years old runs up to the stage and says, "You, you have a big dick, big dick." (Laughs.) You know, we have a long way to go.

DOES THE FORWARD-THINKING ARTIST HAVE A UNIQUE AWARENESS LEVEL OF WHAT SURROUNDS THEM?

Not all artists are created equal so I think it depends on the artist, and I think the people that we end up noticing are the exceptions. Like talking to Henry Threadgill about being in the war in Vietnam and what he created after the war. His awareness of the events of the world is perhaps at a different level and he has experienced a lot in his life.

But there are so many artists who are not yet publicized. Legions and legions of classical piano players that are not playing Carnegie Hall, and if I was to think of us as a population, then there would be few soothsayers amongst us. But like you said, you really get to understand yourself and maybe get more in tune with it because hopefully, you get to spend more time with yourself. Your art form makes your living for you. But I wouldn't say that we are any higher or privileged people, I think that everybody is privileged. There are those people who are very in tune with the world and those who are not.

DO YOU THINK IT'S MORE DIFFICULT FOR A STUDENT TO BE CREATIVE IN TODAY'S SOCIETY?

No, because people have garage bands—you play in your garage! (Laughs.) What more creation or inspiration do you need? I think the media has distributed the idea in America that you need to be rich and pretty at twenty-two, and that's a problem.

Even when I was in college, I was asking Jaki Byard, "Well, how can I get a record; what should I be doing?" And Jaki said, "You should be practicing and that's all you should be worried about." And I was like, "Well, there's the answer." He said that I needed to practice and that if I did, everything else would fall into place.

So I remember telling other young musicians who had questions about getting gigs, "What's the use of getting any gigs if you don't have anything to play? You're just going to get fired!" (Laughs.)

I think it's up to everybody to just use their outlets, and most people just don't realize all the outlets that are available to them. If people understood, they wouldn't be so disgruntled with not having a place to play. Sam Rivers had his own loft and then made that a performance space. It's mind over matter. "This is what I want to do; now how can I get it done."

DO YOU HAVE A COMMON PHILOSOPHY THAT YOU PASS ON TO MUSIC STUDENTS?

To always remember yourself because it's just too easy to get wrapped up into John Coltrane. It's a great world to be wrapped up in, but at a certain point you have to remember who you are. I think that that's one of the more important aspects to learn, perhaps the most important one.

IS IT ALSO ABOUT BEING HONEST WITH YOURSELF?

Hopefully, but you can lie yourself to death. I know I have a spending problem on things I think I "need" to have. It's not gambling or drugs, but just those things I think I need to have. I have to have that chair, that piece of art is supposed to come home with me. So I can lie to myself that I don't have a problem, but then here is the real one. I don't practice enough! I can lie to myself until the mood behooves me and then I'll sit at the instrument and finally play something.

IN AN INTERVIEW WITH TIM BERNE, HE MENTIONED THAT HE THOUGHT THERE WAS A POSSIBILITY THAT MILES ONLY PRACTICED IN ORDER TO GET TO THE LEVEL OF PLAYING HE NEEDED TO BE AT IN ORDER TO PLAY HIS COMPOSITIONS. COULD THAT BE YOUR SITUATION AS WELL?

That would make sense and could be true, that could be true. But I don't think I have enough experience in my playing to really sit back and examine it. I'm anxious for that time when enough time has gone by and I can look at it, but then again, maybe someone else should do that because maybe I'll still hear the same shit.

But as far as practicing, I think that after most musicians get to a certain level, they stop practicing but try to improve on certain aspects that they know they lack in, myself included. And there are people who are upstanding citizens of the music like Sam Rivers, Muhal Richard Abrhams, Steve Coleman, Greg Osby, and Henry Threadgill to name a few. I mean, they really push themselves and continue to up their own ante. They are betting themselves when they step on the stage that they can outdo what they did last night, and that's inspirational.

WHAT EXACTLY HAS JAKI BYARD MEANT TO YOU?

I moved to New York when I was eighteen for the specific reason of studying with Jaki. He was teaching at the Manhattan School of Music and I had been listening to all these Mingus and Eric Dolphy recordings and heard something on piano that I really wasn't expecting to hear. And I knew that this was the person that I had to study with, and making that decision to move to New York from Houston is scary because it's such a culture shock. You see black people who you thought might be in your family speaking Spanish and it just throws everything off. You just cannot take anything for granted in any person that you see.

I had lessons with Jaki once a week and listened to him play and tell stories; he was like my guardian who I could tell all of my problems to. The very first time that I walked into a lesson, there were two pianos side by side and we played duo. And he was like, "Damn, you play too loud! This is not a Herbie Hancock and Chick Corea record." So I never played loud again. Jaki is one of those people where you better grasp what you went over during the lesson the first time, because he would not let you live it down if you messed up again.

I couldn't have asked for a better experience as a student, and I studied with him for four straight years. He was a grandfather figure that taught me his music and told me things about stride playing and the use of the left hand; how to touch the piano, how to respect the instrument, and how to get a specific touch and sound out of the instrument.

And there were times that I was also able to talk to him about his life and I was able to ask him the same questions that you are asking. He talked about being in the Army and meeting Kenny Drew and meeting Sam Rivers, Charlie Parker, and Monk. This was better than any book that I'm going to read. It's coming straight from the source, and that's the kind of experience I wanted to have when I got to New York; something that I couldn't get in Miami or San Francisco.

I always like to say that he was waiting for me to come to New York so that I could study with him. He was just a great human being and it was easy for him to express his personality through the instrument. And that's something that we all say that we are able to do, but very few of us are able to do that. He was able to express his humorous side, his vicious and mean side, as well as his respect for tradition and history. He was able to get all of that out of the instrument.

CECIL TAYLOR SAID THAT "MUSIC HAS TO DO WITH A LOT OF AREAS WHICH ARE MAGICAL RATHER THAN LOGICAL; THE GREAT ARTISTS, RATHER THAN JUST GETTING INVOLVED WITH DISCIPLINE, GET TO UNDERSTAND LOVE AND ALLOW THE LOVE TO TAKE SHAPE." HOW WOULD YOU EXPLAIN YOUR APPROACH?

When you play in a situation with two people that you love and respect dearly, and I'm talking about Nasheet Waits and Tarus Mateen, and you know that they are never going to lead you astray, then it does become magical. You can get lucky and feel this unbelievable amount of chemistry between the musicians you are performing with. You produce something that you know is unique to that moment in time and I'll usually let the audience know, "I don't know what you all are hearing but this is some of the baddest shit you'll ever see." (Laughs.) Those are unbelievably great feelings because you recognize how the body is in tune with its own blood, with the instrument, and if the rest of the guys are in tune, then you are all in tune with each other creating this mass of sound. That is very magical and is not to be taken for granted.

WHAT DO YOU LOOK FOR FROM DRUMMERS AND BASS PLAYERS AND HOW MUCH OF IT HAS TO DO WITH THEIR RHYTHMIC APPROACH WITH EACH OTHER?

Well first of all, I have to like them. (Laughs.) After we get off the bandstand, we have to be able to have a discussion, or not have a discussion and be able to go to dinner and just be cool with each other. That is such an important part. But it's more than that; it's about them knowing that I care enough about them that they don't have to feel as if they have to please me and can just be themselves. I greatly trust them with my music and that's what I'm really looking for, a person that doesn't take the obvious approach to anything. Just because they see free food doesn't mean they have to eat it.

WHEN WERE YOU AWARE THAT YOU HAD FOUND YOUR OWN VOICE?

I still don't consider having my own voice by a long shot because I'm still hearing all of the references in my own music. So, I have a long way to go. (Laughs.) I mean people like Threadgill, he really has his own voice. How he composes and how he plays the saxophone and the flute, the instrumentation he chooses . . . that's amazing! Steve Coleman and the bands that he puts together and Brad Mehldau with his group. They really have that thing that so many people are trying to copy. And I think musicians like that have really found their core and are comfortable with addressing it every night they get on stage.

If anything, a mark of what I do is with the musicians that I decide to hire and how the band functions. You can clearly hear the order between the soloists, but many times it comes together in a very loose but coordinated way. When you think the piano solo is still going on, it has actually transformed into a drum solo without you really knowing where the bar line ended. But none of that stuff is new. Mingus's group did that great. But like I said, I'm still hearing all of the references and feel like I have a long way to go before I get that. At least have a child before I start to think I have my own voice. And that's truly your own voice. (Laughs.)

IS HUMILITY IMPORTANT TO THE CREATIVE PROCESS?

I think so. When you come into contact with the people that you want to learn from, you have to exhibit that to be actually able to learn anything. Especially if you run into people like Jimmy Heath, Andrew Hill, or Sam Rivers; you meet these people that are sometimes three times your age. You have to exhibit humility to actually just absorb anything. So I think that's a major part of any person's lifestyle, that you can respect your elders, truly respect them, and then perhaps you can learn from them and then really take that into account into what you do.

HAS YOUR LIFE IN JAZZ SO FAR BEEN EVERYTHING THAT YOU THOUGHT IT WOULD BE?

It has exceeded every expectation. I have had the freedom I have wanted with Blue Note Records and they let me do what I want to do. They let me work with the musicians that I want to work with and let me choose the artwork. I've also married the woman that I really love. I play the gigs that I want to play and I work with the people that I have admired and have wanted to play with. It has just been a true fairy tale from the moment I graduated.

Greg Osby hired me without ever hearing me. He trusted me because he liked how I talked about music. I didn't have to prove anything to him and he took me on tour. The first night he heard me was in Vienna and you can't ask for a better fairy tale than that.

I have also been fortunate to be surrounded by people who have my best interest in mind and who are showing me things that they thought I could handle. And that entire process has been a true blessing, a true blessing.

28

IKUE MORI

Born and raised in Tokyo, Japan, Ikue Mori is a sculptor of sound. Ingeniously programming drum machines, samplers, and computers, she radically integrates shapes, colors, and pulses into abstract, soundscape masterpieces.

DID YOU HAVE A MUSICAL BACKGROUND WHILE GROWING UP IN JAPAN?

I was born and raised in Tokyo, Japan, and moved to NY in 1977. I studied music in elementary school and learned how to play a variety of instruments. And by growing up in the mixed pop culture of Tokyo, I was always surrounded by many different kinds of music and musicians, whose inherently sexist and macho attitudes about discipline discouraged me from picking up music as a career. I remained simply a fan.

ARE THERE SPECIFIC INFLUENCES THAT YOU HAVE TAKEN FROM THE MUSIC CULTURE OF JAPAN?

Though I began looking more towards the West for musical inspiration, my use of timing, way of counting, and use of space and silence has always been deeply Japanese, which is very evident from my very first work with DNA up to the present. It was not until years later that I was able to rediscover the beauty and weight of the traditional Japanese music that I grew up with.

WHAT'S HAPPENING WITH THE NOISE MUSIC SCENE IN JAPAN?

DNA was one of the original noise bands, creating radical rhythms and dissonant sounds. I think the No Wave scene of the late '70s was very influential on the
present Noise music scene. In the '80s, John Zorn was spending half his time in
Japan and was very instrumental in introducing the Japanese Noise music scene to
the world with musicians like Yamataka Eye, Akita (Merzbow), Haino Keiji, etc.
The scene is now very large and influential.

YOU HAVE HAD A LONG COLLABORATION AND FRIENDSHIP WITH JOHN ZORN. HOW
HAS HE INFLUENCED YOU?

We met around 1982 when he invited me to play in Locus Solus with Wayne
Horvitz. John introduced me to the world of improvisation and to a whole new
community of musicians. Through him, I met musicians like Fred Frith, Tom
Cora, Davey Williams, Jim Staley, as well as dancers and filmmakers, many of
whom I still work with today. He is one of the few people in the world who can
make you believe that anything is possible, and he still keeps pushing me to go beyond my limits. Not by creating pressure, but by showing me how to make it possible. I think many musicians who have worked with him have experienced this. I
also owe a lot to him for my rediscovery of Japanese culture. Through him, I have
found great art, film, and music I would never have known otherwise. Most of all,
his music moves and inspires me.

IS THERE AN EMOTIONAL INVOLVEMENT FOR YOU IN YOUR PERSONAL RELATION-
SHIP WITH SOUND?

For me, emotional involvement has more to do with composition than with
sound itself. My sound sources are made out of virtual instruments, and on their
own they don't have any feelings until they are processed through my system and
mixed together. And by layering and recombining beats and notes, manipulating
various pitches and intensities, new harmonies and dissonances can be created
that could help express certain emotions. Additionally, my processing system includes adding different effects, through filters, chopped up, stretched out, sped
up, and spaced out. These sounds are stored and brought out whenever needed. I
often randomize the beginning and ending point of a sound and continually alter
the speed and pitch so that it sounds different each time around, which keeps
things fresh. It's important to have total control over your system, but it's also important to include the option of relinquishing control so as not to exclude the element of surprise, mystery, and magic.

HOW FAMILIAR ARE YOU WITH THE POWER OF PROCESSING SOUNDS THROUGH
COMPUTERS THAT CAN MANIPULATE HOW THE MIND RESPONDS TO SOUND? IS THIS A
FACTOR IN WHAT YOU ARE ATTEMPTING TO DO WITH YOUR COMPOSITIONS?

I have been working with my "electronic instrument" for over ten years, trying
to create a personal sound while developing my playing skills. I started with one
drum machine together with a regular drum set and eventually realized that by ig-

noring conventional drum machine rules, along with eliminating the quantitating mode to keep regular beats, you can create much more intriguing rhythms and sounds, and by also programming voice and pitch, you can come up with very simple melodies with different tones.

Additionally, I also found that by adding more drum machines and mixing pre-programming with live performance, I could create a personal language that would be as recognizable and reactive to any musical situation as a conventional instrument. These new possibilities of the drum machine created my own sound world that is at the nexus between organic and digital, and between what is considered real and what is unreal. So switching from three drum machines to a laptop has been a major change.

Also, when I began transferring the files of my drum machine sounds, I first began using the laptop simply for more processing power. Now the possibilities of the instrument have expanded my language and my ability to interact with musicians, and my musical future seems more rich and varied than I could have ever imagined.

Thus, the light-speed development of technology has made it possible for musicians like myself to create sounds using high-power machines such as the laptop computer and software like MAX/MSP. But it is ultimately music that I want to make and not something that is merely technologically impressive.

DO YOU HAVE A PARTICULAR VISION FOR YOUR MUSIC GOING INTO THE FUTURE?

I want to incorporate more visuals into my work. And, recently, I have been doing performances that combine sound with visual elements, e.g., an animated piece I made based on Balinese mythological paintings. I would also like to make short experimental films and score them myself, creating a complete world where visuals and sounds interact organically.

WHAT INSPIRES YOU OR INFLUENCES YOUR CREATIVE PROCESS?

I like films, paintings, writings, music, food, anything that moves me. And I think what has always inspired me and keeps pushing me to expand is the musical community that I work in (largely improvised and experimental). These musicians really push me to develop a personal language, and it has happened slowly over time and continues to grow day by day. Musical personality, sensitivity, great sounds, and ability to interact and react with other musicians are for me what makes music great.

YOU HAVE NOW LIVED IN NEW YORK FOR QUITE SOME TIME. DID THE EVENTS OF 9/11 HAVE AN AFFECT ON YOU AS AN INDIVIDUAL AND AS AN ARTIST? DID IT AFFECT YOUR COMPOSITIONS OR YOUR CREATIVE PROCESS?

It was impossible not to be affected by that event while watching the tower falling down with thousands of people dying in that moment in front of you. The world has changed. There is no safe place anymore. My outer life has not changed—I still live in the same place, I am traveling more and more, but something has changed—in my inner world. I now have an urgent feeling to produce more projects, finish pieces, and make new compositions. I try to live in a more Zen way, moment by moment, one day at time. I feel that my mission as an artist is to fight with any kind of fascism—musical fascists, gender fascists—who accept only pure forms and draw borderlines between people, preventing bonding and evolution. It is very important for me to work in a diversified environment with many different kinds of artists.

29

DAVID MURRAY

The power and passion from David Murray is immediately identifiable. He remains fearless, unpredictable, and always profound, influenced by his deep interest in gospel, soul, and global cultures that he communicates through his creative spirit. It's the essence of who he is.

HAVE WE LOST OUR PATIENCE AND INTEREST TO BE CHALLENGED?

I have fifty students all over the world who are besieged by the information highway via the computer. Printed-out solos are now available from all of the great jazz musicians, whereas in the past that information would have to be transcribed, which was part of the creative process and learning experience. Thirty years ago, I couldn't have majored in John Coltrane, but now you can. And many don't understand the hard work because it isn't mentioned in the sound bites and we even have a sound-bite president. And because today's information is in short phrases, our attention span doesn't have to work to understand what's coming at you. I mean, our kids are besieged by information and they are throwing out a lot of information from the past and I don't blame them. They believe that if you are not on TV or in the tabloids, you are nobody! But they need to understand that the grueling and personal kind of work is still necessary for your development as a student in jazz. There are no shortcuts to success.

HAVE WE HIT A CULTURAL LOW POINT?

Ten years ago, MTV took over our children and nobody noticed. Our kids today are a product of MTV. Every neighborhood in the world is becoming more and more similar because they have this product and the kids are becoming more up-to-date than the parents, but the MTV mentality also perpetuates sarcasm.

IS THERE A DIFFERENT SET OF CHALLENGES THAT THE STUDENTS FACE TODAY?

Many teachers are telling students that the only way to become a musician is to learn and play a lot of standards. That's not being creative; that's repetitive as hell. I want my students to realize who they are! The kids today have some bright ideas but they are not eager to rise to the occasion. This generation is lazy! They think they can learn about music and learn how to play the instrument right away and that's what we're dealing with.

And unfortunately, many of today's music institutions try to deaden the creative aspect of the musician as a young artist. They try to form a kid a certain way instead of bringing out the creativity of the individual. And they are not inspiring these kids to write their own compositions and become a part of what they are doing. This is the way to develop a young artist to develop his or her own music as they grow and become creative.

ARE JAZZ TRADITIONALISTS HAVING A DIFFICULT TIME ACCEPTING THAT A MUSIC FORM CONSIDERED "AMERICAN" NOW HAS MORE VISIBLE INTERNATIONAL AND DIVERSE ASPECTS WITHIN IT?

Let's talk about Europe as an example. Europe has never really wanted to accept the recertification of bebop in terms of what was coming out of Lincoln Center. Many European musicians are trying to include more of their own founding concepts from European cultures and interject that into what we call jazz. But by putting that in, something has to be taken out, and it's usually the blues because it's difficult for Europeans to play blues, especially in the slow format. That's because your soul is on the floor crying and you may not want to reveal it. It's much easier to disguise the blues when you are playing in a fast tempo.

But European jazz has been very successful these last four years. I have been to concerts where I was the only African American playing on Saturday night and always during prime time. The festival has been going on since Thursday and I was the only nigger there. And in Europe, that's the shit. And when I say they didn't follow the Lincoln Center movement, the Europeans made a wise decision because they wanted to be more creative in their own way. And if there was ever a group of white people that made a really good decision, that was it, because they made themselves and their music visible. They stood up in the jazz community and we now have European jazz. I mean, I'm not carrying the flag for European jazz but I do recognize it. But every now and then, they have to hire me and people like me, just to know what the real thing is.

Subsequently, the Europeans have come up with their own form of jazz from their own classical history. They understand that you have to be who you are in order to propagate what you are about. Nobody is going to follow you if you are not true to yourself. If you look back at the history of the black musicians from the AACM, they tried to play like classical composers. I mean, check out Anthony Braxton.

But let me also say this, part of the problem is with dance. Everybody in Cuba can dance. Everybody can do the salsa; they can do the rumba, the mambo, and do it with all four extremities moving. But white people cannot dance. They cannot dance in America and they cannot dance in Europe. It's like watching John Travolta in the movie *Saturday Night Fever*. It might be fun to watch, but you know he didn't create those moves.

I don't know what Fidel Castro is feeding those people, but there is something rhythmically happening. Awhile back, I hired a few string players in Cuba and they played the jazz bebop tunes that I wrote better than the musicians in New York. And you know, bebop is another language and if you don't understand it, you will not be able to articulate it on a violin, cello, or on a bass.

IS IT POSSIBLE THAT WITH ALL THE STRIFE AND TURMOIL HAPPENING IN THE WORLD TODAY THAT A NEW TYPE OF CREATIVITY MIGHT COME FORTH?

I certainly hope so because this shit is getting so tired. Something has to give and maybe it will be something like a phoenix which was born out of confusion. A lot of things are born out of confusion like what's going on in Haiti right now with Aristide. There are 200 years of freedom in Haiti this year and nobody is dealing with that. I mean, France got rich off of Haiti and its sugar. It's a big world that not everybody understands and the conventional Western philosophy goes out the window when you go to those places. That's why it is important to go to places like Haiti. I like to visit other parts of the world and try to understand their culture and how they live. I want to see things for myself and that's why I speak the way I speak.

I READ THAT YOU WERE TRYING TO START A MUSIC SCHOOL IN SENEGAL.

It was a dream that I had, but I just could not get the instrument companies in France to provide the instruments for the people and that's where things fell down. I couldn't get the support, though the interest from the people of Senegal was there, because even if these people had the will to play this music, they didn't have the instruments. I mean everybody there has a drum because they can make a drum, but nobody has a trombone and nobody has a saxophone.

But Cuba is actually the place that I go to more often and I'm trying to implement programs there. If we would let Cuba be Cuba and America would get its fucking foot off their necks, we would see so much creativity from these people because it is one of the most creative countries in the world. I wonder why.

CAN YOU CONNECT CREATIVITY IN TODAY'S ENVIRONMENT SOCIALLY, POLITICALLY, OR SPIRITUALLY?

Hell yeah, because I do it every day of my life. Every time I get on stage, I'm trying to adhere to my music. And a true artist should be a semaphore of his times, and I try. It's being well read and well informed; it's knowing what he is doing and trying to give it back to the people in a musical form. Music influences a lot of people, and I have had my music influence people who do art, who do dance, who do drama, and it's important to be exactly who you are and it's not necessary to go any further than that. Musicians have to find ways to survive in a way that allows them to be able to do exactly what they want to do.

DO YOU HAVE A COMMON PHILOSOPHY THAT YOU TRY TO IMPART WITH YOUR STUDENTS?

To strive for creativity and when I say creativity, to try and keep a spark inside of you with your approach to music. In other words, don't be a closed person. Also learn about the scientific aspects of the music along with the feel-good aspects of the music. You have to be curious in order for the music to be good.

WHAT INSPIRES YOU?

The people and souls that are around me, my children and my lady; my love.

HAS THE JAZZ WORLD CAUGHT UP TO DAVID MURRAY?

I think some would think of me as contemporary but also one who is trying to do something along the avant-garde.

WHAT DO YOU ENVISION FOR THE FUTURE OF JAZZ AND FOR YOURSELF PERSONALLY?

I wish that jazz musicians could have an easier time making a living playing the music that they love. This is my hope. But right now, I see a lot of things that suggest the opposite. I see people studying this music, but the more that they study, the less they are appreciated.

WHAT IS THE IMPORTANCE OF JAZZ?

Jazz can put its mark on any kind of music and make it more brilliant. It's like jazz is the teacher and funk is the preacher. If you look at jazz as the teacher, then every other kind of music becomes the preacher. Jazz can make other music more sophisticated and more worldly.

DO YOU HAVE YOUR OWN PERSONAL PHILOSOPHY?

To look at the positive rather than the negative, and it's like what Sun Ra says, "I'm like a bird, you don't have to listen to me, but I'm there."

PAAL NILSSEN-LOVE

He plays in several of the most progressive and innovative bands today (Atomic, Scorch Trio, School Days, The Thing, and the Peter Brotzmann Tentet just to name a few), but the chances are that if you live in the United States, you have never heard of those bands or Norwegian drummer Paal Nilssen-Love.

It's not often that an individual comes along with a way of playing his or her instrument that is completely unique from what came before. Sure, there are influences, but if you want a view of the future of creative music, follow the career of Paal Nilssen-Love—he'll be a part of it.

YOU GREW UP IN NORWAY AND, IF I REMEMBER CORRECTLY, YOUR PARENTS OWNED A JAZZ CLUB. WERE YOU ABLE TO CHECK OUT THE PERFORMANCES AT A YOUNG AGE AND DID YOU EVER GET A CHANCE TO SIT IN?

Yes, they had the jazz club from 1979 to 1986 and before my dad moved to Norway, he ran a concert series at a pub in Red Hill, England. So yes, I was exposed to many shows between the ages of five to ten. There were loads of great bands such as Arthur Blythe, David Murray, Don Pullen, Steve Lacy, Misha Mengelberg, John Stevens, Tony Oxley (who let me beat his drums for ten minutes after the show), and Art Blakey, who tried to get me on stage but I didn't dare. . . .

JUST HOW INFLUENTIAL WAS ART BLAKEY?

He and his playing had a great impact on me, but I've always enjoyed the Messengers a lot. Especially the early bands with Lee Morgan, Benny Golson, and the band with Wayne Shorter was great too. Art Blakey's drumming was one of a kind. He accompanied the soloist in such a supportive way with his use of extreme and sudden dynamics. He could consistently vary the density and push the music and swing it with the heaviest hi-hat strokes on 2 and 4. He also used a simple pattern by orchestrating it on different drums, creating a complex polyrhythm which could last several bars before ending at the top. And his use of Afro-Cuban rhythms could be pretty intense.

It's very rare that an instrumentalist comes along that has a unique style of playing that doesn't seem to be heavily influenced by any particular player. How exactly did your way of playing the drums develop?

I learned a lot from my dad's records and obviously from the shows at the jazz club. When I was about fifteen or sixteen, I began playing with saxophonist Frode Gjerstad and trumpeter Didrik Ingvaldsen, which had an influence on my playing and musical interest. The music was improvised with some written material, and both Frode and Didrik believed that the musician's individual voice should determine the direction of the music. Prior to this, I had a great time playing in local rock bands and that experience had an effect on where I am today.

In 1992, I attended a summer jazz course and met Ingebrigt Haker-Flaten and Håvard Wiik, and later that fall, we took a visit to Trondheim where we started a Coltrane-ish group called Element. I remember the saxophone player pointing out that he enjoyed the Elvin kind of feel that I had in my drumming, but the funny thing was that I hadn't listened to the Coltrane quartet very much, at least not with the intention of copying the style of Elvin Jones. In fact, I spent more time listening to Alan Skidmore, Ali Haurand, and Tony Oxley playing their version of *Lonnie's Lament*. Anyway, the comment influenced me to check out Elvin Jones more.

When I listen to a record with a drummer I like, I always listen to what's going on between the drummer and the soloist. For example, there is always a lot of interaction going on in the bands that include Elvin Jones, Art Blakey, Tony Oxley, or John Stevens. I've always liked different drummers and ethnic music, and I see it all as one pallet that I have the privilege of choosing from. Subsequently, I listen and adapt to whatever attracts my ear, and some of the music that has affected me most comes from Korea (traditional), Cuba, and Brazil from the '60s and early '70s. Drummers such as Steve McCall, Phillip Wilson, Ed Blackwell, John Stevens, and many others have all influenced me.

Your playing is very dense, but in a way that creates a palette and energy for the other members of the band to work from, and there is always a particular tension. It's quite unusual.

High density and energy are both needed to keep the music alive, but I also believe that all levels of density should be considered and that one should always take the approach that you are going to try and create and experience something new

every time. This also includes when you're practicing, where you need to get beyond only playing scales or rudiments.

THE BAND ATOMIC IS ONE OF THE MOST INNOVATIVE BANDS IN MUSIC TODAY, YET
IS HARDLY KNOWN OUTSIDE OF EUROPE. IS THE MUSIC TOO PROGRESSIVE OR IS THE
U.S. MUSIC INDUSTRY JUST NOT INTERESTED IN MARKETING MUSIC FROM EUROPE?

I'm not sure. To some extent, it has to do with distribution within the record industry. Atomic's music is on the label Jazzland and that's a sublabel of Universal.
The absurd thing is that though it's on a major label, it's impossible to find in stores
in the U.S. Canada is OK but the U.S. is fucked when it comes to how Universal
deals with independent music. I guess they don't see it as profitable as Diana Krall
or any other product of the music industry and maybe it's too difficult for them to
create a package around the band. They need to be able to label the music and
since we are playing music that's influenced by both American and European jazz
along with other contemporary music, they find it hard to classify and market the
product. Therefore you end up doing more underground gigs, but the audience is
there and the music gets out there as long as we are willing to take it there. It's as
much up to the musician as the audience, and as long as the two most important
ends meet, the music will get out there.

IN MY OPINION, ATOMIC PLAYS MUSIC THAT IS VERY ACCESSIBLE AND I THINK THAT
GOES FOR THE BAND SCHOOL DAYS AS WELL.

I think you're right. These two bands are more conventional and the fact that
both write out the compositions makes the music more accessible. Also, the parts
that are free improvised are split up into duos so it immediately has a clear structure to it. It's funny though, Atomic was supposedly way too free for a festival in
Norway not too long ago. It just shows what different ears hear.

THE ELEMENT OF TIME IS CRITICAL IN MUSIC, YET I FIND THERE ARE VERY FEW
THAT CAN PLACE THEIR OWN PERSONAL STAMP ON IT. MOST MUSICIANS SEEM CON-
TENT JUST TO BE ABLE TO PLAY ON THE BEAT OR ON THE FRONT OR BACK END OF IT.
FEW KNOW HOW TO TAKE OWNERSHIP AND MAKE IT PART OF THEIR MUSICAL PER-
SONALITY. HOWEVER, AT TIMES, INGEBRIGT HÅKER-FLATEN AND YOURSELF ARE
ABLE TO DO JUST THAT AND IT BECOMES A VERY SPECIAL LIVING THING THAT INFLU-
ENCES THE ENTIRE CHARACTER OF THE GROUP SOUND.

I felt there was something to build on from the very first time that I played with
Ingebrigt. After moving to Trondheim and attending the music conservatoire, we
were playing in eight different bands at one point and I think since we were dealing with so many different styles (balkan, freejazz, fusion, Coltrane, etc.) we became pretty strong together and could pick up any signal immediately and were
able to build up some ferocious rhythms together. We've now played together for
about twelve years so things should be together by now.

But it's also about feeling each other's presence and about being together but also against each other. We push and pull but not at the same time and try to create a time that has tension where we're split on each side of the beat and moving the boat together.

Do you have your own relationship with time?

Time is something you can hear, but you also have to feel it. It's got to be in your guts. If you can't feel it, and need a metronome, you're lost. I have never used a metronome to practice time and believe that you've got to be strong enough without it. It's better to practice time with a record you like. And time is something that can be stretched a lot. I like working with long "1"s, oval time, 4/4 bars with no "1." Everything has its time and you don't need to hear it. The greatest moment is when you can feel it move you and can't place where it is but it feels like something so incredibly strong that you can't avoid it.

Are there particular factors that you feel are important within improvisation?

First of all, I think humbleness is one of the most important factors. Also, being able to meet other musicians while being as receptive as what you expect from him or her. Also being strong within yourself and as an improviser so things come across clearly. And to push yourself all the time, both physical and mentally. Most important, *big ears*!

How important is chemistry between musicians in the creative process?

I would say it's very important that the musicians you play with are people that you like and people that you like to communicate offstage with too. Nothing is worse than getting on stage with an asshole, no matter how great a musician they might be. You are dealing with pretty heavy things and it has to work with people who you communicate well with. Things have to come through clear.

Cecil Taylor said that "music has to do with a lot of areas which are magical rather than logical; the great artists, rather than just getting involved with discipline, get to understand love and allow the love to take shape." Can you describe where your music is from?

I can agree with Taylor's quote but it's hard to tell where the music comes from. Sometimes you feel that you're more of a medium for the music and that you are a tool that carves the curves. And sometimes within a free-improvising situation, one can feel that the music is very magical and that you have to treat it right and not be an obstacle to the music. It's as if the music takes over and lives through you and one has to be very humble and leave your ego and let loose. The music comes from the situation you're in, with the people that you're with, and the place that you're at. Everything affects the music and you just have to tell the story of that time, of that day, and of your life.

WHEN YOU LOOK AT ANY ART FORM, THERE ARE THOSE THAT CREATE THAT SEEM
TO HAVE A FINGER ON THE PULSE OF WHAT'S HAPPENING AT THAT TIME. DOES THE
FORWARD-THINKING ARTIST HAVE A UNIQUE AWARENESS LEVEL AND IS THERE A RE-
SPONSIBILITY THAT COMES WITH THAT AWARENESS?

Artists, whatever their expression is, should be on the ball all the time. As long
as you produce in your own time and are not going back in time, the art you produce is fresh. I had a discussion not too long ago with a college student who
wanted to play music but without listening to anyone else who played his same instrument. He didn't want to be influenced by anyone else. But that's impossible.
You will always be affected by other art forms and other people's meanings and expression and you can't escape the history that lies within the music you play.
Everything one does is in relationship to whatever has happened before and is
happening presently. Therefore, there is responsibility to be up-to-date at all times
and know what's going on around you.

CAN YOU CONNECT THE MUSIC YOU PLAY POLITICALLY, SOCIALLY, OR SPIRITUALLY?

Absolutely, in all ways and levels. It's all connected. The music will always be affected by the political situation of the world, society, social surroundings, and spiritual awareness. Music is such a part of yourself, and whatever is happening
around you, it affects the music. And music is also an outlet for political statement.
Music is strong and can change quite a few things if it is let loose.

HAVE WE BECOME A SOCIETY WITHOUT THE PATIENCE TO BE CHALLENGED, OPEN
ONLY TO THINGS THAT ARE EASILY ACCESSIBLE?

That's a major problem these days because people feel there isn't any time, nor
have they the patience to sit down and let the mind work on something they are
unfamiliar with. Society today is structured around fast action where everything
should happen quickly and take very little of people's time. People want everything
served, ready to digest, which includes music, literature, film, etc.

For me, I would like the days to be longer and feel that I need more time to
conceive my goals and wants, but it's getting crazy when I try to do two things at
once just to save time. But that's how it is these days. It's so important that people
get out and see and hear bands live, see movies at the theaters that receive little
advertising, and go out and meet other people to talk and think.

ARE WE BECOMING MORE ACCEPTING OF EACH OTHER'S CULTURES?

In some communities yes, but there's still lot of fear of foreign cultures and people. People accept the existence of other cultures but not necessarily the actual
culture, which is a pity. One cannot change different cultures and there's no reason why one should. It's much better to learn about those cultures.

IS CREATIVITY ENCOURAGED TODAY?

To some extent yes, but as mentioned before, it doesn't always go through. Musicians and artists have a responsibility to encourage each other along with the listeners' and the viewers' creativity. The public schools are an important factor that doesn't always stimulate the creative mind of young people. Kids spend way too much time at school without any musical or visual stimuli, and the crap that's on TV has nothing to do with a creative mind. People need to wake up their kids and themselves twice.

I HAPPEN TO BELIEVE THAT THIS IS ONE OF THE MOST CREATIVE TIMES IN JAZZ HISTORY, BUT PEOPLE ARE NOT AWARE OF THE DIVERSITY OF MUSIC AVAILABLE TO THEM. WHAT WILL TAKE TO CLOSE THIS GAP?

Mental awareness. People just need to understand that they need to check out other bands or records too, not just the ones they read about in the paper. People also need to shut off their perceptions of what music should sound like based upon the rules of the styles and the retroactive thinking of those rules. It is up to the presenters and the musicians. The media will just have to follow if one is strong enough.

YOU RECENTLY OVERCAME A VERY SERIOUS HEALTH ISSUE. HAS IT CHANGED YOUR THOUGHTS OR VIEWS ON MUSIC AND LIFE?

At the point when I became ill, I was already working way too much and not taking one single day off. Gigs were happening everyday and everywhere. So, I needed a break and maybe the illness was the message. But now, I'm working just as much, but trying to slow down a little. When you get your life back you really love it, you love the people who care and you love the music more than ever. The music was in me all the time during treatment, but at a distance which felt good in a way. It was pretty amazing to be playing again, and I remember waking up the next morning after the first gig, being in a state that I've never experienced before

CAN YOU PUT INTO WORDS WHAT MUSIC MEANS TO YOU?

Music means more than everything—it's given me the reason to live. And when you can give the audience a reason to live through your music, it's twice the payback. Music is life and life is music; not always pleasant, not always good, but something that can enrich you.

㉛

GREG OSBY

I have found that with forward-thinking artists, their music can be a direct reflection of who they are. That's largely my interest in these very creative individuals—in how they think and how they view the world through their own eyes. Greg Osby is fearless in expressing his convictions, and I think you'll find that his compositions reflect that very character. He is a creator and a fresh voice in a world that has a tendency to fall victim to the past.

ARE YOU STILL DOING THINGS YOUR OWN WAY?

I have no other way, and creatively speaking, I customize my career so I'm able to make choices without interruptions. And though I'm a collaborator at heart, I still need to adhere to my initial ideas and concepts.

IT WOULD BE DIFFICULT TO MEET EVERYONE'S EXPECTATIONS ANYWAY.

You just can't please everyone or beat yourself up trying to please writers who may have written unfavorably about you in the past or by trying to pander to the tastes of label executives and fans. As an artist, you want to sleep at night knowing what went into the stew was an ingredient of your own design.

I don't want to sound self-indulgent, but it's not about pandering to what people want or about what's popular because you can box yourself in based upon those expectations and parameters. I would rather let the music write itself based upon the initial germs of thought and maintain that focus. Otherwise you'll get off track worrying about awards and accolades.

ARE JAZZ TRADITIONALISTS HAVING A DIFFICULT TIME ACCEPTING THAT A MUSIC
FORM CONSIDERED "AMERICAN" NOW HAS MORE VISIBLE INTERNATIONAL AND DI-
VERSE ASPECTS WITHIN IT?

The problem is overkill. The floodgates are open with an overabundance of sub-
standard product because everyone has access to some kind of recording medium,
whether they are ready to present a project meant for public consumption or not.
So in order for people to get to the real gemstones, they have to sit through the
muck. They have to get a machete and hack through the jungle of CDs that are not
really developed and print quality. They haven't played long enough or shared any
experience that would give them music to market of permanency. Most of it is disposable, but you can still find accomplished musicians everywhere you go. Everywhere I go, whether it's Germany, Russia, Spain, Italy, Brazil, Australia, or whatever, I find great musicians who are often on par with American musicians, who in
many respects have gotten lazy and taken for granted the demands of this art form.
You have a lot of prominent musicians wrestling with the laurels and not realizing
that there are people in New Zealand who can blow their socks off. The music was
originated here but it doesn't mean it cannot be perfected somewhere else.

ARE PART OF THE ROOTS OF JAZZ FROM AFRICA?

Yes, but as an art form, jazz is the epitome of fusion. Of course it has West
African root elements with functional drumming as well as a great deal of symbolism. But it also emerged heavily with Western European sensibilities as far as
harmony. So a lot of the rhythm, the feel, the soul, the swing is African, but a lot
of the structural elements are largely European. That's what made the music what
it is. Those are the things that need to be referred to and relied upon to fortify and
strengthen it, but many people are just maintaining the precedent as it stands
without being concerned with moving it to the next level. But we need to take
heed and follow the lead of Coltrane, Mingus, and Miles and continue to press forward and not idealize the music as some type of museum piece frozen in time. It
should be perpetual.

IS JAZZ A THING, OR AN APPROACH AND PROCESS TO MAKING MUSIC?

It's all of the above but it's also a mentality and a way of life. It can be readily apparent if the music doesn't contain the stylistic characteristics of a jazz musician living a jazz life. You can tell when the music is largely academic or from a book or from
records. You can tell they are not professionals that don't travel because they don't
think with that aptitude. It's obvious and especially now when there are 100,000
tenor players copying the flavor of the day. You should have individual personalities
and everyone should sound different as you and I sound different in our vocal patterns, mannerisms, and our complete character profile. The lack of individualism
and motivity towards assuming and maintaining a personal approach and a personality in the music is killing a large part of what this music is suppose to be about.
When someone plays, it should evoke imagery of someone who is like no other.

Are academic programs placing enough emphasis on the importance of this?

I'm a veteran of the institutionalized approach to jazz education from teaching at many well-known universities, and I have been at odds with their methodology in approaching music. I think it should be individualized based upon the aptitude and aspirations of each student as opposed to this broad stroke and grand sweep of everybody given the same information and forced to adhere to the same list of requirements. There isn't any reason why someone in music school should be forced to study and be held responsible for anything not having to do with the jazz life. There should be more emphasis on business, self-promotion, and the attainment of individualism that will make you stand out and make you more appealing to label executives because they throw away thousands of audition CDs daily that sound like they came out of a Xerox machine.

- There seem to be younger musicians not wanting to be tied to what jazz did in the past. They are moving in different directions trying to find their own identity.

There is a danger of being dismissive of a precedent or the lineage of the music. Many people are reckless because they don't want to do the work, but in order to get away from something, you have to be aware of it. You have to know how it worked, how it was applied, and what it derived from. You have to know the root source, otherwise it's escapism and people are just trying to circumvent deep study. So there is a danger in that cavalier attitude of "wanting to do my own thing." That's why we have a great deal of people who are not really well versed in the history of this music. They play their own music and play it fairly well, but put them in another environment and they sink like a rock because they don't know anyone else's music and have given its due.

Miles Davis was criticized for incorporating pop influences into his music but jazz has always taken from pop influences. Is there anything different in what Miles was doing or what is being done today by a number of jazz musicians?

Well, in the '30s, '40s, and '50s, there was less divide between the genres because many jazz musicians during that period openly improvised within the confines of the forms of those popular tunes which had a great deal of chord changes, bridges, and development. As time progressed, especially in the 1960s when rock and roll came around, popular music was reduced to one or two chords with a lot of screaming, hollering, and a lot of guitar. There was less an environment for musicians to improvise with and now with electronics, it's gotten worse! That has hurt the scene at large because a lot of people at one time were introduced to jazz through an instrumental version of a popular song they may have recognized. But you can't do that today. I cannot introduce the uninitiated to jazz by playing a pop tune of the day because the songs from Britney Spears and °NSYNC have only two repetitive chords, have no development without anything for me to play on. That's why jazz has been relegated as this bastard child within contemporary music. It doesn't contain any appealing elements that are recognizable to and by young people. So until popular music becomes interesting again, we can't play that music and it's going to remain difficult to reel people in.

DOES HIP-HOP HAVE ELEMENTS FROM THE FOUNDATION OF JAZZ?

At one time, but now it's become disposable and pretty much a waste of record deals in my opinion because most of these people are idiots and it's become a circus. In many instances, it's buffoonery at its finest with very little profundity being uttered. Hip-hop may have been different at one time but there was a lot more creativity in the production and construction of the music. It was more or less a cut-and-paste music where they sampled little snippets of recordings that didn't resemble or have anything to do with each other. It was a collage of sound textures that created an environment and pallet for rappers who artfully and rhythmically created rhymes, short stories, and poems. But once the sampling walls became more strident and artists went after these rappers for sampling their wares, there were exuberant lawsuits and now it's been reduced to two notes on a keyboard with children's nursery rhymes. It's not interesting anymore and all they talk about is money, so it's really disposable.

CAN YOU TALK ABOUT M-BASE AND THE BASIS FOR STARTING IT?

I found it necessary to seek out a group of younger players, players in my peer group that were interested in incorporating elements from music that existed prior to our arrival in New York as well as music that existed at the time. I also found many improvising musicians dismissive of what was going on in contemporary terms so I wanted to use everything that existed as a building block, as a stepping-stone, and not stay transfixed in a rapt state or try to create a bygone era. There was also this vast influx of younger players from all over the country who came to New York well prepared, proficient, articulate, and ready to learn. This was the beginning of what was unfortunately called the "young lions period."

We were also the last beneficiaries of the apprenticeship system and had the grand opportunity to play with our heroes. But after us, a lot of people passed on and stopped having groups so we became the bandleaders younger players started to look towards. But we wanted it organized. I met fellow saxophonist Steve Coleman and found we had a great deal in common and a great deal of aspiration to revitalize the scene and not just make it this "young lions" thing. We didn't want to reinforce that even though we did play traditional music but we also wanted something that was reflective of what was going on now. We wanted an experimental environment where we could write new music and talk about new concepts, new approaches, and implement things that were of our own concoction.

Once we were organized, we met once or twice a week in our basements or apartments and talked about music. It was really a self-propellant entity where if one of the members had a meeting with a music executive, an attorney, or had a session in the studio, we would address the group and detail our experiences. Consequently, we all lived vicariously through each other's experiences and when we had to confront those experiences on our own, we were well prepared.

We also pooled our money and paid for our own studio time and put on our own concerts as well as starting an outreach program for student teaching with a musicians' referral service. And through these efforts, a lot of the journalistic elite took note and started to call us "12th and Brooklyn," but we wanted to nip that in the bud. Whenever you think of harmolodics, you invariably think of Ornette Coleman because that's what he named his music. But we didn't want anyone to coin a phrase as something as ridiculous as bebop which is a phrase that musicians abhorred. So we decided to call our music M-BASE that is an acronym that stands for "Macro–Basic Array of Structured Extemporization." Roughly meaning a large base, a large group of musicians whose main purpose is to learn and teach each other and to present new methods of composition and environments for improvisation.

IS THERE A COMMON PHILOSOPHY THAT YOU TRY TO IMPART ON YOUNG JAZZ MUSICIANS?

It's a new day as far as being a practicing musician and trying to sustain an existence. You have to choose between playing an instrument and playing in creative circles. You can play for money where there is not a great deal of creativity but you're a faceless, nameless commodity who is doing what they are told and basically a hired gun. Or you can make less money and sleep better at night by expressing yourself based upon your creative ideals.

I advise younger players to prepare and to avail yourself of the information—free information, mind you—about everybody's job who is involved in this business. You have to be able to speak with them articulately about what you are dealing with at the moment. You need to be able to talk to recording engineers, attorneys, and music executives and will need to know how the record company and contract works. How promotion, marketing, and distribution work.

Around the '40s or '50s, you went around with a dog collar and people pointed you in the direction you needed to go. That's why a lot of musicians were shafted and died penniless because they didn't have their business together. They were gypped out of all their money by lawyers, managers, and record company executives who took all of their royalties, their spoils, and now today, you have to know everybody's job to know they're not doing that to you.

ONE OF THE PROBLEMS WITH DOCUMENTATION FOCUSING ON JAZZ, SUCH AS KEN BURNS'S SERIES, IS THAT THEY SPEND MOST OF THE TIME CONCENTRATING ON WHAT JAZZ CREATED IN THE PAST TENSE AND LITTLE ON WHAT THE MUSIC IS CREATING AT THE MOMENT, WHICH TO ME IS THE ESSENCE OF THIS GREAT MUSIC WE CALL JAZZ. ISN'T THIS A LOST OPPORTUNITY TO EDUCATE POTENTIAL ASPIRING JAZZ STUDENTS AND PEOPLE AS TO WHAT IS AVAILABLE TO THEM?

Well, perhaps if he would have had a more variable list of advisors but it was obvious who his advisors were because they're all friends of mine. I know how they think, what they prioritize, and that was reflected in the documentary. They spent several episodes talking about Louis Armstrong and several more talking about Duke Ellington, so whose philosophy does that reflect? Had Ken Burns had a more variable list of advisors, the film would have been a lot broader and much more comprehensive. Perhaps they ran out of budget when they came to the more recent period or maybe they ran out of steam, ran out of ideas, or maybe everybody got cotton mouth and became tired of talking. The point is, it was unfortunate that he stopped when he did. He was in fast-forward from the late '50s and '60s with some of the most profound contributors to the music of American culture and if you blinked, you would have missed it. And that was just unfortunate. They spent so much time in the mid-1900s as opposed to dealing with what's leading up to now.

Another aspect that was really disappointing is that he talked about the dark side of the most profound contributors to the music. He talked about their drug addictions and alcohol addictions, which is really nonessential. It took up time where he could have provided worthwhile, useful, and retainable information. That stuff was disposable more or less.

THERE ARE ALREADY SO MANY NEGATIVE STEREOTYPES. WHY NOT FOCUS ON THE POSITIVE?

The thing about documentaries, especially something like this, which was mass-produced, is that they will be referenced in academic circles. There's no point in all that. If you look at the movie *Amadeus*, it was readily apparent that they considered Mozart a child prodigy, a genius who changed music and had these God-given gifts. He was amazing. Even for all his quirkiness and eccentricities, the things he did were astounding. He had inner demons, was haunted by his father, and died a pauper. Still, the symphonies and the concertos that he composed as a young person were portrayed with love. But when you see movies like *Round Midnight* and *The Charlie Parker Story*, they always portray the jazz musician as down on his luck, depraved, dependent upon some golden goose who has rescued him from the depths of hell. They can't take care of themselves; they're groveling, drooling somewhere in the shadows. The lighting is grim, dark, and gray. In many respects, the Ken Burns documentary perpetuated that.

THROUGHOUT ALL THE ARTS, THERE HAVE BEEN MANY WELL-KNOWN AND CREATIVE PEOPLE WITH HIGHLY ADDICTIVE PERSONALITIES. YET IT DOES SEEM THAT MANY JAZZ OR BLACK ARTISTS USUALLY GET PORTRAYED IN THIS NEGATIVE LIGHT. IT CONTINUES TO OCCUR.

It's just history repeating itself. People will glamorize the things that provide drama, and it's tabloid mentality. It's voyeurism for people who want to peek into the dark side of freakish behavior, sexual deviancy, drug addiction, alcoholism, the dark secrets and sordid past. The documentary could have spent a good deal of time talking about innovation, experimentation, and great achievements by musicians and could have been a lot more effective than it was.

IF MILES WOULD HAVE BEEN ALIVE, WOULD HE HAVE BEEN INCLUDED AS A RESOURCE?

It's possible, but I'd like to touch upon something you said earlier. He was criticized but by the time he was doing Michael Jackson and Cindy Lauper covers, he had nothing left to prove. He was having a lot of fun and surrounded himself with musicians that I won't say didn't deserve to share the stage with him, but they weren't really on his level. They just provided a sonic backdrop for him to be a personality and not Miles Davis the musician that he once was. He was having fun and wasn't out to change the whole face or the tide of music. Subsequently, he wasn't this vortex of energy that he once was and it shouldn't have been expected of him. And people unfortunately and selfishly attacked him for that. A lot of musicians attacked him for that but that's their shortcoming and not his.

THOUGH MILES WASN'T PLAYING A LOT DURING THIS LATER PERIOD, HE COULD STILL PLAY ONE NOTE AND YOU KNEW IT WAS HIM.

Certainly. It was his sound, his personality, his approach, his attack, and his technique. Everything was definable and unmistakable and that's what it's all about. He could have played one note per tune and it would have been just as valid had he played one hundred. And that's something that takes musicians a lifetime to achieve and some people never attain that because that's not a point of emphasis or focus. They want to display technique, velocity, volume, and all the other kind of things that are not necessarily priorities or the prerequisite to identification.

OUR CULTURE TODAY APPRECIATES ART BUT SEEMS TO HAVE DIFFICULTY WITH CREATIVITY THAT IS NOT EASILY EXPLAINED OR IDENTIFIABLE. WILL THIS BE A SIGNIFICANT OBSTACLE TO OVERCOME FOR CREATIVE MUSIC?

Well, I think the conditioning that takes place for understanding has to be dealt with at a very young age. It's very common for us musicians to see entire families coming out to see us in Europe. They come out to see pure bona fide American jazz that's not cut or watered down and recognize it as a valid and credible United States export. They cultivate this thinking in the minds of the young people so when they grow up, they appreciate it as something to be embraced, to be treasured, and virtued. And that's what we need to deal with in this country because most people identify the music as my grandfather's music or something heard in cartoons or in the backdrop for a slapstick comedy, silent films, or something ridiculous. That's the association and imagery it conjures up when they hear jazz. The only thing that serves as a bridge for younger people and jazz is probably hip-hop and they just hear it in snippets. They may hear a sampled fragment from a jazz recording but they can't identify the source of the artist or where it's from or what period it represents. It's throwaway. It goes in one ear and out the other and they really don't retain that information. And unfortunately, the most prevailing so-called jazz presentation right now is this so-called smooth jazz, which really isn't jazz at all. And the people that are popular within that, that whole structure, they're really not jazz musicians. They're pop musicians and what they play is pop music. If you take the vocalist out of any pop song or Mariah Carey song, what you have is this so called smooth jazz. It's the same environment, the same sugar coating, the same instruments, and has the same disposable nature. Even the improvised elements are very much prepared. They play the same way all of the time and it adheres to a formula, which isn't about individuality. Jazz now has to find a way to shake the association of being under the same umbrella and grand veil of so-called smooth jazz—instrumental jazz. You have to learn how to appreciate the elements, the relationships, know the history, how things work, and the lineage of it to develop an appreciation for it. It's not an easy sell.

DO YOU THINK WE HAVE BECOME A SOCIETY THAT NO LONGER HAS THE PATIENCE TO BE CHALLENGED AND IS ONLY OPEN TO THINGS THAT ARE EASILY ACCESSIBLE?

Americans in particular and perhaps not so much in Europe because they don't have the same access to a lot of things that we do. I find that people from other countries read more but yes, Americans have short attention spans and since we're victimized by the multimedianess of contemporary culture with emphasis on what is visual and not necessarily what's heard. Yeah, we're suffering. But all things are cyclical and these things have to run their course. They have to because how many pretty girls and belly buttons can you stand?

IS IT MORE DIFFICULT FOR YOUNG MUSICIANS TO BE CREATIVE TODAY?

When I came to New York in 1980 or so and then officially moved to New York in late 1982, there were tons of jam sessions. In every major borough, Brooklyn, Queens, the Bronx, and certainly Manhattan, with the exception of Staten Island, there were jam sessions. You could go on a daily basis and see who was hot and who wasn't. We listened to the new musicians in town to see if they were ready to compete or if they needed a few more months to hone their talent. You could weigh your skill level against the more accomplished players and find out exactly what your weak points were and what you needed to work on. But all of that is gone. There are only a few places for a younger player and you have musicians lining up out the door to get in and have their fifteen minutes of fame. And by the fact that there are not many places to play, these musicians get up and overstay their welcome. They're frustrated so they get there and play a long time and by the time the night is over, most have not had an opportunity to play.

So I don't know what to tell a young cat to do. They ask me, "Where should I go?" and I don't know. There are only a couple of places to play and there are too many musicians. Therefore they only get a chance to play in school, but that's not the same thing because they are only playing with people on their own level. One guy is sad and so they are all sad and it's hard to weigh yourself against a group of sadness.

CECIL TAYLOR SAID THAT "MUSIC HAS TO DO WITH A LOT OF AREAS WHICH ARE MAGICAL RATHER THAN LOGICAL; THE GREAT ARTISTS, RATHER THAN JUST GETTING INVOLVED WITH DISCIPLINE, GET TO UNDERSTAND LOVE AND ALLOW THE LOVE TO TAKE SHAPE." HOW MUCH OF YOUR MUSIC IS FROM LOGIC AND HOW MUCH FROM THIS OTHER PLACE THAT CECIL TAYLOR DESCRIBES?

There's a great deal of fundamental logic in just about everything I embark upon in music because I cannot and will not allow myself to recklessly enter into a situation or environment without deducing what needs to be done. I have to analyze the situation and weigh my various approaches, compounds, and needs in order to make a successful contribution. Jumping in headfirst is like jumping into a pool without assessing the depth of the water. This is very important to me and I have my own opinions about players who just recklessly charge in with guns ablazing, playing real loud and fast without taste or character. Without regard to tone or without trying to fit into what everyone else is doing. It's like some loud drummers who don't care about the ensemble but only about bringing attention to themselves. Or even piano players that just because they have ten fingers, want to make sure they use them all. They're whole presentation is like a run-on sentence without punctuation. They don't breathe or stop because they don't have to and I like to avoid that kind of recklessness.

IF THE PERFECT CREATIVE SITUATION IS COMPLETE FREEDOM, SHOULDN'T THIS CREATIVE PROCESS HAVE INTENT? ISN'T THERE RESPONSIBILITY, WITH ITS OWN SET OF DISCIPLINES THAT COMES WITH THAT FREEDOM?

Freedom of expression is the result of knowing what choices to make. If you don't know what choices to make through study and acknowledgment of history and making yourself aware of the environment you're in, then how are you to know the decisions you are making are going to be sound? Many people have and are dismissive of the precedents that have been established within the music. It's like running out into traffic with a blindfold on. You have to know. You have to have your sensibilities honed and you have to know the game. You have to know the laws in order to break them, to alter them, or to modify them.

AS A PERSON OF COLOR, ARE YOU AWARE OF WHERE YOUR INSPIRATION OR CRE-ATIVITY COMES FROM?

That's a very interesting question but I would have to contend that there are certain biological characteristics that are inherent in people from different ethnic origins and backgrounds. It's self-evident when you see children of one ethnic group embrace certain characteristics in music or they find a beat or a rhythm.

They latch onto certain melodic circumstances and some people just don't. People can argue that but it's self-evident. I don't want to say that that means someone is dominant but some people are predisposed to certain tendencies and that's just the way it is. But I don't want to generalize because that's like saying all Asians are computer whizzes and all Indians are predisposed to being doctors. It's quite ridiculous but there is an abundance of aptitudes such as young black children that can dance as soon as they can walk. They can find the beat or the rhythm. That's almost racist in and of itself in saying that all black children are predisposed to be entertainers or basketball players.

CAN YOU CONNECT MUSIC POLITICALLY, SPIRITUALLY, OR SOCIALLY?

I try not to be detached from what's going on, but outwardly I'm not making any bold political statements because the politics that I abide by are my own politics. I don't abide by the politics of a sixty-plus-year-old silver-haired white guy in Congress. We don't share the same aptitude, the same aspirations, nor are we born of the same environment. There isn't any way that they can see my world or have any empathy for it. So the politics and ideals that I'm presenting in my music are based upon an historical precedent of personal philosophies of self-preservation, motivation, and a progressive, reckless, relentless curious spirit. Which also includes continued growth and prosperity through development and continued learning and that's what it should be about and not about taking arts programs out of schools to provide money for national defense or close libraries so that we can manufacture more biological synthetic viruses. They have their agenda and I have mine.

WHAT HAVE YOU LEARNED ABOUT YOURSELF FROM ALL OF THE RISKS YOU HAVE TAKEN?

It sounds cliché, but you cannot please everyone. However, I try not to be a self-indulgent or an artist saying, "Yeah, I'm playing for myself and the hell with the audience." A lot of people do but they remain poor. I'm not in it for the money either but genuinely to produce work and to share it with people who are interested. I'm not interested in appeasing people who turn a blind ear to the music or people who have it in for me and will never like it. I'm not trying to convince them. I'm trying to convince people who are into new ideas, new approaches, and convince them there are other ways that possibly may inspire them to see yet another option or to take another path, whatever that discipline may be and it may not even be music. There are ways to assume and maintain variables in whatever you do, and hopefully, I'm an example for that and I may be inspirational to some degree. I'm hyped about these things and really excited about it. I just like to share and hopefully draw in people who are interested.

WHAT IS IT ABOUT JAZZ AND THE ART FORM THAT IS IMPORTANT TO YOU?

That you can't hide behind it and you're either proficient or you're not. It's like these older jazz cats after listening to younger players, "Ah, he ain't playin' nothin'."

They're all gruff and grimy and all the technique in the world cannot save you if the statements that you make are not reflective of experience or serious aptitude towards that which you are trying to talk about. Perhaps the best analogy would be the guys recently released from prison. When up for parole they voraciously read a lot of books for three months in the penitentiary library and then come out on the street trying to talk like they read *War and Peace* while using bad syntax. Killing sentences dramatically and functionally, which is like musicians who try to act grandiose in their portrayal of romanticism in the profundity of the jazz life and they are eighteen years old. Or they may be thirty years old but they still don't have a story to tell. They can only tell a tall tale because they hide behind technique and bravado but you can't hide behind a smokescreen in jazz. Unlike other music where people are swayed or distracted by dancing girls, pyro-techniques, and the big stage show. It's more of a spectacle. But jazz is stripped bare with four or five guys on stage and it's as honest as you can get. Either you have it or you don't and either you're doing it or you're not.

WHAT DO YOU ENVISION FOR JAZZ OR FOR YOURSELF PERSONALLY?

I see a healthy future because players are becoming more proficient at an earlier age. The transition from sad to proficient is a lot shorter because of the abundance of intellectual means that's available. It's a good thing. Now we just need an environment for them to hone those skills so that they can see what works and what doesn't. People in my peer group need to actively look to the younger players so that we can nurture and school them and point them in the right direction. I received it from Dizzy Gillespie, Freddie Hubbard, Woody Shaw, McCoy Tyner, Muhl Richard Abhrams, Andrew Hill, Jim Hall, and on and on. I went on the road as an apprentice with these people and saw the life of the road and all the dos and don'ts. That's the only way it's going to survive. Just because they have some talent right out of college doesn't mean you can't expect them to be the golden goose or savior for your label. Invariably, they are still stepping on each other's feet because they don't know what to do. And signing too early actually stunts their growth, and the really sad part is that if they don't make good on the investment, the label drops them like a hot potato and they become damaged goods at twenty-one. Now the only thing they can do is go slumming toward little independent labels in Europe. They are like has-beens before they are twenty-five and they don't grow but stay at the same level. But if they get with someone older and experienced, they can grow progressively and become better and better.

DO YOU HAVE A PHILOSOPHY OR WAY OF LOOKING AT LIFE THAT YOU WOULD BE WILLING TO SHARE?

I try the best I can to maintain a sense of innocence and curiosity and remain a student of life. It keeps me active and thinking about what's next, which is all I can do. Once I get comfortable and resolve that I know it all or believe I have made my grand statement, well, that's the kiss of death and I have seen it happen. But you are only as good as your last profound statement or offering and I don't want that to be the snapshot that I'm referring to for the rest of my life frozen in time. At the conclusion of any recording session or any performance, I'm thinking about tomorrow or what I'm doing next . . . always! That's fodder for progression and is all I need. I don't want my band to become comfortable and start daydreaming so I have to keep the hot coals aflame underfoot. Otherwise it's time to get new cats. I can't replace myself so the best I can do is to stay innocent and maintain that I don't know everything.

32

EVAN PARKER

It may be almost impossible to be involved in free improvisational forms and not be influenced by the compositional genius of Evan Parker. As a saxophonist, he has created one of the most original voices in the history of the instrument and, after several decades, remains one of music's most important pioneers.

TODAY OUR CULTURE HERE IN THE U.S. APPRECIATES ART BUT SEEMS TO HAVE DIFFICULTY WITH CREATIVITY THAT IS NOT EASILY EXPLAINED, UNDERSTOOD, OR IDENTIFIABLE. IS THIS HAPPENING IN EUROPE AND DO YOU THINK THIS IS A SIGNIFICANT OBSTACLE TO OVERCOME FOR CREATIVE MUSIC?

I would say we probably benefit from those people who are looking outside the established culture, the officially provided stuff. The ones sick of the idea of being treated as consumers who want a more active part in the music or want more engagement from the music and want more of a challenge. Again, it's a minority but I think it's a minority that will, if anything, grow. I think the more homogenized and standardized the official culture becomes, the more people will seek information elsewhere and I think we're seeing that now. You can extrapolate from that the resistance to global capitalism with large demonstrations happening not just in Europe but also in America. These are mostly young people not happy with being told how and what to consume and maybe we have something that could be of interest for some of them.

ARE JAZZ PURISTS IN THE U.S. HAVING A DIFFICULT TIME ACCEPTING THAT A MU-
SIC FORM CONSIDERED "AMERICAN" NOW HAS MORE VISIBLE INTERNATIONAL AND
DIVERSE ASPECTS WITHIN IT?

I see a trend in American journalism and criticism that does provide that point
of view. But I equally well know American writers who understand the European
scene better than a lot of the European critics. I think it's pretty obvious that jazz
has always been a music that has taken inputs from different cultures and different sources. This is not to take anything away from the great achievements of the
classic phases of jazz in America, not at all. One of its successes was to become a
world language that was then interpreted in different ways or responded to in different ways by non-American cultures all over the world. This is a tradition that
Americans can be very pleased about and they can be proud of the fact that it traveled well. What can't be done is to make those same people feel any particular af-
fection for the responses and interpretations that come back in slightly other languages, other dialects, and other forms. We win some and we lose some.

For myself, I started to play because of classic modern jazz from Charlie Parker
onward. But my understanding of that tradition was that it was a dynamic one and
your creative imperative was to find something new. The idea that jazz is a classical music is something we associate with a younger generation of musicians and
OK, that's the way they see it. The chief spokesman I suppose would be Wynton
Marsalis. There were exponents of classic jazz who were resistant to the notions of
freedom from Ornette Coleman onward and probably before that. It shouldn't be
forgotten that many of the swing-era musicians were hostile towards bebop so the
whole thing is cycles of attitudes that are repeated. They are repeated generation
upon generation and every so often you have a generation that revives some previous style. The traditional jazz revival here in the '50s included people who discovered Bunk Johnson and the original New Orleans style of playing and they
wanted to go back to that. That gradually turned into something here that was
called Trad Jazz that you probably called Dixieland more often. I was never very
interested in that but I'm interested in the original stuff and I think that's the difference. Some people want the music to stay still, become classical and codified
with all the rules and regulations neatly checked in boxes, and other people want
to add some new boxes and change a few rules.

THERE IS LITERALLY TONS OF INFORMATION ON THE CHRONOLOGY AND HISTORY
OF JAZZ BUT RARELY ON THE HISTORY OF FREE OR IMPROVISED MUSIC OUTSIDE OF
ALBERT AYLER AND ORNETTE COLEMAN. SINCE YOU STARTED IN IMPROVISED MU-
SIC, HAVE YOU OBSERVED ANY SHIFT IN STYLES OR IS IT STILL EXPANDING UPON THE
IDEAS THAT YOU FIRST ENCOUNTERED WHEN YOU FIRST CAME INTO THIS MUSIC?

Once you say anything goes then anything is quite a big category. So anything
has been happening ever since in the name of anything goes. Anything can be any
number of somethings. I'm just responsible for some of those somethings.

SO YOU DON'T WANT TO BE A SPOKESPERSON FOR OTHERS?

Well no, I suppose we have our own originals inside the music and our own less originals where people are dependent upon other people's discoveries or approaches and are playing a kind of generic free music that may not be that interesting. In the same way that people took from the originals in other styles of music. There are generic forms of all types of music if the critics want to jump through the history and name the names. Of course, I could beat my chest proudly and say X, Y, Z about myself but so could every other guy playing the saxophone. This is not for me to say.

KARLHEINZ STOCKHAUSEN SAID THE ARTIST HAS LONG BEEN REGARDED AS THE INDIVIDUAL WHO REFLECTED THE SPIRIT OF THEIR TIME. THAT THERE HAVE ALWAYS BEEN DIFFERENT KINDS OF ARTISTS: THOSE THAT ARE A MIRROR OF THEIR TIME, AND THE VERY FEW WHO HAVE VISIONARY POWER. IS IT POSSIBLE THAT WHAT'S HAPPENING IN CREATIVE MUSIC IS TOO FORWARD THINKING FOR MUCH OF OUR SOCIETY TODAY OR HAS THIS ALWAYS BEEN THE CHALLENGE FOR FORWARD-THINKING COMPOSERS? IS THE MUSIC TOO COMPLEX FOR MOST LISTENERS?

It's very possible that the music is too complex for most listeners, but we are not playing for most listeners. We are playing for ourselves, for the music, and for the people that are interested. I hope that the music is visionary or at least represents an interesting response to the spirit of the time. These times are materialistic times with very low levels of public discourse and consumer patterns and very low levels of ecological and political awareness. So given that I don't think that the people who listen to our music are likely to share those average kinds of views, I suppose I would claim that we are visionary. The Stockhausen category of visionary—even if that's largely an intuitive vision, an intuitive understanding of reactive and reacting against anything but that kind of approach. I also think it has social relevance and it's a question of people that write about it, talking to other people about it, which I know you are doing by writing this book. And gradually people that have an appetite for that kind of something to work with, something to think about, something to chew on, something to study and even learn will be attracted to it. And people that think of music as a way of switching off and relaxing and whatever they call it, then OK, there's plenty of stuff prepared especially for them.

IS IT POSSIBLE THAT A NEW TYPE OF CREATIVE MUSIC MIGHT COME OUT OF ALL THAT IS GOING ON GLOBALLY TODAY?

Yes. There is a piece of graffiti that perhaps didn't originate in London but I saw it on a wall in Shoreditch—it said, "War is so last century." Yesterday, I also read a quote from Oscar Wilde that touched on the same idea that was something like: All the while people think that war is sinful, they'll find it interesting. It's only when they see it's vulgar, that the world will turn away from it. And I think more and more that we see clearly that the people didn't want this war. Certain political forces and certain business forces wanted this war but ordinary people didn't want it. It was of dubious legality in terms of UN mandates and international law. Without being at all pleased about it, all the things that were articulated by people who were against the war are coming true. The troops are bogged down now and the situation is not so easy to resolve for outsiders. Whether it would have ever been resolvable for insiders is another question, but this approach was obviously not just morally wrong but tactically inept. I think the people are ahead of the politicians a lot of the time now and there is a feeling that there must be a better way, a better way for manufacturers to make a living rather than making weapons and looking for new markets for weapons all around the world all of the time. This is boring, this is last century, and it's even arguably two centuries old. And a few people have gradually, certainly the enlightened ones and plenty of them in America are sick of this kind of vulgarity in the Oscar Wilde sense.

THERE IS A HELPLESS FEELING WITH MANY HERE IN THE U.S. AND I KNOW THAT MOST OF THE PEOPLE THAT I KNOW OR INTERACT WITH FEEL THE SAME WAY. I'M NOT SURE IF IT APPEARS THIS WAY FOR THOSE INTERNATIONALLY BUT FOR MANY OF US, THERE APPEARS TO BE DEFENSIVENESS ABOUT THE AGGRESSION AND ABOUT BEING A PART OF WHAT'S GOING TO BE A FACTOR IN THE FUTURE WORLD.

I don't think you have to worry; it's very well understood here that there is opposition inside of America. In fact, the basic thing even goes back to the original question as to whether Bush was even really elected, whether he really has a mandate, and whether he should be president. We can see how frustrating it must be for people there to be dealing with this situation but there is only one way to deal with it and that's to voice your opinions and to join together with others and hope that the situation improves. I mean the election of Schwarzenegger, the governor of California, is not a very encouraging sign. All the while the media is in the hands of big business, it's hard to get any other ideas across but I think that as people start to switch away from media-business-controlled news and go more and more to the Internet for the true stories, it is likely that the controlling powers will learn to manipulate that too. We must stay alert.

I HOPE THAT IN SOME WAY OUTSIDE OF PEOPLE USING THE INTERNET AS A WAY OF ACQUIRING NEWS, PEOPLE WILL ALSO FIND A WAY TO COMMUNICATE WITH EACH OTHER GLOBALLY AND PERHAPS SOMEHOW FIND A WAY TO INFLUENCE THE CHOICES AND DIRECTION OF OUR LEADERS.

It's already happening. I mean there was very intense communication prior to the invasion, the war, or whatever you want to call it. I think Marc Ribot has been responsible for an initiative to try to better communicate the feeling of frustration that you are talking about so that Europeans don't assume that all Americans support this kind of activity.

IS IT MORE DIFFICULT FOR A STUDENT TO BE CREATIVE IN TODAY'S SOCIETY? IS THERE A DIFFERENT SET OF CHALLENGES THE STUDENTS FACE TODAY?

No, I think the problem is always the same. It's like, this is what's there, what are you going to do in response to it? But there are changes of course with each generation but what you do in response to it is really a matter of your own intuitions and your own emotional response.

DO YOU HAVE A PHILOSOPHY THAT YOU TRY TO IMPART AMONG STUDENTS OR YOUNG MUSICIANS?

I think that that's a very hard thing to sum up in a few sentences during an interview. Yeah, I won't attempt that.

SO IT IS IMPORTANT TO YOU?

Well, they say that a donkey carrying a lot of books is still a donkey. I might be one of those.

THERE IS CLEARLY A LACK OF UNDERSTANDING WITHIN THE U.S. OF WHAT IS MEANT BY THE TERM "FREE JAZZ." FOR THOSE OF US LISTENERS WHO THINK WE HAVE SOMEWHAT OF AN UNDERSTANDING, WE HEAR THE FORM AND THE DEVELOPMENT OF THAT FORM OVER THE COURSE OF A PIECE TAKE SHAPE. THAT WOULD DESCRIBE A CLEAR DISCIPLINE WITHIN THE MUSIC FROM THE START UNTIL THE COMPLETION OF THE PIECE. THE QUESTION MANY OF US HAVE IS, WHO IS LEADING THE DEVELOPMENT OF THE FORM AND WHAT HAPPENS IF THERE IS CREATIVE INPUT OR ENERGY THAT DIFFERS BETWEEN THE MUSICIANS? DOES THIS ENHANCE THE CREATIVITY AND ENERGY OF THE MUSIC OR DOES THE FORM START TO LOSE ITS FUNCTION?

This notion of form, the whole thing is the form, what happens is the form. The idea of applying architectural principles to a dynamic form that's revealed in time is not terribly useful, I don't think. What happens in the time that it takes to happen, that's the form. Whether you call something logical, surprising, or illogical therefore surprising, and whether surprises are good or surprises are bad, all of these issues are dealt with in particular improvisations by particular players over and over again. But the fact remains that this music unfolds in time and the form takes the time that it takes to be revealed. And this is not like saying, OK, so we'll repeat the structure twenty-six times. This is not to say that you cannot use cyclic elements and repetitions, but those elements and repetitions are both subject to fresh interpretations in the moment so that the final form is not fixed in a box but is fixed in the course of the making of the piece.

TENSION SEEMS TO BE A SIGNIFICANT PART OF THE CREATIVE PROCESS IN IMPROVISED MUSIC. HOW DO YOU GO ABOUT CONSTRUCTING THAT ASPECT OF THE MUSIC?

Tension is one of the words that's typically used as one of a pair with release. Dominant and tonic would be equivalent to on-beat and off-beat. Which is the tension and which is the release? As the music complexifies and as our attitudes towards what's fresh are determined by what is already well-known and what remains to be discovered, then the whole notion of what constitutes tension changes with time. I don't think there are specific techniques to generate tension or specific techniques to generate resolution in free improvisation. These are issues that are, once again, determined in the course of the piece. But what might constitute resolution in a free improvisation may very well be a rhythmic cadence as much as a harmonic shift from closed-voice sounds to open-voice sounds or whatever the classic harmonic cadence forms might take in free improvisation. That's very often done rhythmically more than harmonically. Some people say rhythm, what rhythm? If you don't hear it, you don't hear it. Some people hear it, some people don't. We're back to the other question.

And I suppose by the same token the music is its own best explanation. We can talk for another five hours and we still wouldn't really explain the music. The music explains itself. And by exposure to the music and by exposure to the history of the music, this is the way somebody will come to an understanding of how the music works. But if they don't like the sound of it, why should they bother, and I'm the first to agree. If you don't like the sound of it, don't bother. I'm not proselytizing in that sense except by being there and being ready to play. But I'm not trying to convert people who don't have a degree of initial curiosity. It's very common to find the first reaction of, "The first time I heard you I thought you were crazy. I don't know what made me come back. Something made me come back. And now, I think I get it or now I think you're the greatest thing on the planet." This is the kind of pattern that I hear from people. They have not necessarily fallen in love with it or get it the very first time that they hear it, but there is something about it that fascinates them and brings them back and it's only a small percentage. So again, we're repeating elements of the answers to previous questions but it's all one question in the end I guess.

THE FOLLOWING IS A QUOTE FROM CECIL TAYLOR: "MUSIC HAS TO DO WITH A LOT OF AREAS WHICH ARE MAGICAL RATHER THAN LOGICAL; THE GREAT ARTISTS, RATHER THAN JUST GETTING INVOLVED WITH DISCIPLINE, GET TO UNDERSTAND LOVE AND ALLOW THE LOVE TO TAKE SHAPE." HOW MUCH OF YOUR MUSIC IS FROM LOGIC AND HOW MUCH FROM THIS OTHER PLACE THAT CECIL TAYLOR DESCRIBES?

When I use the word "logic" about music, I think it should probably be in quote marks because of course music is not from the place of logic. You could find yourself in a situation here if you believe that, then you will probably believe in formally and balanced equations and therefore X plus Y equals just X plus Y. Therefore, something interesting has happened because of that but that's not what I mean by logic. Sometimes a surprise can be an illogical thing to happen but then you are talking about a very strange notion, a very strange use of the word "logic." As usual, when Cecil talks about the music, he says something very profound and very, very important. We need a return to the role of the musician as a shaman or as someone capable of evoking good thoughts in the audience or provoking response. Provoking thought, provoking response because people need to wake up. For any number of reasons, they need to wake up. But primarily because of the stranglehold of big business on the planet and they are killing the planet and it's got to stop. The population explosion has got to stop. There are so many things that are wrong with the trends at the moment. The ice caps are melting, what more has to happen before people start to think about the patterns of their consumption and their personal responsibility?

IT'S QUITE DEPRESSING ACTUALLY.

This is a complex world but if we can link those kinds of thoughts with the music, I would hope that that does some good. Let people know that the musicians are concerned. Most of the musicians that I know in this field of music are concerned and are trying to do something.

CAN YOU TALK ABOUT HOW YOUR MUSICAL THINKING HAS EVOLVED TOWARDS COMPOSITION FROM YOUR EARLIEST WRITINGS TO THE PRESENT? WHAT WERE THE SIGNIFICANT FACTORS THAT HAVE EVOLVED IN YOUR MUSIC?

Again, I think this is best answered by listening to the music itself. In some ways, I think the basic assumptions remain the same but sometimes the ways in which it's expressed are more under control, more sophisticated, but I don't know. Again, I feel that this is an answer that somebody else should answer but I hope it's still alive. My main job is to keep my music alive and input into the music alive. Of course, the longer you go on, the more accretions of habit and stylistic considerations come into it. The skills are improved but the habits are more extensive; it's a question of the musician's relationship with their own habits. It then becomes a crucial thing for keeping it alive.

WITH MANY JAZZ MUSICIANS, THE LISTENER IS A CONSIDERATION WHEN THE PIECE IS DEVELOPED ON PAPER. HOWEVER, WITH YOUR MUSIC, I HEAR SOMEONE THAT IS TAKING A FORM AND LOOKING FOR ALL THE POSSIBILITIES OF DEVELOPMENT OF THAT FORM.

First of all, it has to be for the people I'm playing with and for myself, but it has to be right and if it's right, then it's ready for other people if they're interested. But if I start thinking about what people would like then this would indulge in the most absurd kind of generalization about other human beings. That's part of the thinking that's taking the planet the wrong way. People thinking that they know how a lot of other people think. I don't know how people think but I know how I think and I know how the musicians that I work with think well enough in order to organize a concert or two. Beyond that, it's a question of individual choices about other people's responses of whether they choose to come or whether they choose to do something else. That's up to them, but it's pretty obvious to me that if somebody likes sitting home and watching these so-called reality-TV programs, they're not likely to come out and listen to me.

CAN YOU DESCRIBE YOUR APPROACH AND PROCESS AND WHAT YOU ARE ATTEMPTING TO DO WITHIN THE CONTEXT OF THE MUSIC? ARE YOU GETTING CLOSER TO THE SOUND THAT YOU HEAR OR DOES IT KEEP CHANGING?

Well, if I had an absolutely clear idea of how I wanted the music to sound, I wouldn't improvise. I'm interested in finding out what the music is going to sound like that I improvise. OK, certain results please me better than other results where I follow those avenues of pleasing results. But that's not with the aim of duplicating already pleasing results but following the path of those results to some new places, hopefully. And the potential for evolution in particular combinations of musicians interests me enormously, and obviously staying together with Schlippenbach and Lovens for more than thirty years means that I still find where we go with that stuff interesting. I have been playing with Barry Guy and Paul Lytton almost as long, which means that I find working with them still interesting. However, other combinations and relationships seem to have come to a natural end at different points with fresh relationships starting all the time. I have the advantage of living in a city with a large pool of players to draw from with wonderful opportunities in which to perform on a regular basis. That's it. So when new things come then, OK, see where the life is and where it's leading and go with it.

You cannot get angry if the music doesn't come out at a certain place or a certain way. It's just not a very intelligent thing for somebody interested in improvisation to do. You have to accept that you're only partially in control of the result and you have to enjoy that, the risk, and the risk sometimes means failing. OK, not failing too badly but failing in an interesting way. Not always making it clear where you consider the failure to have been and if somebody wants to go through the records, they'll see and find out that, well, it didn't last long or that lasted hell of a long time. What's the difference between those two things? Again, it's the critic's job to do that, not for me to explain all these mysteries beyond a certain point, you know. I can give you a clue but I can't tell you the whole answer.

A MUSICIAN'S RELATIONSHIP WITH TIME AND HOW THEY DEAL WITH IT DOES NOT GET OPENLY DISCUSSED THAT OFTEN. CAN YOU DISCUSS YOUR APPROACH WITH TIME?

There is an American scientist, mathematician, or philosopher, Charles Arthur Muses, whose views on time appeal to me very much indeed. There is a diagram that comes with his book, *Destiny and Control of Human Systems*, where he plots the various ways of seeing time above and below an axis— future–past, conscious and unconscious. At the middle of it is an individual breaking into the so-called moment and I think the cliché of the moment is somehow overdone. Most of us live in a place inhabited by memories that is also driven by desires. Each of those things can be either conscious or subconscious so the complexities of all of those things make up what I take to be the time in which we live. Any moment of time includes those four axes, which is like a compass. Four points of a compass around the moment in time in the conscious moment of time of an individual . . . or the being moment in time of an individual. Because, as I've said, above is perhaps conscious but below is unconscious. Ahead is future and behind is past, but all of those things are in the being time of an individual. Some of that finds its equivalents in the music and certain techniques can only be developed through repetition.

Certain understandings can only come about through discovery and those understandings can only be reapplied when those insights and techniques are re-called. So the whole notion of being in the moment is a little more complicated than it at first appears. You also have to have somewhere you want to go and that's also in this moment where you live. The future is also in that moment or your view of the future branched as it may be at many different points where a decision needs to be made. That's about it. If anybody wants to know further, they should check out Charles Arthur Muses. A great American philosopher and it's very hard to find his stuff. A very remarkable man, the more you investigate, the more re-markable.

DRUMMERS AND BASS PLAYERS CAN COME UP WITH THEIR OWN LANGUAGE WITHIN THE CONTEXT OF WHAT'S HAPPENING IN A LIVE SITUATION. WHAT DO YOU LOOK FOR FROM DRUMMERS AND BASS PLAYERS AND HOW MUCH OF IT HAS TO DO WITH THEIR RHYTHMIC APPROACH WITH EACH OTHER?

What I want is a sense that somebody is there to find what the music can be and not to show what they already know, although that's a fine distinction. They have to bring something. They have to bring a bunch of stuff with them from the past but be looking to the future. Why do some things work and other things don't work too well? I don't know. The questions are about compatibility coming from ques-tions of predispositions, preferences, tastes, styles, and congruence. Some people sound great on their own but you put two of them together and they sort of can-cel out one another. Some people understand the mechanisms of cancellations well enough so that doesn't happen. That's what keeps it interesting. I have noth-ing against routine if people want to bring routine but someone has to come fresh. Stay alive. They have to be in that moment where anything can happen or feel that anything can happen. The stuff you bring is just the place to start from. It's the stuff you discover that's the reason for going there.

WHERE DOES YOUR INSPIRATION COME FROM OR WHAT INFLUENCES YOUR CRE-ATIVITY?

You know, that varies at different times but I tend not to listen to other impro-vised music on record. I'm so busy with my own stuff and with the things that I would like to issue on my label that I don't really get a chance to listen to what is going on very properly. And the explosion of the exponential growth of recordings of improvised music also makes it very difficult to have a very good overview of the whole thing. Subsequently, I rely on recommendations from other people, but if I hear people playing live that impress me, I may go back and look for some record-ings. Outside of that, as a record collector, I would say that I more or less only col-lect ethnic classical recordings, field recordings from other cultures, especially en-dangered cultures. Those of course can be a source of amazement, absolute amazement. But then again, a donkey with a big load of records on his back is still a donkey. I have some good records of what they call ethnic music. Ethnic music, where did this term get started? I'm interested in music from endangered cultures, minority cultures, known global cultures. I'm not especially interested in world music once it's been pasteurized, homogenized, and served up, re-served up—then I'm not so interested. I'm interested in the real field recordings from Folkways onward. That's the kind of stuff I collect.

WHAT DO YOU ENVISION THE FUTURE OF CREATIVE MUSIC TO BE AND FOR YOURSELF PERSONALLY?

The future of music remains there . . . in the imagination. If somebody can think of it and if somebody can imagine it, that's where it's going to go next. That's the one part of the job of being in the time: You have to know what is possible, what is the future. How is the future beckoning to you? Muses talks about imagination as memory of the future. We just have to keep our imaginations sharp and listen hard to what's going on. Whenever an idea is tested, see what can be done with that idea. See what makes sense.

In a situation where anything goes, it's going to be very hard to shock anybody anymore in the subculture that I operate in. Nobody is going to be shocked in whatever I do and even if they were shocked, they would never admit that they were shocked. And I can't think of anything I'm interested in doing that they would find shocking. So it's really not about shock, it's more about inventiveness and freshness. And life, living life forward, which is the only way it goes.

DO YOU HAVE A PHILOSOPHY OR SOME WAY OF LOOKING AT LIFE THAT YOU WOULD BE WILLING TO SHARE?

I would say that the most profound influences in terms of my view would be John Coltrane, Idries Shah, and Charles Muses. Perhaps coming a little further down the line would be political philosophers like Bakunin and Kropotkin—contemporaries of Marx who were critical of his theories and for very good reasons that have subsequently been proven to be right. Muses says in his book *Destiny and Control in Human Systems* that the great tragedy of our times is that too many people spend their lives doing work that is contrary to their own natures. That might be it in a nutshell.

WILLIAM PARKER

"It is the role of the artist to incite political, social, and spiritual revolution, to awaken us from our sleep and never let us forget our obligations as human beings, to light the fire of human compassion."

—William Parker

There has never been a bassist/drummer collaboration quite like that of William Parker and Hamid Drake. Able to manipulate time, rhythmic shape, and feel; they can influence the temperature and weight of the music without ever losing the center of the piece.

YOU RECENTLY PERFORMED IN RUSSIA. WERE THE AUDIENCES PRETTY HIP TO THE MUSIC?

The people were very much into the music and are just happy to have something going on. Hamid Drake and I performed concerts in Moscow and St. Petersburg and the festival, now in its sixth or seventh year, has an audience that's still building and developing.

We also didn't know what time we were going to play until the day of the concert. They use paintings rather than posters, which really don't provide much information. The location of the event isn't even provided but somehow people find out. The place was full, they enjoyed the music, and everything seemed to work out OK.

ARE WE GETTING ANY CLOSER TO BRIDGING THE GAP BETWEEN OUR DIFFERENT CULTURES?

I think we have a long way to go. New York is a melting pot with people from all over the world but we are not familiar or educated with regard to other cultures, music, poetry, or history. We are into American culture and this is when traveling as well. It's obvious with the musicians I know, and we work in Europe 95 percent of the time. You will not see French musicians performing in New York, and when the ICP Orchestra travels to New York, they are sponsored by the French government, not the American government. We need a minister of culture that's going to take the job seriously. We are all human beings and should be able to do a study exchange with countries like France and Sweden. It should be mandatory in all educational institutions.

Upon arriving in Russia, someone was to pick us up at 4:00 A.M. but didn't arrive until 5:30 A.M. and *they were on foot*. Living in America, we often don't have any idea how other people in the world live. Some people cannot get up in the morning and take a shower and we cannot even get close to understanding that way of life.

IS IT POSSIBLE THAT A NEW TYPE OF CREATIVITY MIGHT COME OUT OF ALL THAT IS GOING ON GLOBALLY?

Our ears, hearts, and souls are always yearning for something creative, but we have been numbed. Our sense of touch, feel, and taste has been deadened and our impulse to reach out to creativity has been damaged. We have given up our individuality by trying to fit in and are never encouraged to explore and told that our individuality is OK. We are always being told what we need to have and not encouraged to just be ourselves. People have a need and desire for creativity, but for many people, it's dormant or has not been awakened. Our minds are open, but our feelings are not and we may want to intellectually adjust to things before we feel them. It's an entirely different area than having things reach you intellectually.

IS THERE ENCOURAGEMENT FOR ARTISTIC FREEDOM TODAY?

In Europe, there are international jazz festivals being held in cities half the size of New York. And it's not their music so they don't have to do these festivals. They could say, "We have unemployed Italians, why should we pay for you to come over here to play music?" I have observed this in Italy, Holland, France, and in Norway.

I played in Poland for two weeks in 1980 and marshal law had just been declared. There were long lines of people trying to get food and they even had to sign a list in order to get meat. Most people would have canceled the festival but they didn't cancel the festival and they didn't even think about not having the music. They went ahead with their commitment.

In America, you can get a degree in art but when you get out of school, what do you do? You work a day job, paint, put it into a corner, and then you do another painting. But in Holland, the government buys paintings, places them in libraries, and the public can borrow them as you would a library book and then take it back and get another painting.

Artists are the easiest type of profession to employ and every school in America that has an auditorium could have an art gallery, hold elections, or concerts where students could meet musicians which could be funded through the government. President Jimmy Carter implemented the CETA arts program (Comprehensive Employment and Training Act), which hired musicians with theater companies. I auditioned and was given a job with Theater Forgotten, a theater which provided performance for forgotten people such as those in prisons. I wrote music for theater puppet shows and also performed with a band called the Juess Quartet. The theater also did concerts, workshops, and plays for a year but when Ronald Reagan became president he cut the program. I knew it worked because you could begin to see the temperament of New York change. People would ask, "Where's the concert at lunchtime?" You could find artists painting murals and it was wonderful!

A ten-year program where children could be exposed to art and music on a pretty regular level is needed. A support system would be required, but after a period of time these types of programs would support themselves just from the ticket sales alone because these same young children will eventually start going to the theater on their own.

Do artists have a higher awareness level?

There are many artists who are in touch with their profound side and are what you would call special people. There are also those who are not, but still have layers of professionalism attached to their art. Even at the lowest levels, art that is thought mundane can ignite, catch fire, and the artist can step over the line to another dimension. That's the wonder and beauty of it. Even when you don't want it to, it can get out of hand and work better than you anticipated. Again, there are artists who are very, very good at it and know how to work this magic more consistently than others but I think this has to do with training.

People are not told that music can heal nor provided the aesthetic behind why they are doing what they are doing. Music can change people's lives but what's the purpose of the music? Does it distract or take away from whom they call the "pure artist"? This is the artist that doesn't want to have any political or social meaning to their work. But someone could have a song called "The Greatest Revolutionary Is a Flower." The things that are the most beautiful are the things that change us the most.

What is beauty to you?

Beauty is what makes anything in life work on a level beyond our comprehension. It's a doorway that leads to the greater good in mankind. It's also connected to nature and brings out the best in us. What is beautiful? A sunrise. What is beautiful? A sunset. What is beautiful? A flower. These things are way beyond that which we can create. They are things that we can tap into but we don't necessarily have to create them because we are also part of that creation and are beautiful too. What's beautiful? What's music? What's art? All of these things are closely connected but the consistent answer is the result that they consistently bring. The overwhelming feeling to give, to share, and create something that's a reflection of what you think is beautiful.

DIDN'T YOU ALSO STUDY A METHOD OF RELATING IDEAS OF VISION, COLOR, AND SOUND?

I've always felt that acquiring music knowledge was basically an autodidact process. I had ideas and theories about improvisation and their relationships when I was playing very intensely. Like colors of heat. Having a red flame, a blue flame, and a white flame. The amount of energy you use to make sound vibrate is connected with particular colors. If you are playing high sounds or harmonics, they floated upwards. If you looked up, you saw sky that was blue and cloudlike. With thick bass lines, you have trees going into the ground so they were brown. Melodies come up from the ground and are green, yellow, and orange. There are also clusters of sound, which couldn't be anything else but brown. You also have horizons, which are your meditations, your drones and repetitive rhythms. These things all have long cycles. The sun takes a bit of time to rise and fall and the sky remains a certain color. So if you observe these things, the idea was that each musician should catalog what a certain note was for them, what that sound means for them.

One of the first thoughts I had when playing the bass was that the strings were bands of light and the bow was a prism. When you ran light through a prism, you had harmonics, and the harmonics are the nutrients of the sound. You have the sound of the sound, which is like the taste of the food, but the nutrients of the food have an entirely different perspective. If you play one string, it's from the idea that, "I'm going to play this note and this is going to happen. If I play this sound, someone is going to move in a certain way." This is a call to a certain feeling and spirit which gave me the strength to find meaning in every sound and tone that I made.

Right now, I'm reinvestigating these ideas because it's a lifelong process and you still want it to be magical in a way. But there is always fear because we don't necessarily want to dissect the flower. You still want to have respect for the mystery. It doesn't have to be scientifically proven but you have to know that it's important and know that well. There is sound and there is music. The colors are just relating sounds to colors and the amount of energy to make these colors. Like a ballad might be a certain color and certain rhythm might be a certain color. But then again, another musician might have an entirely different system of how he or she relates to his or her sound.

CAN YOU DISCUSS YOUR RELATIONSHIP WITH SOUND?

Music is anything that is beautiful, and sound is the poetry and the dance that makes the music work. A catalytic element that makes music beautiful and sometimes music manifests itself in different ways.

If I spent all day working in the desert and someone came up with a nice cold glass of lemonade, that's music. If you are a little league baseball player and the coach gives you a brand new uniform, that's music. Sound is one way in which music manifests itself. When I started playing music, I studied fundamentals and would try to copy bass lines off of records but I wasn't very successful. So I thought perhaps I wasn't supposed to play the bass lines in the same way as Richard Davis. I won't imitate him, but see if I can do something that will work in that particular music. Again, the greatest teacher is the music itself and the key is to let go.

My students will ask about finding their own sound but finding your sound is like finding your nose. You find it by not looking. The more you look, the further away you'll get. When you first stumble awkwardly with your first sounds, those are your first steps towards originality. You have a musical DNA in the same way that you have a life DNA. Music was here before we were, so all we are doing is tapping into it, trying to get it through us, and the key is to just let go. Once I realized how to let go, music would not leave me alone and I composed a record about this process called *Flowers Grow in My Room*. It's a combination of letting go and flowing with what you let go. It's a matter of shutting off the idea of history in your head.

Charlie Parker did not play everything that can be played, and no matter how beautiful and how much music Louis Armstrong played, he'll never be able to play as good as you because he's not supposed to. He's Louie Armstrong and you are you. You cannot be a better Louie Armstrong and Louie Armstrong can't be a better you. It's just a matter of tapping into your energy and flowing with it. It's like a contradiction. It's flowing with it, holding onto it and letting it go at the same time. That's the key to tapping into one's relationship with sound. It's not really about being a musician or being an anything. It's about flowing with it until you feel comfortable with whatever you are going to be and do it in a way without your ego getting in the way and losing any of the magic.

CAN SPIRITUALITY BE REFLECTIVE OF ONE'S CULTURE, COLOR, OR DOES IT EXIST ON A DIFFERENT LEVEL?

Spirituality is a work in progress. It unfolds in so many different ways and when we think we have it pegged, we find another entirely different aspect to its existence. For some, spirituality is the core of the music so they believe that the music is not them, but a vehicle in which God works through them. I assume that when you play music, it's not you. It's coming through you because it's not consistent with your personality. For example, sometimes musicians don't understand what's happening to them. Such as Mingus getting physically violent and then playing such beautiful music. Charlie Parker could be in very bad shape but when he put his horn in his mouth, things happened. Chet Baker supposedly didn't take a trumpet lesson in his life and was heavy into drugs, but when he played, some magical things happened. But off the bandstand, he was very destructive. You begin to believe that what is called spirituality are gifts that are given to people. Some people accept them gracefully, and some people don't. But whether you accept it or not, it's a gift.

I think a lot of people resist and cannot blend the two together. There are musicians from Africa who talk about healing drums and how the shamans deal with music as a healing force. It's quite different from going to a classical music concert, but again, it's not about style and improvisation compared with nonimprovisation. The healing part of music doesn't come from style or from whether it's written or improvised and that's what's wonderful about it.

I once played with an older Cuban arts band and they told me that the real music of every culture is never recorded. What's exported from different countries is sort of one thing but the real music is on the same level as what you would call "creative music." That's when I had the idea that if you took musicians from Korea, Japan, and Africa who are on the same level and put them in a room together and said, "Let's play." No written music, just a downbeat, boom! We could all play and communicate.

CAN YOU EXPLAIN YOUR RELATIONSHIP WITH TIME IN A MUSICAL SENSE?

A person from the BBC asked me to define free music and I explained that free music is where you are free to do whatever you want to do. If you were a painter and I said, "I only want you to paint bebop and with bebop, only use the colors red, blue, and green. And with Dixieland music, only use purple, red, and black." But free music is any color, sound, or texture that exists. You are free to use them without someone telling you how or when to use them.

This was very evident when I was playing with Cecil Taylor in the sense that dealing with time, you could play time continuous. You could play a metered time 6, you could play a 3, you could play 7, and you could play that continuously or you could change time signatures with every beat. And then time became pulse. And before pulse, you had impulse, which again was an entirely different theory because it was almost like you were what the time was. It's like anticipation. Or time became melody, rhythm, and all these other things, and you saw all these different ways of playing of what they call time.

When I met Billy Higgins, I was a kid playing the drums and Billy was the son of another musician. He used to invite me over to his house, which was in Brooklyn on St. Marks Avenue. I would go out there a couple of times a week and we would play duets and dance with the time.

Time became many things and had transformed itself. It's the life of the music. The breath of the music was time. It's no longer only about numbers as it graduated into all these other things. When I played with Cecil Taylor, I could do anything I wanted because the music was working 99 percent of the time. I could play a tango, a waltz, or play something I didn't even know. The only criteria was that it had to work. And how do you know when it's going to work? How do you know when to play fast or when to play slow? In the navigation of sound, how do you know when to just let go?

There is a warehouse of language—a musical language of sound. The skill is in knowing when and how to use it and how to place them so that they become their own entity. You don't try to own them but try to let them be, and by letting them be, you also learn how to control them without a fearful control. If you are one with something, you are really not controlling it because it's doing what it wants to do and you're doing what you want to do but you are one. Time is an element and rhythm is an element. All of these are elements of music and elements of harmony. The mystery always has to be there too and once you have this realization, the fear of losing it goes away. You don't lose it just because you touched it. It's such a mystery and is beyond us.

I play with a group called the Music Ensemble where we play total improvised music. After playing three sets for three or four nights in a row, you think, "Wow, that first set was fantastic, we're never going to top that." Then you play the second set and you say, "That was totally different. I didn't know I had that much language." You start out playing the same thing and then you realize it's not the same thing. It's never the same, which is like life. You wake up every day and it's a different day. Even though it's the same Monday morning at 7:00, it's a different Monday and a different 7:00. That's why it's like an improvisation and you can never tire of it. It's always moving, always changing, and is always in a different spot in time. Again, these are things one discovers from doing it repetitiously and you can never catch up to these concepts of why things are beautiful and endless.

WHAT MAKES YOUR RELATIONSHIP WITH HAMID DRAKE UNIQUE?

There is a high level of telepathic communication that exists between us. Hamid is a kindred spirit and we have never discussed what we're going to play and that's from the very first time we ever played together. It's just very, very natural and beautiful.

I recently performed concerts in Europe with the "Raining on the Moon" band and Hamid couldn't make the tour so we used another drummer who was very good. But when Hamid returned, he totally broke up the rhythms. He was playing Kimbay rhythms on the cymbals along with many different time patterns. And Hamid has a burning joy that comes through and joy is a very important word, which is very different from happy. So there is joy and the music is constantly changing, going wherever it wants to go.

You also need to be able to listen for long periods of time and listen to various quartets and trios. After several weeks, you begin to see the long range of where the music can go. You get an inkling of the possibilities. It's also very innovative to change the rhythms into chance, where he's playing half of the rhythm and I'm playing the other half. It's like learning to take the most awkward thing and turn it into something that works. It's a quality that Milt Jackson and Art Farmer used to have. Milt Jackson could turn solo after solo in connecting the patterns and phrasing of anything that he played. Art Farmer as well. He could play an entire set of ballads at the same tempo, which wasn't boring, and that's like the most difficult thing in the world to do.

These rhythms and patterns start out from anywhere and always end up in unpredictable places. It shows you that it's an unstoppable thing. Thus, combinations of where you enter into the music, where you stop, and where you develop it is quite amazing and always surprises me.

Also in dealing with time, we can lock into a fast or slow time or we can go into the blues. We can use all of the elements of not only black music, but all elements of music. I recently started playing Native American music and Oscar Pettiford said that the Indian contribution to jazz was 4/4 time. So I've been using those rhythms. I have been using broken rhythms from different places and the amounts of things there are to play are just endless.

When you step into this small arena of music, you realize that what you thought would be a small part of your life has really become part of your life. The people you continuously play with over a thirty-year period are like your family, like your brothers and sisters. What it means is that I have a support system, and it's very important to have people you can relate to on the road because when I'm not on the road, I don't necessarily call Hamid but it's very important to have him because he's a very, very special human being, which is still being revealed. I'm lucky to meet so many people but Hamid is very, very special and at the top of the list of those people.

Are you still going through a process of self-discovery?

Things that were planted as early as 1972 are beginning to come into my life, but you always have to grow because one eventually discovers that you have to modify things. To fit the standard now, I must be more open to this person or that person or I must be less open because I'm going in a different direction. It would block progress to continue to do or not do certain things. I am hopefully changing and growing in different ways and I'm really happy about that.

Do you have a lasting impression of the time you spent with Jimmy Garrison?

Whenever you heard Jimmy Garrison, he was on. He kind of played the same way with a lot of different groups but he had a very special, magical feel on that instrument. That helped me with the idea that you have to find your center in the music. He was able to find his center all of the time and really concentrate. You have to find the center and stay centered throughout your musical life and through each musical thing that you are doing. I was eighteen when I studied with him, and at the time, he was John Coltrane's bassist. We didn't always talk about music but it was great for me to see how a musician lived. It gave me a good foundation that it was possible to work as a musician but the main thing was to be yourself.

I once saw Ron Carter, Jimmy Garrison, and Reggie Workman all play the same bass and they all sounded different. I realized that each of them was able to maintain their sound with the same bass and it was a really good learning experience. I also learned about being oneself while studying with Richard Davis as he was into playing classical music while Jimmy Garrison was just interested in playing music, which is a little different concept.

You also spent time with Coltrane.

Trane was very spontaneous and relied on and gave the musicians a lot of freedom. He didn't speak very much but was really into the power of spontaneity and trusting the musicians. If you had to tell somebody what to do, it wasn't like the best thing to do. But whenever possible, if people could learn or feel what you needed, then it worked out a lot better for him. He emphasized the importance of just being a straight-up person.

Do you have a personal philosophy?

The importance of learning to accept those things which you cannot control. These are things that come about like death, or like the cycles of life. If you really want to have longevity, you have to accept life and want to change life—at the same time. You need to be able to balance those two things and find your joy center, keep the ability to laugh. In the same way that you can be lighthearted, but very serious, know that all the music during every day and every second of your life is very, very important. Nobody can dispute that.

34

JOSHUA REDMAN

Joshua Redman is inspiring and influencing a new generation of players with his fresh virtuosic interpretations of traditional idioms. With rhythmic finesse and maturity of a much more experienced player, he seamlessly integrates his charismatic soulfulness into his warm and radiant musical sensibilities.

YOU HAVE BEGUN TO MOVE IN NEW MUSICAL DIRECTIONS AND WITH THE DOWN-TURN IN INTEREST IN JAZZ, IS THE INDUSTRY BECOMING MORE RELUCTANT TO SUPPORT PROJECTS MOVING INTO NEW DIRECTIONS?

It's certainly a risk but my whole life in music has kind of been a risk. I didn't plan to be a professional musician. I've been very fortunate and very successful but it's still a risk relative to the kind of stable career I could have had if I had continued with my schooling and ended up going to law school and doing whatever with that. It's a challenge and I wasn't thinking of the state of the music industry and the obstacles that would present themselves or the apprehensiveness that exists in the business when I chose to move in this direction. I've always made my musical choices based on musical criteria and the time was right for me creatively and musically. Even though this band has a different sound and different instrumentations, we're dealing with different styles and for me, it is a natural extension of everything that I've done. It's not like I was playing super-traditional jazz and all of a sudden I buffed out with a mohawk and dancing girls in high shorts.

I feel like a lot of the concepts that we're dealing with in this band, along with the approach, attitude, and even the sound coming from the things I have worked on with other bands, is the natural next step and extension. As far as the record company goes, they have been very supportive of me and, once again, is something that has been very fortunate. They have always let me make the choices that I have wanted to make. I think that's partly because I did prove myself to be successful for them early on. There are more commercial choices that I could have made given the state of the business, but they have supported me in the choices that I have made and I'm fortunate for that.

THE INDUSTRY TODAY SEEMS TO HAVE DIFFICULTY WITH CREATIVITY THAT IS NOT EASILY EXPLAINED, UNDERSTOOD, OR IDENTIFIABLE. IS THERE TOO MUCH DIVERSITY FOR BOTH THE INDUSTRY AND THE LISTENER TO DIGEST?

That's a tough question. First of all, with creativity, absolutely not. I think that diversity is a good thing and from a creative standpoint, it's wonderful. It's wonderful for the long-term artistic health and growth of this music. There are so many different artists out there committed to music, committed to finding an original way to express themselves and doing different, exciting, original things.

For the industry, it presents a challenge and a problem that the industry has yet to fully embrace, let alone solve. Yes, we are dealing with an industry and market that is shrinking, yet at the same time there is more different music available. I don't know too much about the marketing of music, but I think there is an issue of dilution going on here. An industry that can't really figure out how to sell a few different artists or types of music certainly is going to have a bigger problem when there is ten times that many. But ultimately, that's a challenge that the industry will have to solve and adapt to. We certainly shouldn't pose it as something of a problem for the art form because I don't think it is. It's a boon for the art. It's a problem for the business.

As far as audiences go, there is so much information, music, and so many different artists out there. The average listener or even aficionado can't even begin to familiarize themselves with even 1 percent of what's out there. I'm talking about people that are already interested in jazz. There's way too much out there to familiarize yourself with or even be aware of. So how do you make the choices? You take the guidance from something someone has said or written on TV or the radio or an article. It's a problem for the industry, the audiences, and it's a problem in terms of exposure and I'm not really sure how this is all going to shake down.

DO YOU THINK MARKETING PEOPLE AS INDIVIDUAL VOICES RATHER THAN STYLE IS A BETTER APPROACH?

The industry has yet to figure out how to market artists based on their art. No artist is purely marketed based on the art they are creating. It's a package, it's an image, and it can be as superficial as a look or as intellectual as a concept or theory, but it's still something that surrounds the art. It's also the context, presentation, attitude, and the look and feel. It's not the music itself because how can you really market the music. Music is to be heard, lived, experienced, and enjoyed, but you can't market it. I don't mean to be pessimistic but what is the answer?

I certainly hope the industry can find a way to market artists as individuals rather than being representative of a style. All individuals that have been marketed in music have been marketed by more than just who they are. That's what marketing is. That's what hype is. That's what publicity is. The individual and the music becomes larger than life and representative of something greater.

HAVE WE BECOME A SOCIETY WITHOUT THE PATIENCE TO BE CHALLENGED, OPEN ONLY TO THINGS THAT ARE EASILY ACCESSIBLE?

I think a modern, Western, industrialized, computerized, informationalized culture is an impatient culture. American culture is and perhaps has been for some time. We are used to getting our necessary data, filtering that data, getting our sound bites fast, and moving on with our lives. Unfortunately, that kind of attitude that might allow us to live faster, doesn't necessarily allow us to live richly. I think that's true of a general trend in our culture. That trend has had negative implications for creative music but for every rule there is an exception. For every mainstream trend there is an alternative and I think that there are those exceptions in our culture because of what is dominant in attitudes. I think there are people who are seeking something else, something that requires more patience that can be more deeply enriching and satisfying. I think it's those people that are seeking that in addition to the elements in our culture that embrace creative music and music like jazz.

I can't speak to where this world is heading, whether this will continue or will there eventually be mass backlash against the information made. And believe me, even though we are talking about the negative aspects of the information age, I'm part of this age and spend my fair share on my computer and surf the web. I like to get my information fast as well. It's not a good or evil. In fact, this trend is kind of an amoral evil. It's not good or bad. It exists and the challenge is how we are able to integrate the recent developments with what I think is ultimately a human need for depth, enrichment, and meaning that some of the more creative arts can give us.

ARE TRADITIONALISTS HAVING A DIFFICULT TIME ACCEPTING THAT A MUSIC FORM CONSIDERED "AMERICAN" NOW HAS INTERNATIONAL AND DIVERSE ASPECTS WITHIN IT?

Do I think there are people who are afraid of that? Yes! Do I think their fears are justified? No! Jazz is a music of American origin and specifically African American which has evolved into this incredible art form that belongs to the world and is played all over the world. Jazz is a world music now. Is jazz purely an American art form anymore? Absolutely not. Should it be? No!

I think it's a testament to the brilliance, the genius, and creativity of the original creators who were American. This music has had the power and the appeal all over the world and I think that the opening up of jazz to different influences and different sounds and cultures is a wholly positive thing.

This may be a subtext of your question, but is there some type of dilution going on? Are we losing the essence or the core of jazz through the absorption of all these other sounds? I think the answer is no because even though there is all this eclecticism in the music and pollination, there is still a very, very strong and vital jazz core. A lot of the artists and myself included that are interested in exploring the relationship between jazz and other styles are not doing that exclusively. A musician might have a project of some kind of fusion and I hate to use that term because it's so dated and so loaded a term. But some kind of experiment in jazz, combining with other influences. Most of those musicians are still doing things that we still consider more within the jazz core. I think there are always going to be people that are afraid and a fear of change is common. It's a common human tendency. But I don't think the music is in any danger. All that is exciting, is real and positive in the music, in jazz, will continue; it's strong.

MANY JAZZ JOURNALISTS HAVE A DIFFICULT TIME IDENTIFYING OR EXPRESSING THE SIGNIFICANCE OF JAZZ PRODUCED DURING THE LAST THIRTY- TO FORTY-YEAR PERIOD. SOME ARE NOT EVEN WILLING TO ATTEMPT THIS, AND THERE ARE EVEN THOSE WHO SEEM TO MAKE AN EFFORT TO DIMINISH ANY OF THE SUCCESSES. HOW WOULD YOU DESCRIBE MUSIC OF THIS PERIOD TO STUDENTS FIFTY YEARS FROM NOW?

All respect to the question, which is a great question, but my own feeling is that I don't think I could give you an adequate answer. Then again, I don't think that anyone could give you an adequate answer to that question because we cannot see ourselves nor should we see ourselves through a historical lens. I don't believe that we could have a historical consciousness nor should we have a historical consciousness about ourselves. We can have a consciousness about how we relate with the past, that kind of consciousness, but not a consciousness about what our relevance is for the future and how we will be regarded fifty years from now.

I think there is a danger to think in those terms because that kind of thinking can not only lead very quickly to a kind of conceit, but it can be dangerous from an egoistic standpoint. Also, it takes us out of the moment. If we are too concerned with how history is going to judge or perceive us, it can hamper our creativity. I truly believe that in fifty years, people will look back at creative jazz of this period and appreciate the originality and creativity of the music. I think moreso than people necessarily appreciate it today, and one of the problems with how people view jazz today is that people are still trying to view today's jazz through the same lens that they viewed an earlier time in jazz history. They are still trying to use the same conceptual apparatus. What I mean by that is that there was a time in the history of jazz, from the birth of the music and let's say through the late '60s, where jazz history could be viewed in a very linear way. You could see and make a very convincing argument that through a very linear evolution of the music, you can see how each style in each decade or in each period of jazz, that there was a dominant style. There was a cutting-edge style and so that style or those styles followed in a kind of very linear evolutionary way from what preceded it. You can see how New Orleans jazz produced swing-based jazz, how swing jazz which produced bebop which broke off into cool and hard bop, which broke off into various forms of free jazz, and all of which opened up the possibilities for jazz fusion. Then at a certain point I think the linear evolution breaks down or you can say that the tree branched off.

It's more complicated. You cannot try to view jazz in those terms and jazz artists or jazz styles in those terms any longer. I think part of the problem is that people are still searching for something that's never going to come. They are searching for the next bebop, the next Charlie Parker, Ornette Coleman, or next Louis Armstrong. That will never come and that doesn't mean that there won't be artists as equally as brilliant and inspirational and that the music won't be as equally beautiful. There are not going to be the same kinds of dominant revolutions in the music and that's not a bad thing. I think the maturity of this music is that there are going to be plenty of revolutions but I think they are going to be of a more personal and quiet nature.

IS IT MORE DIFFICULT FOR ASPIRING YOUNG MUSICIANS OR STUDENTS TO BE CRE-ATIVE IN TODAY'S SOCIETY?

I don't believe that it's more difficult for students to be creative today because creativity is so deeply a part of the human essence and human spirit. It's there for all of us, it's on the surface. It's a thin opaque layer surrounding our creativity that our culture has kind of manufactured. We can't necessarily see what's right beneath the surface, but as soon as we start to splash away, that thin layer comes off and it's all there. I think the potential for creativity has not diminished at all.

DO YOU HAVE A COMMON PHILOSOPHY THAT YOU TRY TO IMPART WITH YOUNG MU-SICIANS?

I don't do a lot of education because I don't feel qualified yet to do it. I haven't done a lesson in my life and I tend not to do formal clinics. I have done my fair share, I just don't feel qualified to be educator. I mean, I'm still trying to figure out what I'm doing before I try to tell someone else what to do. I have had a lot of contact with young musicians through doing some of these things and through meeting them on the road at gigs.

There are a few things that I try to impart to them that are very basic and are almost cliché but I think they are cliché because there is something essential about them. I think one is, listen. And maybe that's not so obvious because there is so much knowledge and skill that is more developed with each generation. Each generation learns a little faster so there's no shortage of that. But that stuff doesn't mean anything without musical sensitivity and empathy. Those things come from listening. Musicians can develop their skill to a very high level yet still not develop their capacity to really listen with empathy and sensitivity so I do try to stress that. Jazz is not just playing about what you know, what you've studied, or what you've accomplished. It's about discovering something in the moment and discovering something through your interaction with the relationships to the other musicians you are playing with. This requires a very, very deep and profound commitment to listening. So that's one thing that I try to stress.

Also, I try to stress being in the moment as an improviser and hopefully as a human being. I'm thirty-four years old and I'm still working on that. Just making sure that whenever you do step up to the mic as a player, step up on the bandstand, you're there in the moment trying to play what you feel in the moment. That's the challenge and that's the inspiration of jazz.

IS JAZZ A THING OR AN APPROACH OR PROCESS TO MAKING MUSIC?

I think that there are two factors to jazz and those are the two. There's jazz as a style and there's jazz as an approach. Jazz as a style is something which gets constantly in flux and constantly changing, yet there are some constants. We can still speak about stylistic elements that remain a part of jazz. The contributions of some of the musicians such as Louis Armstrong, Charlie Parker, Miles Davis, Thelonius Monk, and Ornette Coleman. That list goes on and on, I mean Duke Ellington. What they contributed to the vocabulary of jazz, to the idiom of jazz, remains and still reverberates. All of those things make up the style of jazz in addition to melodic ideas, phrases, harmonic structures, song forms, textural ideas, modes of band interaction of the repertoire. These are all the things that make up the vocabulary and the style of jazz.

There is also the jazz approach. I think the spirit of jazz is the primary essence of jazz. That is ultimately an approach of adventurousness, risk, spontaneity, immediacy, and honesty. It's improvisation, and not improvisation purely as one guy taking a solo but improvisation as a whole esthetic commitment. That I think is the heart and soul of jazz. That's the attitude, the spirit, and that's what's primary.

DO YOU HAVE A VISION OF WHERE YOU WANT YOUR MUSIC TO GO LOOKING FORWARD OR DO YOU CONCENTRATE ON THE HERE AND NOW?

I believe in the commitment of the here and now but I also believe my music has developed and will continue to develop. My vision is very simple and I certainly embrace change and evolution. I'll continue to find ways to express myself honestly and creatively as a musician and continue to find new ways to do that. To push myself into situations where I can grow, learn, and develop things with other musicians. I think that's a vision and I think that's enough of a vision. If I had a clear vision as to what my music would look like or sound like, then it wouldn't be much fun getting there. It wouldn't be much of an adventure. Part of the true joy of music is the discovery and it's great to have a vision. But people that have too clear of a vision ultimately may be shutting themselves off from creative possibilities because you can have vision and then you can have tunnel vision. I think the clearer your vision of your future, perhaps the more in danger you are of running towards the clear vision with a single-minded purpose. You may not see what's coming around your periphery, which ultimately might be much more exciting and more interesting.

THE FOLLOWING IS A QUOTE FROM CECIL TAYLOR: "MUSIC HAS TO DO WITH A LOT OF AREAS WHICH ARE MAGICAL RATHER THAN LOGICAL; THE GREAT ARTISTS, RATHER THAN JUST GETTING INVOLVED WITH DISCIPLINE, GET TO UNDERSTAND LOVE AND ALLOW THE LOVE TO TAKE SHAPE." HOW MUCH OF YOUR MUSIC IS FROM LOGIC AND HOW MUCH FROM THIS OTHER PLACE THAT CECIL TAYLOR DESCRIBES?

I agree with the spirit part of the quote. And I think that the source of music, at least for me, is emotion and spirit. I think of love in that sense. There certainly is a need, especially for music like jazz, for tremendous intellectual and tremendous logic, but the issue is, who is ultimately calling the shots? I'd like to think that the spirit, the emotion, the feeling, the origins of creativity and musical content are in the spirit of emotion. The mind is incredibly powerful. Logic and intellect are incredibly powerful tools to use in service with emotional force.

IF THE PERFECT CREATIVE SITUATION IS COMPLETE FREEDOM, SHOULD THIS CREATIVE PROCESS HAVE INTENT? ISN'T THERE RESPONSIBILITY, WITH ITS OWN SET OF DISCIPLINES AND CONSIDERATIONS, THAT COMES WITH THAT FREEDOM?

What I feel is my responsibility, and I think this is true off all art, is to express and be true to yourself as much as possible. There certainly is discipline within my approach to my music and hopefully it doesn't hamper the creativity and doesn't come at the expense of anything. There is certainly discipline and I believe in craft and developing my craft as a saxophonist with my instrument as an improviser. I believe in knowledge of different vocabularies, sounds, harmonies, styles, and rhythms. All these things help because they are greater tools and I think the more information I have, more ability I have, more knowledge I have, the more I can refine my craft. The more tools I have to put in service of creative self-expression. The trick is to not allow those tools to become the engines. Not allow it to become ultimately the means to the end of in itself.

Sometimes when people talk about freedom, they are talking about freedom in a set of external conditions. Like the idea that freedom means an absence of equal parameters or boundaries. Freedom of form. That is a type of freedom and certainly a very powerful type of freedom and a valid type of freedom. A lot of great things can come out of that sort of freedom but I think what's more important is the sense of internal freedom. And that's really what freedom of expression is. It's a freedom of expressive content.

The idea and sense that no matter what the parameters or conditions, there's a maximum range of creativity and maximum depth of expressivity on the part of the musicians who are playing in those contexts. So, I think it is quite possible to have a tremendous degree of internal freedom in a context with some external boundaries. In fact, I think some of the most creative and free music often takes place within sets of parameters. Some of the greatest examples of freedom of content, internal freedom, are realized under conditions that aren't completely externally free. I'm not trying to be prescriptive here, I'm just saying that for instance, some people will say that song forms, meters, harmonies, these are all things that are going to hamper freedom because they are forms, they are restricting. I think they can restrict expressions but can also create the conditions for greater freedom. Sometimes the most creative things happen within sets of parameters and boundaries. It's what you make of the limited resources that are available to you.

You HAVE HAD THE OPPORTUNITY TO PLAY WITH A NUMBER OF MUSICIANS FROM
SEVERAL GENERATIONS, CAN YOU DESCRIBE WHAT YOU WERE ABLE TO RECEIVE FROM
THOSE EXPERIENCES?

I think the thing that I learned especially from the older musicians is that, by and large, the truly great musicians, the masters are truly humble. This is something that might sound obvious, but you come to New York, which is the jazz capital of the world, as a young musician and person and you are surrounded by other great young musicians. Some of whom have quite an attitude, tend to be competitive, abrasive, cocky, and negative in a certain way. I'm just talking about one segment of the jazz community. Many of the young musicians that I have played with have been incredibly humble. One thing that I realized from the older musicians—with great achievement comes great humility. That's comforting and inspiring.

WHEN YOU COMPOSE, DO YOU ENVISION WHAT IT IS YOU WANT YOUR MUSIC TO DO
FOR THE LISTENER? DO YOU THINK IN TERMS OF TELLING A STORY, LOOK TO CREATE
MELODY, OR CREATE A CERTAIN FEEL OR MOOD THAT WILL MOVE THE LISTENER?

I think I have a very strong narrative sense as a composer and as an improviser, especially as an improviser. For a long time that was my only form of composition. It continues to be my most developed form of composition as an improviser. I certainly have a sense of telling a story, but I don't think I specifically have a sense of what the impact will be on the listener or what I'm trying to do for the listener. What I can do is try to express myself and create a sound and mood and a set of ideas and feelings that are representative of myself at a point in time. So that's what I'm trying to keep in mind. Yes, I have sense of narrative flow and I certainly have a sense of mood and emotion, but it's not specifically oriented towards how the listener is going to experience it. I think what I try to do is create something for myself, present it and play it as expressively as possible.

WHAT IS IT ABOUT JAZZ AND THE ART FORM THAT IS IMPORTANT TO YOU?

I think improvisation is one of the most essential elements in jazz and is the thing that has drawn me to jazz. The power and potential of improvisation is what has drawn most musicians to the music. There is the challenge and frustration of it on one hand and the exultation and inspiration on the other. I think that jazz is a music which has developed improvisation and holds improvisation as dear as any other music. Perhaps greater than most other music. I think there is also a sense of integrity in jazz and commitment. A kind of uncompromising attitude which is essential to me. A sense of risk and adventure to go along with spontaneity. All these things are essential.

Finally, a sense of dedication, commitment, and sophistication. These are aspects of jazz that are very important that shouldn't be denied. Jazz is a complex music and it is a difficult and demanding music. Through its rigor and through its difficulty, it's created something great. Hopefully, all of this is in service of the spirit and emotion. That's the final idea, that jazz at its best is the ultimate combination of music of the intellectual and emotional. Jazz manifests both of those facets of humanity and reconciles and integrates them in a very unique and special way.

WHAT DO YOU SEE AS THE FUTURE OF JAZZ?

I think the future of jazz will be continued creativity, discovery, originality on the part of many great artists doing many interesting things rooted within the jazz tradition and also departing from it. I think that in the long run, this is all very healthy for the music. I think we live in a very creative time right now musically. Jazz is developing in all sorts of different directions and I think that there are great musicians doing tremendous work. That's going to continue.

There is a very healthy attitude out there among jazz musicians right now despite the unhealthy state of the industry. I think jazz musicians these days are more open-minded, less factional, less ideological, less exclusive, and even more so than when I first got to New York twelve years ago. I feel there is less of a sense of different tribes in the jazz community and more of a sense of a wonderful intersection of different individuals coming together in different combinations in creative music. Hopefully that will continue.

DO YOU HAVE A PHILOSOPHY OR WAY OF LOOKING AT LIFE THAT YOU ARE WILLING TO SHARE?

I should preface it by saying that just because it's a philosophy doesn't mean it's a practice. My philosophy of life is my philosophy of jazz. Live in the moment and experience, discover, and express in the moment. I'm much better at doing that as a jazz musician than I am as a human being. So hopefully, my experience as a jazz musician can teach me how to do that as a human being. Living in the moment with inspiration, creativity, commitment, and humility.

35

MARIA SCHNEIDER

Imagine a musical ballet of gentle raindrops in distinct textural shapes and colors, a visual soundscape tapestry of dense, complex melodies—imagine a gorgeous, sensuous rainbow of sound.

WHEN DID YOU FIRST KNOW THAT YOU WANTED TO GET INVOLVED IN MUSIC?

I fell in love with music when I was five, which was when I first heard somebody play piano that really brought personality to music. That was my first time really hearing and seeing somebody play and I thought, "Wow, I want that!" And so growing up, I always felt I would do music but I just didn't know what form that it would take. It took a lot of years before I figured out that I was going to be a composer. I mean, finding myself as a jazz composer just sort of happened and evolved slowly over time through school, by the people I was exposed to, and the music that I loved. I just wasn't happy composing in the classical world and had much more of an affinity for the jazz world.

WHAT I LIKE ABOUT YOUR COMPOSITIONS IS THAT I HEAR YOUR INNER VOICE AND YOUR OWN CREATIVE SPIRIT. IT'S AS IF YOU WRITE THE PIECES AND IT'S UP TO THE PLAYERS TO FIND THE CONNECTION WITH THE EMOTIONAL ELEMENT THAT YOU ARE TRYING TO EXPRESS THROUGH THE ARRANGEMENT. HOW DO YOU GO ABOUT DRAWING THE EMOTIONAL ASPECT OUT OF THE PLAYERS?

It takes awhile because when they first play a piece, it doesn't have the shape and feel that I had in mind. They all have to get comfortable and when they can hear the notes and also hear how they relate to each other, then they can take it and shape it.

I give instructions but I usually don't go deep into an emotional explanation of my music. I explain the articulation, or I sing how I would like the lines phrased. Then over time, they find the music. To me, the really fun thing about music is getting to a certain emotional place that can be put into sound, and then codify that into notes on a piece of paper. The players can then look at the notes and decode them with their own instruments and make the air vibrate by plucking a string, hitting a drum or whatever, and the combination of all those things in the end translates the emotion that went into it at the beginning. That's the mystical thing.

The spiritual intent that first went into the music hopefully comes out the other side after being filtered through all of these different things. That's the mystery of it and I have no explanation of how that works; it just does.

DO YOU HAVE THE MUSICIANS IN MIND WHEN YOU WRITE YOUR COMPOSITIONS?

They play a huge part because I don't think I could have come to this musical place if it had not been for these particular musicians playing and shaping my music. Musicians always bring something to the music that I didn't count on. They'll find things dynamically in the music that goes beyond what I was even thinking and those things give me ideas for future pieces. So I am definitely writing for my players, and in terms of the solos—absolutely.

IS THERE AN EMOTIONAL INVOLVEMENT FOR YOU WITH YOUR RELATIONSHIP WITH SOUND?

Yes, of course. Music definitely touches emotions and emotions are expressed through music. I think it's a bit mystical as to how that works but yeah, I think the main reason that I do music is because of expression.

It's funny, last night I started reading this biography that a friend wrote on the choreographer George Balanchine. For years, I have described my music as sculptural—these ephemeral sound sculptures. But then I realized that the reason I'm inspired by dance is because it's sculpture with the added dimension of time. And I always think of dancing when I'm writing my music because for me, dancing is expression; and music is expression and emotion and all of those things. If music wasn't wrapped up in emotion, I wouldn't be doing it, that's for sure.

HOW IMPORTANT IS BAND CHEMISTRY WITH THE MUSIC THAT YOU ARE TRYING TO BRING TO LIFE?

Most of the musicians in the band have been playing together for ten to fifteen years and I think that the sound of the band has really evolved. But it's funny, the last time we played a gig, the bass trombone player made a comment about the band being like a flock of birds and it's really true because the music has become so malleable. If one person solos, everybody immediately reacts because everyone is so in tune with each other. It's become this deep, collective, and intuitive thing, or maybe it's chemistry. That's just so important because a lot of the music is written, and the written stuff has to have a very blended sound. And for the improvised aspect, everyone has to have a certain chemistry.

IS CHEMISTRY SOMETHING THAT CAN BE DEVELOPED OR MUST IT BE THERE FROM THE BEGINNING?

I think that to a certain degree, it can be developed, but it can also be both. I recently made a couple of changes in my band and there was suddenly this fresh chemistry. And even though these were players that I have really loved for many, many years, I made the decision to make a change because I was ready for that kind of fresh chemistry.

IT SEEMS TO ME THAT A GROUP OF MUSICIANS THAT HAVE BEEN PLAYING TOGETHER FOR OVER TEN YEARS HAVE DEVELOPED RELATIONSHIPS WITH EACH OTHER AND WITH THE MUSIC. AND WITH RELATIONSHIPS, SOME WILL GROW CLOSER AND SOME GROW APART.

Yeah, definitely, definitely. For me, it was also a feeling of needing a change. To have some new surprises coming at me and to bring me to a new place.

YOU HAVE TALKED ABOUT HAVING YOUR OWN RELATIONSHIP WITH THE EMOTIONAL ASPECTS OF MUSIC AND SOUND, BUT ARE YOU AWARE OF THE RELATIONSHIP BETWEEN THE EMOTIONAL ASPECT THAT BRIDGES THE GAP BETWEEN THE LISTENER AND YOUR COMPOSITIONS?

Well, I hope that that's what I'm transmitting. To me, the music is as important as what is being passed through the music. And the music is this conduit for something else deeper. And I don't make music just to make music; I make music to communicate something. Music is nice but if it doesn't do something to me. . . .

I hear jazz all of the time where I'll think, that's interesting, but it does absolutely nothing to me. And it's not that I want my heart bleeding every time I hear music, but I do need my spirit moved in some way with either joy, feeling inspired, melancholy, or something. I need emotion and I certainly do hope that my music does something for the listener in that way.

WITHIN YOUR COMPOSITIONS, HOW DO YOU ASSOCIATE BETWEEN COLOR, FORM, SHAPES, OR FEELING? DO THEY ALL HAVE EQUAL WEIGHT WITHIN YOUR CREATIVE PROCESS?

There isn't one thing that I think is more important than the other. I use the musical things required to get whatever it is I'm trying to get across. So it's not that melody is everything or that harmony is everything or that texture, dynamics, or rhythm is everything. (Laughs.) To me, I can't say that one of those things are most important; they all come together and come to the forefront in different amounts depending on what it is I'm trying to get across. Certainly color and texture are big parts of my music but there are always other things included like melodic development and rhythm. It's kind of like three-dimensional chess. (Laughs.)

IN A DOWNBEAT ARTICLE WITH PAUL DEBARROS, YOU SAID THAT YOU DON'T HAVE MANY IDEAS, AND I THOUGHT TO MYSELF, "WHAT IS SHE TALKING ABOUT? I'M STILL TRYING TO DIGEST THEM."

(Laughs.) I'm not a person that can sit down and the music will flow out of me. I have to coax myself a little bit and once it gets going, then I can't tear myself away. I think I talked about Kenny Werner in that article where he said, "Maria, I just can't stop the ideas, they just keep coming!" And I'm thinking, "Oh, please!"

BUT THERE IS ALSO A DENSITY WITH ALL THESE DIFFERENT LEVELS OF IDEAS GOING ON.

Well, there is definitely a lot of detail and intricacy in my writing. I know that.

IS THERE A CERTAIN AMOUNT OF HUMILITY REQUIRED FOR THE CREATIVE PROCESS?

I really don't think so. There are musicians that think they are God's gift to man and play music that is at an incredibly high level. And then there are musicians that are very self-deprecating or the exact opposite of having a huge ego. (Laughs.) Then there are some that are somewhere in the middle and are humble; and I think strong and creative music doesn't depend on any of those things. I think strong music depends on a musician just being dedicated to developing their craft and being dedicated to developing themselves, whatever that is.

To me, the most important thing that music has to have is personality, and whatever a person's personality is, that's what makes it special and what makes each person unique. If one person is humble and one person is arrogant, it really doesn't mean anything except that those two people are probably bound to write very different music.

WHAT INSPIRES YOU?

If I knew exactly what inspired me, I would have written something today. (Laughs.)

Deep life experiences inspire me whether it's past or present. I find inspiration in art that goes deep inside of me and deadlines can inspire me pretty quickly too. (Laughs.) It's amazing what you can come up with when you have to.

When I write, I'll come up with a musical idea, but in the beginning, I'm just looking for sounds that have personality and character. I'll work with an idea and then all of a sudden, the idea will attach itself to a memory of something in my life or something that I am going through, a person I know, a feeling I had, and then the sound grows fueled by this memory or this other musical thing and that's usually the process that takes place in my composing.

I HOPE YOU ARE NOT TIRED OF BEING ASKED THIS NEXT QUESTION . . .
Of being a woman?

WELL, YEAH.

(Both laugh.) No, it's OK. It's been awhile since somebody has asked me but I don't have much to say about it actually.

WELL, I GUESS MY ISSUE WITH IT IS THAT WOMEN MUSICIANS DON'T SEEM TO GET THE SAME RESPECT IN MAINSTREAM JAZZ IN THE SAME WAY THAT MEN DO. AND EVEN WHEN THEY DO, IT'S NOT REALLY RELATIVE IN THE SAME WAY THAT IT IS FOR MEN.

Maybe I'm just oblivious, but I haven't perceived that people haven't given me the same fair shake that men get.

THAT'S GREAT!

I've won a ton of *Downbeat* polls, people come to my concerts, I work with groups all of the time that are all men and they hire me. I also work at colleges. I'm working more than most men doing what I'm doing so I can't really look at it and say, "Oh, I'm being treated unfairly in some way." I don't feel that. But if you talk about Ingrid Jensen where people feel shocked because they don't expect this woman to get up and play trumpet like she does, well the truth is, there hasn't been a whole hell of a lot of women trumpet players that play like Ingrid. So, it is a bit of a shock. Most people see it and hear it and they are like, "Holy shit!" This woman can play, and you know, Ingrid works a ton. She travels constantly.

So I'm not really feeling deprived in any kind of way. But I may be naive because maybe there are things that I'm not being called for because of that, but I really don't know. I just don't feel like I have been missing out on anything in my life. What do you think?

I'M AWARE THAT A WOMAN CAN COME ON THE SCENE BECAUSE OF A CERTAIN LOOK OR SEX APPEAL AND GET THE ATTENTION IN A YEAR THAT IT MAY TAKE SOMEONE ELSE FIVE TO TEN YEARS.

Well, that can happen to men too. If Harry Connick didn't quite look like Harry Connick, maybe he wouldn't have been so successful.

GOOD POINT.

I mean, it happens with race a lot too. There are white male musicians that will complain that, "Wow, you know, there are so many of us and we don't get a fair shake." I hear people complain about that and you always hear that a record company is listening to music with their eyes. But I believe that most musicians, regardless of what the commercial world does, just want to make music and just want to play. And if people want to hear it for what it is, great, and if they don't, it's not going to stop musicians from doing what they are doing. At least most musicians, so I don't get too hung up on most of those things.

I READ AN INTERVIEW WHERE YOU MENTIONED THAT YOU BELIEVE WHAT YOU DO IS VERY FEMALE. I ALWAYS TEND TO THINK THAT THE CREATIVE SPIRIT IS WITHOUT GENDER AND COMES FROM A DIFFERENT PLACE. COULD IT BE THAT THE FEMALE ASPECT INFLUENCES HOW YOU WORK WITH THE CREATIVE ELEMENT?

I think it's impossible for any of us to say. You know how when you are in a relationship and somebody says that maybe you are with that person because you had this relationship with your mother or your father and you say, well maybe, but I think I would have fallen in love with this person anyway. It's so hard to know in life, to extract what elements contribute to what we do, but certainly, I think that one has to accept that probability.

There are many, many different things that come into play in why people do what they do. For instance, what makes up your music? What things are you inclined to do because it's your spirit? What things are you inclined to write because you grew up in southwest Minnesota with a mother that played a lot of Chopin, Copeland, and standard songs around the house? What are you inclined to come up with because you always sang soprano in a choir as opposed to always singing bass in a choir, or because you enjoyed looking feminine and wearing dresses as opposed to something else? In my case, I grew up being very feminine wearing dresses but also going duck hunting with my father. (Laughs.) And how do those things come out in your music?

I just don't think we can help but be influenced by our sexual perspectives on the world. Not to say that my music is going to sound girlish because I'm a woman, but women and men are different in a lot of ways; we just are (laughs) and I just can't imagine that it doesn't affect something in your way of making music.

Just as your family and where you grew up and what you studied and what you listened to is going to have an effect. I think it's just one of many things that comes into people's music and I think that people get so uptight talking about it, because they are so scared of either being perceived as sexist or racist or having somebody being sexist or racist towards you. I'm just not afraid of talking about it because we are what we are and, yeah, it would be impossible to say what my music would be if I was a man because my whole life would be different. But I'm sure that my music has many female aspects to it, but whatever they are, I don't know.

DO YOU MIND TALKING ABOUT THE INFLUENCE BOB BROOKMEYER HAS HAD ON YOU AND YOUR WORK?

Well, Bob's biggest influence on me has been with form and development. He has this knack of being able to take a few notes and make them very conversational and very developmental as opposed to just arranging that song. To me, Bob is the master of formal development in jazz and he's the guy who stretched form in a very effective way in the idiom by using classical developmental techniques, and that influenced me a lot. And to this day, I still believe that formal development is his biggest contribution towards jazz.

I GET A SENSE THAT HE IS AN INDIVIDUAL WITH A HIGH LEVEL OF INTEGRITY.

Yeah, that's definitely right.

YOU ALSO DEDICATED THE RECORD *EVANESCENCE* TO GIL EVANS.

Hearing Gil's music really made me want to be a jazz composer because the thing that I heard in his music was this fusion of written and improvised music into a statement that was bigger than any of those two forces. And it was very expressive; expressive of the player and expressive of the composer and it felt very, very alive and beautiful.

I was studying classical music the first time I heard his music and feeling really judged by whatever stylistic materials I was using. Like if your music was tonal, you were just completely insipid and ridiculous and your music had to be something you could almost write a theory to, otherwise it wasn't deemed worthy. But Gil's music was so intricate, tonal, and expressive, though it wasn't rigid. Everything didn't have to be what he said it was but there was all this openness. And with Miles playing on those things, it was just so deep. And at that point, I really started wanting to write for jazz musicians. But, it was a social thing too.

To me, the thought of having to compose a piece that has to be the same every time as opposed to having people contribute to it is kind of lonely. Like when Ingrid Jenson steps in on a night where she is really inspired and plays something really great, it's her piece as much as it is my piece and I just love that. It's also the way I want to live my life and not just with the music that I want to make.

WHEN THERE IS STRIFE IN THE WORLD OR IN SOCIETY, PEOPLE BEGIN TO LOOK FOR THINGS WITH MORE DEPTH. ARE YOU SEEING THAT IN THE ARTS TODAY?

No, sadly not, but I wish it was true. I think we are in a time when people are not thinking for themselves. And with this last election, it appeared that people wanted to be told what to do. When people are free thinkers, they are attracted to the arts and of wanting to be artists. They want to think on their own and be confronted with questions. I mean, it's like what you were saying earlier; it's not only finding answers, but finding the questions. And I don't think people want to be faced with questions right now. They just want to have answers, and that's not conducive to an artistic society.

DO THE EVENTS HAPPENING IN THE WORLD TODAY AFFECT YOU OR YOUR CREATIVE PROCESS?

Yes it does, and when 9/11 happened, I was so down that I didn't do anything for almost a year in terms of creativity. I was so depressed.

You know, something amazing happened a couple of days after the election. Scott Robinson, who plays in my band, gave a concert playing duo that was free and so incredible. What they created was so beautiful that it made me forget about the election entirely. And I thought, you know, let the world blow each other up if that's what they want. And these people who profess religion and value violence the way that they do . . . one day, when these people realize that they have given all of their rights away, maybe they'll wake up. And I have a feeling that we are going to reach a very critical and alarming point where that is going to happen.

PERHAPS WE JUST HAVEN'T HIT A LOW ENOUGH POINT FOR PEOPLE TO BE MORE APPRECIATIVE.

I believe that our culture and society is going to hit such a low point that we'll then realize we are not even living in a democratic society anymore. People will also start to realize what this lack of separation between church and state is really going to mean for our society.

And perhaps the more alarming part is the apathy on the part of so many people. I mean, how many people didn't vote? Wasn't it something like only 10 percent of eighteen to twenty-four year olds that voted? So I'm sorry, but in this day and age, if our young people are feeling so entitled to having whatever they have and not realizing that the responsibility rests on all of us to keep this going. . . . Wow, this is really frightening and maybe these are the people that are going to hopefully wake up first. Maybe faster than turning around the people that are such believers in having Jesus in the White House.

DO YOU THINK IT'S DENIAL OR JUST NOT KNOWING?

I think it's not knowing. People are numbed out on TV and just have no idea.

DOES THE ARTIST HAVE A UNIQUE AWARENESS LEVEL OF WHAT SURROUNDS THEM?

I think they do because they travel and meet and interact with people of different cultures so they don't see the world through one eyeglass. I recently had a conversation with a friend of mine who grew up with a very, very religious background, and that person sees life filtered through their religious beliefs and that's with everything. And I realized that this person's political beliefs are what they are because this person has such a one-dimensional look at the world and that's what they were taught as a child. They were taught that this is in the such and such writings and therefore everything just relates to that. As opposed to somebody who travels and meets people and has the opportunity to observe different looks at Christianity, Judaism, of being Muslim, of being atheist; or of being into some sort of unique mysticism and seeing the value and beauty of all of these different perspectives.

Jim Hall played just a few days before the election and was telling people to vote and said that because musicians travel, they get to see the world and they have a unique vision of the world that other people just don't have very often.

So I realized that even though my friend is a really, really brilliant person, religion was a way to control his mind. And religion can control huge groups of people at such a young age. And then they become scared their whole lives and cannot think outside that box. It becomes a fixed truth for them. This version of God and this version of this and that and what is right or wrong and what you should and shouldn't eat comes from whatever they were taught. For me it's like, wow, I just cannot relate to it.

I ALSO FIND THIS CLOSED-MINDED ATTITUDE IN JAZZ AND IT CAN REALLY BE UPSETTING.

Oh yeah, yeah. Don't even get me going on what is jazz. I cannot stand that because the thing is, I don't even care what jazz is. To me, jazz is a name for a music and isn't an idiom for people who make music to try and fulfill what the idiom proclaimed itself to be. It's a music that warranted having a name given to it but what was valuable about the music was that it was free expression that developed in its own way. However, you can suddenly stop that development by giving it a name, so it's almost the same as religion.

Suddenly you give it a name and then you have to give it rules and then you are controlling the audience. This is jazz and this isn't jazz, and I can't stand those things. Again, it's about questions and answers. Why are we afraid to live our lives with unanswered questions? Why do we look to some religion for answers to some questions that that religion cannot answer? There are questions that we are not meant to answer.

DO YOU BELIEVE THAT THE ARTIST HAS A ROLE AND RESPONSIBILITY WITHIN SOCIETY?

No, I don't think so. I think we all have a role and responsibility but the artist fulfills having an important role by being an artist, and that role is to express themselves. Everything we see around us is everything that the world perceives as reality. But what the artist believes in and trusts is another reality. And ultimately, the artists are touching, expressing, and bringing that sort of alternative reality into form through art and music. It brings into form where we can touch it and people can have access to it through some medium that we recognize as being real.

It becomes a conduit for other people to touch that place. And to me, this is what is amazing. We believe and trust in that world and that that's how we make a living that's going to pay our bills. (Laughs.) You know, it's pretty insane. But to me, it's just a really important spiritual function in the world, to keep people in touch with that place.

DO YOU BELIEVE WE ARE CLOSING THE GAP BETWEEN OUR CULTURAL DIFFERENCES IN THE WORLD TODAY?

You know, the world is so bizarre because we are all connected when it comes to making money and commerce. The governments of France and the United States have such strong disagreements about Iraq but, on the other hand, a French magazine just gave me an award and I'm going to go there and connect with those people.

There are just so many different levels in which people and cultures connect and I remember when we were bombing Yugoslavia, I had a friend there who I was e-mailing back and forth. Man, it's so completely screwed up. Music connects us but also other things in life connect us and I just think, on one hand, cultures are disconnected and, on another hand, there are a lot of Muslims that want to live in the United States even though we have this war. I'm sure there are also a lot of Iraqis that would like to work and live here and then there are others who just despise us. Man, the world is . . . I just can't begin to make comments about the world that way. I mean, I'm just so grateful that I'm in the world of music that isn't something that's about competing or killing.

ARE YOU STILL AS DRIVEN AS YOU WERE FIFTEEN YEARS AGO?

Yeah, but not this month. (Laughs.) I'm feeling like a slug but I'm kind of enjoying it. I have worked incredibly hard the last two years. When I finish a recording, I always chill a little bit because it's kind of intense doing one of those records.

HAS YOUR CAREER THUS FAR TURNED OUT THE WAY YOU ENVISIONED?

Well, I never really set out with a vision and I had no idea of what I was going to do. I knew I wanted to write music and become a better writer but I didn't really guess that I could make a living at it. If somebody would have told me that I would accomplish the things that I have with the people I have had the opportunity to play with, I just would not have believed it.

I have no ideas for the future but I would like to do a film someday on what I do well and maybe write for dance. I hope I do lots of exciting projects and collaborations with people. I just like working with people.

AND FINALLY, DO YOU HAVE A PARTICULAR WAY OF LOOKING AT LIFE OR CERTAIN PHILOSOPHY THAT YOU WOULDN'T MIND SHARING?

I wouldn't say that I have a particular philosophy because the minute I have one, it changes. (Laughs.) But I would say that I spend some time each day thinking about life. I had some pretty heavy experiences two years ago that made me really assess how valuable life is, and just how lucky we are to be here and have all these opportunities, so I don't take things for granted as much as I used to. I just try to live each day and live in a way that feels good while using my own gut instincts for what's right and wrong to guide me.

36

WADADA LEO SMITH

I think only in America could a person of Leo Smith's talent not be recognized. I think Leo Smith is a genius, and whenever the thrust of his work becomes known, then he will get the respect he deserves. I only hope it will happen while he's on the planet.

—Anthony Braxton

WHEN WERE YOU AWARE THAT YOU HAD YOUR LOVE FOR MUSIC?

I became curious about the world between the ages of twelve and thirteen and began to think about music in a very serious way. I went to my mother and asked when I could date and she said when I was thirteen. But I really wasn't interested in dating but in finding out when I could have some sense of independence.

WAS THERE A POINT WHEN YOU HAD A SPIRITUAL AWAKENING AS FAR AS WHAT THE POSSIBILITIES WERE IN MUSIC FOR YOU?

I began to read Marcus Aurelius's *Meditation* at the age of twelve, which is a pretty famous book about a Roman emperor who was more spiritually inclined than he was militarily or politically. He talked about observing phenomena and ideas in life, which I found fascinating. He also spoke about being able to see that music or art had a very different meaning than what was ordinarily attributed.

WHEN WAS THE AACM (ASSOCIATION FOR THE ADVANCEMENT OF CREATIVE MUSICIANS) ESTABLISHED?

About two or three years before I was a member in 1965. It was started by Muhal Richard Abrams, Steve McCall, Phil Cohran, Jodie Christian, and a couple of others. The Art Ensemble of Chicago, Anthony Braxton, and a few others came later but arrived before I did.

HOW WERE YOU MADE AWARE OF THE AACM?

I met this fellow in the Army at Fort Carson, Colorado, who talked about this guy who was very serious and made great music. It was Anthony Braxton. He gave me Anthony's telephone number and we met in Chicago, played music, and had a great time.

WAS THE AACM ESTABLISHED OUT OF NECESSITY OR OUT OF COMMON INTEREST?

There is a great connection with society in African culture, both secret and aboveground. Almost all musical organizations are connected with any organized society. Coming from that tradition, it was important to have a social context in which to engage the audience and look at the problems that that particular engagement presented. We wanted to be self-sufficient on all levels. From organizing our own performances to recording our own music, interpreting what our music meant and presenting it in a context that was totally harmonious with the way we thought as a collective people. When the AACM was devised, all of those principles became part of the by-laws. And those bylaws are very specific about those elements and those contexts, even to the point of calling it "creative music."

DID YOU KNOW MUCH ABOUT THE AACM WHEN YOU MET ANTHONY BRAXTON?

No, but when I arrived in Chicago, the AACM name and persona was all over town. I saw a sign that said the Joseph Jarman Quartet ensemble was performing and I was so excited that I couldn't wait for the show which I believe was on a Sunday evening at the coffeehouse. When I stepped inside that door, it was like stepping into a new heaven. Jodi, Christopher Gaddy, Thurman Barker, and Charles Clark were playing and the music was so exciting. Lester Bowie, Roscoe Mitchell, and a number of other AACM members were in the audience and I met all of them that night. And the next weekend, Roscoe introduced me as a member of the AACM and this was towards the beginning of 1967.

WAS THERE A MUTUAL SEARCH FOR WISDOM AND SPIRITUALITY THAT CAME ALONG WITH THE MUSIC?

Every meeting would include moments of meditation and silence. Every meeting. Everyone had a connection with a deeper meaning of what they were doing along with a deeper social meaning of what the collective meant and how important it was. We didn't always understand the importance but because the collective was very powerful, it brought people back into the circle almost instantly. You really didn't stray. If you made a mistake, you were lifted right back up again; both in conceptual understanding and the intellectual connection with those concepts.

QUITE A FEW MUSICIANS SEEM TO LOSE SOME OF THEIR PEAK CREATIVE POWERS AS THEY REACH MIDDLE AGE. HOWEVER, MANY MEMBERS OF THE AACM SUCH AS YOURSELF AND ANTHONY BRAXTON CONTINUE TO PRODUCE CREATIVE MUSIC IN A WAY THAT SEEMS TO TRANSCEND TIME. WHAT IS HAPPENING?

I have made this observation as well. Duke Ellington, Miles Davis, and Jelly Roll Morton were creative their entire lives. This will occur in the individual who is a transitional artist and is continuously changing, but it has to be evident from the very beginning. Beethoven, Stravinsky, and Yanachek were this way along with writers such as Shakespeare and Langston Hughes. All of these people reflected what I would call transitional artistry; an artist that doesn't sell down. In my teachings, I have an analogy that says: "On the way up the mountain, they see many flowers; they observe them in deep depth but don't pluck them. They observe and look for other flowers."

WHAT I THINK IS UNUSUAL IS THAT THERE ARE SO MANY MEMBERS OF THE AACM THAT FIT WHAT YOU JUST DESCRIBED.

I think it is too. This group of artists is quite unusual and quite an exceptional group of people. When you look at the works of Henry Threadgill and Anthony Braxton, they were apart from each other but continuously growing. I see the same thing when I view John Zorn and David Douglas. I see that same parallel line where they are not plucking the flower to take it home, but are observing and continuing to move forward once they have finished observing it.

DURING THE CIVIL RIGHTS MOVEMENT OF THE '60S, IT HAS BEEN SAID THAT THE POLITICAL POWERS-THAT-BE FEARED FREE IMPROVISATIONAL MUSIC BECAUSE IT ELEVATED THE CONSCIOUSNESS OF THE INDIVIDUAL.

That's absolutely true and if you read Consener's book on Coltrane, it says specifically what you just said. During the '60s in Chicago, policemen were even planted as musicians to observe our habits and practices in the AACM.

THESE WERE POLICEMEN THAT POSED THEMSELVES AS MUSICIANS?

They actually played instruments. They infiltrated and were part of our organization for about a half a year. They observed everything about the group and made their report to Mayor Daly and his task team. One of our secretaries ran into one of them in uniform about a year later and the guy actually admitted that they were investigating what we were doing.

Our music had the same kind of fire and energy of Martin Luther King, H. Rap Brown, and Stokely Carmichael so we called our music, "Free Music." It had the same type of energy. For my colleagues such as Mr. Braxton, Leroy Jenkins, and Richard Abrams and myself, it was quite clear to us that if the music had made its way into mainstream African American or American society, we would have a very different society today. The places in which we live would be in much better condition. We believe that.

DID THE MEMBERS OF THE AACM HAVE A HIGHER AWARENESS LEVEL OF THE
POWER AND THE ENERGY OF THIS MUSIC AND WHAT KEPT THE MUSIC FROM MOVING
FORWARD AT THAT TIME?

You can tell people the truth about something but if they don't hear it from news
mediums such as in newspapers, magazines, or television, it doesn't register.
There's a disconnect. For example, black DJs would not play our music but college
stations would. However, college radio stations reached a different set of intellect
than those that really should have been participating.

This disconnect was not something that was normal or usual; it was something
that has been conditioned into African American society by a term we called
"mental slavery." In the rest of the world, it's an arrogant slavery, arrogance against
these types of inclusions.

WERE THE MUSICIANS OF THE AACM PURPOSELY TRYING TO CREATE MUSIC THAT
WAS POLITICAL OR SPIRITUAL IN TRYING TO REACH OTHERS?

It was natural propensity or natural understanding of our lives and what was
needed in order to be whole or complete. However, those elements were a by-
product after we began. For example, I wrote my first composition at the age of
twelve, but I thought of myself simply as a composer trying to write music that
came straight out of my heart without any set formalized distance. I had only been
playing the trumpet for a couple of months so it came out of that impetus. But
once you get started and begin to see the road opening up before you, you see
what's wrong because it's like a light that goes into a dark desert and as the light
moves forward, it only illuminates the spot in which it strikes. But if the light is
taken from a vertical angle and made horizontal, it shows a clear path to where you
are going. That's what happens with an artist upon understanding what happens in
our society.

WAS THERE A FRUSTRATION AMONGST THOSE WITHIN THE AACM BECAUSE OF
THE KNOWLEDGE AND AWARENESS OF WHAT NEEDED TO BE DONE?

We were very much aware of what we were doing and what was happening in
society. It created a sense of frustration but the ones that have the true spirit; they
know that, ultimately, victory is on their side. They also know that change is very
gradual. Take the ant as an analogy. In order to cross a stream of water, the ants
will make a bridge in order to take the rest of the ants across. Ultimately, those
ants realize that you have to make a sacrifice in order for a real change to occur
and I think that we understand that too.

DID THE MUSIC OF THAT TIME REFLECT THE STRUGGLE OF AFRICAN OR BLACK
AMERICANS?

It specifically reflected the struggle of black America, which is the struggle of
humanity. Becoming free was awakened during the '20s by people such as Marcus
Garvey and Philip Randolph. They began to show a resistance against a set for-

mula, which went against all human rights. All people who were denied those rights and colonized by Europe began to break away. Thus, a demonstration was held to educate how these things could be done. I contend that black liberation is liberation for the whole planet. If people who are black are not liberated, then no society is liberated.

HOW DID THE CIVIL RIGHTS MOVEMENT PERSONALLY AFFECT YOU?

I wasn't afraid and went anywhere I wanted to go. But every so often we would play in a white country club in Mississippi, which had a segregated society. And in that country club, we would have to go in through the back door and sit in the kitchen until it was time to play. The manager of the club would have us line up behind him and walk us through the white audience to get to the stage. And while we played, he would stand by the side of the bandstand in order to keep people from coming up and, specifically, drunk white women from engaging in any kind of conversation or activity. But there was a piano player in the band by the name of Gabbo. And every time we were getting ready to play this club, he would get pissed off and get very drunk or he wouldn't even show up. And no one, including me, understood what was going on but I was only a thirteen-year-old kid. But he objected to the way the band was being treated.

But on one particular night, the manager didn't stay on the stage during the show and a drunken white woman came over and sat at the piano along with Gabbo while he played. The lights immediately came on and the dance was over. They brought us out and that was it.

Now this is a personal story. One night while also in Mississippi, I was walking through town while taking my girlfriend home and a cop pulled up to us very fast and about six white guys jump out of the car to beat me up. And then one of the guys says, "That's Leo and he plays at the Country Club." They all jumped back into the car and took off. If I was Leo that didn't play at the Country Club, I may have been beaten worse or might have been killed.

HOW OLD WERE YOU AGAIN?

That was fifty years ago when I was thirteen.

IS IT POSSIBLE THAT A NEW CREATIVITY MIGHT COME OUT OF WHAT IS HAPPENING GLOBALLY TODAY?

I think it has been going on for the last fifteen or twenty years. When new ideas and new musical language begin to generate, it takes awhile before it reaches the surface. And right now, it's kind of boiling up to the surface. Hip-hop and electronic music are part of many various forms of new music that are becoming part of the mainstream. This is a reflection of what's happening right now and all those things are generating new languages and aesthetics, along with new systems, and once someone begins to organize that in a more creative manner, something new will surface from it.

Today in electronics, some creators are using new processing within their tones and are opening up new areas of development. These developments are going to lead to something very unique and rare but definitely indicative of what our society is turning out today.

The world today is seeking unity. And future music will not necessarily be about the merging of things and solos, but a distinct music where the creative collective is the most powerful known. It will be in an ensemble that will be forever changing. Consequently, it won't be rooted in just a single band but in various different bands. John Zorn, Anthony Braxton, and many other people along with myself are doing that right now.

With our global connection through wars and the economy today, there isn't going to be a way back towards narrow and pretentious music anymore. And I think communication is going to play the biggest part because the tradition of Islam, which I study, teaches that all of the developments such as air and space travel have to produce another meaning to what life is about.

DO THE EVENTS HAPPENING IN THE WORLD TODAY INFLUENCE YOUR CREATIVE PROCESS?

I think so. When I name a piece of music, it's systemic and symbolic. I use the phenomena of magic as the elemental point in how I develop a piece of music. For example, I use musical constructions and designs that have nothing to do with pitch, note, or rhythm. But the use of colors, shapes, and images can be referenced scientifically and biologically and, through imagination, can create another world.

For example, I have a piece named after the systemic construction of clouds. When clouds begin to attract to one another, they cause an updraft, which creates several levels of activity such as rain or sleet. This activity moves in a certain way so that the inner portion is heavier and more condensed than the outer parts. When these aspects become crystallized such as with rain or hail, they become heavier and fall back down. That has a symbolic musical principle and is a very important point. It's not an A or B flat anymore. You are researching through the material in a scientific artistic way that makes the piece happen. And, the first piece of symbolic music was done over thirty-five years ago.

YOU HAVE SAID THAT THE PEOPLE OF AFRICA BELIEVE THAT RHYTHM EXISTED AT THE BEGINNING OF TIME AND WAS THOUGHT TO BE THE ABSOLUTE CREATOR OF THE WORLDS AND THEIR INHABITANTS. THAT, THEREFORE, IT RUNS THROUGH ALL OF US. I'M NOT SURE THAT EVERYONE HAS THIS LEVEL OF AWARENESS OR REALITY.

Well, they don't and, generally speaking, our society lives without guidance. And we live without guidance because of materialism. Materialism tends to make one feel more powerful by having more material possessions than someone else. But in fact, that may not be true but the person lives as if it is true and much of society thinks this way. However, there is also a group of people that is not connected to either one of those elements that drifts and has absolutely no guidance whatsoever.

HAVE WE BECAME A MORE VISUAL KIND OF SOCIETY AND TOOK FOR GRANTED OR
PLACED LESS SIGNIFICANCE ON VARIOUS ELEMENTS OF SOUND?

Things have changed because people have begun to isolate themselves. For instance, I can sit at home and watch television or put on a DVD and not need interaction with anyone. But during earlier periods of almost every society, there was
more engagement between people and some type of connection. And when it becomes energy stored in systems for commodities, it kind of declassifies that a little bit. But it should not entrap one because that declassification should bring out
more of the real person.

When I watch television, I'm more aware of the propaganda than I would be
if I had a different kind of reality. I know that everything on television wants me
to buy or think something. So I have to watch that with the right perspective.
DVDs, CDs, and other forms of commodities trivialize things to the point where
the ordinary person gets trapped into thinking they need more of these commodities.

But the person who has spiritual intact in their being will try to find a connection or allow it to move them to another state. That's very different than being
gratified in a more materialistic way. Some say music is very powerful, but music
in itself is not powerful. No art is powerful but if it makes contact and transports
you from your ordinary state, it can be extraordinary. You can have a fresh view of
everything that's old and that's also another way of engaging fresh and new artistic
or intellectual properties within our society.

When we buy CDs, DVDs, or books, we don't own any of it. What's on the DVD,
the CD, or inside the novel is the key or the formula of what you should be realizing about it. It is not the thing itself. It can show you a portal to where another dimension is opening and that's all. The artist wants you to forget about where you
have been and be transformed to some other state of what is much richer, more
powerful, and has the fruits of illumination. Once again, that's the power of art and
the objects are only the key to that door but not the door. They cannot open it.

ARE WE CLOSING THE GAP BETWEEN OUR DIFFERENT CULTURES?

Artists and scientists have already closed the gap and I think nutritionists and
certain specialists will begin to close the gap. But in the human spectrum, most human beings in society are politicized by people that usually don't want people to see
the world as it really is. Human beings as a whole have a much larger gap to close.

CAN YOU DISCUSS YOUR PERSONAL RELATIONSHIP WITH TIME IN A MUSICAL SENSE?

Most of the things that I like, such as rhythm, are on a metrical level and deal
with proportions. The relationship with time and space is also a kind of relativity
of activity happening. Each individual has a responsibility for it to move and the
collective of these individual movements transfer a horizontal space which creates
what I call rhythm.

WHERE DOES YOUR INSPIRATION COME FROM OR WHAT INFLUENCES YOUR CRE-
ATIVITY.

Allah or God and I say that in the deepest meaning. I believe that the question
itself is the manifestation of God or Allah. And this manifestation, no matter where
it's going is that realization. And so, everything that I do, I attribute to this place.

CAN YOU DESCRIBE WHAT YOU ARE TRYING TO DO WITH YOUR MUSIC TODAY?

I'm trying to create a horizontal and vertical universe that is continuously evolving and has the same characteristics as the universe that I live in.

CECIL TAYLOR SAID THAT "MUSIC HAS TO DO WITH A LOT OF AREAS WHICH ARE
MAGICAL RATHER THAN LOGICAL; THE GREAT ARTISTS, RATHER THAN JUST GETTING
INVOLVED WITH DISCIPLINE, GET TO UNDERSTAND LOVE AND ALLOW THE LOVE TO
TAKE SHAPE." HOW MUCH OF YOUR MUSIC IS FROM LOGIC AND HOW MUCH FROM THIS
OTHER PLACE THAT CECIL TAYLOR DESCRIBES?

In a truly visionary sense, all of it comes from love and it comes from love because it starts with love. And love itself has a communicative quality that can touch
another person's heart.

To get that music out of you into this realm to where it can be communicated
requires an enormous amount of skill. It could be individual or personal. Reflection, meditation, or contemplation and design. For example, you can give people
a piece of music with notes on a piece of paper or you can dictate them from the
piano as Cecil does. I have played with Cecil and Cecil and the piano itself is a
score for the music. He makes his scores from the piano spontaneously after each
player because he has thought about it for a month or a night or a year, of what he
wants to give you. He and the piano become one and that becomes the score. It's
what everyone in his ensemble must be able to relate to in order to become successful. But in order for him to get there, he had a tremendous wealth of formal
training, of personal training and what I meant by personal is by his own initiative
and research. I think that's the hallmark of a great artist.

Love is the starting point, which is the great way that this rich form of communication or this energy form is coming from, but underneath that energy is a world
of information that is generating the kind of energy that can touch another person,
that can cause them to be transformed. And the ultimate goal is to transform society through art.

NOTE

1. Anthony Braxton with Graham Lock, *Forces in Motion* (New York, Da Capo Press,
1988), 53.

KEN VANDERMARK

In a world that has difficulty and attitude toward unfamiliar and creative thought, Ken Vandermark is a visionary exploring possibilities with improvisational and compositional forms.

A recipient of the MacArthur Foundation Genius Grant, he has used the funding to support his interest in bringing together some of today's most innovative and forward-thinking musicians and composers in the global arts community.

Embracing music and life without compromise, Vandermark is a bold and brilliant presence, relentless in his passion for creative and artistic ascension.

HAVE WE BECOME A SOCIETY THAT NO LONGER HAS THE PATIENCE TO BE CHALLENGED AND IS ONLY OPEN TO THINGS THAT ARE EASILY ACCESSIBLE?

For me, it's really difficult to understand how the current administration in power has been able to completely dominate political and cultural thought the way it has. The people I am surrounded by are incredibly critical of this administration but it's clear there's huge support by the American people for what this government is doing. This is connected to the question you've asked, which is in regard to this information age. Things are becoming more and more accelerated with information and imagery bombarding us from every side. You can't get into an elevator, you can't go into a bar, and you can't get into a bus. . . . No matter where you go, there are sounds of some kind of music, some kind of advertising—it's everywhere! People no longer have the patience to contemplate something and the news is a perfect example. There are obvious exceptions, but mass media has dumbed down its information, making it very quick and readily available to a certain kind of mentality.

My day-to-day experience is an exception to this; I don't understand it and it discourages me. It depresses me on a lot of levels because we are living in an incredibly complicated time and unless there can be dialogue, intense dialogue about complicated ideas in ways that can be articulated to the mass public, we're screwed!

IS THERE A CHANCE THAT BECAUSE OF THE CURRENT GLOBAL CLIMATE THAT PEOPLE COULD FIND A NEW APPRECIATION FOR THOSE THINGS THAT HAVE MORE DEPTH OR CREATIVE AND ARTISTIC VALUE?

There's a total shift in the way we receive information and people in their twenties can deal with complexity from sounds and visual elements more readily and are not going to get overwhelmed by huge amounts of information. They can pick out what's necessary and are able to deal with potentially more complex art forms because it's connected to their general day-to-day existence. That may be connected to the kinds of music and art that they are going to be interested in. But for someone like myself or maybe someone older than me, dealing with new forms of technology can be overwhelming. There's like seventy things here, which ones do I deal with?

This group of younger people is going to experience frustration with status quo sensibility and lots of them are just sick and tired of mainstream music. Radio and MTV has become so corporatized, manufactured, and homogenized in the truest sense of the word that they're just bored out of their skulls. They're scrambling on the Internet to find things they like and find new bands they haven't heard. So I think that there are a lot of connections. It's technology, it's politics, it's the age group, and it's cycles that culturally happen. On some level, it doesn't surprise me that there is a group of people actively trying to find something that's an alternative to the common culture.

DOES SOCIETY TODAY HAVE DIFFICULTY WITH CREATIVITY THAT IS NOT EASILY EXPLAINED, UNDERSTOOD, OR IDENTIFIABLE AND WILL THIS BE A SIGNIFICANT OBSTACLE TO OVERCOME FOR CREATIVE MUSIC OR THE ARTS IN GENERAL?

If you look at the development of that music from the beginning of the twentieth century, there has been a very rapid growth rate. But if you look at the parallels from Western tonal music, the kind of music that was being played at the very beginning of the century was harmonically more simplified in a lot of its elements. Louis Armstrong was an incredibly complex musician so I'm not suggesting at all that people fit some generalization or were simplistic. For example, if you compare the harmonic and rhythmic systems that were being used previously to those of Cecil Taylor, there are obviously some developments that have happened. But in a simplistic way, you can draw a parallel from tonal music in Western culture to the progression of more dense chords and complicated rhythms in jazz.

In the twentieth century, jazz history was in this incredibly accelerated process of development but at the end of the '60s, something happened with that development. There was this very strong reaction against that development in the '80s and for the first time in jazz history, there was a really large-based neoconservative movement that was similar to the '50s, where there was a resurgence of interest in Dixieland music. With Wynton Marsalis and the crew surrounding him, there was a big neoconservative movement and that makes sense because there has to be a period of reassessment to make sense of these developments. The problem for me is that this neoconservative movement became so strict in its definitions of what was and what wasn't art. It's like a box.

If you look at a lot of the cultural institutions and the way that they are connected to politics, it would seem that there would be a real fight to convince the art status quo to be interested in challenging work. Whereas, the creativity that comes out right now is from a totally different place and actually has a lot more to say about being alive right now.

There's going to be a fight in that status quo between the established artists and the way they believe things should be done. I think we are in a shift period where the stuff coming up now is going to be problematic for that status quo and that's connected to politics.

ARE JAZZ TRADITIONALISTS HAVING A DIFFICULT TIME ACCEPTING THAT A MUSIC FORM CONSIDERED "AMERICAN" NOW HAS MORE VISIBLE INTERNATIONAL AND DIVERSE ASPECTS WITHIN IT?

You have a group of people that are connected to part of the past and that past is really important to them. They see influences coming in and altering their sense of tradition and that tradition gets lost and then it's gone. There's protectiveness to that, and just as the beboppers saw the influence of Ornette Coleman and Cecil Taylor, the pre-bebop players saw the influence of Charlie Parker and Dizzy Gillespie. Miles Davis is a perfect example of a guy that was completely cutting edge and then Ornette Coleman, Eric Dolphy, and Cecil Taylor came along and it's like, this is crap! Miles had broken through all these things just as they were breaking through them and at some point he began to recognize the correlation but not initially in the late '50s. It's protecting the work you've done because it has to remain valid. Is anybody going to care about the work that we did or is it just going to get thrown out with the next new thing that comes in?

Lasting art is going to stand up to time. That doesn't change the fact there are musicians who understand and have devoted their entire life to working with certain methods. And as new methods come from outside the United States within jazz and start affecting the perception of what's important, innovative, and interesting—that's a threat to their livelihood. There's defensiveness about outside influences and I think it makes a lot of sense. Art's going to do what it's going to do. If you look at the music historically, there have always been outside influences in jazz. Look at Duke Ellington's music. He was influenced in the '20s and '30s from people integrating into the United States in addition to the touring he did outside the United States. And Coltrane was influenced by music from the East.

European composed music also had an impact on people who were dealing with composition. Charlie Parker was interested in Stravinsky and wanted to study with Varese. The music of Charlie Parker is 100 percent as valid as Varese but it indicates there is an interest in cross-pollination. It's always been part of improvised music coming out of the United States, and to say that now that's going to have to stop if the music is going to remain jazz, I don't see how that's going to happen. It gets into this whole thing of defining what jazz is, which gets into some really complicated cultural issues that deal with race too. Because you cannot say that jazz in terms of its source, its innovations and influence, is separate from black American culture. It's completely developed and defined by that culture.

If you look at jazz audiences today, they are not predominately black and that includes performing artists too. So if black Americans are not coming out to hear the music and especially if black American children are not coming out to hear the music, then it's not surprising they're not going to be interested in playing that music as an adult. So now what's going to happen to the music that we call jazz? That's a huge change and maybe it's a change for the worse, but you can't force through definition what jazz is. It's like any kind of art; it has its own set of threads. It's a very complicated and touchy subject because the things that define music in this country come out of the black American experience and those influences have affected European and Asian interests in the music too. All the primary influences that are connected to jazz are coming out of the black American experience as far as I see it. I don't see how anyone can make an argument against that.

So what's going to happen to the music now? I don't have an answer for that and I think it's out of our hands. I would be incredibly naive and ignorant to suggest that I understand black American culture. I'm not a black American. I'm totally influenced by it, and it's completely changed my life down to my DNA, but I'm not a black American. And if I can't understand or appreciate what it means to be a black American culturally, socially, and politically, then how can somebody in Europe or Asia really say that they could possibly understand the answer to what that culture is and how it would affect the art?

As participation from people outside black American culture increases, there is no question the music is going to change radically because the source has shifted. That's a real issue and is neither positive nor negative, it's just reality. I'm really curious, fifty years from now, what happens? Is improvised music or jazz—is it just an anachronism? Or does it become something totally unrecognizable to someone who thinks they knew what jazz is because of this move away from the culture that developed and defined it. And the only way for someone today to sound vaguely like jazz in a Coltrane and Miles classic quintet way, is to completely work counter to the way that the music works. Because improvised music is of its time in every possible way that you can define it. And to sound like classic jazz now, you've got to re-create and imitate the sounds, rhythms, harmonics, melodic approaches of something that's like OK, mid-'50s. We're talking forty-five or fifty years ago at this point. As soon as you start doing that, you're killing the creative drive of the music. It has to follow a timeline. It's not an art that's based on re-creation. It's based on creation, which is consistent with almost any art.

One of the problems in this country is that race is still a touchy and loaded issue and it's a sad statement about what little distance we've come in the United States.

Jazz is tied to race issues in this country and we have to be able to discuss these things and I find that when I talk about subjects that are connected to race, I find myself walking on eggshells. There are so many different ways to interpret what I am trying to say and if I'm not as articulate as I need to be, and not as informed as I need to be on the subject, it's not from lack of trying. And yet to have someone that's a white middle-class American try to talk about race relations in the United States, it's a problem because I can't fully appreciate a huge part of the situation.

A discussion of the subject really needs to happen from all the parties involved, and I find that those circumstances arise so rarely without them becoming combative. That's a really strong statement about how screwed up race relations are in this country. I want to point this out because it's the kind of thing where some people just won't talk about it because it's a really loaded subject. It touches on so many very sensitive and painful aspects of the problems in the United States. Yet I would rather try and talk about it and do the best that I can to articulate my own subjective point of view, rather than leave it not discussed. To be honest, I think it's a bit risky because it's so easy to misinterpret or mishear what I'm trying to say. I have nothing but respect for the people who have been developing this music, both black and white. From the friends that I have who are black American and the things I have seen them deal with socially, culturally, and politically, there are serious lasting problems going on with how black Americans are treated, and it's important to discuss in forums like this or nothing is going to change and that would be the biggest crime.

IS IT POSSIBLE THAT WHAT'S HAPPENING IN CREATIVE MUSIC IS TOO FORWARD THINKING OR COMPLEX FOR MUCH OF OUR SOCIETY?

The most creative and unique music of any period has always been ignored or was under the radar. Thelonious Monk was almost a household name and that's kind of astounding. Almost all the great classic jazz records with rare exception were made on small independent labels such as Bluenote, Riverside, Prestige, Dial, and Savoy. That's not unlike now, whether in Europe, Asia, Canada, or here. You're talking about people who are passionate about the music and trying to get people documented that are overlooked by the mainstream.

Columbia Records is a weird exception because Miles Davis did some of his greatest work on Columbia. There are other examples like Duke Ellington as well, but generally speaking, it's been people working independently outside the mainstream. And I think the people who are doing some of the most interesting work now, like you said, are artists that others don't know about.

ONE OF THE PROBLEMS WITH DOCUMENTATION FOCUSING ON JAZZ, SUCH AS KEN BURNS'S SERIES, IS THAT IT SPENDS MOST OF ITS TIME CONCENTRATING ON WHAT JAZZ CREATED IN THE PAST TENSE AND LITTLE ON WHAT THE MUSIC IS CREATING AT THE MOMENT, WHICH IS THE ESSENCE OF THIS GREAT MUSIC WE CALL JAZZ. DOESN'T THIS SEEM SHORTSIGHTED, PERHAPS A LOST OPPORTUNITY TO EDUCATE POTENTIAL ASPIRING JAZZ STUDENTS AND EDUCATE PEOPLE TO WHAT JAZZ IS REALLY ABOUT AND WHAT IS AVAILABLE TO THEM?

One of the problems with art is it's hard for people to assess what's really happening connected to the present. The artists that get signed to a major label frequently are people who have done work that's associated with the past because people can assess it or think that they can assess it. There are very few writers who actually talk about artists that are doing things right now that have real weight. Some people are trying to do that obviously but the overwhelming majority of information about the music is about its past. In some ways that makes sense but there is certainly a discrepancy there.

At the beginning of their careers, Louis Armstrong, Duke Ellington, and Thelonious Monk were looked at as outsiders. Amazingly, Monk was even looked at as someone that was not technically capable of playing the piano that well. At some point, there was enough weight in their art for people to accept the fact that they were great artists. However, when many artists are allowed to do their work, they end up being misunderstood. This is especially true for someone like Duke Ellington, who was still being criticized for not being able to compose long-form pieces even towards the end of his career.

It doesn't surprise me that the people who get funding to document jazz usually receive it for stuff that has been assessed as art. There are no qualifiers that say the people doing great work right now such as Matt Maneri, Joe Morris, William Parker, or Peter Brotzmann are going to be as lasting as the work of Charlie Parker. So we'll talk about Charlie Parker more because that's a qualified and quantified thing as great art in America. The irony is that improvised music is attached to its own time, the present, and very infrequently is it discussed in its own period.

Institutions like schools place emphasis on music that has history, and I would say the emphasis is much more on harmonically derived elements and music that's attached to tonal harmony as opposed to music that comes out of the end of the '50s. There is like a ton of development going on inside and outside the United States that has really moved the music into different places. That's why it continues to thrive. It may not get written about or acknowledged like in a Ken Burns series, where I think the last episode dealt with the '60s and was pushed into thirty or forty-five minutes of time. In terms of chronology, that's half the period of the music. It's absurd! Whether you like the music or not, it has continued to change and shift.

People in mainstream jazz magazines still talk about Albert Ayler as a charlatan and I think that's a very simple illustration of the kind of problem that we are faced with. If Jackson Pollack is seen as a genius, then translating that to music, Albert Ayler should be seen as a genius. His approach to the saxophone and sound radically changed the possibilities for music and yet he is very unknown. In terms of the general thrust of the writing, Albert Ayler is a footnote and he shouldn't be. There is some kind of critical assessment issue with the music as far as the way I perceive it.

IS THERE A CHANCE THAT AT SOME POINT OVER THE GENERATIONS WE BECAME A MORE VISUAL KIND OF SOCIETY AND TOOK FOR GRANTED OR PLACED LESS SIGNIFICANCE ON VARIOUS ELEMENTS OF SOUND?

Historically, it would seem that the visual arts have a long history of respect in Western culture. Jazz is this weird anomalous music that isn't highbrow enough for people to consider as art music and too esoteric to be considered pop music. It's stuck in this ghetto somewhere. And it's ironic because it may be the most inclusive approach to music in terms of its sources and ability to take influences from all kinds of music and organically apply it to the thread of improvisation and narrative expression.

There is an issue with improvised music that I wrestle with all the time. If you keep it doing what it should be doing, then how do you make it valid to a world that doesn't want something to be ephemeral. People want to know that it's the best band or the greatest performance. Everything is quantified and qualified but this music isn't designed for that. It's designed for experience in real time and it's about risk. If you take risk, then sometimes things fail. Even in the process of something failing, it's totally crucial to the aspect of what's going on and that creates tons of problems.

As far as I can tell, the motivations connected with the Lincoln Center are to try and codify the jazz vision of Ken Burns, Wynton Marsalis, Stanley Crouch and promote that as the thing that will replace symphonic music in this country. There is a huge amount of funding in support of that vision and that vision cannot include things that are contrary to that thread. If you read comments by people who are very strongly sided with that vision, they get very critical about music that doesn't fit into it. But the frustration that I have is with the vast majority of the funding that goes towards this vision and they know that and are trying to control it. That's why they become very defensive about things that don't fit into their paradigm because it challenges what may or may not be happening with the music and the funding for it.

I think a lot of the people that are associated with the Lincoln Center viewpoint really honestly believe they are saving jazz and the art form and that they are keeping it alive. From my perspective, they are totally into a museum piece. They are turning it into those paintings on the wall so everyone can say that this is a classic, this is a masterpiece. But I don't need to actually look at the damn thing because I know that that's what it supposed to be.

DO YOU HAVE A PHILOSOPHY THAT YOU TRY TO IMPART ON YOUNGER MUSICIANS OR STUDENTS?

The most creative musicians working today, like those of the past, have been individualists that have their own innovative and personal approach. And anytime I'm playing with people who are younger than me, I try to emphasize the fact that you've got to find your own voice, pursue your own ideas, and understand that the ideas that you have as an individual are completely valid and need to be pursued. The ideas and explanations for why I have done things a certain way are just personal solutions. It's very necessary for people to find their own set of solutions to the problems they are faced with and to pursue those influences that strike them the most. Therefore, you cannot give people the answers to the problems you have found. You have to suggest the problems and suggest that you have to go solve them yourself.

WHAT CHARACTERISTICS DO YOU LOOK FOR IN THE MUSICIANS YOU COLLABORATE
WITH?

My favorite musicians are people who are extremely open-minded and open to
the tools they have available as players. I very rarely play with people that are only
familiar with one type of music or are only interested in jazz and not interested in
playing music that isn't connected with jazz and improvised music.

At times, the musicians of the Vandermark 5 need to be able to work with materials that have nothing to do with jazz, and if they are not familiar with the music or not motivated to explore things on their own, the band wouldn't work. That's
much more common for musicians now and certainly for musicians that I work
with who are even much older than me. Most have come from backgrounds where
they are extremely aware of many developments of music, whether it's improvised,
composed, or music that's not connected to jazz at all. I can't imagine playing with
someone who wasn't like that. I know that there are people who are only concerned or focused on one kind of music and I can see why there might be merits
in that. You can explore deeper in terms of the relationship within a specific set of
limitations. There is certainly merit in doing that but I don't work with people with
that focus. For the kind of music that I play, the broader your sensibilities, the
more potential tools you have to express your individuality.

YOU SEEM TO HAVE MORE CONTROL OVER THE RHYTHMIC DYNAMICS OF THE MU-
SIC THAN MOST. HOW MUCH OF THAT ASPECT OF YOUR MUSIC IS TAKEN INTO CON-
SIDERATION WITH THE MUSICIANS THAT YOU ARE INVOLVED WITH?

The way I play and write for groups tends to deal with rhythm, which is one of
the most critical elements I'm dealing with. Rhythm is a consistent factor in all the
different kinds of music, and there are a variety of rhythms attached to the way different people and music deal with time. I'm not a harmonically oriented player.
I'm a melodically/rhythmically oriented player and I've always heard music that
way. When I hear groups play and I find something lacking in the performance, it's
usually connected to the way they deal with rhythm or tempo in a way I don't find
interesting.

Since the beginning of the Vandermark 5, the ensemble has dealt with exploring the different possibilities in rhythm. That's why I think a small part of what the
group does is related to jazz time and the way that time feels rhythmically. It also
has the kind of propulsion that incorporates a lot of elements of more open time
that may come out of Cecil Taylor's music. This is wave energy as opposed to strict
pulse energy. The group is also incorporating rhythmic feels completely out of improvised music such as funk, or different kinds of traditional world music that has
nothing to do with jazz.

DRUMMERS SEEM TO BE A KEY ELEMENT WITHIN THE CHEMISTRY OF YOUR GROUPS.

For me, the most essential musician in the group is the drummer. I think the
drummer defines more aspects of the music than any other individual and so my

relationship to the drummer in each group is the most important relationship I have musically. Drummers define the dynamic level, the rhythmic flow more than anybody else in the group and end up affecting structural indications more than anyone else along with every element of the music. For instance, if you have a mediocre horn section with a great drummer, that band will sound really good, but if you have a great horn section with a horrendous drummer, the band will sound bad. You cannot overcome a bad drummer and a great drummer will make the music really come alive. This again is tied to the way I approach things which is more from a rhythmic base than from anything else so that relationship is completely connected to me. They are inseparable.

There is an issue of chemistry and communication that doesn't seem to get talked about that much which is about the way individuals relate to each other and less about individual skills. You have great players who don't communicate well just as you can have really cool people who can't have a conversation. They just don't communicate. The key is really about group communication and chemistry, and chemistry can be incredibly unpredictable but there are times that you cannot anticipate the way a group of people are going to work in a room. So chemistry is like this X factor.

Look at the Miles Davis group after Coltrane left. He tried to find that chemistry again but had to totally revamp the group. The group with Wayne Shorter had a different rhythm section with a totally different approach and yet that group had amazing chemistry. Miles was a genius at putting groups together, but even someone as brilliant as Miles Davis at organizing ensembles had to find an entirely different set of chemistry before he could find a group that was as strong as the group he had with Coltrane. That's a mysterious element to the music, which is really essential and for some reason doesn't get looked at very much.

Mingus was able to put groups together that were just completely burnin'. That group with Dolphy and Jackie Byard was one of the greatest groups I have ever heard. There were more famous and versatile drummers than Danny Richmond but no one would have sounded as good in that band. You could have had Philly Jo Jones in that band and it wouldn't have made any sense. It may have sounded all right but the thing that Danny Richmond and Mingus had was one of the great bass and drummer relations in the history of the music. And that was chemistry.

ONE OF THE ASPECTS OF THE MUSIC THAT YOU ARE INVOLVED IN IS THAT EVERY INDIVIDUAL WITHIN EACH BAND HAS A UNIQUE VOICE AND AN EQUAL SAY OF WHAT'S HAPPENING WITHIN THE LIVE CREATIVE PROCESS. DO YOU MIND TALKING ABOUT YOUR APPROACH AND HOW YOU INCORPORATE THE RELATIONSHIP BETWEEN THE INDIVIDUALS YOU HAVE IN MIND WITH YOUR COMPOSITIONS?

Trying to write for who's in the band is a huge part of the composing aspect. The Vandermark 5 is a group that's been very stable for many years and part of the challenge is writing material that continues to develop as the individuals have changed and developed over time. That's a primary importance on a compositional level. I'm always happier when I'm working with people whom I'm familiar with because it gives me much more grounding in terms of how I can write for the ensemble. There-fore, it's less about instrumentation and more about the individuals. Putting a bal-anced group together in terms of the instruments is obviously important but more im-portant is who the players are and what their musical personalities are and how I'm going to organize that aspect of the music.

I read something from Cecil Taylor where he said that composing starts when the band is selected, or something to that effect, and I think that that's completely true. Once a group is put together, the compositional process has actually started in my head and I think a lot of music is written, without sounding overly romantic about it, in my subconscious. Also, when I tap into the creative process of trying to put stuff down, a lot of it has accessed already in my mind because of my aware-ness of who the band is. And that's completely attached to the individuals in the band and is of utmost importance to me.

MANY OF THE MUSICIANS THAT I THINK ARE SOME OF THE STRONGER SOLOISTS TELL A STORY BUT WAIT UNTIL THEY GET TO THEIR SOLO TO DO IT. BUT YOUR NAR-RATIVE APPROACH STARTS RIGHT AT THE BEGINNING OF THE COMPOSITION.

Yeah, that's a big part of it. The piece itself has got to tell a story that informs the narratives of the soloists, the improvisers, and the way that they interact in the hierarchy of the piece. Certain pieces are fluid within the hierarchy and others are more conventional in terms of the rhythm section and soloist. But from the be-ginning of the piece, there has to be a tone set that affects the choices of the play-ers in terms of interpreting the score and then taking that much further and im-provising on that score. If that's not going to happen, then there is no point in having the piece. Get rid of the piece. If the piece is not affecting or having an im-pact on what's going on in the overall story, like you said from the beginning of the first note until the end, then there is something ineffective about the piece or there is something wrong about the way that the improvisers are dealing with the material. The piece then is just a crutch. It's not structurally or creatively impact-ing the music in a way that's important or inspiring the performance so it's just there as a matter of course. It's a convention. And if the compositions are just a mere convention, then get rid of them. There's no point.

MILES DAVIS SAID THAT "THE RIGHT NOTES CAN FERTILIZE THE SOUND OF A COM-POSITION, THAT IT CAN MAKE THE SOUND GROW, MUCH LIKE ADDING LEMON TO FISH OR VEGETABLES THAT BRING OUT THE FLAVOR. THAT IT'S YOUR SWEAT." WITH MANY OF YOUR COMPOSITIONS, YOU SEEM TO EMPHASIZE WHERE AND HOW YOU USE SOUND TEXTURES AND COLORS. I HAVE ALSO NOTICED THAT WHEN SOMEONE IS SOLOING, YOU ARE LOOKING FOR A PLACE TO ADD SOUND TO ENRICH WHAT'S HAPPENING IN THE MUSIC. CAN YOU DESCRIBE THAT PROCESS, YOUR APPROACH, AND WHAT YOU ARE ATTEMPTING TO DO WITHIN THE CONTEXT OF THE MUSIC WITH REGARD TO SOUND?

I would agree with your observation because that gets back to this idea of clar-ity that I was talking about. I would also say that the correlation you make with

Miles Davis's music is really insightful to be honest because in the last year or year and a half, I have been studying his music in terms of listening and examining his different periods. Duke Ellington and Miles Davis have had the most impact on my ideas in terms of the jazz perspective. Part of that is because they both continued to change and shift their sensibility over the course of their careers as performers, composers, and improvisers.

John Coltrane is another example of someone who was constantly searching. If you look at his earlier styles and notice where he ended up with Interstellar Space, there are a lot of shifts and changes, so Coltrane is another person who had a voice and wanted to hear that voice in different contexts over the course of time. I think with Miles and Ellington, there is a thing about the clarity in which they deal with sound, both in primary composition and secondary elements that work behind the soloists or are integrated into the improvised material. Gill Evans did this perhaps not better than them but certainly as well. The line between improvisation and composition is sometimes blurred in a way that can be very effective but the music always remains very clear.

CECIL TAYLOR SAID THAT "MUSIC HAS TO DO WITH A LOT OF AREAS WHICH ARE MAGICAL RATHER THAN LOGICAL; THE GREAT ARTISTS, RATHER THAN JUST GETTING INVOLVED WITH DISCIPLINE, GET TO UNDERSTAND LOVE AND ALLOW THE LOVE TO TAKE SHAPE." HOW MUCH OF YOUR MUSIC IS FROM LOGIC AND HOW MUCH FROM THIS OTHER PLACE THAT CECIL TAYLOR DESCRIBES?

That's a really, really good question. When I'm writing and composing, I would say that that process is kind of coming from an unconscious place. I guess the place Cecil is talking about is magical because I don't really understand it too well and I don't really want to. I feel fortunate that this music comes to me and I'll leave it at that.

When I'm writing a new piece, I believe in the unconscious or subconscious way that my mind works. There is a deeper level beneath my conscious understanding and there is also a part of my mind that is not working consciously in a way that I can articulate where a lot of this music comes from. It's something that's really mysterious without getting too romanticized about it, but I think Cecil Taylor's description of it as being magic is appropriate.

People talk about artists being conduits to something else and that's another way of looking at it. That whole aspect is perhaps the most important element in the process of trying to be creative because that's where it all comes from. It's the source in terms of organizing themes, making arrangements, organizing structure, and let's say the architecture of a composition in terms of how interactive it gets with the players.

With the pieces I'm working on, I'm not writing from the idea of a system, as I don't have a system that I use for composing and arranging, even if I'm using logic within the pieces after the initial steps. It's more that each individual piece sets up its own set of parameters, meanings, and needs. So I really deal with the composition on an individual basis, which is also connected to the individuals that play the pieces. When I'm writing the pieces, nine times out of ten, it's for a specific ensemble and the people who are going to be playing it affect the character of the piece. The arrangement, materials, architecture, and structure of those pieces are affected specifically by the way that piece sounds to me and how it needs to function as a piece. It isn't like an overarching sensibility where I do these ten things for every piece and then it's done.

WHEN MANY PEOPLE LISTEN TO CREATIVE OR IMPROVISED MUSIC, THEY HAVE DIF-FICULTY GETTING BY THE COMPLEXITY OF THE MUSIC TO GET TO THE EMOTIONAL EL-EMENT OF THE PIECE. YET WITHIN YOUR COMPOSITIONS, THERE IS AN EMOTIONAL ELEMENT WITHOUT COMPROMISING THE MUSIC THAT PEOPLE CAN RELATE TO.

It's hard for me to say because there is no way for me to be objective when I'm in the middle of the process. I'm not writing the pieces to please or expand the audience. I'm trying to write these pieces to challenge the players and to expand the possibilities of what I am hearing myself. And hopefully I'm getting to a place where there is more clarity in the ideas and that may be connected to what you are talking about—emotional communication.

A band has to play with clarity, a lot of passion, and have an emotional connection to the music that they are playing. It has to be important to them that they are playing this music that has something to say about them as people. An audience can feel that whether they understand or don't understand the material or the history and that has been my goal. To try and create bands and musical situations where that happens.

If you are at a concert where people are there to hopefully have an open mind about what they might experience, you can communicate to them and have an impact on their experience. If the band is not doing its job, which to me is being clear, being connected to the material, and having something to say, then you can't expect the audience to walk away with an impression that they have experienced something that had meaning because the meaning isn't being projected from the band. All of these things you are talking about are really crucial to the overall broader picture of accomplishing of what I hope to do—what I see as the possibility to present improvised music to a much broader audience.

WHERE DOES YOUR INSPIRATION COME FROM OR WHAT INFLUENCES YOUR CRE-ATIVITY?

I find that I'm inspired by, for lack of a better word, creative thinking. I get really excited by talking with people who have a lot of passion about what they do, and at times it has nothing to do with music at all. The visual arts have had a huge impact on the way I think about music. So it's more about creative thinking. For me to remain creative as a musician, I need my mind inspired and questioned by outside sources. It becomes too insular if everything becomes all about music all of the time.

All of the arts are an expression of the individual and the relationship to society.

Jazz, as an improvised music, goes even further because it's such a direct expression of whomever I am in this moment. Even if it's a recording, that's who I was at that time very specifically. And if you haven't had any interests or experiences, what's it going to sound like when you play? So I think that without question, the people who are very passionate not just about music but about being alive have very strong ties to other kinds of things outside of music.

YOU HAVE TAKEN A NUMBER OF RISKS IN YOUR CAREER. WHAT HAVE YOU LEARNED ABOUT BOTH MUSIC AND YOURSELF?

I've put the vast majority of the MacArthur money back into the music and a lot of people think I'm crazy. There are economic and artistic risks and to me, those things are not really risks. I think the choices I made about wanting to put my money back into the music was the only clear logical thing to do. Because those things mean that the music can continue and we can have experiences that would otherwise not be possible and that's what the whole point is.

Artistically, I feel very strongly that if I'm going to be responsible about what I'm doing as a musician, then I have to do what I have to do and that's not a risk. I don't think it's a risk in the true sense of the word to go out and play the music with the people I play with. Even when I become extremely frustrated to the point of it being painful, those kinds of risks, in the objective light of day, are just part of the job and that's what I'm supposed to be doing.

There is a risk that I have only recently become aware of in the last year and that is the risk of my relationship with my wife. This is unfortunate because it shows how slow I am at really seeing outside myself, which is more of a reflection of my selfishness. In order for me to survive artistically and economically, I have to tour. If I stay in Chicago, I cannot make enough money to be of any help at home, so that puts me in a position of where I have to leave. Consequently, that places a huge amount of stress on my wife Ellen and on our relationship. She's an amazing person and has her own very intense life. She's a doctor and if I'm gone, it's not as if her life is not fulfilling or anything ridiculous like that. It's just something that doesn't get talked about in terms of sacrifice, and I would say that that's the risk of sacrifice that I'm making. I am risking the success of our relationship as two people who really care about each other by going away all of the time. And we work really hard at making it function, but it's a very, very difficult thing.

From musical standpoints, I really believe in the process of playing. I've subscribed to that since I started and it's very difficult to say that I can't go out and work with people whose playing and creativity are really important to me. At the same time, I'm not willing to sacrifice my relationship with Ellen in order to continue to play music because I wouldn't be able to continue to play music without her. She's a huge part of why I'm able to do what I do and it's very, very painful and difficult to know how to sort it out. We work very hard on it but I can't say I've found a balance between being away and being home. That's a real balance and that's tough.

YOU HAVE THE REPUTATION OF BEING ONE OF THE HARDEST-DRIVING ARTISTS TO-
DAY. YOU HAVE MORE PROJECTS GOING ON AT ANY GIVEN MOMENT THAN MOST MUSI-
CIANS EVEN THINK ABOUT IN A GIVEN YEAR. WHAT'S DRIVING YOU?

I get really excited about music and it's very difficult to express this in a way that doesn't sound like a romantic exaggeration. My whole sensibility is shaped by music and my interest in finding out what it can do. It's what I do all day and I have to force myself not to be consumed by it, which is one of the healthy things about my relationship with Ellen.

I'm motivated by possibilities and nothing is more exciting to me than playing somewhere and realizing the potential of the situation. It's chasing that possibility and each and everyone has a different set of potentials so I can't imagine saying, "I don't want to do that." I just can't even imagine that. I know that there are people who criticize me as being an opportunist and that I overextend myself, but I'm just skimming the surface of what I'm trying to do.

I went through a two-year period where people weren't playing with me when I first arrived in Chicago. That has motivated me to help younger musicians as much as I can because I had a very difficult time when I was first here. I still remember what it was like to not have those opportunities very, very clearly.

I have also encountered a lot of things over the last year that has kind of brought this question to the forefront. Two very close friends were diagnosed with cancer and, thankfully, both seem to have made a full recovery. But when someone ten years younger than you is potentially going to die, it really drives some things home. Mats Gustufsson took nearly a half a year off to take stock in what he wanted to do. Peter Kowald passed away before anyone expected and it seemed like he would live forever.

And it's strange, I don't have a good answer for what drives me. Maybe it's a type of fatalism along with the knowledge that people I'm close to are going to be disappearing. I feel this overwhelming weight that there's not enough time with a horrible sense of dread that I'll be shut off from all these things that could have been if I had taken the time to do them. And maybe it's fear, but there is something in me that really makes me overly conscious that life is pretty ephemeral. I don't want to be in a position where I've regretted not taking a chance and have not participated in the day.

38

CUONG VU

Born in Vietnam, Cuong Vu grew up in Seattle and attended the New England Conservatory of Music. He has developed a voice on trumpet that is completely his own, with a remarkable talent for creating visual impressionistic soundscapes that can be both intimate and haunting. The sound and spirit of his work is unmistakable.

DOES SOCIETY TODAY HAVE DIFFICULTY WITH CREATIVITY THAT IS NOT EASILY EXPLAINED OR UNDERSTOOD?

I'm not sure that it's the sign of our times that is causing society to experience what you are suggesting. Back in the early 1900s, people freaked out and rioted at Stravinsky's premier of the *Rite of Spring*. Schoenberg was an outcast. Hell, early in music history, people went to war over a major 3rd, arguing whether it was a dissonance or a consonant. Time will always point out the people who were ahead of their times. Aside from having time to absorb new things, as has always been the case, I don't think that this obstacle could ever be overcome.

However, I can say it is more difficult for forward-thinking artists to put out their work and make a living at it than ever before because of the technological advancements in delivering entertainment products to mass consumers. Artists have much more to compete with than ever before.

ARE YOU PERSONALLY AFFECTED BY THE EVENTS HAPPENING IN THE WORLD TODAY AND DOES IT INFLUENCE YOUR CREATIVE PROCESS?

I'm extremely affected. Probably more so mentally and emotionally than immediately or physically, given the sheltered existence of most Americans. In fact, I feel despair and hopelessness for mankind especially after last week (Iraq invasion), though I knew it was inevitable. I think we are living in extremely dark times even though most of us can't see this. And I sometimes wonder myself if it is really all that bad. But again, that's because we Americans are sheltered from seeing what is really out there and what our leaders are doing to other people in order to keep us sheltered, dumb, and "happy."

If it influences my creative process, which I'm sure it does, it is definitely subconscious. I don't address music that way . . . that is, in a programmatic way, so the influences aren't intentional. People have said that my last two records were extremely dark, so. . . .

ARE WE CLOSING THE GAP BETWEEN OUR GLOBAL CULTURES?

I'm not sure if technology is helping us close any gaps. Music, and art in general, are about sharing ideas and communication, so I think it's inherent that musicians and artists are more able to overlook differences while they often value and are excited by the differences.

But there are plenty of instances of intolerance within music and art. For instance, why does Wynton Marsalis dismiss almost any music that is outside of what he considers to be jazz as inferior or even garbage? Why do so many people follow that way of thinking? Why are there people within the avant-garde community that dismiss any kind of music that has consonant harmonies? Could it be that most societies breed a way of thinking that links things which are different or unfamiliar with fear?

DO YOU HAVE A PHILOSOPHY THAT YOU TRY TO IMPART AMONGST STUDENTS OR YOUNG MUSICIANS?

I try to emphasize the importance of being honest and to embrace and understand insecurities instead of overcompensating for them, to accept whatever shortcomings you have. Because once this has taken place, no one can knock you down, at least not for long. And more importantly, when you know your weaknesses, you can strengthen them more easily and readily and become better more quickly.

ARE JAZZ TRADITIONALISTS HAVING A DIFFICULT TIME ACCEPTING THAT A MUSIC FORM CONSIDERED "AMERICAN" NOW HAS MORE VISIBLE INTERNATIONAL AND DIVERSE ASPECTS WITHIN IT?

I have no reference point for answering this question. The whole jazz traditionalist mentality is something I've never understood, emphasized with, nor cared for, so. . . .

IN A PREVIOUS CONVERSATION THAT WE HAD, YOU MENTIONED THAT YOU DEVELOPED YOUR SOUND BY ACCIDENT. THAT ONE HAS TO BE OPEN FOR THE ACCIDENT TO HAPPEN. COULD YOU ELABORATE FURTHER?

It's not that one has to be open for the accident to happen, but that one has to be open to dealing with the accident when it occurs. A lot of the coolest and greatest things occur unintentionally and completely outside of what is planned. You have to be open enough to recognize that it could be a cool thing and be able to go with it when it happens. Another aspect to this idea is that it addresses logic, magic, and the conscious and subconscious. How many times have we all done things that we didn't intend to do, that we didn't think we could do? So yeah, the coming together of the two is what makes this music interesting to me, so, as you've indicated, that is hugely important to how I want to hear this music.

HOW SIGNIFICANT IS CHEMISTRY TO THE SOUND AND ENERGY THAT YOU ARE TRYING TO CREATE WITH YOUR MUSIC AND OVERALL SOUND?

Chemistry plays a huge role in the music that we are making and it allows me to have a great deal of trust in the guys and really go with what they bring to the music while letting that play a huge role in defining many aspects of the music. When you have good chemistry, it seems like almost every decision that is made by any individual is a good decision because it is taken care of and respected by the others. When you have that, there is less thinking required which allows you to be more instinctive/intuitive. For me, intuition and instincts are what gets us to the "new" and unexpected places, which is what I find exciting and transcendent. Without good chemistry, I would have to put a lot more work into specifying what I want and controlling more aspects of the music, which could then easily become pretty rigid, predictable, and probably even stale.

ONE OF THE REASONS I AM ATTRACTED TO YOUR MUSIC IS BECAUSE THERE IS AN ASPECT THAT GOES BEYOND THE BASIC ELEMENTS OF RHYTHMIC FEEL. I HEAR A FASCINATION WITH SOUND WITH YOUR COMPOSITIONS, BUT IN A WAY THAT IS ABLE TO CONSTRUCT A BRIDGE FROM THE SHAPE OF THE MUSIC TO A VERY HUMANISTIC QUALITY. HOW MUCH DO THE ELEMENTAL ASPECTS OF SOUND PLAY A PART WITHIN YOUR CREATIVE THINKING OR PROCESS WITH MUSIC?

I'm very interested in the most elemental and fundamental aspects of sound. I often find that the further you get into a sound, the more moving that sound can be. There is a lot of information and detail that can be found that way that is so basic in a primal sense that it is more powerful and complex to me than a series of complex chordal relationships wound together by some extremely "hip" and complex set of polyrhythms. I think that most musicians forget this aspect of music, and even while many are technically proficient and are well versed in the knowledge of "music theory" and all that, they still sound like they have no reason for doing what they're doing aside from showing people what they can do in a strongman's weight-lifting competition type of manner.

YOU PREVIOUSLY MENTIONED THAT JOE MANERI HAD A SIGNIFICANT INFLUENCE ON YOU. CAN YOU EXPLAIN?

The most important thing Joe impressed upon me was the spirit of going for and searching for the unknown. Just trying to make music without depending on the musical devices that have been proven, done, and overdone. My experience with him helped me learn about my values about music and realize that many of the values that stand outside of the mainstream are valuable and legit.

I also learned how to really listen. There was a lot of info but much of it was intangible. Just being around the guy was inspiring and you couldn't help but learn a lot from what he had to say. It's hard to explain. Anyone who gives him a chance and is open will experience what I'm talking about from just being around him.

Outside of Joe, I would also say that my peers are the ones who have challenged and influenced me the most. The people I love to play with are the people that I respect most, so they have a lot of impact on how I think about things. We spend a lot of time sharing ideas whether it's discussing or debating, and in the end, the most important thing that comes out of that is finding out what I think and value and solidifying those thoughts and ideas. It's really all about finding your own path and your own way of doing things that addresses your strengths and weaknesses.

39

DAVID S. WARE

His voice on saxophone is a spiritual awakening of titanic proportions. His delivery, bold and daunting. His presence, a progressive foundation of unapologetic conviction and passion.

YOU MENTIONED MOVING INTO A NEW SPIRITUAL DIRECTION SINCE WE LAST SPOKE. CAN YOU EXPLAIN?

I have given my music over to a certain form of divinity called Ganesh. This is part of the Sanatana Dharma, or the eternal teachings, and these teachings are revealed every time the universe is born and in every cycle of creation. It's also said that all religions come out of these teachings. So I no longer play for David S. Ware and I don't play to gain anything, it's more about the message and the force behind the music is why I play.

SO ALL OF YOUR CREATIVITY COMES FROM THIS PLACE?

Yes, it comes from this place or this being, and it's not an imaginary figure. I have been experiencing a very personal reality through meditation and a more personal relationship with divinity.

IS THIS NEW SPIRITUALITY HAVING AN INFLUENCE ON THE DIRECTION OF YOUR MUSIC?

I would say that I'm at a new beginning because I have come to a point where doing things in my name and for my own personal gain no longer motivate me. I'm tired of doing that.

So I have found a way to keep things going in a very positive light and it feels as if everything is new and I can stay excited about what I am doing. And with the condition of the world, it's not an easy thing to do.

IS YOUR MUSIC A REFLECTION OF THE THINGS YOU ARE SENSITIVE TO, OR DOES IT REFLECT YOUR NEW SPIRITUALITY?

That is the fundamental difference that I have with a lot of cats that have been involved with this. I'm saying that music is actually a realm that exists without us. Creativity does not depend upon the state of the world.

SO IT'S DETACHED FROM IT?

Detached from it completely and the music comes from our nervous system.

BUT I HEAR SENSITIVITY FROM YOUR MUSIC.

It has to be there because I have been going inside of myself and God is the source of caring, not man. I am trying to be humble but I have been in touch with that reality through the great ancient science of meditation. So it has to project into my playing.

HOW ARE YOU ABLE TO COMMUNICATE THIS SPIRITUAL PLACE THROUGH YOUR SAXOPHONE?

Through meditation and by becoming one with whatever I am engaged with or might be focusing on. When I play, I'm trying to live and be in that moment, and when I meditate, I tap into very deep regions of the mind. There is a place that's like an ocean and you settle down to the bottom of that ocean which eventually becomes meditation. It's similar to nirvana or total stillness but not just your stillness. It's a universal stillness. Before the big bang, there was something, and it came from that something and can be described many different ways, but it's basically described as God. It's pure consciousness and a consciousness aware of itself.

IS THERE A DIFFERENT MENTAL OR SPIRITUAL STATE YOU'RE IN WHEN YOU PLAY IN CONTRAST TO WHEN YOU COMPOSE?

I don't go into a trance to play or compose. This is an ongoing or automatic transference of consciousness. When you go into that meditative state, you go to that pure consciousness state and when you come out of it, you maintain some of it. That's the process and why a person that meditates seriously needs discipline because you have to do it religiously to see the full process unfold.

WHEN PLAYING LIVE, HOW MUCH OF YOUR MUSIC COMES FROM A SPIRITUAL PLACE IN CONTRAST TO WHAT IS INFLUENCED BY THE BAND MEMBERS YOU ARE PLAYING WITH?

I have been working with these cats for a long time and it's destiny that brought us together because we all have a certain spiritual awareness. We are able to understand the same language, and over the years, we just keep refining it and refining it. It's a particular dialect that we all understand.

HAS THE BAND BEEN ABLE TO REACH A COLLECTIVE SPIRITUAL REALITY?

We don't talk about it but know that that's the case. You just know. That's what keeps us together and we live in a time where cats can't stay together. There's a common purpose and most of it is unsaid but it does exist. That's why it's not fulfilling for me to freelance and work with all different kinds of cats. That doesn't work for me as music is more intimate than that. I have to be intimate with these cats on a certain level in order to make this music and give it that special quality.

DO YOU HAVE A VISION FOR YOUR MUSIC GOING INTO THE FUTURE?

I'm being brought deeper into the teachings which gives me an understanding of what my life purpose is, which does not change. Consequently, it also broadens the scope to place me deeper into my life purpose which is to know God, the God within.

I also want to proclaim to everyone that listens to my music that I am only a vehicle and this music doesn't belong to me, it belongs to the universe. It truly does.

MOST PEOPLE CANNOT CONNECT WITH THIS MYSTERIOUS PLACE. THEY DON'T KNOW.

I realize that people don't know because if they did, music would not be in the state that's it's in. They wouldn't accept all this garbage that is happening, which in my mind has no message to it. If it has any message at all, it's about how to get more entangled in the world and how to have more materialistic things. And this world doesn't need more materialism, it needs more spirituality.

YOU HAVE ALSO FOUND A WAY TO COME UP WITH YOUR OWN MUSICAL VOICE.

You have to realize who you are and your place in the galaxy of artists. I have that realization and I've known that for a long time, which certainly helps to solidify all the elements that I'm working with.

I KNOW YOU PREFER NOT TO SPEAK ABOUT YOUR PAST MUSICAL TRAINING BUT DO YOU MIND TOUCHING ON IT?

I was only seventeen years old at the time and was not able to get along with the teachers and their attitudes about music and how they felt things should be. The real problem was that they couldn't respect my heroes. They couldn't say that so-and-so is a good musician though their way of doing things are outside of their teaching methods. They couldn't admit to not understanding this music rather than say that so-and-so is garbage. Remember, I'm seventeen years old at this time and that turned me off! There were a lot of things that I could have benefited from, but instead, they were not open to the realm that I felt close with and I just couldn't relate to them. My heroes are garbage, I mean, what is that? It was like getting kicked in the teeth, so I had to get out of there.

IT'S INTERESTING THAT WHEN PEOPLE CANNOT UNDERSTAND OR COMPREHEND SOMETHING, THEY PUSH IT ASIDE.

It's disrespectful, but they did respect me as a musician and for what I was doing. They would accept a dissonant note on a certain chord coming from me but they wouldn't accept it from the guy standing next to me. That was because they knew that that's where my ear, my sense of improvisation and beauty was really coming from. So they respected me and I think that's very important.

I now get students coming from various East Coast music schools that are way underdeveloped in the basics, but at the same time, they have this sense of grandeur about what they want to do with music. When I was seventeen, I had my basics together and that's why these cats respected me. I was developing my own language at seventeen years old. But there is a big difference if you don't understand the basics and think you are going to go out there and change the face of music. That's ludicrous!

WHAT DO YOU BELIEVE IS THE DIFFERENCE BETWEEN THE FOUNDATION YOU WERE ABLE TO RECEIVE COMPARED TO WHAT THE STUDENTS RECEIVE TODAY?

Everything is instant success with this young generation. They don't want to put any time into anything and I'm saying that from the cats who have come to me. They say they love jazz. Well fine, I love things too! I love car racing and I love a lot of things but that doesn't mean that I should become a professional at it. Some don't even have enough talent to know that they don't have the talent. There are students in music school that are not music-school material but the school has taken them in because their parents have money so they are accepted when they shouldn't be.

There was a very high level of musicianship in the '60s but from what I have seen, it's a whole different story today. The schools are to be faulted and the students are to be faulted. The fault lies on both sides. And then again, it's the time in which we live.

IS JAZZ A THING OR A WAY OF THINKING?

Yeah, well, one thing is for sure, jazz is not stagnant. The tradition of jazz is basically one hundred years old with different sounds and styles that have been created by musicians. There is a certain order and intelligence that's working along a certain progression and every area of music has that. That's what separates it from sounding like something over there.

The sound is definable and it has more subtle lines of thought with a certain rhythmic pulse that defines it from classical music where the rhythm in classical is totally different but the notes are the same. You can take the same lines, the same exact notes, and the same phrase, but if you play it with a different rhythm and dif-

ferent rhythmic pulse, you get a different musicality. Jazz has all of these subtle elements of how a note is projected and you can feel all of the history and lineage
behind it and feel where it came from. The same goes for classical. If you play that
music a certain way, you automatically get a certain feel behind it.

Young people love jazz but they don't have that special something, they don't
have that stamp. The stamp is what gives what you are doing an identity, but they
don't have it. They don't have their own personal unique sound and feel for the
music. They don't have a sound, period.

In a way, you could say that jazz is something that you cannot really develop. It's
something that's in your blood and you either have it or you don't. You can't really
teach it. Not really. You can teach a lot of things like theory, but the projection, the
feel, and the sound, you can't really teach that.

EVEN THOUGH MOST MUSICIANS MAY NEVER BECOME GREAT ARTISTS, CAN THEY
BECOME CREATIVE BY WORKING AT THE RIGHT THINGS?

Certain musicians have become very commercially successful today though they
are not playing jazz, but who has the authority to say that? I'm talking about the
projection of how the music is being played and the feeling and creativity behind
it. Some of these guys are really only playing one tune, and in sense, there is nothing wrong with that but the public doesn't know. The level is so low now that the
public doesn't even realize it. So these musicians are being called jazz and the reason it can be called jazz is because the real thing, like what you are working on, is
never brought up into the light. The real thing has always been kept underground
and you're not recognized until you are almost dead. It's a hell of a time that we
live in, artistically, musically, and overall. It's a different day.

YOU OBVIOUSLY HAVE VERY STRONG BELIEFS ABOUT JAZZ, BUT AT THE SAME
TIME, THERE ARE PEOPLE THAT DON'T PERCEIVE WHAT YOU OR MANY OTHER PEO-
PLE ARE DOING AS JAZZ; YET YOU COME FROM THE SAME TRADITION. WHAT ARE
THEY MISSING?

That's true, that's true, and Coltrane was trying to do that as well. The press has
praised us left and right but in reality, can we work in the Vanguard or the Olympic
Center? No. We have even played many festivals throughout the world but there
are certain festivals that don't want us. We're too out there for such and such festivals. They keep their doors closed to us because they have this idea that the audiences are not ready for our music and that's BS because they are ready for the
music. They are ready to hear it but the promoters are afraid. They look at us as
taking a chance and its all bullshit. The audiences are ready for us but the doors
are still closed.

There is a younger audience with a limited knowledge about jazz, which is really better because they don't have all this crap in their head about what it's supposed to be. They are open to our sound and are ready to go but we can't get to
them because of the promoters.

Man, I tell you, I have never experienced a night like the night we opened for Sonic Youth at the Manhattan Center. That night had a different open feeling in the midst of new water and new opportunity. It was that fresh and there was a fresh spirit playing for those kids. Right now, I don't see any better situation as far as potential than with the kids we played for that night.

THE FOLLOWING IS A QUOTE FROM CECIL TAYLOR: "MUSIC HAS TO DO WITH A LOT OF AREAS WHICH ARE MAGICAL RATHER THAN LOGICAL; THE GREAT ARTISTS, RATHER THAN JUST GETTING INVOLVED WITH DISCIPLINE, GET TO UNDERSTAND LOVE AND AL-LOW THE LOVE TO TAKE SHAPE." HOW MUCH OF YOUR MUSIC IS FROM LOGIC AND HOW MUCH FROM THIS OTHER PLACE THAT CECIL TAYLOR DESCRIBES?

In the common way of looking at things, assumptions are made that artists are joined from the magical spheres. Yes, that's true, but everyone has to realize that those magical spheres have their own logic, another form of logic. It's infinite orders of logic within the universal language and cosmic range of music. We as human beings have limited ourselves to thinking that there is only one type of logic or that this is right and this is wrong. It's not about that type of rigidity and limited perspectives.

We now live in a time where we have to really push beyond our limited faculties, push beyond what we know to get into the unknown and learn how to operate in that place. That's what spirituality is all about. Over the years, the Cecil Taylors have learned how to operate in the so-called magical realm. It's just different from what has come before with a different order of elements that are just as valid, just as intelligent, and just as scientific as anything else. It's just a different order. Not necessarily higher, just different.

IF THE PERFECT CREATIVE SITUATION IS COMPLETE FREEDOM, ISN'T THERE RE-SPONSIBILITY WITH ITS OWN SET OF DISCIPLINES AND CONSIDERATIONS THAT COMES WITH THAT FREEDOM?

I think it should support life and there is a responsibility. High-minded things can be used in a wrong way just as spiritual powers can be used not in the right way. There are forces that you need to understand and you have to have a devotion to creativity and use it in creative avenues. You do have a responsibility in how it should be used and you're consciousness is the authority on this. Your own awareness is the authority. There's a voice inside that guides all of us, and all you have to do is listen and it's not going to lead you wrong. Most of the time it's going to guide you to uplifting situations, but it's also about intent as the intent of what you are meaning to do is very important. My intent has always been to uplift myself along with those who listen. I'm trying to discover God, discover the creator. I'm trying to learn where all of this sprung from because of this thing we call life. I'm trying to be closer to where it all came from and where it's all going and what it all means. The meaning of it, that's the intent of my music. That quality of uplifting can always be recognized.

IS THERE A COMMON PHILOSOPHY THAT YOU TRY TO IMPART ON YOUNGER STU-
DENTS OR ASPIRING MUSICIANS?

That any advancement they're making is going to be because of the basic fundamentals. It's also working with the element of swing though you can't learn it.
Swing in jazz, what is swing? When they play, I know if they have it or they don't.
You can't really teach it but I can describe what it's supposed to be and that's all I
can do. But if they can't swing, they can't swing. They also need to understand
where the foundation of jazz is from and also need to have a story to tell. If you
have a story to tell then you have a sound. The sound comes from having a story
to tell and knowing who you are. After working on their sound for five minutes,
cats will tell you, "Yeah man, I'm working on my sound, blah, blah, blah." But the
sound is really the essence of who you are! You need to know who you are and be
able to read that connection with yourself on a couple of different levels. It's your
superficial self in terms of who you are, where you were born along with your
background. It's your parents along with your experiences in the world and how
much money you have and all of those superficial things. You then have to go beyond all that to the real self, your spiritual self. If they know who they are in terms
of the world perspective, they usually are a lot closer to being open to who they
are spiritually.

CAN YOU CONNECT YOUR MUSIC POLITICALLY?

There are a lot of cats involved with this arena of the music that make strong
connections with political struggle and that particular movement, but I'm not one
of those cats. I grew up in the '60s with the civil rights movement and was very
aware of it but I never once related that to the music I was listening to. And I was
listening to heavy Coltrane, heavy Archie Shepp, and heavy Pharoah Sanders. I
never once put the two together because I don't think the two belong together. To
me, the music was an entity unto itself and didn't need political struggle or to be
linked with Malcolm X. It wasn't maintained on the basis of racial inequality and
all of that. That's real, but to me, the two just didn't go together and I never put
the two together. When I listened to Sonny Rollins, I didn't get anything like that
from the music.

There is a creative reservoir that exists apart from our reality that's like a place
of enlightenment, a pure reality. It has to do with intentions, and as human beings,
we have a nervous system that is capable of expressing the whole range of everything that exists in terms of human experience. It reflects a pure consciousness, a
God reality, and it can reflect the lowest of humanity too. It also has to do with who
we are physically, the type of beings that we are physically.

Still, you can very easily put unrighteous struggle together with any music, but
I never felt the intent of the music was to reflect what the black man was experiencing in that particular period. I think that high art is a thing unto itself. It's a
beauty that has the ability to change our condition, the human condition to a
higher condition. It doesn't mean you need to struggle to do that.

IF SOMEONE HAS GONE THROUGH SOME SORT OF FORCED HUMAN CONDITION
SUCH AS WHAT THE BLACK OR AFRICAN AMERICAN MAY HAVE GONE THROUGH IN THE
'60S, THAT'S PART OF WHO THEY ARE. HOW DOES THAT PERSON SUBCONSCIOUSLY NOT
BECOME AFFECTED BY THAT TO WHERE IT DOESN'T AFFECT THEIR INDIVIDUALITY OR
INDIVIDUAL EXPRESSION?

My process of how I do things and the way I see things are different. I'm not
denying struggle. I'm just saying that we have been conditioned to say that we
need struggle to rise above it. No, no, I say no. There is a philosophy that says you
don't necessarily have to struggle to be enlightened. You could write volumes on
this and go into intellectual gymnasiums about the subject of struggle and how we
are related to it and how deep it is in our philosophy as progressive human beings.
For me, it's more about beauty, about knowing about the thing in itself and where
you can go from there. Beauty is only the beginning for me, it's not the end, it's the
beginning. The intent of my music is to make people aware, period!

WHAT IS IT ABOUT JAZZ AND THE ART THAT IS IMPORTANT TO YOU?

Jazz is a form, a vehicle for the artist to transcend, and it should uplift your life.
When I say uplift, it doesn't necessarily have to be from a struggle. It's a clear understanding of being on a path where you understand more and more and become
more conscious. It's a form or vehicle for spiritual transcendence and that's what
jazz is for me.

When people talk about peace in this society, they are talking about the absence of
war. But that's not true peace. That's just the absence of war. You have a state of non-
war that's just stagnant and they think its peace. But that's not peace, that's just a state
of being neutral. My music is not about being in a neutral place, it's about ascension.

WHO ARE THE MUSICIANS THAT HAVE INFLUENCED YOU?

There are other musicians such as Sonny Rollins that have influenced me.
There was and still is Sonny Rollins. He is sort of a father figure, brother figure to
me. In him, I could see that it's not only about being a great horn player, it's about
being a solid human being. It's about the search for something that transcends the
work-a-day world.

IS YOUR MUSIC A REFLECTION OF THAT SEARCH?

I certainly hope it is. For example, how could an artist support this war on Iraq?
War is wrong. It's wrong period! It's not, "we have to protect America." A human
life is a human life. The Iraqis are living beings that were created in the image of
God just like Americans and everyone else. We shouldn't have the superiority
complex that believes we have to rule the world and that our way is the way, they
have to be under our kind of government, and all of this arrogance.

The true artist cannot see it that way. The reason we can be artists is because
there is a universal language; there is something in the music that transcends time,

place, and circumstance. It transcends race, color, creed, and religion and so does the spirit of man. The soul of man is in the same reality as music in that it transcends everything and that is what truly makes us brother and sisters. Blood is deeper than water, and spirit is deeper than blood.

War is wrong but the only thing that will stop it is when humanity comes to the realization of why it is wrong. It's wrong because we are all the same. We are true brothers and sisters in spirit. If people cannot understand it, it's because to truly understand, you have to go beyond it.

For George Bush, war is the answer for every problem. This cat is in a time warp. He is an idiot bozo cowboy with his finger on the trigger and he is going to turn the whole world into hell if it continues to go on. They talk about America being the greatest country and we may have that potential, but at the same time, we also have the potential to be the worst. It takes spirituality to see that, and these people haven't learned anything about history and have never experienced war in their own land, which is why they are so quick to go to war. I have never felt or seen America want to go to war so quickly. We are starting war because we want them to live under our system and that's wrong.

WHAT DO YOU ENVISION FOR JAZZ AND FOR YOURSELF PERSONALLY?

That's a really good question and I don't know, but it's not getting any easier. It's getting tougher and tougher. In terms of our children and when I say our children, I'm talking about the ones who want to continue the lineage that we're on. Jazz is going to be something that they are going to have to love and that's the only reason to be in it. They are going to have to be on the ascension in order to do it because we are all connected and the world has to be in a good place in order for there to be moneys for the arts. To have money available for the arts, it's a mother. Therefore you are going to need people that understand a little bit of something that's real, which includes every continent. The cowboy in the White House is making it so far-reaching for anybody that is seriously thinking about going into the arts. Thus they are going to have to be real messengers in order to really have a lifetime involvement in this art form called jazz.

DO YOU HAVE A PHILOSOPHY OR SOME WAY OF LOOKING AT LIFE THAT YOU WOULD LIKE TO SHARE?

Every human being is unique and you're halfway there if you have the realization of your purpose in the human body. Because the body is like a vehicle that will allow you to go out into the world and do whatever it is you were meant to do. It won't matter how much resistance you'll meet because you know within yourself that you are going forward and will stay on this path that you have chosen for yourself. In one form or another, your life is about helping human beings and helping yourself to rise above. You have the understanding that humanity is really where we are and that we are all truly brothers and sisters.

40

OTOMO YOSHIHIDE

Born in Yokohama, Japan, guitarist and turntablist Otomo Yoshihide has been experimenting with sounds from the time he was a young teenager. His vast explorations include working with sampler viruses which act in much the same way as a computer virus. When applied to music, the sampler invades, multiplies, and transforms the sound into new sound worlds.

A student of ethnomusical history, Otomo is a brilliant prolific composer, exploring worlds of improvisation and musical philosophies while combining the influences of every genre of music imaginable.

THE MUSICAL DIRECTION YOU HAVE TAKEN HAS CROSSED MANY BOUNDARIES BUT YOU HAVE CONSISTENTLY COME BACK TO JAZZ, WHICH SEEMS TO BE HIGHLY INFLUENTIAL WITH YOUR WORK.

Jazz has by no means been the only major influence in my musical life. I've been influenced by many musical forms of all kinds. But, as you indicate, it is a fact that the influence of jazz has been bigger than that of other types of music. To me, the biggest difference between jazz and other music is that the "songs" of each era and the "avant-garde improvisation" of each era coexist in an unforced way within the special ensemble style and sound color of jazz. This is the case with Ellington and Gil Evans, for example. Unfortunately, though, that subtle balance only lasted until around the mid-'70s, that's my personal feeling. I've heard hardly any of the jazz played after that time and consequently, I haven't been influenced by it. In terms of the music that came after that period, what was a lot more interesting to me was, for instance, the improvisational music of Derek Bailey and AMM; the Japanese free music of Masayuki Takayanagi and others; the kind of punk music played on the album *No New York* and by the Pop Group; and the music of such artists as John Zorn, Heiner Goebbels, and Alfred Harth. These styles of music were not always based solely on the themes of "song" and "improvisation," but they showed us a very interesting "something" that was clearly of their particular era. Just as jazz did in the past. The music I create always fluctuates as if drawing an ellipse between two main points: how to organize and listen to something like "song" and a kind of "sound" that is sound itself, completely distinct from "song." The jazz that interests me always contains both of these aspects, and I feel there's a great significance in the fact that it is created not in an academic environment, but in clubs and other "street"-type places.

YOUR MUSIC IS A GOOD EXAMPLE OF THE DIVERSITY OF MUSIC HAPPENING TODAY AND IT HAS BEEN SAID THAT IT IS VIRTUALLY IMPOSSIBLE TO CATEGORIZE.

My work branches off in so many directions; I can't explain it very well even to myself. I've even worked on incompatible projects at the same time, embracing contradictions. Reality, not only music, is so varied and filled with contradictions that it's difficult to grasp. Whenever you try to reconcile a contradiction, another one springs up. It may be that the simplest and most impressive way of eliminating contradictions is through violence, war, and terrorism, because it forces a single answer on people. But in the end, it doesn't resolve contradictions in any real sense. I believe music is the furthest thing from that. I believe that a way of life in which one nestles into contradictory reality and within that reality, looks and listens closely, rather than just seeking clear-cut answers is the essence of creation. That's why I can never come up with a clear, simple explanation. If my works interest you, please listen to them. The various things that can be heard in them are your reality and also my reality. And that will surely be something that is interesting to you.

CAN YOUR EXPERIMENTAL SOUND COMPOSITIONS BE IDENTIFIED WITH THE ONKYO SCHOOL?

It may be convenient to have the category "onkyo" to help people find CDs by me or someone else on a CD store shelf, but I don't think it has any meaning beyond that. It's certainly true that the Tokyo musicians labeled "onkyo" have very interesting creative methods, and I think I'm partly responsible for the fact that the Japanese word "onkyo" entered and came to be used regularly in English. But I also think that using a word coined in a particular period to refer to certain musical tendencies is a very dangerous thing. In fact, there's a slight difference between what in Japan is called the "onkyo-ha" (onkyo school) and what the English "onkyo" refers to. In Japan, the word has been used even in reference to a certain trend in pop music. It did not originally refer only to regular Off Site musicians by any means. Furthermore, I don't want to set down the kinds of clearly defined borders called "schools," or make hierarchical or historical fabrications. In reality, what we're doing is more open; there's a gradation-like blending with the methods of many people.

CAN YOU DESCRIBE A LITTLE BIT OF THE HISTORY OF THE ONKYO SCHOOL AND IS IT EXCLUSIVE OF THE MUSIC COMING FROM JAPAN?

I think that when you say onkyo, you're probably referring to the people who gather at Off Site, such as Taku Sugimoto, Tetuzi Akiyama, Toshimaru Nakamura, Sachiko M, etc. As I said in my answer to the previous question, I tend to resist the idea of regarding their activity as the "onkyo school." What they're doing is freer and more open than that; it can't be lumped together as a single trend. I think each of these artists finds his or her own methods within the contradictory intermingling of various tendencies, just as I do in my music. If I had to cite a common characteristic, though, I'd say it's their unique stance in relation to the existing musical language, and their radical attitude towards listening. I've been greatly influenced by these things.

IS IT MORE DIFFICULT FOR A STUDENT TO BE CREATIVE IN TODAY'S SOCIETY?

I think that being creative is a difficult thing regardless of era or period or status. And in any era, students who attempt to be creative are not so numerous, but they certainly do exist. I don't believe that former times were more creative or that the present time is more creative. The past and present can't be compared because the circumstances are too different.

YOU HAVE ALSO SAID THAT FREE JAZZ OF THE '70S IN JAPAN WAS NOT JUST MUSIC, BUT A PHILOSOPHY. CAN YOU EXPLAIN WHAT YOU MEANT BY THAT AND IS THERE A PHILOSOPHY WITH NEW FREE JAZZ OR MUSIC MOVEMENTS TODAY?

I'm sorry but I don't remember exactly when, where, or in what context I said that. In any case, it happened that the Japanese free-jazz movement of the '70s, prior to the start of direct exchange with musicians from the American free-jazz scene and European improvised music, began with records and books; it was something quite conceptual. I also think the first-generation musicians were under pressure due to the necessity of proving that they had an original style, different from that of American or European musicians . . . that they were not mere imitators. On top of that, it was a period in Japanese society when many young people were saying "no" to the kinds of old social systems represented by the conservative administration that had been in power since the end of World War II. These young people supported the counterculture of the time (which later became mainstream pop culture); but within this movement, the first-generation free-jazz musicians distanced themselves, in turn, from that kind of youth culture, and went underground.

In the period starting in the mid-'70s, the various youth movements suffered setbacks and were pressured into making more realistic choices. I think it was a period when the counterculture turned mainstream (when young people turned into well-behaved grown-ups) and underground culture went further underground. In that context, my interest in free jazz as a teenager in the mid-'70s wasn't just a matter of taste, I think it was equivalent to considering the question of how to live. At the time, of course, I wasn't thinking about it that way; I simply thought it was the "coolest" music. If asked whether this kind of thing exists today, I'd probably say yes. I don't know if it's in the music called free jazz. Personally, I don't think that either jazz or free jazz has that kind of power anymore, but I've realized that in each era, at least since I got into music, that musical forms of that kind are always emerging and disappearing. In my own case, at least, I always have the idea that my music equals "how to live"; and so, to me, it's the same thing as philosophy. But this isn't the kind of thing that can easily be expressed in words.

DO YOU HAVE A PHILOSOPHY THAT YOU TRY TO IMPART AMONG STUDENTS OR YOUNG MUSICIANS?

This may seem to contradict the previous answer, but I don't make music with the intention of imparting a philosophy to anyone. All I do is play music, no more and no less. If you draw a philosophy from it, that's your choice. But I don't think music is a good way to express a philosophy. It's just that music is something closely linked to ways of living.

WITH TODAY'S NEW INFORMATION AGE, SOME PEOPLE BELIEVE THAT AMERICA'S SOCIETY NO LONGER HAS THE PATIENCE TO BE CHALLENGED, OPEN ONLY TO THINGS THAT ARE EASILY ACCESSIBLE. ARE YOU FINDING THIS TO BE TRUE IN JAPAN AS WELL?

I don't live in America, so I don't know exactly what it's like there. But in regard to information, it's a fact that over the past ten years the situation in Japan has changed completely from how it was in the preceding twenty years. Before, obtaining information was really a difficult thing, in the same way that it was hard to get a hold of a record. Now, though, we're saturated with information. I think we've entered an era when the question is not how to get information, but how to eliminate the information you don't need and select only the information you want. I don't think this is a good thing, since it's created the kind of society which to a remarkable extent extinguishes people's tolerance for values other than their own, in regard to information, even though the reality of today's world requires that people with different values live together while holding onto their contradictions. At this point I don't think art, and not only music, can do anything if it ignores this problem. I have concerns, too, about the fact that American-made standards, as exemplified by McDonald's and the top-ten music charts, are taking hold throughout the world. On the other hand, I disagree in part with the tendency towards the nationalistic independence of separate, unique cultures.

DO YOU THINK JAZZ PURISTS HAVE A DIFFICULT TIME ACCEPTING THAT A MUSIC FORM (JAZZ) CONSIDERED "AMERICAN" NOW HAS MORE INTERNATIONAL AND DIVERSE ASPECTS WITHIN IT?

Frankly speaking, the style called jazz today has a nostalgic meaning, something that should be preserved in a museum, a great expressive form; in reality, that seems to be the only meaning it has. Of course, I recognize that even now there exists terrific jazz, and I'm not saying this in order to negate that music. It's just that I have no feeling of interest or necessity in regard to playing in a jazz-like way. That isn't my function and I don't feel that kind of historical inevitability.

The reason I used the word "jazz" in the name of my band is that, along with the personal respect I feel towards the various benefits I gained from jazz, I have hope for music that is *not* the kind of artifact-like jazz that's taught in schools. Generally speaking, I think that even now, the great "something" that jazz gave us in a certain period of the twentieth century is quietly taking root in various forms of music that have nothing to do with the "jazz" style. To me, that's what the thing called jazz is now. That's why I don't think there's any need to call it jazz anymore. Looking at it in a positive way, you could say that jazz has moved ahead of the human race and broken down the walls of race and ethnicity.

IN FIFTY YEARS, WHAT WILL A JAZZ HISTORIAN WHO TEACHES STUDENTS SAY ABOUT THIS PERIOD? HOW WOULD HE OR SHE DESCRIBE IT?

As a period when people could no longer talk about jazz in terms of an evolutionary theory of a single line of history. To put it in a poetic way, when the ethnicity called jazz had blended into numerous musics and disappeared, but as a result, various musical forms had gained a richness they hadn't had before. So it may have been a time when it was all right to throw away the concept of ethnicity.

KARLHEINZ STOCKHAUSEN SAID THE ARTIST HAS LONG BEEN REGARDED AS THE INDIVIDUAL WHO REFLECTED THE SPIRIT OF THEIR TIME. THAT THERE HAVE ALWAYS BEEN DIFFERENT KINDS OF ARTISTS: THOSE THAT ARE MIRRORS OF THEIR TIME, AND THE VERY FEW WHO HAVE VISIONARY POWER. IS IT POSSIBLE THAT WHAT'S HAPPENING IN CREATIVE MUSIC IS TOO FORWARD THINKING FOR MUCH OF OUR SOCIETY TODAY OR HAS THIS ALWAYS BEEN THE CHALLENGE FOR FORWARD-THINKING COMPOSERS? IS IT POSSIBLE THAT THE MUSIC IS JUST TOO COMPLEX FOR MOST LISTENERS?

I don't know in what context Stockhausen said that, so I can't comment on it. But I think that over the several centuries prior to the twentieth, music strongly influenced by European culture moved in a direction in which creators always made more complex things than previous creators had. At this point I can't believe blindly in that process. I see possibilities in music other than the kind which proceeds on the idea that music is something created and disseminated in an enlightening way only by musicians.

HOW MUCH OF THE POPULARITY OF CREATIVE MUSIC HAS TO DO WITH A LISTENER HAVING A DIFFERENT WAY OF THINKING OR MINDSET?

In any case, I don't believe today's music consists only of listening to things that musicians have created in a one-sided way. I think that the partnership resulting from bidirectionality between listeners and creators is becoming the central point in the creation of music.

ROY CAMPBELL HAS SAID THAT HE THOUGHT THOSE WITHIN THE UNITED STATES POLITICAL SYSTEM FELT THAT FREE JAZZ WAS BECOMING A DANGEROUS MUSIC BY IN-FLUENCING PART OF THE CIVIL RIGHTS AND ANTIWAR PROTEST MOVEMENTS OF THE '60S IN THE U.S. THAT THE MUSIC HAD A CERTAIN ENERGY AND OPENED DOORS ALONG WITH ELEVATING THE CONSCIOUSNESS OF LISTENERS. I HAVE ALSO READ THAT WITHIN YOUR OWN PERSONAL RESEARCH, THAT YOU HAVE FOUND DURING TIMES OF WAR, AUTHORITIES MAY HAVE CONTROLLED MUSIC IN JAPAN. CAN YOU EXPLAIN HOW THIS WAS DONE AND IS IT STILL BEING DONE TODAY?

I don't know in what context Roy Campbell said that, so I can't comment on it. In regard to the topic "Japan's wartime regulation of music," which I researched when I was in university, it's more accurate to say that the influential musicians of the time worked in cooperation with the war effort than to say that the authorities controlled music through the power of the state. At that time, I couldn't believe it, but now, having seen the general support for the war that America has been con-ducting, I've come to think it's possible. Human beings and even the kind of rela-tively peaceful human beings who make music, for example, will go to war for a just cause. It seems likely that at the time, those Japanese musicians believed that justice was on Japan's side, and they cooperated in the war effort for that reason. Which is why I can't believe in "justice." That's the conclusion I've reached.

IN A PREVIOUS INTERVIEW, YOU MENTIONED THAT WHEN FREE MUSIC WORKS BEST FOR YOU, THAT IT'S THE PROCESS THAT IS MOST IMPORTANT. COULD YOU PLEASE TALK ABOUT THAT IMPORTANCE TO YOU AND THE PROCESS IN ITS VARIOUS FORMS.

I personally think that the creative process itself is the most important aspect of music. I don't play music in order to confirm an outcome that I'm already sure of. As I play, I always have a sense of something I don't even understand. In the same way, I don't compose in order to express something that I have in my mind; I'm interested in the kind of music where during the process of listening to the sounds that emerge, I keep discovering relationships between familiar sounds and new sounds. Inherent in music is the fact that as soon as you play something, it's gone. Therefore, rather than treasuring things that are complete, I like the kind of ap-proach that involves paying close attention to things that are disappearing.

MILES DAVIS HAS SAID THAT THE RIGHT NOTES CAN FERTILIZE THE SOUND OF A COMPOSITION, THAT IT CAN MAKE THE SOUND GROW. MUCH LIKE ADDING LEMON TO FISH OR VEGETABLES THAT BRING OUT THE FLAVOR. YOU SEEM TO EMPHASIZE WHERE AND HOW YOU USE SOUND TEXTURES AND COLORS.

To me, sound texture—including sound color—is very important, and not only in jazz. There are even cases where it's the whole of what I create. But unlike harmony and rhythm, sound color and texture are things that I'm incapable of analyzing and putting into words. Honestly speaking, I simply feel that some-thing is either OK or not.

THE FOLLOWING IS A QUOTE FROM CECIL TAYLOR: "MUSIC HAS TO DO WITH A LOT OF AREAS WHICH ARE MAGICAL RATHER THAN LOGICAL; THE GREAT ARTISTS, RATHER THAN JUST GETTING INVOLVED WITH DISCIPLINE, GET TO UNDERSTAND LOVE AND AL-LOW THE LOVE TO TAKE SHAPE." HOW MUCH OF YOUR MUSIC IS FROM LOGIC AND HOW MUCH FROM THIS OTHER PLACE THAT CECIL TAYLOR DESCRIBES?

Almost none of what I've created has been logical. It's true that when I'm asked questions, I try to answer in a logical way, but when I'm actually making some-thing, it's almost completely a matter of feeling. I'm not thinking in a theoretical way that can be verbalized. The truth is that I'm putting out sounds that I have a good feeling about. In poetic terms this might be called "magical," and some peo-ple might call it "love," but I don't think that way either. My reality is that I make music as if I were simply living. Of course, a poet would probably say that living consists of both "magic" and "love."

HOW MUCH OF WHAT YOU COMPOSE IS STRUCTURED AND HOW MUCH IMPROVISED? CAN YOU EXPLAIN YOUR COMPOSITIONAL PROCESS?

It varies depending on the work or project and the conditions of the venue. The only thing I can state unequivocally is that I've never produced anything that's ei-ther 100 percent composed or 100 percent improvised, and I don't believe that such a thing exists. Even solos that seem improvised are, to an important extent, composed, and a number of my works labeled compositions consist almost wholly of improvisation. In fact, I feel there's a certain incongruity in making a clear dis-tinction between the two as the border between them is vague. What's more, I think it's only because Western music invented the written score and came up with the idea of individuals creating music in the first place, that the concepts of things like compositions and copyrights came about. You could also say that the excessive dominance of those Western concepts was what caused people to turn to improv-isation. It's true that copyright law has retained a lot of that dominance, and that musical economics revolve around those standards as well, but in fact, the music being made by myself and others has to a great extent freed itself from that kind of thing. Actually, even the concept of the composer has little meaning now, in my opinion.

IT HAS BEEN SAID THAT THE PERFECT CREATIVE SITUATION IS COMPLETE FREE-DOM. HOWEVER, SHOULDN'T THE CREATIVE PROCESS HAVE INTENT? ISN'T THERE A RESPONSIBILITY, WITH ITS OWN SET OF DISCIPLINES AND CONSIDERATIONS, THAT COMES WITH THAT FREEDOM?

To begin with, I don't understand the concept of "complete freedom." Freedom as a human rights issue is, of course, very important. But freedom in the creation of music is a different thing. Because issues of individual psychology and the organization of multiple intentions come into play, I don't think the problem is whether or not it's free. I think the most important aspect of creation is how to organize as sound, the friction and distance that occur between differing ways of thinking and contradictory ideas. Therefore, the theme is not "becoming free," but, on the contrary, recognizing limitations and finding ways to work with them.

IN A PREVIOUS INTERVIEW YOU MENTIONED THAT "THE EXPERIENCE OF BEAUTY IS ALWAYS LINKED TO DANGER. THE DANGER IS A CESSATION OF THOUGHT." COULD YOU PLEASE GO INTO MORE EXPLANATION OF WHAT YOU MEANT BY THIS?

For human beings, the feeling that something is "beautiful" is a very important source of energy in creation and in life. Once people experience something as being beautiful, they tend to become blind and it's exactly the same as when they fall in love. In that respect, "beauty" in music is a source of emotion, but it's also very close to the state of cessation of thought. Of course, if you simply want to enjoy music, this isn't a problem at all. But if you're a person who creates music or a listener who attempts to feel something through music, you should fix your gaze on the something that lies beyond beauty. The reason is that when the concept of beauty becomes fixed, it very quickly turns into cliquish conservatism, and judging things solely on the basis of beauty turns into simply forcing personal tastes on others. The ability to experience beauty, free from logic, is probably something that human beings need to have. The problem, however, is the tendency to believe that that beauty is universal. That's what I meant when I said that beauty is always linked to danger.

CREATIVE MUSIC CAN REQUIRE MUSICIANS TO TAKE A NUMBER OF RISKS IN THEIR CAREERS. WHAT HAVE YOU LEARNED ABOUT BOTH MUSIC AND YOURSELF?

I'm not interested in risk-free music—in the same way that a risk-free life is boring. But just because something is risky, that doesn't mean it's good. Doing something out of recklessness or ignorance is different from taking a risk in order to discover something.

YOU HAVE PLAYED IN A NUMBER OF DIVERSE SETTINGS WITH MANY DIFFERENT MUSICIANS. HOW DOES THIS INFLUENCE OR CHANGE YOUR CREATIVE PROCESS OR THE RESULT OF THE MUSIC BEING PERFORMED OR COMPOSED?

Playing with other people isn't necessarily essential to me and it is sometimes even important not to play with other people. In the past, more than now, I enjoyed playing with someone else, especially a musician I liked. I don't really know, specifically, in what ways that influenced me, but now I'm not as enthusiastic as I used to be about performing in a group. I think of it as something relaxed and informal, comparable to going out for a meal with friends. Certainly it's enjoyable, but I no longer have the feeling that I always want to be doing group performances. And when I really like the musicians, I find it more enjoyable to watch their performance from the audience than to perform with them.

WHAT ARE THE FACTORS THAT INFLUENCE YOUR DECISIONS IN A LIVE SETTING?

It depends on the conditions, but I think the quality of the sound system and the acoustics of the venue influence me the most, especially when I play turntables and electronics. The attitude of the staff members and my relationship with the audience are important factors, too.

AND FINALLY, DO YOU HAVE A PHILOSOPHY OR SOME WAY OF LOOKING AT LIFE THAT YOU WOULD LIKE TO SHARE?

I wonder if it's possible to have a society where mere individuals with different ways of thinking can coexist in a gentle way by sharing the things they have in common while holding onto their own ideas—a society with a tolerant system, rather than one that controls people through religion or ethnicity or violence or state power. In any case, I don't want to be part of a society dominated by what America calls "justice" or a society made up of a single religious theory.

41

JOHN ZORN

As I sit and wonder what to write about John Zorn, a sea of words and thoughts surrounds and encapsulates me. Never has a composer lived who is as diverse and perplexing as Zorn. His world of sound, of beauty, of creativity, is one of mystery; a living and infinite creative universe which has unapologetically chosen him that perhaps not even he can understand.

It's his music that disturbs many, and inspires others, but there is another side of Zorn that is important. He refused to be a part of this project until satisfied that there was a representation of innovative women and people of color included. He has created his own music publishing company Tzadik not only to ensure there was an avenue to produce his work without compromise, but to provide a resource for creative musicians in a society that has difficulty with artistic vision.

Never has an artist been so misunderstood, even maligned, but what's fascinating is that his vast and diverse body of work is always there for those who risk opening the door. He is continually identified with jazz, but the only correlation is that he plays the sax. He is thought of as a player, yet his genius is in composition. We continually want to frame him, categorize him, define him, yet his visionary work is one without genre, without boundaries. There isn't a category, there isn't a box. There is only the work and the mystery that is Zorn, and perhaps it's best that it remains this way.

THE COMPOSITIONAL HYDROLYTH

From the CD MAGICK by John Zorn

Many good things come with age, and for me the most telling has been a certain realization. An understanding. Not the kind of understanding that happens in the front of the brain, because the most important things in life cannot be grasped in such places. There is a deeper, more intuitive understanding. The understanding that Mysteries, to remain Mysteries, must remain Mysteries, and are not meant to be understood. Unraveled, yes. But never fully, because it is the Mystery itself that is the reality. The Mystery gives birth to the Search, and the Search is life.

Music is one of the great Mysteries. It gives life. It is not a career, not a business, nor a craft. It is a gift . . . and a great responsibility. Because one can never know where the creative spark comes from or why it exists, it must be treasured as Mystery. For the most part I believe that creativity chooses you, not the other way around. When it is with you the universe makes sense and the struggles have meaning. When it leaves there is an emptiness. A void. Meaning eludes you. Simply waiting for its return is painful, and is often exacerbated by very human needs: for shelter, food and drink, a sense of belonging . . . understanding and love. One can passively exercise patience and wait for visions to return, or one can take action and explore the esoteric traditions that have been used throughout the ages as catalysts for change: Magic, Alchemy, Shamanism, and the like. In recent years I have become interested in how these techniques can be used as an aid in compositional practicum.

Through study and transformation, whether it be fasting, ritual, incantation, study, spell, trance, or meditation, one can learn to access the power of creativity almost at will. This is not about inducing change through drugs, or altering levels of perception within yourself, but rather about tapping a living energy force that exists at all times everywhere. Call it what you will—Magic, self-hypnosis, alchemical transformation—it is something to be respected, because if it is not taken seriously it can destroy you.

The process of composing music is often at its best when the piece is seemingly writing itself and the composer is merely an observer. These two pieces came about in such an atmosphere, and months or preparation were involved before putting pencil to paper. *Sortilege* was written in a flash of inspiration and took less than a week to complete. *Necronomicon* was begun on Candlemas Eve (February 1) and completed on the Grand Sabbath of the year, Walpurgisnacht, the eve of May Day (April 30). Both pieces transcended my expectations and my abilities. I cannot explain them. They are part of the Mystery.

42

PAT METHENY

Closing

There might not be a more telling and timeless piece about the creative process than the keynote address that Pat Metheny provided at the IAJE conference in New York City, in January 2001.

What a pleasure it is for me to be invited to talk to you all today.

I feel so proud to be a part of the jazz community. The life that I have been able to lead as player and composer and improviser over these years has been fantastic beyond anything I ever could have imagined when I first started playing.

In a lot of ways, my own career has roughly paralleled the evolution of the IAJE itself. I started playing music professionally in 1968 when I was about fourteen, growing up around the Kansas City area—and the IAJE, of course, was founded just next door over in Manhattan, Kansas, at right around that same time. And it is really just unbelievable to see a few decades down the road how it has evolved into this huge worldwide organization that has done so much to further the music and, maybe just as important, as we see here today, to foster a sense of community for all of us who are involved in the evolution and study of this wonderful way of playing and thinking.

There is no question that jazz education is in better shape now than ever. Thirty years ago, in the small town that I grew up in out there, although we had an excellent music program developed by one of the best band directors in the state, there was no jazz band, no jazz program at all; there weren't even any saxophones in the marching band!

The fact that I can go back to Lee's Summit now, and see that they have several ensembles available to kids that are interested, is just one of countless examples that can be found all over the world of the power and pervasive influence of this movement.

Nevertheless, as we stand here at the beginning of this new century as jazz musicians, we find ourselves living in a culture that often seems to be oblivious, if not outright hostile to musical creativity as most of us in this room would define it. As millennium-era musicians and educators, we find ourselves with some major challenges ahead of us, as a community, and as individuals.

But in spite of these challenges—in fact, I personally believe it may wind up being *because* of some of these very challenges, and the real pressures that they will put on us to redefine ourselves, for even our very survival—jazz will likely continue to thrive, although possibly in unexpected ways.

It is jazz's very nature to change, to develop and adapt to the circumstances of its environment. The evidence of this lies in the incredible diversity of music and musicians that have evolved, and lived and flourished, under the wide umbrella of the word "jazz" itself from the very beginning.

Jazz is an idea that is more powerful than the details of its history—a concept bigger than any single one of its partisans could ever hope to define.

However, as a participant in the cause, retaining one's optimism can be a difficult task in a culture that often appears to be indifferent to the kind of personal creativity that is embodied in the quest for excellence in jazz. As I talk to other musicians and other members of the larger community, it seems like I keep hearing these somewhat gloomy forecasts for the music's future, as the sand beneath our feet continues to shift in these changing times—particularly in the last couple of years.

But I feel that the apparent limitations of opportunity are actually deceptive. Even though I do see certain disturbing changes taking place among the traditional outlets for playing, for touring, funding for school music programs, possible cuts in funding for the NEA, PBS, etc., I actually also sense that an even more amazing set of potentials is just ahead of us on the not-too-distant horizon.

We are on the verge of entering a world where the potential for communication itself is about to explode beyond almost anything we can even imagine, and jazz is about nothing if not the essence of communication. On a very basic level that is sometimes easy to forget or overlook, jazz is actually well suited to excel in this new climate in many ways.

And as long as we, the purveyors of the form, are not discouraged by the short-term growing pains that appear to be inevitable in changing times like these—and most important, as long as we keep our eyes on, and faith in, the long-term power and influence that is embodied in the very nature of the music itself and the way that it is made—we have the opportunity to remain engaged in the collective research that is the lifeblood and uniting element of our community: basically, the pursuit of trying to play some great music, and to uplift and inform the spirits of the folks who would come to hear it.

To accomplish this, we have to stay vigilant in our efforts to address that most difficult task that faces each and every generation of jazz musicians, regardless of their era or stylistic bent: the task of coming up with musical goods that are challenging and uncompromising, yet fully and utterly compelling to our audiences, and even in this era of increasingly short attention spans, to *cause* listeners to seek out the musical universe that we are hoping to hip them to.

And as long as we can come up with the music, music that delivers on our promise of giving them something that they can't find anywhere else, something that enriches them the same way *we* have all been enriched by the musicians that have influenced and inspired all of *us* to become players and teachers and students and fans, then we have an excellent chance of not only surviving, but taking the music to the people in a way that has historically been elusive.

In fact, I believe there is lots of evidence that this *is* happening. To me, jazz has been expanding and growing and broadening, stylistically and in terms of the materials that it draws from as its sources, steadily since its inception. The globalization of the music is now fully underway and there are endless musical opportunities for musicians in pretty much every corner of the globe to learn and address their own musical issues through the prism of the jazz language.

One of the great beauties in the invention of this form, of this platform, of this process, is jazz's almost unlimited capacity to allow human beings to find out things about themselves and the culture that they live in through the process of reconciling their own personal experiences with the experiences of others through the blessing of improvisational and organizational inspiration in sound.

In recent years, with the centennial of this music approaching and the beginning of a new century, we have spent a lot of time basking in the glory of the achievements of the masters in this form. Tribute records, films, reissues, reissues of reissues, more tribute records, tribute records in tribute to other tribute records . . . you name it! There are great things about that too, even a certain comfort in that kind of activity, a sense of feeling more connected to the past, a sense of genuine appreciation on all of our parts of amazing accomplishments, and hopefully an always renewed awareness of the incredibly high standards that have been set throughout jazz's history. But I feel that to spend too much time doing that can also breed a certain kind of complacency towards one of the major elements that has historically been a primary ingredient in the success, and survival, of this music.

There is an important and consistent element in the jazz tradition of young people coming along and molding—reinventing—the nature of the form itself to fit their times and their circumstances, as only they could possibly know how to do. Whether it was the invention and evolution of the drum set, or the impulse to expand the forms and cadences of the popular songs of the day to accommodate new ways of playing, or the desire to incorporate the newest folk instruments of the time (like the electric guitar), or possibly even nowadays the wild new sounds that permeate an entire culture, there has often been a group of young musicians somewhere saying "what if" to the status quo of jazz culture, sometimes even saying stronger two-word phrases than that, but always in the name, and the natural spirit, of moving the music to a new place.

Myself, I have always, and somewhat actively, resisted the mythology that says that we all need to "return" to some kind of a safe place where the proverbial "tradition" resides, in order for jazz to be considered *"real"* jazz.

As much as I encourage and value the need to understand the roots of this music, in the most specific and detailed ways possible, I also feel that it is worth noting that most attempts to recreate the past in jazz, even by musicians attempting to recreate their *own* pasts, while often enjoyable, have rarely been made of the fabric of that elusive material that seems to be present whenever and wherever there are musicians who are pushing, and remaking in the likeness of their *own* generation, the boundaries of the music.

In this sense, I believe the form is actually somewhat unforgiving. It seems to *demand*, in fact, that each new generation makes peace with something specific that is uniquely theirs. There is something about *that* particular negotiation that informs the music with a kind of living, breathing, molecular structure than can never be recreated or even accurately simulated by any other means. Whether it is the addressing of a newly invented musical instrument technique or technology or even the reaction to something that they aren't crazy about in the previous generations, this is an essential element that *all* of the most successful generations in jazz have had in common: that they have sophisticatedly illuminated some aspect of their culture in a way that could not be found in any other form—or at any other time—and therefore have *naturally* drawn an audience to it that was attracted to jazz to find out something, in return, about themselves.

For this reason, I always encourage musicians (who are of course citizens of the world first, and jazz musicians second) to address *all* of the music that they love and that they are attracted to as people, regardless of its style, regardless of its content, as a unified set of materials when they consider their full options—and potentials—as modern-day jazz musicians.

Of course, for a lot of you who are students out there, you may be thinking, "What the hell is this guy talking about, I just want to sound good and not make too many clams at the next jam session when I take my solo on 'Autumn Leaves'!!" And yes, I agree absolutely that that may well be the first item on your "to do" list. But I feel this too, and this is something that I've noticed over the years and throughout the music's evolution: that when you are around a certain age—I would say that that age generally falls sometime between twelve and twenty-two—you actually have access to something, a certain kind of energy, that is really valuable, something really rare, and something most people never have again to quite the same degree of intensity at any other point in their lives.

It seems like somewhere about that time in a musician's life, you can hear the emerging sound of your *own* generation of musicians. It lives inside of you, and it often rings loud and clear. And it often sounds nothing like anything that has ever been heard before. Listen to *that* as closely as you can. Listen to it with the same attention and curiosity that you reserve for your heroes on records.

My contention has always been that jazz is, and I hope will always be, a form of folk music, but a very, very serious and sophisticated folk music. Almost a kind of scientific folk music. When I say folk music, I am talking about the tradition of musicians using every aspect, all the materials, all the sounds and moves and vibes and spirits of their time in a musical way. The attempts to make jazz something more like classical music, like baroque music for instance, with a defined set of rules and regulations and boundaries and qualities that *must* be present and observed and respected at all times, have always made me uncomfortable. That's not because I am not all for jazz being given that kind of respect, but because I feel that the basic desire for self-expression—in whichever of its manifestations that its participants care to address at a given time—is such a primary presence in the fabric of what makes "jazz" *jazz*, that it is *crazy* to *not* take advantage of that fact by relegating it to some predetermined model of supposed authenticity.

And, please, let's never forget that this is a genre built to harbor irreverence, or even dissent, in addition to earnest devotion. The diversity of jazz is a big part of what makes the street-level variety of the form so vital.

What I mean by that is that right now, there are probably kids in this room that have their finger on a certain pulse that none of us over twenty-five could likely ever even imagine. And in that pulse possibly lie the ideas that could very well alter the future course of jazz, keeping it current and alive. And if this music *will* survive as a primary point of departure for a young kid's dreams, it will be because he or she feels that their investment in it as individuals will result in something that they can really call their own, not something they are borrowing or simply emulating, but rather something that they can show to the world that is uniquely theirs and *sounds* like it is theirs.

To the educators out there that are saying, "Yeah, that's all great and everything, but it is hard enough for me to get the kids to all play in tune and stop and start together at the same time on their way through a basic chart . . . ," I understand, and I agree completely that the teaching of the fundamentals of the music is central and essential.

But, just as one example, let's say one day next semester you might look up, and there may be a kid that is hanging off to the side who would love to participate somehow. And say in this case he may even have a beat-box or a microphone or a turntable or a computer, or who knows what else under his arm. And he is curious. Maybe . . . go ahead and invite him in. Jam with him. Have one of the kids write or make up some kind of a piece to do with him. To some, this may seem like the worst kind of anti-jazz, even, god forbid, "fusion"!! Or they might see it as an encounter that, while maybe being fun, could never result in *"real"* jazz at all.

But to me, it would be *exactly* that kind of gesture—a gesture of inclusion and curiosity and communication and *hope*—that *is* the spiritual engine of jazz. It is *that* spirit that has kept jazz's momentum going forward so successfully for all these years, in spite of whatever cultural blockades have been erected along the way.

I guess what my message here is today, as we all launch off into our various extremely individualized little niches within the larger community of jazz and music, is that the openness to experiment, to really be in the moment, not only the specific musical moment, but the larger view of time and culture, is not really an option for jazz musicians at any level—it is a necessity if the music is going to go on.

I know that in my own work, I love playing standards, I love playing the blues and working on trying to make sense of the infinite details that all of my favorite musicians throughout history have laid out so generously for our examination and enrichment. But I also know that for every hour I spend working on those essential, fundamental materials, I need to spend three more hours working on how I can reconcile those materials with the vital information that has to do with the things that I see and feel and hear around me each day, things that are real to me right now, right this second. And I also humbly acknowledge and accept that my reality is, for better or for worse, *different* and incomparable to any one else's—not the least, probably, my biggest heroes in jazz history.

Each band director or educator here has his or her own reality, with its own limitations, and its own potentials. Each student here has their own reality, their own cache of materials learned, and I am certain, a far larger cache of things that they need to know.

The challenge that I make for myself each time out, whether it is a single note, a single gig, a new record, whatever, is first of all to try to sound good and deal with the material and the situation at hand in hopefully an effective and musical way, but also to try to find some aspect of what I can offer to that moment in time that honors and respects the less quantifiable qualities of the tradition that I am talking about. A tradition that includes—and demands—pushing it, pulling it, questioning it, and even changing it.

As musicians, educators, journalists, industry executives, students, all of us, we all have an exciting opportunity to take jazz to places it has never gone, to turn it into a music that millions of people everywhere (people that don't even know how much they love it yet) will find out what *we* all already know: that the nature of this music has the ability to transform people, to enlighten them and enrich them in ways that *only* this music can.

But in order for that to happen, we all have to rise to this challenge, and it's a big one: the challenge to recreate and reinvent the music to a new paradigm resonant to *this* era, a new time. It's simply not gonna cut it to just keep looking back, emulating what has already been done with just a slightly different spin on it. We have to get to work to a degree that we haven't seen for a while now on a broad level within the jazz community; we have to get our collective imagination working hard on a vision that is more concerned with what this music can *become* than what it has already *been*.

We need to put on more interesting and better concerts! We need to make more interesting records that really connect with people! We need to play better! We need to practice more!—*We need to move the music forward!* You know what excites me? The thought of a kind of jazz that sounds *nothing* like the jazz of the twentieth century, that is an entirely different thing, a new kind of animal, but one that is still unmistakably connected to the larger jazz tradition. The twentieth century is over. The challenge for us is to discover what that new thing might be through our own individual research, by rising to the occasion of the upcoming centennial of this music's birth with ideas that honor the premise of resonant, organic innovation that has been the hallmark of the form from day one, the kind of innovation that springs naturally from the curiosity that is imbedded in everyone who gets hooked on jazz. It's there, collectively, between us. All we have to do is listen hard to find it, identify it, and it will grow into something special and unique.

Along the way, mistakes *will* be made. Not all things tried will work out. But that impulse, the impulse to *try things*, is perhaps the most attractive—and sometimes the most underutilized—intrinsic quality that the promise of jazz education offers to its students. If young people can really view their time spent learning about jazz as something that will offer them an outlet to dream about things that are resonant and applicable to their day-to-day lives, man, we would see an explosion of interest in participating in jazz education that would dwarf even the amazing growth that has happened over the past thirty years.

I can't wait to hear what everyone is going to do here over the next few days, and over the next few years! Thanks so much for listening.

"We say that the . . . genius is always ahead of his time. True, but only because he's so thoroughly of his time."

—Jack Kerouac, 1959

INDEX

AACM, 44, 73, 105, 148, 151–55, 158, 185, 213, 271–74
Abrams, Muhal Richard, 73, 105, 150, 204, 272, 273
Academy of Ancient Music, 123
Adams, Pepper, 87
Adderley, Cannonball, 172
Aebi, Irene, 146
Aguilera, Christina, 202
Akita (Merzbow), 208
Akiyama, Tetuzi, 308
Ali, Rashied, 73
Allen, Carl, 173
Allen, Geri, 105
Amati, Nicolo, 144
AMM, 307
Anderson, Fred, 1, 87, 89, 90, 152
Aphrodite, 144
Aristotle, 141
Arman, Paul, 89
Armstrong, Louis, 134, 247, 255, 257, 280, 284
Art Ensemble of Chicago, 59, 83, 150, 152, 154, 158, 272
Atomic, 215, 217
Aurelius, Marcus, 271
Auster, Paul, 117

Axe, Maia, 154
Ayler, Albert, 86, 87, 116, 117, 234, 284

Bach, 38, 58, 129, 192
Bacon, Francis, 106
BAG, 105
Bailey, Derek, 2, 30, 114, 123, 307
Baker, Chet, 247
Bakunin, 242
Balanchine, George, 262
Bang, Billy, 59
Baraka, Amiri, 62, 86
Barker, Thurman, 272
Barnes, Danny, 102
Baron Down, 18
Baron, Joey, 9, 83
Barron, Kenny, 38, 172
Barry Guy New Orchestra, 129
Barry, Robert, 31
Bartok, 184
Bartz, Gary, 172
Bechet, Sydney, 69
Beethoven, 87, 121, 273
Bennink, Han, 30, 32
Berkeley, George, 143
Berklee, 96
Berne, Tim, 19, 83, 204

Birdland, 172
Bjork, 105
Black, Jim, 83
Blackman, Cindy, 72
Blackwell, Ed, 89
Blade, Brian, 100
Blakey, Art, 73, 83, 87, 176, 201, 215, 216
Bley, Paul, 65
Blues People, 62
Blythe, Arthur, 215
Booker T & the MG's, 14
Bowie, David, 58
Bowie, Lester, 83, 158, 171, 272
Bradfield, Polly, 145
Bradley's, 172
Braxton, Anthony, 53, 59, 62, 63–65, 77, 80,
    105, 271–73, 276
Briggs, Karen, 36
Brookmeyer, Bob, 171, 266
Brotherhood of Breath, 104
Brotzmann, Peter, 29, 43, 44–46, 77, 113,
    114, 126, 284
Brown, Clifford, 80
Brown, H. Rap, 273
Brown, James, 171
Brown, Ray, 34, 38, 175, 176
Bruce, Lenny, 10
Bruno, Giordano, 141
Bryars, Gavin, 2
Buchenwald, 32
Burns, Ken, 20, 59, 70, 107, 156, 181, 193,
    225, 226, 283–85
Burton, Gary, 97
Bush, George, 53, 54, 78, 202, 236, 305
Byard, Jaki, 200, 203, 287
Byrd, Donald, 175
Byron, Don, 83

Cage, John, 15, 121, 157
Cain, Michael, 67
Caine, Uri, 83
Cal Arts, 13
Camerata Berne Chamber Orchestra, 129
Campanella, Thomaso, 141
Campbell, Roy, 311
Carey, Mariah, 228
Carmichael, Stokely, 151, 273
Carrington, Terri Lynn, 72

Carter, Betty, 170, 176
Carter, Elliott, 50, 167
Carter, Jimmy, 244
Carter, Regina, 34
Carter, Ron, 174, 175, 250
Cash, Johnny, 15
Castendos, Carlos, 63
Castro, Fidel, 213
Catlett, Sid, 14
Celan, Paul, 32
Chambers, Joe, 173
Chambers, Paul, 162, 175
Cherry, Don, 69, 87, 92
Chopin, 265
Christian, Charlie, 7
Christian, Jodi, 272
Christiansen, Jon, 65
Clapton, Eric, 133
Clark, Charles, 272
Clarke, Kenny, 14, 73
Clayton, John, 35
Clinton, Bill, 169
Cobb, Jimmy, 14
Cohen, Greg, 16, 83
Cohran, Phil, 272
Coleman, George, 172
Coleman, Ornette, 50, 64, 83, 90, 98, 133,
    185, 186, 225, 234, 255, 257, 281
Coleman, Steve, 83, 204, 206, 224
Coltrane, Alice, 73
Coltrane, John, 33, 38, 64, 65, 69, 72–74,
    87, 90, 98, 104, 114, 133, 167, 175, 177,
    192, 196, 203, 209, 216, 222, 242, 250,
    273, 282, 287, 289, 301, 303
Columbia University, 156
Company, 2
Connick, Harry, 265
Conrad, Tony, 145
Consener, 273
Copeland, 265
Cora, Tom, 208
Corea, Chick, 132, 204
Cornish College of the Arts, 189
Crispell, Marilyn, 56, 124, 125, 129
Crouch, Stanley, 20, 285
Cream, 133
Cullum, Jamie, 170
Cunningham, Merce, 121

Dance for a Dead Prince, 35
Davis, Anthony, 59, 105
Davis, Miles, 14, 22, 27, 38, 66, 68, 72–74, 83, 97, 100, 104–6, 114, 132–34, 167, 171, 175, 182, 195, 196, 204, 222, 223, 227, 257, 273, 281–83, 287–89, 311
Davis, Richard, 250
Dawson, Roger, 124
Debarros, Paul, 264
Debussy, 38
DeJohnette, Jack, 14, 66, 132, 173, 174
Dial, Gary, 13
Dolphy, Eric, 204, 281, 287
Donaldson, Jeff, 150
Douglas, Dave, 75, 273
Dour, Youssou N', 73
Downing, Will, 170
Drake, Hamid, 16, 53, 86, 87, 243, 249, 250
Dresser, Mark, 83
Drew, Kenny, 205
Dupree, Betty, 148

Earth, Wind and Fire, 148
ECM, 63
Element, 216
Ellington, Duke, 4, 18, 134, 177, 226, 257, 272, 281, 283, 284, 289, 306
English Baroque Soloists, 130
Eskellin, Ellery, 18
Evans, Bill, 11, 61, 69, 124, 125
Evans, Gil, 171, 267, 289, 306
Evergreen State College, 189
Eye, Yamataka, 208

Faire, Savoir, 154
Farmer, Art, 249
Favors, Malachi, 73, 158
Feiler, Dror, 113
Feldman, Mark, 83
Feldman, Morton, 14
Felix, Lakjo, 145
Fitzgerald, Ella, 38
Frank's Drum Shop, 89
Freeman, Chico, 73
Freeman, Von, 73
Friedlander, Eric, 83
French Impressionistic Period, 35

Frisell, Bill, 80, 81, 93
Frith, Fred, 83, 103, 208

Gabbo, 275
Gadd, Steve, 173
Gardiner, John Eliot, 123, 129
Garrett, Kenny, 38
Garrison, Jimmy, 73, 250
Garvey, Marcus, 274
Genus, James, 83
Gil, Gilberto, 83
Gillespie, Dizzy, 37, 104, 231, 281
Gjerstad, Frode, 216
Glass, Phillip, 71
Globe Unity Orchestra, 123
Globokar, Vinko, 50
Goebbels, Heiner, 307
Goldsmith's College, 121
Golson, Benny, 215
Gosfield, Annie, 109
Grapelli, Stephane, 34, 38
Grateful Dead, 172
Graves, Milford, 32
Grenadier, Larry, 182
Griffin, Johnny, 69
Guildhall School of Music and Drama, 122
Gully, Terreon, 174
Gush, 113
Gustafsson, Mats, 31, 43, 77, 112, 126, 292
Guy, Barry, 65, 121

Hadid, Zaha, 124
Haker-Flaten, Ingebrigt, 216, 217
Hall, Arsenio, 172
Hall, Jim, 11, 268
Hamilton, Jeff, 173
Hancock, Herbie, 132, 170, 204
Hardman, Bill, 80
Hargrove, Roy, 170
Harris, Eddie, 73
Harris, Jerome, 67
Hart, Billy, 173
Harth, Alfred, 307
Haurand, Ali, 216
Hayden, Charlie, 12
Hayes, Louis, 14
Haynes, Roy, 14, 73, 169, 195
Heath, Jimmy, 206

Helfer, Erwin, 184
Hemphill, Julius, 22, 26, 80
Henderson, Joe, 170
Henderson, Wayne, 201
Hendrix, Jimi, 133
Heraclitus, 145
Hermes, 145
Hersch, Fred, 35
Hicks, John, 172
Higgins, Billy, 69, 176, 248
Hill, Andrew, 200, 206
Hill, Lauren, 202
Hines, Earl, 200
Hirsch, Shelly, 108
Hogwood, Christopher, 123
Holiday, Billie, 36
Holland, Dave, 132
Holmes, Richard "Groove," 162
Homburger, Maya, 129, 130
Hoover, J. Edgar, 149
Hornsby, Bruce, 172
Horvitz, Wayne, 208
Hubbard, Freddie, 80, 175, 231
Hughes, Langston, 273
Hunair, Danile, 65

Ibarra, Susie, 3, 83, 138
Ibrahim, Abdullah, 59, 65
ICP Orchestra, 83, 244
Incus records, 2
Indian Classical Music, 89
Ingvaldsen, Didrik, 216
Ives, Charles, 77

Jackson, Al, 14
Jackson, John, 150
Jackson, Melvin, 148
Jackson, Michael, 227
Jackson, Milt, 249
Jamal, Ahmad, 73
Jarman, Joseph, 73, 189, 272
Jarrett, Keith, 61, 65, 66
Jazz Messengers, 83
Jenkins, Leroy, 189, 273
Jenny-Clark, J. F., 65
Jenny, Hans, 144
Jensen, Ingrid, 265, 267
Joachim Kuhn Trio, 65

Johnson, Bunk, 234
Jones, Elvin, 14, 18, 73, 171, 173, 216
Jones, Hank, 169
Jones, Leroi, 62
Jones, Papa Joe, 73
Jones, Philly Joe, 14, 73, 287
Jones, Norah, 68
Jormin, Anders, 65
Juess Quartet, 245

Kabalevsky, 184
Kahn, Hazrat Inayat, 87
Kang, Eyvind, 140
Kanyakumari, A., 145
Karenga, Ron, 151
Keiji, Haino, 208
Kenny G, 38, 176
Kent Opera Company, 123
Kepler, Johannes, 141
Kerouac, Jack, 324
Kerry, John, 53, 78
King Oliver, 134
King, Martin Luther, 10, 77, 151, 273
Klucevsek, Guy, 83
Konitz, Lee, 11
Kosugi, 145
Kowald, Peter, 292
Krall, Diana, 170, 216
Kreisler, Fitz, 145
Krishnan, T. N., 145
Kronos String Quartet, 18, 71
Kropotkin, 242

Lacy, Steve, 83, 112, 146, 215
Lake, Oliver, 59, 67, 105
Lateef, Yusef, 105
Lauper, Cindy, 227
Leandre, Joelle, 3, 108
Lennon, John, 10
Lewis, George, 59, 105, 112, 148
Lewis, Victor, 172, 173
Libeskind, Daniel, 125
Lincoln, Abbey, 170
Lincoln Center, 20, 79, 80, 105, 108, 212,
    285
Lindbergh, Charles, 77
Little Theater Club, 122
Living, Bernhard, 121, 122

Locus Solas, 208
Lokomotiv Konkret, 112
London Classical Players, 123
London Jazz Composers Orchestra, 122, 123, 126, 128, 129
Lovano, Joe, 83, 95
Lytton, Paul, 46, 65, 123–25

Maal, Baba, 73
Malle, Louis, 60
Maneri, Joe, 295, 296
Maneri, Matt, 284
Marsalis, Wynton, 20, 59, 108, 115, 170, 171, 234, 281, 285, 294
Martino, Pat, 160
Mateen, Tarus, 202, 205
Mayor Daly, 273
M-BASE, 224, 225
McBride, Christian, 169
McCall, Steve, 272
McLean, Jackie, 73
McPhee, Joe, 43, 47
Mehldau, Brad, 178, 206
Melford, Myra, 184
Mengelberg, Misha, 83, 215
Menuhin, Yehudi, 130
Metheny, Pat, 6, 73, 176, 191, 317
Mills College, 103
Mingus, Charles, 39, 62, 74, 121, 126, 134, 183, 204, 206, 222, 247, 287
Mitchell, Blue, 175
Mitchell, Joni, 83
Mitchell, Nicole, 154
Mitchell, Roscoe, 73, 159, 272
Moholo, Louis, 32, 53, 123
Monk, Theolonious, 47, 49, 77, 80, 98, 205, 257, 283, 284
Monteverdi Orchestra, 123
Moore, Thomas, 60
Moran, Jason, 199
Morgan, Lee, 175, 215
Mori, Ikue, 83, 108, 207
Morris Brown University, 34
Morris, Butch, 105, 189
Morris, Joe, 284
Morton, Jelly Roll, 273
Motian, Paul, 14, 73, 83, 95
Mozart, 38, 87, 226

MTV, 37, 40
Muhammad, Idris, 173
Murray, David, 105, 211, 215
Muses, Charles Arthur, 240–42
Music Ensemble, 249
The Mysticism of Sound and Music, 87

Najee, 38
Nakamura, Toshimaru, 308
Nash, Lewis, 173
Nessa, Chuck, 159
New England Conservatory, 62, 146, 189
New Orleans music, 104
Nichols, Herbie, 200
Nichols, Maggie, 108, 129
Nilssen-Love, Paal, 43, 47, 77, 215
Nonesuch Records, 94
Nordeson, Kjell, 112
Norrington, Roger, 123
NSYNC, 223

O'Conner, Mark, 36
Odin, 120
Onkyo School, 307, 308
Orr, Buxton, 123
Osborne, Mike, 123
Osby, Greg, 204, 206, 221
Osho, Rajneesh, 92
Oxley, Tony, 2, 215, 216

Paganini, 35
Paracelsus, 143
Parker, Charlie, 4, 62, 77, 80, 87, 95, 108, 177, 192, 205, 226, 234, 247, 255, 281, 284
Parker, Evan, 2, 30, 65, 114, 123, 124, 126, 233
Parker, William, 16, 23, 30, 53, 91, 243, 284
Parkins, Zeena, 108
Partch, Harry, 77
Patchen, Kenneth, 40, 52
Patrick, Pat, 73
Pattitucci, John, 170
Patton, John, 73
Peanuts Club, 123
Pearson, Mike, 44, 45, 52
Peart, Neal, 171
Penderecki, Krystof, 123

Penn, Clarence, 83
Peoples, Tommy, 145
Pepper, Art, 87
Perkins, Walter, 31
Peter Brotzmann Tentet, 215
Peterson, Oscar, 171
Pettiford, Oscar, 250
Pierrot, Alice, 145
Plugged Nickel, 74
Pollock, Jackson, 121, 284
Pomeroy, Herb, 14
Ponty, Jean-Luc, 34, 38
Potter, Chris, 83
Power Noise Trio, 112
Pullen, Don, 184, 215
Purdie, Bernard, 171, 173
Pythagoras, 141

Rajam, N., 145
Randolph, Philip, 274
Rands, Bernard, 123
Reagan, Ronald, 245
Reason, Dana, 108
Redd, Vi, 170
Redding, Otis, 14
Redman, Joshua, 170, 176, 252
Resnais, Alaine, 32
Ribot, Marc, 236
Rich, Buddy, 17
Richmond, Danny, 287
Richter, Gerhard, 100
Riley, Howard, 123
Riperton, Minnie, 150
Rivers, Sam, 203–6
Roach, Max, 51, 73
Robinson, Scott, 268
Roelofs, Anne-Marie, 108
Rolling Stones, 94
Rollins, Sonny, 27, 33, 69, 74, 97, 113, 175,
    304
Roseman, Josh, 18, 83
Rossy, Jorge, 182, 183
Rothko, Mark, 121
Rove, Karl, 51
Rubenstein, Arthur, 18
Rudolph, Adam, 88
Rumi, 189
Russell, George, 105
Rutherford, Paul, 50, 122, 123

Sachiko M, 308
Said, Edward, 49, 80
Sandel, Sten, 113
Sappho, 140, 145
Sarin, Michael, 83
Saunders, Pharoah, 65, 74, 303
Schneider, Maria, 170, 171, 261
Schwarzenegger, Arnold, 236
School Days, 215, 217
Schurch, Dorothea, 108
Schweitzer, Irene, 108, 129
Scotts, Ronnie, 122, 126
Shah, Idries, 242
Shakespeare, William, 277
Shaw, Marlena, 170
Shaw, Woody, 80, 83, 175, 231
Shepik, Brad, 83
Shepp, Archie, 303
Shorter, Wayne, 132, 173, 201, 216
Silver, Horace, 133, 201
Skidmore, Alan, 216
Smith, Stuff, 145
Smith, Wadada Leo, 51, 59, 105, 271
Smith, Willie "the Lion," 200
Songline/Tonefield Productions, 94
Sonic Youth, 105, 302
Sonore, 48
Spears, Britney, 223
Speed, Chris, 83
Staley, Jim, 208
Stenson, Bobo, 65
Stevens, John, 122, 123, 215, 216
Stitt, Sonny, 170
Stockhausen, Karlheinz, 97, 167, 235, 310
Stravinsky, 273, 293
Strid, Raymond, 113, 117
Sugimoto, Taku, 308
Sun Ra, 31, 59, 64, 73, 104, 214
Surman, John, 69, 70
Suso, Foday Musa, 71
Swell, Steve, 18

Taborn, Craig, 22
Takayanagi, Masayuki, 307
Tapies, Antonio, 118
Tardy, Greg, 83
Tatum, Art, 200
Taylor, Cecil, 5, 22, 32, 38, 59, 60, 61,
    63–65, 76, 88, 89, 99, 106, 116, 127, 128,

133, 164, 166, 171, 173, 177, 181, 194, 205, 218, 229, 238, 248, 258, 278, 281, 286, 288, 289, 302, 312
Taylor, Chad, 154
Terkel, Studs, 150
The Thing, 215
Thomas, Ron, 167
Thompson, Kim, 72
Threadgill, Henry, 77, 80, 83, 105, 184, 189, 203, 204, 206
Time Warner, 94
Tor, 120
Townsend, Lee, 94
Travolta, John, 213
Tyner, McCoy, 65, 231
Tzadik, 110

Vandermark, Ellen, 291, 292
Vandermark, Ken, 22, 31, 43, 44, 114, 115, 279
Vandermark 5, 286, 287
Van Gelder, Rudy, 162
Velvet Lounge, 90
Verve Records, 35, 36, 40
Village Gate, 172
Vivaldi, 129
Von Schlippenbach, Alexander, 240
Vu, Cuong, 293

Wachsmann, Phil, 46, 54, 123
Waits, Nasheet, 205
Waller, Fats, 147
Wallin, Per-Henrik, 112
Walton, Cedar, 172
Ware, David S., 297

Washington, Kenny, 173
Watson, Bobby, 172
Watts, Trevor, 122, 123
Weather Report, 83, 173
Webern, Anton, 83
Werner, Kenny, 264
Wexler, Haskell, 150
Wheeler, Kenny, 123
White, Michael, 140, 145
Wiik, Håvard, 216
Wilde, Oscar, 235, 236
Williams, Davey, 208
Williams, James, 172
Williams, Mary Lou, 83, 170
Williams, Tony, 14, 15, 73, 132, 172
Wodraszka, Christine, 108
Wolff, Michael, 172
Woodring, Jim, 100, 101
Workman, Reggie, 59, 250
Wright, Lizz, 170

X, Malcom, 303
Xiao-Fen, Min, 3

Yahel, Sam, 100
Yanachek, 273
Yanni, 36
Yoshihide, Otomo, 306
Young, Whitney, 151

Zawinul, Joe, 173
Zevon, Warren, 95
Zittano, Jimmy, 14, 15
Zorn, John, 6, 83, 110, 187, 208, 273, 276, 307, 315, 316